The Troubl Democracy

Political Modernity in the 21st Century

edited by Gerard Rosich and
Peter Wagner

EDINBURGH
University Press

© editorial matter and organisation Gerard Rosich and Peter Wagner, 2016 , 2017
© the chapters their several authors, 2016 , 2017

Edinburgh University Press Ltd
The Tun – Holyrood Road
12 (2f) Jackson's Entry
Edinburgh EH8 8PJ
www.euppublishing.com

First published in hardback by Edinburgh University Press 2016

Typeset in 11/13 Sabon by
Servis Filmsetting Ltd, Stockport, Cheshire,
and printed and bound in Great Britain by
CPI Group (UK) Ltd, Croydon CR0 4YY

A CIP record for this book is available from the British Library

ISBN 978 1 4744 0798 4 (hardback)
ISBN 978 1 4744 2839 2 (paperback)
ISBN 978 1 4744 0799 1 (webready PDF)
ISBN 978 1 4744 0800 4 (epub)

The right of the contributors to be identified as authors of this work has been
asserted in accordance with the Copyright, Designs and Patents Act 1988 and
the Copyright and Related Rights Regulations 2003 (SI No. 2498).

Contents

Acknowledgements

This book is a result of the work of the research group *Trajectories of Modernity: Comparing Non-European and European Varieties* (TRAMOD), funded by the European Research Council (ERC) as Advanced Grant no. 249438 and based at the University of Barcelona. The editors would like to thank ERC for providing generous funding; the contributors for their commitment and patience in a long editorial process; and all members of the research group for intense discussions on the current state of democracy in the world.

Contributors

Ivor Chipkin is Director of the Public Affairs Research Institute (PARI) at the University of the Witwatersrand, Johannesburg. He completed his PhD at the Ecole Normale Supérieure in France and was based at the Wits Institute for Social and Economic Research (WISER) between 2001 and 2004. In 2005, he received an Oppenheimer fellowship and took up a position at St Antony's College at the University of Oxford. He spent four years in the Democracy and Governance Programme at the Human Sciences Research Council, where he acquired an intimate knowledge of government departments and agencies. In 2007, he published *Do South Africans Exist? Nationalism, Democracy and the Identity of 'the People'* with Wits University Press. He is currently finishing a new book on the history of public sector reform in South Africa and its consequences for development and democracy.

Carlos A. Forment is Associate Professor in the Department of Sociology and Politics at the New School for Social Research, New York City, and Research Professor in the Division of Human Studies at the Universidad Nacional General Sarmiento, Buenos Aires. He is the author of *Democracy in Latin America, 1760–1900, Vol. I* (2003) and *La Formacion de la Sociedad Civil y la Democracia en el Peru* (2012) and co-editor of *Shifting Frontiers of Citizenship: The Latin American Experience* (2013). He recently published: 'Ordinary ethics and the emergence of plebeian democracy across the Global South: Buenos Aires' La Salada Market', *Current Anthropology* (September 2015). He is currently working on two book manuscripts: *Sociability and Everyday Forms of Nationhood in Nineteenth Century Latin America* and *The Emergence of Plebeian Citizenship Across the Global South: Democratic Life in Buenos Aires in the Wake of Neoliberalism*.

Geneviève Fraisse is a philosopher and historian of feminist thought, Director of Research (emeritus) at the National Centre for Scientific Research (CNRS), Paris. Her work deals with epistemology and politics, the genealogy of democracy, concepts of emancipation and the problematisation of the sex/gender debate. Her numerous publications include: *Muse de la raison, démocratie et exclusion des femmes en France*, 1989 (Engl. tr.: *Reason's Muse*); *Les Femmes et leur histoire*, 1998; *Les Deux gouvernements: la famille et la cité*, 2000; *Du consentement*, 2007; *Le Privilège de Simone de Beauvoir*, 2008; *A côté du genre, sexe et philosophie de l'égalité*, 2010; *Les excès du genre, concept, image, nudité*, 2014. She is the co-editor of vol. 4 of the *Histoire des femmes en Occident*, Volume IV, 1991 (Engl. tr.: *A History of Women*).

Manuel Antonio Garretón is a sociologist and has been Professor at the University of Chile since 1994. He has been Visiting Professor of numerous universities in Latin America, Europe and the USA. He received the National Prize in Social Science and Humanities and the Kalman Silvert Award (LASA). Among his books: *The Chilean Political Process* (1989); *Fear at the Edge: State Terror and Resistance in Latin America* (1992, co-editor); *La sociedad en que vivi(re)mos: Introducción sociológica al cambio de siglo* (2000, 2015); *Latin America in the 21st Century: Toward a New Sociopolitical Matrix* (co-author, 2003); *Incomplete Democracy: Political Democratization in Chile and Latin America* (2003); *Las ciencias sociales en la trama de Chile y América Latina: Estudios sobre transformaciones sociopolíticas y movimiento social* (2014).

Andreas Kalyvas teaches political theory at The New School for Social Research, New York. His research interests are situated at the intersection of politics, law and history, with a thematic focus on democracy, sovereignty, constituent power, resistance and citizenship. He is the author of *Democracy and the Politics of the Extraordinary: Weber, Schmitt, Arendt* (2008) and the co-author of *Liberal Beginnings: Making a Republic for the Moderns* (2008). He is currently completing a book-length manuscript on dictatorship and its formative impact on the political constitution of modernity.

Nathalie Karagiannis is a sociologist who also holds degrees in law and political science. Her interests have included the relation between the social and the political, the ambiguities of solidarity, democracy. She has published *Avoiding Responsibility: The Politics and Discourse of European Development Policy* (2004); *European Solidarity* (ed., Liverpool University Press, 2007); and *Varieties of World-Making: Beyond Globalization* (co-ed., 2007). In 2014, she published *Saranta*, a book of poetry, together with the artist Christina Nakou.

Gerard Rosich is currently a doctoral researcher within the ERC Advanced Grant Research Project *Trajectories of Modernity*. His work is on the modern foundations of politics, focusing on the concept of autonomy from its birth in classical Greece to the present day and evaluating its conceptual adequacy in terms of understanding the current global transformations. His research interests include ancient Greek political foundations, modern theories of autonomy and cosmopolitan studies. His most recent publication is (as co-author) 'The limits of recognition: history, otherness and autonomy' in Peter Wagner (ed.), *African, American and European Trajectories of Modernity: Past Oppression, Future Justice? Annual of European and Global Studies vol. 2* (Edinburgh University Press, 2015).

Tracy B. Strong is Professor of Political Theory and Philosophy at the University of Southampton and Distinguished Professor, emeritus, at the University of California, San Diego. He is the author of many books and articles, most recently of *Politics without Vision: Thinking without a Banister in the Twentieth Century* (2012). He is presently working on the politico-theoretical importance of the affectual in nineteenth-century American literature.

Peter Wagner is ICREA Research Professor at the University of Barcelona and has been Principal Investigator of the ERC Advanced Grant project *Trajectories of Modernity* (2010–15). His recent publications include *Progress: A Reconstruction* (2015; French edition: *Sauver le progrès*); *Modernity: Understanding the Present* (2012); and *Modernity as Experience and Interpretation* (2008), as well as the co-edited volumes *African, American and European Trajectories of Modernity* (2015); *The Greek Polis and the Invention of Democracy: A Politico-Cultural Transformation and its Interpretations* (with Johann Arnason and Kurt Raaflaub, 2013) and *Varieties of World-Making: Beyond Globalization* (with Nathalie Karagiannis, 2007).

Lea Ypi is Associate Professor in Political Theory at the London School of Economics and Adjunct Associate Professor of Philosophy at the Australian National University. She is interested in issues of global justice (including migration and colonialism), democratic theory (with particular focus on parties) and the philosophy of the Enlightenment (especially Kant). She co-edits *The Journal of Political Philosophy* and is the author of *Global Justice and Avant-Garde*

Political Agency (2012) and, with Jonathan White, *The Meaning of Partisanship* (forthcoming). She was recently a joint recipient of the British Academy Brian Barry Prize for excellence in political science.

1 Introduction: Re-Interpreting Democracy for Our Time

Gerard Rosich and Peter Wagner

We live, supposedly, in the era of freedom and democracy. Never have human rights, many of which are rights to freedom, and democracy been as widely discussed and accepted as key political reference points across the globe as today. Certainly, these commitments are not adhered to everywhere. But recent debate and practice even suggest that external actors have both the right and the responsibility to promote freedom and democracy in regions of the globe where they are not – not yet, as many are inclined to think – fully accepted. This is, so to say, the official view of current politics.

This volume elaborates a very different, much more critical angle on the political condition of the present time. But it also suggests that this official view has to be taken seriously, that it cannot be rejected as merely ideological, as masking domination, as many critics pretend. The official view is based on two key assumptions, one conceptual and the other empirical-historical: that freedom and democracy can attain a coherent, stable form and that this form has been reached in major parts of the world and is about to be achieved in most others, individualisation and democratisation being among the most powerful dynamics of our time. In contrast, this volume maintains that the commitments to freedom and democracy are highly ambiguous and volatile, that they constitute a field of tensions that, in *conceptual* terms, is devoid of any inclinations towards stability.[1] In *historical* perspective, furthermore, it suggests that freedom and democracy may have had achieved a temporary, and far from unproblematic, stability in some parts of the world several decades ago, roughly around 1960, but that this stability is long gone and unlikely to return in any similar form.[2]

To characterise the conceptual and empirical agenda of this volume further, we shall start out by capturing some key features of that historical moment: at about 1960, the contemporary description of the political situation in terms of co-existing worlds expressed this sense of relative stability and smooth, gradual change. The 'First World', despite the existence of some authoritarian regimes, was modern and had domestically achieved the institutional combination of personal freedom and inclusive democracy. The 'Second World' of existing socialism had embarked on a different path towards political modernity, indeed claiming to establish a radical alternative, but there were signs of convergence between the 'First' and 'Second' Worlds in the face of functional requirements of modern society. The 'Third World', in turn, had not yet achieved either democracy or the functional efficacy of modern society, but it was just somewhat behind on the world-historical trajectory of 'modernisation and development', as the jargon of the time had it. Half a century later, the picture could not be more different: the specificity of the 'Second World' has all but disappeared; the societies of the 'First World' move between acute crisis and long-term stagnation or decline; and in the former 'Third World' we allegedly find a combination of 'emerging societies' and 'failed states', the logic of which is difficult to decipher.

The widespread description of 1960s democracy as stable and coherent was mirrored in the social and political theory of the time – and this theoretical legacy keeps haunting us and prevents us from capturing the ambiguities inherent in the commitment to democracy and from elaborating a compelling diagnosis of democracy's current state. Within the Western scholarly debates of the 1950s and 1960s it was widely assumed that modern societies had acquired their ultimate form, which was both normatively and functionally superior to other societies: traditional societies of the past as well as societies that had not succeeded in becoming modern in the present.[3] In particular, modern societies also had endowed themselves with modern political institutions, combining freedom with efficiency. Accordingly, political theory's foremost, if not exclusive, task was to provide the existing political forms with coherent conceptual underpinnings. In the hegemonic view, political modernity, even though this term was not used at the time, could conceptually be characterised by the following distinct features:

Modern democracy had led to the creation of political collectivities that had clear boundaries to the outside, and intelligible and rather coherent social structures inside – a 'well-ordered society', to refer to John Rawls's terminology.[4] Firstly, the form of political modernity is the democratic nation-state, in which the alleged homogeneity of the nation paves the way for the emergence of a general, collective will in popular sovereignty. Sovereignty was seen as the condition for democracy as collective self-determination in these two senses: the collectivity had to be sufficiently closed and separate from others to master its own fate, on the one hand; and it had to be able to substantively determine its fate through internal communication, deliberation and decision, on the other (for critical discussions, see Chapters 2 and 3 below).

Under another aspect, secondly, the political form of modern society is the liberal constitutional state of law, which combines the commitment to individual liberty with constitutional guarantees, thus eternalising the liberal achievement and limiting the power of potentially tyrannical majorities.[5] This form was seen as creating the lastingly appropriate balance between individual autonomy and collective autonomy, between personal freedom and democracy. The individual liberty at issue here was conceptualised as equal freedom. Formal inequality and domination was supposed to be abolished by a stroke of law, overcoming discrimination by gender and race, among other criteria (see Chapter 5).

Significantly, thirdly, this political arrangement was seen as inherently stable and, thus, of lasting duration once it had been successfully established. The stability was to be based on 'natural' features, on the one hand, most importantly on the internal homogeneity of the collectivity as grounded in the nation and on the human endowment with reason as a condition for the exercise of individual liberty. On the other hand, this stability also required the appropriate institutional construction, in particular for the balance between individual and collective self-determination and for the organisation of representative processes of deliberation from which the common will could truly emerge. While the 'natural' features only had to be discovered, the institutional features were to be enshrined in modern constitutions. Whether through discovery or institutional architecture, though, once they were at hand, the correct political principles were not expected to be placed in doubt again (see Chapter 4).

Fourthly, the modern polity after the Second World War was also considered to have finally solved the 'social question' or 'labour question' that had haunted many societies from the middle of the nineteenth to the middle of the twentieth century.[6] Until then, political domination of a minority over a majority had often gone along with socio-economic exploitation, not rarely entailing poverty and starvation. Inclusive egalitarian democracy, introduced in a range of countries after the First World War, arguably made any such arrangement untenable. Electoral majorities would claim an end to socio-economic subjection. Though repeatedly interrupted by experiences of authoritarianism and totalitarianism, too often neglected in linear accounts of political history, the democratic welfare state would institutionalise social solidarity by redistributing the surplus generated by the smoothly managed functioning of a market economy (see Chapters 6 to 9).

This was the conceptually driven image of modern democracy that prevailed by 1960, and it was apparently supported by some evidence from so-called advanced industrial societies, mostly in the West – or, to use current language, the global North. Several of the contributions to this volume, in particular in its first half, aim to demonstrate that this image was misconceived from its beginnings and to uncover the conceptual flaws that underpinned its construction in the first place. In the present, furthermore, it is clear that the sense of certainty that prevailed during the 1960s about the accomplishments of modern democracy has disappeared, even though many observers are still at a loss to understand what has happened in the meantime. To grasp the meaning and significance of the transformations of democracy since the 1960s is a second objective of this volume.

We can start here with some first summary description: over the past half century, there has been an accumulation of political transformations that in their sum have radically reshaped the political condition of our time. The movements for decolonisation and national liberation in the 'Third World' gained momentum during the 1960s, but they were initially misconceived as merely a step ahead towards the 'modernisation and development' that the 'First World' had already accomplished. The events in Teheran in 1979, often referred to as the Iranian Revolution, should at the latest have shaken this view. As specific as the Iranian circumstances were, they can now be seen as an opening towards a broader understanding of political possibilities in the present, since then intensified not only by the strengthening of political Islam but also by 'emerging' novel political self-understandings reaching from the variety of 'progressivist' political majorities in Latin America, to the transformation-oriented post-apartheid polity in South Africa, to post-communist China.

In turn, the years of intensified protest at the end of the 1960s and during the early 1970s were much more than a short 'crisis of governability'[7] from which one could easily return to elite government and citizen apathy as usual.[8] Significantly, though, the protests did not entail 'legitimacy problems' that 'late capitalism' would be unable to overcome, as critical theorists maintained at the time.[9] In socio-economic terms, the accommodating response of elites in many Western polities – in contrast to persistence or reinstauration of authoritarian regimes in Latin America, South-East Asia and South Africa – restored legitimacy for a moment, but also deepened the fiscal crisis of the Keynesian welfare states. The so-called rise of neo-liberalism is best considered as the next step of elite response to the threat of the withering away of profitable production possibilities. It involved the weakening of protective labour legislation and the attempt to crush trade-union power, as is well known, but also the 'structural adjustment policies' in the global South[10] and the relocation of major sectors of industrial production from the supposedly 'advanced industrial societies' to initially East Asia and now many parts of the globe.[11]

In politico-cultural terms, and despite the intentions of the early protest activists, a major consequence of the movements that started in the 1960s was a weakening of the collective concepts the political use of which had marked the preceding one-and-a-half centuries: nation, class, state and also society. These collective conventions and regulations had not only stabilised democracy temporarily in the West but also contributed to giving meaning to social life. Their dismantling was certainly partly brought about by elites who saw their power endangered, both through institutional changes and cultural re-significations mainly achieved by large mass-media conglomerates. But these conventions and regulations were also under attack by people, mainly by middle classes consolidated precisely by a collective concept such as 'the welfare state' and now majoritarian in electoral terms, who experienced them as constraining their liberties and capacities for self-realisation.[12] Thus, a double-pronged attack, highly differently motivated, on collective conventions led to the destabilisation of the existing form of democracy. Rather than the conceptually coherent and empirically successful high point of political modernity, this form turned out to be a temporary phenomenon rooted in a contingent historical constellation. (For further details on the recent transformation of democracy see Chapter 2 by Gerard Rosich, with a focus on the relation between inter- and intra-societal developments, and Chapter 6 by Manuel Antonio Garretón, with a focus on Latin America.)

The fall of Soviet socialism in the decade after the rise of the first neoliberal governments to power – first by violent means in Chile, and then by electoral majorities in the United Kingdom and the United States of America – then appears to confirm the de-collectivising tendency of recent political change. Globalisation, seen in connection with the decline of the nation-state, and individualisation, entailing the weakening of the capacity for collective action, become the keywords for describing socio-political change during the 1990s. In the conceptual terms introduced above, the frame in which collective self-determination was to be exercised, the nation-state, was seen as increasingly lacking the supposedly indivisible sovereignty in relation to other such entities that was at the core of modern democracy. And in turn, the citizens, whose commitment to the polity – conceptualised in various ways – was foundational for democracy, may have become better informed and more inclined to make their voices heard, but at the same time they oriented themselves more to individual self-realisation than the accomplishment of collective objectives – or so at least much of current socio-political debate in the North has it.

It is in this double light that this book explores the political condition of our time: based on the insight into the fundamental ambiguity within the commitment to democracy and into the lack of stability of modern political institutions, on the one hand, and on the observation of an actual unravelling of political arrangements from the 1960s onwards that has radically altered the conditions for political action and the justifications for political institutions over the past few decades, on the other. Combining conceptual reflection with historical analysis and empirical observation, this book provides both a rethinking of the time-honoured concept of political modernity and important elements for assessing the condition of democracy in and for the twenty-first century.

The chapters of the book address these issues with variable emphasis. In the first few chapters (Chapters 2–5) the critical scrutiny of key concepts of political modernity through investigations in the history of political thought prevails: autonomy, sovereignty, constituent power, democracy and its failing, gender. A second set of chapters (Chapters 6–9) offers selective analyses of current settings for political action as defining experiences for the democracy of the twenty-first century, focusing on experiences in the global South: in Latin America and South Africa, in some comparison with the North. Throughout these analyses, political experiences are not seen as cases to be subsumed under existing concepts, but as sites of novel concept-formation, or in other words, of re-interpretations of democracy. The conceptual criticism and retrieval combined with the focus on political re-interpretations pave the way for exploring the possible directions such re-interpretations may globally take in a third and concluding set of chapters (Chapters 10–12).

This three-step sequence can also be described in terms of the historico-conceptual constellation that marks our current time: (1) In Western political thought one had long assumed to have found lasting answers to all key questions of democracy. (2) But those answers have neither had lasting validity in their regions of origin nor have they been found similarly applicable in other world regions, where different interpretations have emerged. (3) In the current global constellation, it has become clear that no lasting answers exist and that a reconsideration of existing answers is ongoing.

The constitution of democracy: challenging the dominant interpretations

The analyses in the first half of the volume address all the key questions for which one had long assumed that Western democracy had found a lasting answer. Gerard Rosich, in Chapter 2, challenges the double founding assumption of external boundedness and internal coherence of the modern polity. Starting out from a series of political paradoxes that have emerged since the end of the Second World War, he shows that the autonomy of a polity, a key presupposition for collective self-determination, can be taken for granted neither in terms of the relation to other polities, which are relations of interdependence rather than independence, nor in terms of the internal capacity for decisive political action. Thus, the supposed subject of self-determination – the people, the nation, the citizenry, in different terminologies – needs to make a claim to autonomy in the sense of separate existence and capacity to act while at the same time knowing that neither of the two conditions are fulfilled.

Andreas Kalyvas, in Chapter 3, elaborates further on the second aspect of autonomy, the capacity to act collectively, or as a collectivity. Retrieving the history of the concept of sovereignty in European debates, he demonstrates a deep bifurcation in political thought that mostly goes unnoticed because the history of the concept tends to be written from the angle of the 'winner'. Standard accounts of political modernity suggest that the concept of state sovereignty emerged in the historical context of the Westphalian system of territorially-bounded absolutist states and was effectively transformed into the concept of popular sovereignty at the moment of the French Revolution. This view, significantly, suggests that sovereignty is as absolute after the transformation as it was before and therefore remains within the notion that the sovereign governs the people, separating self-determination from government and creating what has been called the 'democratic paradox'.[13] In his nuanced reconstruction, Andreas Kalyvas demonstrates that there has been a conceptual alternative, centred on some notion of constituent power that avoids both democratic regression and paradox, and should be revived to provide for a broader and, in the light of conceptual history, largely alternative view of democracy.

The combination of 'government of the people, by the people, for the people', as Abraham Lincoln famously put it in the Gettysburg Address, therefore, contains many more complications than are usually acknowledged in the mainstream discourse on democracy. Nathalie Karagiannis, in Chapter 4, addresses the circular nature of such a formula by investigating the failing of democracy, such as in the invocation of the state of exception or the rise of totalitarianism. In both of these 'modern' political situations, the end of democracy is brought about from within a democratic condition, thus these are cases of the self-cancellation of democracy. By comparing ancient and modern debates about such self-cancellation, Nathalie Karagiannis demonstrates that an understanding of such self-cancellation that goes beyond stating a 'paradox' requires a conceptual distinction between the political and the social. The former is seen to consist in those relations among people and among institutions within the *polis* that aim at deciding about the polity's fate, and the latter to be those relations among people and among institutions within the *polis* to which such decisions about the polity's fate apply and which they create (we will return to this distinction below). In democracy, there is always a tension between the political and the social, which brings about change. The cancellation of democracy, in turn, occurs when the social is identified with the political, when this tension is abolished. In contrast to modernist political thought, thus, democracy should be thought of as constitutively unstable, fragile. The aim to stabilise democracy is itself often endangering democracy.

A key component of the conceptual stabilisation of democracy has been the elaboration of an abstract notion of freedom. The idea that the interaction of free individuals would lead to a stable and peaceful political order required not only that such freedom would be equally available to all individuals, but also that these individuals as citizens would abstract from all other differences that exist between them. This has been a key contention of social-contract theory from Thomas Hobbes and John Locke to John Rawls and a fundamental assumption, whether admitted or not, of most conceptualisations of the modern polity. It was acknowledged that some actually existing differences constituted political inequality, but such inequality was defined as discrimination that would be overcome in the historically progressive course of political modernity. The key examples of such discrimination were race and gender, and they were to be overcome by the abolition of slavery, colonial subordination and domestic subservience and by the granting of equal rights to human beings of all skin colours and to women and men alike. Indeed the notion of abstract equal freedom, while being an indispensable cornerstone of the prevailing theoretical edifice of democracy, makes it impossible to conceptualise the mere possibility of lasting and politically relevant effects of past domination. The granting of formal equality, in such a view, claims to eradicate with one stroke political discrimination, while what the concept of abstract formal equality in effect does is eradicate the possibility of making historical injustice a relevant issue in modern polities.

In Chapter 5, Geneviève Fraisse discusses the historical exclusion of women from, and persistently reluctant inclusion of women in, democracy from the angle of the historical temporality of female emancipation. While gender equality in the modern polity was on the agenda from the moment of the French Revolution, it kept being deferred far into the twentieth century, and was then seen as having already taken place, thus neutralising the possibility of an emancipatory or revolutionary historical event. And even at the current moment when formal gender equality exists in many polities across the globe, political debates often show an asymmetry on gender issues which makes it difficult to conceive of women's emancipation as an objective in its own right, as other than instrumental to the overall benefit of society and polity. The chapter shows that democracy has not developed a sufficiently rich conceptualisation of equality to adequately include those who, by general admission, have been historically excluded from political participation, women as well as the colonised, the latter often being defined by the colour of their skin.[14]

The major conceptual and historical point of reference for democracy before the eighteenth century was the Greek *polis*, most importantly democratic Athens.[15] In the Greek *polis*, a strong distinction was made between free citizens, who collectively determined the fate of the polity, and other residents, most importantly women and slaves, who took care of material needs. This distinction, which we can see as a version of theorising the relation between the social (or: the economic) and the political, as suggested by Nathalie Karagiannis (Chapter 4), reappeared in European political debates across the seventeenth and eighteenth centuries. The so-called modern political thinkers had male property-owning heads of households in mind when they thought of free citizens of the modern republic, rather than all adult residents, and the conceptual reason for this view was that material independence was seen as a precondition for free and responsible action, as in ancient Athens. Thus, they had to justify why some human beings had to take care of the material needs and others not, normally with the help of substantive ideas of human nature and reason.

After the political revolutions of the late eighteenth century, such justifications were more difficult to sustain.[16] The democratic political imaginary suggested an institutional transformation towards free and equal universal suffrage, which was rarely accomplished before 1919. Full political inclusion was forced on the elites of the persisting Old Regime by social movements, often in the early twentieth century. When inclusive, equal-suffrage democracy arrived, however, critics of democracy had an easy target because the tension between the idea of independence as a condition for citizenship and the fact that the majority of voters depended on others for their livelihood was not resolved.

Has this tension been resolved since? There is a line of reasoning in the history of socio-political thought that suggests that it has. 'Modern' societies are both commercial and democratic societies. A division of social labour exists in them that enhances productivity and wealth on the one hand, and on the other hand makes all members of these societies interdependent with all others, thus creating strong social bonds between them – 'organic solidarity', as Emile Durkheim called this link. This interdependence, well understood, is the new basis for responsible political behaviour, no longer the individual property earned through the right to the product of one's own labour. And it is common to all members, not limited to a class of property owners.

Reviewing the political experiences of the twentieth century, however, the question arises whether the interdependence diagnosed by social theory should not rather be seen as an asymmetric dependence of some citizens on others. More precisely, it is a situation in which a majority depends for their material well-being on the (socio-economic) decisions of a minority, all the while this majority among equal citizens in a democracy holds the (political) power of calling on the resources owned by the minority. This issue was not unknown to the ancient Athenians. Our current vocabulary permits us to see it as a tension between a social situation and a political form; more broadly, it raises the issue of the social preconditions for democracy to be viable.[17] One might want to argue that the welfare states of the twentieth century were a way of mitigating the tension between the political and the social, securing 'mass loyalty' through partial redistribution of profits.[18] In Manuel Antonio Garretón's brief characterisation of the Latin American twentieth-century political experiences as the socio-political model of national-popular regimes (Chapter 6), we can understand these experiences with their authoritarian leanings indeed as a partial arresting of the tension between the social and the political that underlies democracy, in Nathalie Karagiannis's terms. The current crisis of the European welfare states, in turn, suggests to review this experience by concluding that, indeed, the tension between a capitalist organisation of the social and a democratic understanding of the political can be counteracted, but always only temporarily and at the cost of narrowing the understanding of democracy.

Experiences of democracy in the twenty-first century

Garretón's analysis then proceeds further by showing that more recent political experiences in Latin America reveal an unravelling of the twentieth-century model, a disarticulation of its relative coherence, not least in the name of stronger claims to democracy. The earlier socio-political matrix relied on a strong notion of the state and on related collective concepts such as nation and class that underpinned a relatively unproblematic understanding of political action and political change due to the specific way of arresting the tension between the social and the political. Currently, no new coherence is yet recognisable, and the disarticulation has made effective political action much more problematic. At the same time, a both more open and more radical understanding of democracy has emerged in which citizen participation is central and new forms of collective action are in the process of constitution, including novel commitments to cultural rights. These reflections suggest to read the recent emergence of 'progressivist' political majorities, on the one hand, as a specifically Latin American transformation of democracy against the background of the experiences with the earlier socio-political model, and on the other, as part of a global process in which the tension between the social and the political is rearticulated in novel ways.

The subsequent Chapters 7 and 8, by Carlos A. Forment and Ivor Chipkin respectively, demonstrate in more detail how such rearticulation of the tension between the social and political looks like in different settings. Carlos Forment analyses novel forms of workers' solidarity in response to the consequences of neoliberal economic policies in Argentina. The financial crisis and the political reaction to it in terms of structural adjustment policies and deindustrialisation marked the ways in which the Argentinian version of the national-populist socio-political model, which Manuel Antonio Garretón analysed in the preceding chapter, disintegrated. On the road to reconstruction, of which current 'Kirchnerism' is one project that revives national populism under changed conditions, Carlos Forment analyses the recuperation of bankrupt firms, which had fallen victim to deindustrialisation policies, by the workers themselves. Beginning as a defensive strategy in the face of lasting unemployment and loss of dignity as the only alternative, the continuation of production in self-management gains significance beyond the workplace when the practice faces the need for legal underpinnings and political support. The workers who start out by illegally occupying the factories succeed in winning battles at court and gaining political representation. They thus contribute to reshaping the politico-juridical self-understanding of Argentinian democracy, a process that is still under way.

Ivor Chipkin, in Chapter 8, provides a parallel analysis under the very different socio-political conditions of post-apartheid South Africa. Since the end of apartheid, South Africa has established a stable egalitarian-inclusive democracy, in which national elections have regularly provided a strong majority for the transformation-oriented government alliance of the African National Congress, the core organisation of the national liberation movement, with the South African Communist Party and the trade-union federation COSATU. In socio-economic terms, in contrast, the situation presents itself – and is domestically discussed – in much less favourable terms. Social inequality and unemployment remain very high, and despite the emergence of a 'black middle class' the apartheid legacy of segregation and exclusion seems very difficult to overcome in terms of patterns of poverty and inequality. Against this background, Ivor Chipkin analyses the emergence of new forms of urban residence, so-called townhouse complexes, a form of gated community, in the Johannesburg region. These complexes reflect the post-apartheid social situation by virtue of the fact that house-buyers are often members of the new middle class and that they are mixed in terms of the old apartheid racial categories. But they also reflect the post-apartheid political situation, which is marked by insecurity and violence and the lack of enforcement of agreed-upon rules across the whole territory of the polity. Residents opt for a quasi-Hobbesian social contract, which guarantees peace and order within the townhouse complex, and they create new social bonds that may be seen as a crucial underpinning of the egalitarian-inclusive democracy, while at the same time they appear to renounce the prospect of the emergence of a more-than-Hobbesian civil and democratic polity across the whole Republic of South Africa.

While the three preceding chapters analyse transformations of democracy and new democratic experiences in the South, Chapter 9, by Peter Wagner, explicitly confronts Northern and Southern experiences of the relation between democracy and capitalism. The chapter starts out from the common view that the global financial capitalism of our time has undermined the democratic embedding of capitalism in Europe. The limited capacity of democratically elected governments to defend the European welfare state – as well as their unwillingness to do so – leads to citizen disaffection. The European situation, however, is often confused by local observers with the general withering away of the possibility to democratically embed capitalism. The confrontation with Brazil and South Africa, where high-intensity participation leads to transformation-oriented government majorities and expansive social policies within the context of current global capitalism, complicates the picture.

This set of four chapters is much more than a range of empirical and regional-comparative case studies. Their authors persuasively claim that the interpretation of the phenomena they observe requires the innovative use of existing political concepts and, more than that, that the actors in question may be involved in conceptual re-interpretations that are about to transform political modernity. In particular, they demonstrate that the core commitment of political modernity to collective self-determination, to democracy, is not being realised in linear processes of 'democratisation', as much of current political science suggests, and that democracy can never be seen as a lasting accomplishment, as political theory has often aimed to show. Rather, democracy always exists in and through a tension with a socio-historical constellation, which is in need of political interpretation. Relating the conceptual reflections in the first half of this volume, which underlined the general openness of the democratic commitment to a variety of interpretations and its constitutive instability, to the analyses of recent and ongoing socio-historical transformations provided in the subsequent chapters, we have strong reasons to assume that political modernity is currently undergoing a major transformation with yet uncertain outcome.[19] The final set of chapters addresses aspects of the challenge of re-interpretation that we are currently facing.

Re-interpreting democracy for our time

The analyses of recent political experiences in Latin America and South Africa show that we have moved beyond the unravelling of the political arrangements of the 1960s that we discussed above. There is no longer only weakening of existing political institutions and loss of the capacity for political action, as had been the dominant trend over some decades. We witness the emergence of new forms – and new scope – of collective action, of which the Argentinian factory movement is an example, and the political implications of novel social phenomena, of which the South African townhouse movement gives evidence. Furthermore, the dangerous consequences of the preceding loss of political capacity have led to the striving for a new socio-political coherence, the strongest signals of which can be found in current Latin America and also in South Africa, societies of the global South that are not at all 'emerging' – they have long been there – but might be politically exemplary for other regions of the globe.[20]

The current condition of democracy is characterised by a wide gap between that which is necessary and that which is seen as realistically possible – maybe wider than at any time in human history due to the reach of the interaction between all human beings, even though such a comparative assertion is always difficult to argue for. This discrepancy is in the background to the debate in political theory between moralists and realists, to which Lea Ypi refers (Chapter 10). The question of global social justice is for Lea Ypi the reason to recall this debate, because the current globe is marked by utterly unjustifiable injustice and inequality, largely produced by global connectedness, while at the same time political institutions with capacity for action operate within boundaries and limit claims to justice to the residents within those boundaries. For Tracy B. Strong, political urgency exists due to the persistence of war and violence that spread all across the twentieth century, combined now with an ever more widely diffused way of life that threatens the very inhabitability of the earth (Chapter 11). Social injustice, war and violence, and sustainability are key political issues of the twenty-first century, which are rather clearly recognised as such, but for which neither the conceptual registers for political action nor the political institutions that could effectively address them are even remotely in sight (we return to Chapters 10 and 11 below with a view to ways of addressing these issues).

To better grasp the current condition of democracy, let us recall one more time the theory of political modernity that prevailed by 1960 and its sense of certainty. This theory was modern because it upheld the commitment to human self-determination, individually and collectively, and it declared its renunciation of any external source of authority, in particular its rupture with religion, a key item in secular political theory. But at the same time, the approach assumed that in combination of freedom and reason the world could be made safe for democracy, for self-determination. Within polities, social life was considered to be well governed and smoothly progressing. And as these polities were largely independent from each other, the relations between them, international relations, only required a minimum of co-ordination to avoid warfare.[21] As discussed at the outset, the whole conceptual apparatus of political theory was geared towards demonstrating the coherence and stability of the modern polity. This apparatus constituted something like a tradition of political modernity, to paraphrase Jacques Derrida, a recourse for thought and action that is always and unquestionably at hand.[22]

However, as we have tried to show in this brief introduction, this conceptual apparatus is not safely available any longer, and possibly it has already been failing us for a long time. Hannah Arendt spoke about the political experiences of the early twentieth century, and in particular the First World War, preceded by events such as the South African War, as a rupture with tradition.[23] From these experiences onwards, at the latest, no support was any longer available for human beings to lean on when they make collective decisions. Arendt talked about the need to 'think without a banister', a formulation taken up by Tracy Strong in his recent book and in his contribution to this volume, and both these authors suggest that this condition has already prevailed across all the twentieth century.[24]

The short-lived and problematic stabilisation of democracy in the decades after the Second World War created the illusion of a new and modern certainty about political matters; and the unravelling of this political arrangement during the past few decades has shown this belief to be an illusion. Thus, we live a situation of urgency without institutions that have the capacity for adequate action, and without the conceptual tools that can guide the reconstruction of such institutions. At the same time, the conviction is now much more widespread that it is only human beings themselves who can create these concepts and these institutions, in collective self-determination. The concluding set of chapters explores avenues to deal with this novel constellation of modern democracy.

Lea Ypi, in Chapter 10, discusses the issues of radical disagreement, feasibility of political action, and motives for political action as points of dispute between moralists and realists. In the light of our preceding observations, these issues can be seen as marking the contemporary uncertainty about foundations of sound political action. Lea Ypi admits the significance of the issues, but suggests at the same time that the divide between moral necessity and political possibility is not as wide as it is often seen to be. Focusing on matters of global social justice, she re-interprets the controversy in such a way as to sustain a concept of avant-garde agency that takes account of the concerns of both realists and moralists.[25]

Tracy Strong, in Chapter 11, defines democratic politics as the attempt to find agreed-upon solutions to the pressing problems a collectivity of human beings is facing, thus returning to the core of our reflections on the concept of collective self-determination. He briefly sketches both the intellectual and the political trajectory of the twentieth century, the former by radically insisting on the lack of a banister, and the latter by underlining the unprecedented measure of violence, cruelty and activities that endanger human life in general. The absence of a banister suggests that political theory fails when it aims for certainty and timeless solutions. As political problems vary across place and across time, the solutions and the ways to find them will also vary. Political theory has for too long erred on the side of often fine-tuned but ill-guided conceptual elaboration. The current moment is one of challenge to political concepts that have lost, or are about to lose, their context of application. Therefore, the emphasis needs to be placed instead on the analysis of current political experiences and the ways in which they lend themselves to conceptual re-elaboration with a view to addressing urgent current and future political problems.

Chapter 12, by Gerard Rosich and Peter Wagner, tries to spell out this conclusion. It suggests that the currently competing conceptualisations of democracy – as an institutional model, as an ideology that masks domination, as a paradoxical constellation – are not erroneous as such. They all point to observable features of democratic experiences. But they are flawed as general theories of democracy, because they precisely apply to specific situations which are always contingent and temporary. If one wants to capture general features of democracy, then the focus should not be on certainty and stability, but rather on self-transformation – in two senses: their characteristic fragility entails that democracies *undergo* transformations in the face of changing socio-historical circumstances; but democracy as collective self-determination also refers to the *capacity* for self-transformation – possibly demanded by changed circumstances, but actually brought about by the will of the collectivity that self-determines its fate. The current trouble with democracy may precisely be this: that democracy is too often understood as an institutional arrangement in need of conceptual and historical stabilisation rather than as an institutional setting that allows for, even invites, attempts at transforming itself in the face of new requirements or normative demands.

Notes

1. For the expression in a related context, see Johann Arnason, 'Modernity as Project and as Field of Tensions', in Axel Honneth and Hans Joas (eds), *Communicative Action: Essays on Jürgen Habermas's The Theory of Communicative Action* (Cambridge, MA: MIT Press, 1991).
2. For one account of this stability, see Peter Wagner, *A Sociology of Modernity: Liberty and Discipline* (London: Routledge, 1994).
3. Talcott Parsons, *The System of Modern Societies* (Englewood Cliffs, NJ: Prentice-Hall, 1971).
4. John Rawls, *A Theory of Justice* (Cambridge, MA: Harvard University Press, 1971).
5. For one reflection on such a connection, see Jürgen Habermas, 'On the Internal Relation between the Rule of Law and Democracy', in *The Inclusion of the Other: Studies in Political Theory* (Cambridge, MA: MIT Press, 1998), pp. 253–64.
6. For a recent account, focusing on Europe, see Bo Stråth, *Three Utopias of Peace and the Search for a Political Economy* (London: Bloomsbury, 2015).
7. Michel J. Crozier, Samuel P. Huntington and Joji Watanuki, *The Crisis*

of Democracy: Report on the Governability of Democracies to the Trilateral Commission (New York: New York University Press, 1975).

8. The global significance of these protests was captured early by the perceptive but widely misunderstood comparative observer Louis Hartz in *The Founding of New Societies* (New York: Harcourt, Brace & World, 1964).

9. Jürgen Habermas, *Legitimation Crisis* (Boston: Beacon Press, 1975).

10. On Africa, see Achille Mbembe, *On the Postcolony* (Berkeley: University of California Press, 2001).

11. For an early analysis see Volker Froebel, Jürgen Heinrichs and Otto Kreye, *The New International Division of Labour: Structural Unemployment in Industrialised Countries and Industrialisation in Developing Countries* (Cambridge: Cambridge University Press, 1980). For more detail, see the forthcoming special issue of the *European Journal of Social Theory* on 'Modernity and Capitalism', edited by David Casassas and Peter Wagner, vol. 19, no. 2 (2016).

12. See Peter Wagner, *A Sociology of Modernity*, chs 8–10; Luc Boltanski and Eve Chiapello, *The New Spirit of Capitalism* (New York: Verso, 2005); Peter Wagner, 'The project of emancipation and the possibility of politics, or, what's wrong with post-1968 individualism?', *Thesis Eleven*, 68 (February 2002): 31–45.

13. Chantal Mouffe, *The Democratic Paradox* (London: Verso, 2000).

14. For a recent discussion on colonial domination, see Achille Mbembe, *Critique de la raison nègre* (Paris: La Découverte, 2013), and for a critique of the liberal underpinnings of such exclusion, see Charles Mills, 'Decolonizing Western political philosophy', paper presented at the TRAMOD conference on 'Political modernity in the 21st century', University of Barcelona, February 2012.

15. For a comprehensive recent re-assessment of the Greek democratic experience, see Johann Arnason, Kurt Raaflaub and Peter Wagner (eds), *The Greek Polis and the Invention of Democracy* (Malden, MA: Wiley and Blackwell, 2013).

16. The following paragraphs draw on Peter Wagner, 'Transformations of Democracy: Towards a History of Political Thought and Practice in Long-term Perspective', in Arnason et al., *The Greek Polis*, pp. 47–69.

17. For further conceptual elaboration on this issue, see Nathalie Karagiannis and Peter Wagner, 'Varieties of Agonism: Conflict, the Common Good and the Need for Synagonism', *Journal of Social Philosophy*, vol. 39, no. 3 (Fall 2008).

18. See Wolfdieter Narr and Claus Offe (eds), *Wohlfahrtsstaat und Massenloyalität* (Cologne: Kiepenheuer und Witsch, 1975).

19. The need to recast political concepts in the light of the experiences with political action, focusing on the example of the poor in New Delhi, is at the centre of Veena Das, 'The Poor in Political Theory and How to Grow Concepts out of Life', presentation at the TRAMOD conference 'Political modernity in the 21st century', University of Barcelona, February 2012. A large pluri-lingual, pluri-religious polity with a great

internal variety of political constellations, India indeed provides an example of a long-lasting democracy that has always been difficult to integrate into 'Northern' political theory. While it is an exception also in its region, it demands to integrate more explicitly Asian experiences into the conceptualisation of democracy. Major political transformations in Asia are often state-led, but they may be driven by strong social movements in the form of communist movements, historically, as well as, more recently, civil-rights- and participation-oriented movements.

20. For a re-assessment of varieties of democracy against the idea of a Northern model that informs political theory, see Leonardo Avritzer, *Rethinking Democracy* (forthcoming).

21. Significantly, the Cold War was the only major source of uncertainty because the communication between the liberal-capitalist and the socialist world could not entirely be trusted to follow maxims of rationality.

22. Jacques Derrida, *Of Spirit: Heidegger and the Question* (Chicago: University of Chicago Press, 1989).

23. Hannah Arendt, *The Origins of Totalitarianism* [1951] (New York and London: Harvest Books, 1978).

24. Hannah Arendt, 'On Hannah Arendt', in Melvyn Hill (ed.), *Hannah Arendt: The Recovery of the Public World* (New York: St Martin's Press, 1979), pp. 301–39; Tracy B. Strong, *Politics without Vision: Thinking without a Banister in the Twentieth Century* (Chicago: University of Chicago Press, 2012).

25. Her approach can be fruitfully compared with Alessandro Ferrara's reflections on exemplary action. See his *The Force of the Example: Explorations in the Paradigm of Judgment* (New York: Columbia University Press, 2008).

2   Autonomy in and between Polities: Democracy and the Need for Collective Political Selves

Gerard Rosich

In the field of political theory, one finds several paradoxes which signal that now, at the beginning of the twenty-first century, we are living in times of change. Beyond the historical periodisation that one might wish to choose in order to identify on the timeline an event that could shed light on this moment of transformation, there is an absence of clear ideas as to the subterranean currents hidden beneath these events. The widespread use of the term 'globalisation' and its political twin brother, cosmopolitanism, is explained in part by the suggestion that it would seem to offer some kind of response to these 'processes'. Nonetheless, one senses that the term is only useful if it refers to a new reality, namely global connectedness in the broadest sense of the expression. What is paradigmatic about this fact, in relation with the past, would be that globalisation now de facto affects the entire surface of the planet and it would not simply represent an ideal. The problem with a simple confirmation of global connectedness is that it does not contemplate either what the *nexus* might consist of, or what form the *co-* takes, or whether *global* refers to the physical globe of the world or to the human world. One current trend in world history attempts to elucidate how we have come to this new reality, and many people seem to agree that 'globalisation' has its beginnings, *grosso modo*, with modern times.[1] The advantage of this approximation is that it is generally useful when it comes to explaining why the West achieved global dominance after the end of the nineteenth century, but it does not help much at the point where what is to be explained in the study, namely the global economic and political supremacy of the West, is no longer a reality as such: the world is not, if it ever was, *only* Western.

The aim of this chapter is to assess the prospects for democracy, here understood as the commitment to autonomy as self-determination, against this background. It is suggested that democracy is in fundamental conflict with the contemporary individualist under-standing of the polity and with theories that link its endurance under globalisation to cosmopolitanism. The chapter will first present a view on our political present through the notion of paradox in order to indicate the main challenges for democracy in the present and the insufficiency of current dominant theories to correctly grasp those challenges. Secondly, it addresses what has to be understood as hegemonic political thinking from the perspective of the chapter, namely individualist hegemony in connection with the dominant contemporary re-interpretation of cosmopolitanism. And thirdly, it shows how democracy requires a plurality of collective selves, which goes against the assumptions of the hegemonic political thinking.

My objective is to show how, as soon as the plurality of frontiers is contemplated as being among the world's most serious problems, the main assumption of what I shall call contemporary cosmo-politanism, which supposedly provides a solution to the paradoxes discussed below, tends either to reduce the existence of different col-lectivities to a mere sum of individuals or regard them as 'function-ally inefficient' or dangerously superfluous. Furthermore, the same theory is repeatedly used contextually to mask or justify positions of hegemonic power in the guise of universalist discourse.[2] I shall attempt to show that the idea that underpins democracy, namely the concept of autonomy, 'to give oneself one's own law', implies not only historically but also conceptually the existence of a plurality of collectivities.[3]

Although I am reducing all the nuances and divergences of the dif-ferent contemporary re-interpretations of cosmopolitan theories to a single point of view, if 'cosmopolitan' is to be a different concept from '*inter*national', I fail to see the basic difference between the two positions if it does not consist in giving a certain prominence, what-ever form it takes, to the position that one occupies in the 'cosmos' in relation to other political contexts.

Political paradoxes of the present

'Paradox' is one of the concepts that the past 'post-modern' trend promoted in scholarship. Paradoxes would emerge once systemic or structural thinking was no longer theoretically consistent. Persistent internal non-sublatable contradictions or non-subsumable facts have undermined systemic thinking once the social configurations that were thought as realisations of a system could no longer claim normative superiority.[4] Thus paradoxes could be described as the conceptual phenomena which appear once we abandon the idea of a structure that is *realised*. If we accept that theoretical thinking must be more 'modest' in its epistemic objectives and recognise that totalistic reasoning is ill-founded by virtue of its methodological assumptions, reality appears as an interpretative field of experiences where paradoxes can be useful conceptual tools to test our limits for understanding reality when included as *positive* and *informative* contents within the interplay between micro and macro in theoretical analysis. The usefulness of the concept of paradox lies in the fact that it cannot be either solved or dissolved. It questions any clear-cut relation between theoretical normative blueprints and practices or institutions.[5] For the purposes of this chapter, I would like to highlight some of the contemporary paradoxes that can help us to assess the prospects for democracy in the present. A first set of paradoxes is introduced in relation to the understanding of the new political global constellation and a second one regarding the relation between human rights and democracy.

First, a new international order based on human rights and liberal democratic principles would have emerged as a result of the collapse of the Soviet Bloc, thanks to the economic, cultural and political supremacy of the West, with the United States in the lead. There would be no balance-of-power logic because there would only be *one* power. However, while the military ascendancy of the West is true in comparative terms, this way of perceiving things obscures the fact that the world that is now being constructed is ever less Western. New blocs have appeared to counterbalance the Western post-Cold War hegemony. The new balance of powers is no longer tipping to the West. To give one example, China, a supposedly communist country, is the United States' biggest creditor, and the Monroe Doctrine has ceased to be valid for explaining the dynamics of power in Latin America (the political sway of the United States in Latin America is ever more limited and, if it does exist, it is only thanks to the discourse of the struggle against international drug trafficking in Colombia and Mexico), not to mention the changes taking place in the continent of Africa and in South-East Asia. Therefore, there is a power which overwhelms the *others* due to its military capacity but is unable to exercise political hegemony. Furthermore, though we are still living in an order, with regard to units of power, which is based on the Westphalian system of states, one can hardly say that political sovereignty, even in the case of the great powers, continues to be a defining attribute of these units. The most surprising fact regarding this phenomenon is the simultaneity of two processes: the shaping of *great* supraregional political entities in order to confront this new situation and, at the same time, a growing number of states, however *small* they might be, which has occurred in recent years. In the past twenty years, thirty-three new states have appeared, and this is the highest figure for any comparable period over the last two centuries.[6] Against this background, one of the great risks that the world will confront in future is the result of an absence of limits and of a breakdown of the bonds that sustain it. Deterritorialisation, ecological crises and the new borderless capitalism constitute a threat to the viability of the world we share. This is the nature of worldlessness, which Hannah Arendt associates with the boundlessness inherent to the capacity of acting when the world-in-common is not taken into account.[7] Yet the problem is that we live in a world where any limit or frontier that we might establish has no legitimacy in itself since it tends to encourage exclusion, or uphold the status quo, grant privileges, undermine freedoms and so on.

Second, the new way of thinking that detaches human rights from the fact of being a citizen of a particular state turns human rights into a source of justice from a higher order. Since there is no enforcement agency, however, human rights are in practice undermined. This new basis of supranational political legitimacy for the protection of human rights should have led to a reduction in the importance of 'national identities' by transforming them in a certain sense into performative and secondary elements, while also producing diffuse, lax and porous frontiers. Nevertheless, the reality of political borders is that, rather than porous, they have on the contrary turned into real physical barriers, whether they take the form of walls, electric fences, blockades or fortresses in the literal sense. In the heart of countries that are allegedly standard-bearers of human rights, militarised barriers – for example, the United States' border with Mexico or, in Europe, the Spanish border with Morocco in Melilla – are erected to prevent the entry of people, who are sometimes even killed.[8] It seems that as a result of globalisation the loss of political sovereignty, one of the two features characterising the system of states, has given rise to increased intervention in and control of territorial integrity, which is the other characteristic of the nation-state system. This looks very much like a defensive reaction by the states: the greater the loss of political sovereignty, the greater control of territorial integrity. Moreover, the starting point of human rights discourse is essentially political and historical, but its foundation is legal and moral and based on human nature. The abstract nature of the underpinnings of human rights is in radical tension with the contextual nature of political conflicts. At best, the application *in abstracto* of individual human rights in situations of political conflict leaves things unchanged, sometimes aggravates matters and usually serves as an ideological cover for intervention from outside the country concerned, or to give legitimacy to a situation of internal repression.

The resort to individual human rights as a way of resolving conflicts tends to lead to a kind of retributive justice via punishment, but not to peace, reconciliation or stability while, at the same time, turning political discourse into moral discourse.[9] However, though democracy is the time-honoured best political form, the twentieth century has also shown that democracies can be internally and externally terribly unjust forms of government, engaging in both the most destructive colonial adventures and perpetrating the most savage massacres. As Michael Mann puts it, 'civil society may be evil'.[10] In turn, the defence of human rights may be anti-democratic in some contexts. Therefore, it seems that democracy should limit, restrain or self-cancel some of its potentialities.[11] But since the constitution of a democracy as autonomy is the matter of the people as constituent power,[12] it is difficult to see how the self can limit itself in the absolute terms which are required by the foundations of human rights.

Nowadays it is difficult to sustain the idea that if all polities are democratically governed, they will treat each other democratically. This is not only because of matters pertaining to power dynamics but also, and in particular, because it seems that the conditions and bases of their relations are apparently beyond their control. If E. H. Carr could interpret the disaster that was looming between the First World War and the Second World War as the preponderance of utopianism in international relations, by way of the creation of the League of Nations and the associated idea of promoting liberal democracy in plurinational states that had just been created, one can hardly say at present that democracies,[13] as forms of government all around the world, are utopian projects, and any diagnosis made nowadays would surely start out from the ascendancy of the opposite imaginary that E. H. Carr also discusses in his book, namely that of conventional realism – in other words, this would be saying that the dynamics and processes of globalisation are so powerful that it would be utopian to believe that its progress can be modified or controlled.[14] Beyond proclaiming the success, which is very frequently ideological, entailed in the fact that more and more polities have taken the democratic form of government, it would not appear that we are capable of seeing the implications of this for the international order. Thus, cosmopolitanism, a theory at least three centuries old, has been re-interpreted as a result of globalisation. Again paradoxically, at a time when more polities are governed democratically, which might make one imagine that the principle of autonomy would be consolidating in inter-polity relations, we are in fact witnessing three processes that are transforming it or working against it: first, is what is acknowledged as the general loss of autonomy of polities in favour of private actors, which are not subject to their control, in what is seen as an international economy with nation-states but lacking democratically legitimated international regulatory institutions; second, is what is sometimes called new imperialism – and, depending on the interpretation, this either turns one particular democracy, the United States, into a world policeman, or reduces multilateralism to agreements reached in the United Nations Security Council or NATO; and third is the generalised intrastate political exclusion of immigrant workers or refugees from other states, or internal repression of political minorities or other nationalities. One would not need, then, to be very perceptive to understand that one of the great challenges of the twenty-first century is to democratise inter-polity relations precisely at a point in human history where, as a *quaestio facti*, all the peoples occupying the surface of the earth are interconnected. In present-day conditions, it is difficult to imagine a context in which one might keep talking about democracy at the internal level independently of what is happening at the external level. It seems that the two dimensions go hand in hand. Nowadays, and not only for normative reasons, it is very problematic to think about 'the good of the nation' independently of 'the good of the world'. The other side of the coin, however, is not totally clear: what and who would 'the good of the world' represent?[15] If one asked, for example, the republic of France to declare clearly what its interests are, it would be no easy matter to establish which of them are strictly national or depending exclusively on its own sovereignty. The same thing certainly occurs with the United States or China. If one is a stubborn realist and starts out from the idea of balance of powers as the linchpin of the international order, it would be difficult to define with any clarity what a 'power' is today and which or of what kind another counterbalancing 'power' might be. If one wishes to continue analysing international relations from this standpoint, it would first be necessary to recognise a change in the nature of this kind of power, and not only because of technological changes in the military sphere which make wars between 'powers' almost impossible,[16] but also as a result of the degree of interrelationship between these supposed powers. It is against this background that one must analyse the contemporary re-interpretation of cosmopolitanism which is, approximately, the position that considers that the only political response to this new situation must entail the shaping of a suprapolity global entity.

Accordingly, some political responses to changes in recent times suggest that the tie between people and territory is weakening. Or, to be more precise, there are certain different interpretations around the question of what is, or who are the people breaking down the bond from within and converting the political issue into a matter of business conducted only among individuals.[17] From the moment in which the territory in question is the planet as a whole, which would mean that there is no more territory available, the relationship between people and territory, from this perspective, would have dissolved and territory would no longer be understood as a condition of political action or as a relevant ingredient of political organisation.[18] Accordingly, the relationship between people and territory would now be understood only from the paradigm of individual proprietorship of the earth or the notion of competent jurisdiction.[19] In keeping with this logic, it is then held that democracy will only be possible on the global scale if there are just *one* people. My basic understanding is that the constitution of a single people could be incompatible with the principle of autonomy on which democracy is grounded.

The individualist hegemony and the contemporary re-interpretation of cosmopolitanism

Nobody would be surprised by the observation that the second half of the twentieth century witnessed historical transformations that have substantially affected our way of viewing the world. After the end of the Second World War, a political imaginary that had previously been confined to either minority concerns and specialist material, or had only been deemed important in some parts of the world, began to take hegemonic form and to be used, either as a critical weapon or as a legitimising tool, against any way of understanding the human being that did not consider the individual as the unique and singular entity on the basis of which to 'constitute a polity'. One of the lessons that should have been learned from the first 'cosmopolitan' project ever to be carried out, the League of Nations, is that the ostensible solution to the problem that arose with the First World War was based on a totally erroneous diagnosis and, rather than being a solution it, too, intensified the structural problems that were already present before the war. The nation-states created out of the dismembering of ancient empires and guaranteed by the principle of collective security – which depended precisely on the volition of the selfsame nation-states – together with the establishment of liberal democracies that included several minorities or nations in one single territory, did not constitute any panacea that would lead to peace but, rather, one more reason for war.[20] In order to avoid these problems after the Second World War, the individual human being had to be placed at the core of the contemporary re-interpretation of 'cosmopolitanism', and human rights should not be linked, from now on, with being a citizen of any nation-state as happened with the first universal declaration of human rights, the Declaration of the Rights of Man and of the Citizen which was derived from the French Revolution of 1789, when it associated citizenship, nationality and human rights. Instead, it was necessary to create a new independent body, the United Nations, as a guarantor of their *universal* fulfillment. One should not ignore the fact that both international responses to the two world wars, the League of Nations and the United Nations, had their origins in the model of liberalism, in the former case, a liberalism that linked liberal democracy to the form of the nation-state and, in the latter, one that gave priority to the human being beyond the polity to which he or she belonged, in the form of individualist liberalism. For all that, it is still surprising how some of the critiques of this new individualist understanding of human rights are in tune with the other understanding, deriving from the French Revolution, except that now the quality of being a citizen would be in terms of a global polity. Yet one of the historical effects of the individualist position, although it is not shared in any explicit way, is tacitly accepted by numerous critics of the theory, including the most vehement among them: any kind of organisation of society that involves borders and differences between individuals, which is to say the existence of different peoples, is potentially aggressive even when the need for them might be recognised. This leads to a double bind. Either there are only individuals, in which case, any border works against them or, to put it another way using the metaphor of Isaiah Berlin of the 'inner citadel',[21] the only border recognised is that between 'my own skin' and what lies outside it: not only are there just individuals, but any frontier is excluding and dangerous.[22] Any theory that assumes common ground in the shaping of a polity, which therefore excludes on principle those who do not share this ground, is the typical target of this confluence of critiques from these rival positions – with regard to the fact of excluding people on the basis of what is not shared, it is irrelevant if what is held in common is constituted by private interests, culture and shared language or mutual solidarity, although it is perhaps not irrelevant with regard to the form of exclusion. Furthermore, it is possible to construct arguments from the three aspects of the need for common ground that would not recognise the need for different collectivities. There are theories for all possibilities: there can be harmony of private interests among all the citizens of the world, a common hybrid culture that we now call multiculturalism or melting pot, and mutual solidarity, which we might call global social justice.

This communion of diagnosis is based on the assumption that the notion that *all* human beings are free and equal is in tension with the existence of political collectivities that differ from one another.

Hence, it would seem that it is generally accepted, at the level of principles, that there is no democratic criterion that would permit the exclusion of human beings from any polity. Why, then, should there be different peoples if all human beings are free and equal? The form of the question certainly presupposes absolute non-contextual normative contents since, in phenomenological terms, it would not appear that all human beings are free and equal in the same way. Human beings as such, at least while they live on planet earth, are subject to a series of conditions that partially shape their lives and the range of decision-making possibilities open to them. The most significant of these is that they occupy a certain place on the surface of the planet, which is to say they are born in a clearly determinate context, from which they can dissociate themselves in different ways but always *a posteriori*. It is important to highlight this fact because it points to a tension at the heart of globalisation.

If it is true that there is global connectedness, the point from which I connect is always, and as a matter of principle, local. This tension can only be abolished from extreme positions. The first is that which asserts that the place from which a human being connects is exactly the same as that from which another human being connects. The place itself would be irrelevant as all the places are equal. The processes of global homogenisation and standardisation can be understood in this light. On the other hand, saying that all places are equally different is the other version of this notion that place *per se* has no importance. In this regard, multiculturalism performs the same function as homogenisation: invalidate the place or render it superfluous.

The justification of human rights-based multiculturalism partly denies the political significance of place since it detaches culture from the political collectivity. Paradoxically, since culture only has sense if it assumes a collective entity, it would be necessary to create a culture of human rights in order to sustain them, which constitutes a certain naturalisation of culture since this can only be done if it is linked to a particular nature, a universal abstract: Humanity. All the rest would come under the heading of particularism or pertaining to the private sphere.

The second way of understanding place is one in which, while globalisation is acknowledged, only power relations are seen, in which one particular place imposes its norms on all the rest. This position, which might be described as relativist, holds that the place or context determines the extent to which the way of being and self-understanding of human beings precludes any 'equality and freedom' that is shared by everyone. There would be a certain degree of incommensurability among the different contexts. This is how I interpret the journalists' 'clash of civilisations' catchphrase.[23]

One can find in the history of humanity a host of ways in which human beings have come together and organised into collectivities and in which the different collectivities interrelate.

With this commonplace observation I am not assuming any contradistinction between individuals and collectivities or between different collectivities. In fact, any contrast that might result from this would depend on the particular way in which human beings understand themselves in any particular context, and the reasons they give to justify what constitutes them as distinctive political collective entities and with regard to who belongs and who does not. In this sense, it is important to know in each case the reasons which, from the different theories, are offered to explain this fact since, very often, the reasoning as to why there is no longer any need to 'come together in distinct collectivities' holds that this is because the reasons that once made it necessary no longer exist. Thus, although in the course of history explanations have always been given in the terrain of conceptualisations as to why we live in different collectivities, the general form of this *factum* has never been questioned. A relevant precedent for any critique of this *factum* goes back to when Diogenes of Sinope ('the Cynic'), a Greek philosopher of the fifth century BCE, describes himself as *kosmopolites*: 'I am a citizen of the world'. The term was used, for the first time it seems, as a way of automatically opposing the usual practice by his claiming precisely that he is an individual who *lives outside of any collectivity that is not the Kosmos*. In the classical period, a Greek, asked about his origins, would have had to name the *polis* of which he was a citizen. The first time the term 'cosmopolitan' is used, then, is to say that one is a citizen who lives alone and outside of any political collectivity.[24]

The best-known, the most long-lived and influential explanation of this *fact*, is Aristotle's: the human being is, 'by nature, a *zoon politikon*'.[25] Nevertheless, many rival theories have challenged everything that this implied, and every change or historical transformation has entailed changes in conceptualisation as well. Certainly, the fact of explicitly wondering about a practice that has always been the same at the heart of human existence, which is to say asking oneself about *the whys and wherefores of what has always been thus*, should imply some reference to the nature of the human beings who are engaged in the project. It is not very difficult to see that answering the question 'why is what is', when there is no possible comparison with other ways of being, provides no explanation but is rather an observation, since there is no way an explanation can be compared with other hypotheses: we have *always* come together in collectivities, consequently we are constituted by nature in that way. In historical and anthropological terms, the only thing that one could compare with this *factum* would be nomadic collectivities but, even so, they *are* collectivities.[26] However, the principles of what is known as the dominant modern political philosophy spring from a new theory represented by the philosopher Thomas Hobbes, who takes a radical stand against the Aristotelian position and accepts as an explanation of the collectivity a totally counterfactual principle, which cannot be proven empirically either, based on what thenceforth started to be known as the state of nature:

> The majority of previous writers on public Affairs either assume or seek to prove or simply assert that Man is an animal born fit for Society – in the Greek phrase, Zoon politikon [. . .] This Axiom, though very widely accepted is nevertheless false; the error proceeds from a superficial view of human nature. Closer observation of the causes why men seek each other's company and enjoy associating with each other, will easily reach the conclusion that it does not happen because by nature it could not be otherwise, but by chance.[27]

The importance of this coinage consists in its pointing out that the fact that humans live in collectivities is neither necessary nor natural but contingent, and while this is the case at the empirical level, it is not so in terms of principles. Since, in the order of de facto reality, men indeed live in collectivities, if men were able not to do so, it would be necessary to invent a counterfactual situation, the state of nature, in order to illustrate such a situation. Hence the fact that a man lives collectively with other men is only an *effect*, a result but not a condition. The fact that men live together is only an *appearance* for, in reality, they are independent units, except that this reality is of the same type as the entities theorised by the sciences of physics and mathematics, inasmuch as they are invisible and hypothetical like gravity or the atom. This line of thought is what gives rise to liberalism. Clearly, the trap of this position is that it takes man's nature back to another hypothetical dimension, the state of nature and, in principle, this nature is neither demonstrable nor refutable. In addition, just as we saw how the Aristotelian explanation is, at bottom, no explanation, the Hobbesian one is no explanation either, since it has to assume something that is not observable: his principles are not demonstrable but are axioms.[28]

The fact of living together which, as such, seems to go back to the beginning of time, has ceased to be so evident in the eyes of many people, not only theoretically, as in the case of Hobbes, but also empirically: the tendency, process, dynamics, or historical power entailed in globalisation would deny that there is any sense in the necessity of a plurality of differentiated collectivities and would lead us to the establishment of a single collectivity called 'Humanity' which would take as its premise, in keeping with liberal logic, that human beings are taken into account only in their capacity as individuals.

The 1945 Charter of the United Nations and the Universal Declaration of Human Rights of 1948 would be political milestones in this process. One would take into account individuals as entities *in themselves*, as members of the collective macro-entity we call 'Humanity'.[29] This simplification, although it may sound grotesque, appears at the root of many contemporary re-interpretations of cosmopolitan theories that have emerged with respect to globalisation.[30] Beyond the reasons that might be adduced in favour of or against this appraisal, what does seem to be a point of agreement is that, from a historical standpoint, there occurred around the nineteenth century the consolidation of a transformation that would change not only the ways in which human beings related, but also their way of understanding themselves as a result: the World became Global.[31] If there is going to be a world-in-common, it will have to be just *one*. If, until that point one could assume that relations between distinct collectivities were limited both in extension and intension, from the time that the globe was occupied, dominated and known, the interconnectedness would be total and would have significant consequences for the forms that had previously prevailed in the ways in which different elements related to each other.[32]

However, scholars tend to distinguish between the world and the globe, where the world would be a 'man-made artifact', in Arendt's words, and globe would simply refer to the spherical surface of planet Earth and it would exist even if mankind did not. Although the distinction is pertinent, certain conclusions would, however, be derived from it on the basis of the historical development of modernity which would lead to countervailing positions: globalisation would be the 'process' that *de-mundane-ises* the world, makes it less worldly, and takes away its constructed and artificial character, and the historical time to come would be that resulting from the logic of necessity or of economic processes. Forces governing the course of history would have been unleashed. Yet if one upholds the distinction between world and globe, the question as to who would have set off this 'process' only has one answer: humans themselves. Hence, the question, as I understand it, would be this: why, as of a certain historical moment, is the world 'made' taking as a premise the globe of the earth, which entails unicity and naturalisation, but not understanding globalisation as being opposed to the human world. Globalisation is only one particular self-understanding of making the world, which is certainly self-destructive. One of the consequences of understanding the world from the standpoint of the globe is that there cannot be different worlds. Both parts of the distinction, very much used in the Francophone world, between mondialisation – making a human world *common to all*, although there are different ways of doing so – and globalisation start, I believe, from the same principle, namely universality in extension, whether of a shared world that includes all human beings, or that of the finite extension of the globe of the earth. Naturally, the opposite context of a plurality of differ-ent worlds does not mean that they are incommensurable.[33]

The ingenuity and immensity of the question could make one forget that asking it as such has only made sense very recently. Certainly, there was little point in asking it before the end of the Second World War. After that, a generalised perception arose that something basically problematic was occurring in the assumptions on the basis of which human beings constructed polities. Until that happened, apart from a few exceptions in some intellectual circles, the crucial theoretical problem that governed relations between poli-ties was not so much that they were multiple and plural, which was accepted as just one more fact among others, with all the problems deriving from that, in particular those pertaining to the inclusion/exclusion binomial and wars.[34] The importance of collective political entities was not discussed. What was quite a problem and not gener-ally accepted was, rather, the idea that *all of us* were human beings in the same way and/or the question of whether only a few of us were. What was obvious was the difference among peoples, but not the similarity among their members. Therefore, if we were not all equal, boundaries were needed.

All kinds of divisions have appeared in attempts to explain why we are not the same: from the barbarians in comparison with the Greeks, through to Indians in comparison with the Spanish, infidels in comparison with Christians, African 'savages' in comparison with European colonisers, and so forth. This difference tends to be an a priori condition of political action. Extreme cases of difference made people think that not everyone was a human being like 'us'. After 1945 a perception began to take shape,[35] according to which the existence, analytically and historically, of a plurality of polities would presuppose a fundamental inequality among human beings, between those who belong to the polity in question and those who do not, and all the inter-polity dramas and violence would have arisen in response to the connection between exclusion from a polity and the non-human being: the techniques of extermination/dehu-manisation of the Nazi concentration camps in accordance with the National Socialist doctrine of the supremacy of the Aryan race would be its most distinctive manifestation, together with the theories of social Darwinism that were constructed to legitimate nineteenth- and twentieth-century colonialism.[36] It is against this background that the Universal Declaration of Human Rights resounded in 1948, in a very clear expression of this conviction. Article 2 of the Declaration is the most significant for my purposes here:

> *Everyone* is entitled to *all* the rights and freedoms set forth in this Declaration, without distinction of *any kind*, such as race, colour, sex, language, religion, political or other opinion, national or social origin, property, birth or other status. Furthermore, *no distinction* shall be made on the basis of the political, jurisdictional or international status of the country or territory to which a person belongs, whether it be independent, trust, non-self-governing or under any other limitation of sovereignty. (italics mine)

An extreme interpretation of this article could make any frontier established between polities a breach of human rights. One consequence of this is that, after the Second World War, as many writers have pointed out from very different perspectives, the principle of *ius gentium* underwent such a radical transformation that one might even say it has disappeared.[37] Once states were no longer deemed to be the chief actors in international law, the classical internal/external difference that had structured relations between polities faded out as what are known as international relations, or the post-Westphalian era, began to predominate.[38]

A new order that was no longer based on the Westphalian model would entail, in the view of its upholders, the disappearance, or at least irrelevance, of polities. This thesis understands the Westphalian order in terms of the Hobbesian contractualist paradigm and its analogy with the domestic sphere.[39] The analogy consists in considering polities as individuals in the state of nature. What gives rise to the state at the internal level, a positive constitution with a monopoly on co-active power enabling its emergence from the state of nature, however that might be interpreted, is proscribed for states. To continue with the analogy, the world order would be seen as constituted by a set of 'individuals', the polities, without any positive law to bind them together and, therefore, in the absence of any monopoly on force that would equally compel them all, the state of nature between them would be war or anarchy. A long tradition of modern international law mainly considers *ius gentium* in the light of *ius bellum* (conversely, in my view, affirming that wars are a serious, perhaps the most serious, problem in the international order *should* not be the same as stating that the international order appeared in order to regulate war). This lack among states of an all-embracing norm that would unite them and require their compliance would be the factor that has legitimated the principle of non-intervention in inter-polity affairs and, with that, the consistency of state sovereignty. From this perspective, contemporary cosmopolitan critics of the Westphalian system would consider that if a global-scale binding law was desired, it would be necessary – to continue with the analogy – to convert the whole globe into a domestic sphere,[40] and thereby avoid the 'state of nature' among polities and discretionary powers or arbitrariness, in both the external sphere with the possibility of unjust war, and in the internal sphere with the possibility of human rights violations, which characterises the principle of state sovereignty. If this step is to be taken, at least three necessary conditions must be met: there should be global, and not just international, laws; all individuals should be subject to these laws; and there should be courts with universal jurisdiction and a global coercive power. Jürgen Habermas has recently pointed out that the discussion in the core of the international community is no longer about what conception of international law – the realist (state of nature) or the idealist (construction of a system of positive international law) – is the more adequate to tackle injustice, but whether international law or the unilateral policy of one very powerful polity would be the better measure.[41] What Habermas seems to overlook is the fact that this dispute is no longer one between international law and empire, but between international law and global 'private' law. Any critique of the United States' global empire would not entail only the fact that it acts as a global policeman, but that it conceals private interests under the ideology of protecting human rights. Few people question the idea that *some kind of coercive force* with universal jurisdiction is needed to protect human rights but, paradoxically, the justification given as the basis for this protection, namely humanity as the bearer of human rights, can only be invoked, according to contractualist logic, in the domain of natural law. One of the main problems with this approximation is that of defining what human rights are being referred to, and who are the bearer-subjects of these rights, apart from the problem of the source of their legitimacy. In the democratic context, laws and constitutions are variable and disputable. The understanding of human rights as inherent to the human being goes against any democratic understanding of the law. Once the contents are defined, they are valid independently of the context, history, the type of government and their institutionalisation. It is not very difficult to perceive this move as one that amounts to a moralisation of politics, or to realise that the fact that this way of viewing things is a majority view in the United States is not independent from the international role the country plays.[42] Thus, in order to justify the universal reach of positive law or, in other words, the possibility of an eventual *global* co-active force, one must appeal to the universal sway of natural law and the incorporation of certain rights, independently of positive law, in individuals. One has the feeling that the application of contractualist theory to one single global polity where it is assumed that there is nothing outside its ambit actually implies the self-cancellation of the contractualist theory: there would be no criterion that would make it possible to discern what is natural law and what is positive law. Some thinkers call the domain wherein this situation prevails the 'state of exception'. The best known theory that hypothesises the state of exception, which entails a blurring over of the boundary between positive law and nature, as the paradigm of the new international relations, may be found in Giorgio Agamben's 2005 book *State of Exception*. However, this theory can only be sustained, at least theoretically, if the following points are accepted: (1) the analogy between individuals and states in the international order; (2) that the individual is the basic unit; and (3) the contractualist theory of political affairs. It is quite surprising to see how both critics and champions of the international order who share this standpoint agree on the basic premise that it is related to the possibility of war. All contemporary cosmopolitan approaches that start out from this perspective, the construction of a single political entity to curb war, always favour a government based on security, order and the defence of individual rights. At the same time, all theories that are critical of this form of government as being anti-democratic, while yet sharing the idea of war as the fount of the international order, would have to affirm that people, the masses, are always dominated and subject to violence.[43] It should be pointed out, however, that the contractualist theory was only one among several that sought to explain the changes that were occurring.[44] Any understanding of order that makes it equivalent to the rule of law must lead to the idea that the best possible order is that in which the *same law rules everywhere*.[45]

To return to contemporary cosmopolitan theories, it would seem then that, if we cease to organise ourselves in diverse and different ways and take as our starting point the supposition that the plurality of political collectivities has been one of the key problems of history, then, according to this theory, relations of domination between peoples would disappear. If this reality, this fact, disappeared, the problem would also disappear. However, it is not explained how unjust domination appears through the mere fact of the existence of different collectivities.[46] Furthermore, relations of domination between polities which are exclusively based on violence, which is to say that they do not need *any* kind of justification, are notable for their absence in the historical record, at least in the sources that are available to us. Violence has always been justified as a means, but never as an end in itself. Then again, we know that de facto differences do not imply differences in values or, to reword the proposition slightly, it is not possible to derive normative statements from empirical statements. To justify through difference an explicit political domination, it is necessary to bind an epistemological theory to a normative view.[47]

Autonomy, independence and the democratic inescapability of a plurality of political collectivities

In modern times, democracy as the commitment to autonomy is historically linked with the notion of independence as self-determination, as the result of two events that, in the long term, have ended up combining and becoming predominant in the understanding of political affairs. The first, classically illustrated by the French Revolution, entails an internal rupture within a collectivity with all the ties of organic and hierarchical dependence derived from the *ancien régime*. The second, which is normally associated with the 1776 Declaration of Independence of the British colonies in America, occurs externally and constitutes a break with an alien, colonial power.[48] In conceptual terms, it was assumed that in order to give oneself one's own laws, the *self* must be independent from the *others*. The old philosophical concept of *causa sui* re-interpreted as self-determination represents this connection.[49] These two ruptures linked autonomy to independence as self-determination. Indeed, historically speaking, the word 'autonomy' was coined in ancient Greece in order to claim a *polis*'s capacity for dictating its own laws independently of the Athens-based Empire. Claiming the autonomy of a *polis* meant reasserting its independence vis-à-vis the domination-seeking power of Athens.[50] After the advent of Hellenism the word ceased to be used, but it reappeared at the beginning of modernity in the context of the wars of religion and the juridical-theological interpretation of the new order with the principle *cuius regio, eius religio* (whose realm, his religion), which is concerned with freedom of worship against the defence of Catholic orthodoxy by the Holy Roman Empire and is the key principle of the Peace of Augsburg of 1555.[51] Thus, historically speaking, autonomy as a concept emerges in response to universalist claims embodied by empires, and it becomes interpreted as self-determination with the age of revolutions at the end of the eighteenth century.[52]

The most difficult matter to resolve is whether the democratic link between autonomy and independence as self-determination is of a contingent nature, and whether the fact that they have gone hand in hand historically is only a function of the particular conditions wherein they have appeared, or whether there would be some kind of conceptual relationship between independence and autonomy that would make it very unlikely that one would exist without the other.[53] It is, of course, not necessary to understand independence as the fact of not depending in any way at all on anybody or on questions pertaining to territorial control. If that were the case, the only possible connection between independence and autonomy would be liberation due to death, the only situation in which one does not depend on anything at all.[54] By independence, one understands, in this context, whether it is necessary or not to presuppose the existence of a domain external to that in which the principle of autonomy prevails, or whether there should be a plurality of spheres or not.[55] Evidently, whether the principle of autonomy prevails in these other external spheres or otherwise is not irrelevant to the question. As I shall attempt to demonstrate, the concept of 'a people' is what lies behind this definition of independence. Here it is only a negative determination of plurality, not a positive one in the sense of determining what a 'people' is. The question thus raised goes back to the one I stated at the beginning: whether the principle of autonomy requires that there should be, at least as a possibility, a plurality of 'peoples'. Naturally, this is not to deny the possibility of there being *one* single people as defined above, but it does question whether this fact would be compatible with democracy. In other words, and it is important to make this clear, the discussion is whether democracy as such requires a plurality of peoples, and not in relation to other principles or any claim for plurality *per se*. Unfortunately, the cosmopolitan counter-argument would not be able to operate with an empirical counter-example since for those who wish to put forth the thesis I wish to criticise, this is seen today as merely a normative project even though it has an influence on many contemporary events. At present there is not *one* single people inhabiting planet Earth (unless by 'people' we understand humanity, which is precisely the notion I wish to criticise) and, therefore, any criticism aiming to demonstrate its incompatibility with the principle of autonomy would have to operate essentially at the conceptual level, although it can be illustrated with contemporary examples that show this tension.

A minimal definition of autonomy, which does not presuppose normative or empirical contents, would have to leave the elements of its definition maximally indeterminate. In view of this, the definition I would offer almost derives from its own etymology: 'to give oneself one's own law'.[56]

The definition itself offers the elements that make it possible to disentangle it into components. They are conceptually and empirically analysable in terms of both commonalities shared by all contexts where autonomy is the key political interpretative concept, and differences that are due to the variety of possible interpretations of it.[57] The structure of autonomy then implies several concepts: (1) the concept of 'oneself', which refers to the entity whose autonomy is predicated; (2) the concept of 'own', which should be interpreted from a threefold perspective and countering the natural/positive, private/public and own/alien schemata; (3) the concept of 'law', which takes one back to the legality/legitimacy problem and the form of government; and (4) the 'giving', namely the constitutive, active aspect of the principle of autonomy, which should be analysed taking as its starting points both the constituent/constituted dialectic and the question of whether, if one is 'to give oneself one's own law', it is necessary to guarantee certain prior existential and/or economic conditions.

Several implications follow from the general sense of the principle of autonomy. First, the normativity that any sphere presupposes cannot be derived from any external source. This is what is called the re-flexive character of autonomy and is what ensures that every determination is self-determination.

Second, any normativity is, in principle, disputable. Indeed, the fact that the norms that regulate human life in a given ambit can only be legitimated on the basis of the principle of autonomy, that every determinate content has to be recognised as set in place, established, instituted by the determinate object or, in other words, that the ambit on the basis of which the norms are justified is the same as that wherein they are applied, means that the character of this normativity is contingent and therefore revocable. Certainly, if the norm had the character of necessity it could not be modifiable, and it could not have been set in place or established. This is the characteristic that opens the door to the possibility of the transformation of any ambit.

Finally, the conditions on the basis of which the principle of autonomy is established imply that there is no law, order or normativity that is pre-established before autonomy can be exercised. There is only normativity once autonomy is exercised. The opposite situation would be determined by the fact that the law or normativity had already been installed prior to the exercise of the principle of autonomy. The source of law would therefore come from an external sphere. The sphere over which the law prevails would not recognise the origin of the law as its own but as alien. The principle of autonomy must explicitly recognise that the origin of the law is internal to its own ambit and not external. To express it slightly differently, if there is nothing previous to the determination of the law, the only factor that could have been present before it is the origin of the law and, in these conditions, the law can only exist if the origin of the law *realises, makes explicit, is aware, understands, wishes, desires* that the law is applied *to itself*. Alienation or heteronomy is that situation in which *it is not known* that the *self* is the origin of the law. Evidently, awareness of this fact will have a major bearing on what kind of normativity is in force. From the analytical standpoint, the particular collectivity, the people, is always the origin of the law. The other question is how this people perceives itself, and how this knowing or knowledge relates to the possibility of transforming or changing the normativity.[58]

Hence the principle of autonomy entails the self-understanding that the sphere of origin of the law is the same as the sphere in which it is applied. If the principle of autonomy is to be valid there must be self-understanding. In fact, there are practices with a history that amply exceeds the period in which the principle of autonomy prevails, and that are also produced within their own ambit; for example, having children, eating meat, making war, establishing borders, producing goods, etc. The difference with respect to other historical periods is related to the way in which these practices are justified and the legitimacy they presuppose. In the conditions of modernity, it is not possible to justify them without turning to the principle of autonomy. We very often focus more on practices that change as a result of the principle of autonomy but overlook those that remain and need to be justified anew.

The other sense in which we speak of understanding is determined by the fact that, granted that the law is *consciously, explicitly* introduced, the decision must be made as to *which* laws, compatible with the principle of autonomy, are being introduced. Since the principle of autonomy offers no specific content of the norms that are to prevail, in principle there would have to be infinite possible effectuations of the principle, *each one of them obeying the possible interpretations of the principle of autonomy*. Thus, the principle of autonomy presupposes self-understanding and an infinite variety of interpretations. The reverse situation, however, is not true: it is not the case that every instance of self-understanding implies the principle of autonomy.

In this regard, if one assumes the implications of the definition, it would require speaking of the concept's triple sense of radicality.

First, this radicality consists of the fact that, unlike other historical spheres, that which characterises modernity is that it sets no a priori limit to the criterion of autonomy as a source of legitimacy. In conditions of modernity, there is no experience that would *de jure* have to be excluded from the principle of autonomy. The radicality does not lie in the concept itself but in the extension of its domain which is, a priori, unlimited.

Second, the radicality consists of the fact that no normativity, order, legislation or whatever one might wish to call it, has the character of necessity and permanence *per se*, and hence every order is contingent. The possibility of being disputable is inherent to the nature of the self-positioning of any normativity.

Third, the radicality of the principle of autonomy lies in the fact that it is the bedrock on which modernity is founded as a phenomenon. It is true that laying down the principle of autonomy as the foundation of modernity would have certain implications deriving from the aforementioned fact. If every norm is in principle arguable thanks to the principle of autonomy while, at the same time, the principle of autonomy has to constitute the foundation of any norm in the conditions of modernity, this means setting in place as the foundation of an order the very element that makes it possible to question it. The principle of autonomy is, if one might put it like this, an anti-foundational foundation.

I shall conclude now with an analysis of the first of the concepts I have disentangled from the principle of autonomy: the concept of 'oneself'. It should be pointed out that I am not primordially concerned with what makes something be a *self*, this being a problem that is discussed theoretically in relation to the problem of identity, or to what makes the self be *one* or, in other words, the *same* over time. Tackled from this perspective, a certain understanding of the subject of autonomy will always be given priority. I wish to view it from the inclusion/exclusion standpoint in relation to what the principle of autonomy implies: whether the set of those who come under the legislation is, in principle, identical with the set of those who legislate.

If we think about the problem of the polity from the point of view of inclusion/exclusion and consider, as I have supposed, that it is necessary to stop constituting these two elements within this paradigm, contemporary cosmopolitanism offers an answer. The classical problem pertaining to inclusion refers to those members of the polity who, although living within it, are not fully-fledged members. Immigrants and refugees are the classical object. They are excluded by the fact of not being included. However, one cannot overlook the fact that, within this logic, one also finds another problem, of equal or greater importance, related to inclusion. This refers to all those who are included in the polity and do not wish to be, or those who are excluded by the fact of being included. Under this heading one finds all the problems connected with assimilation, secession and so on. Contemporary cosmopolitanism, together with universal human rights discourse, considers that these problems will cease to exist as of the moment in which all human beings are included, and this can only happen under two conditions. Either we all belong to one single polity, or we stop thinking about citizenship as a political *quality* and start seeing it as a *property* inherent to the fact of being a human being. This is the discourse of human rights. (Linking *membership* to nationality is one possibility among several. If it were associated with work, for example, immigrant workers could not be politically excluded but a problem of exclusion would arise with those who do not work or cannot work.)

The evident paradox of this problem is that the relationship in the inclusion/exclusion binomial is one of mutual co-dependence. There is no inclusion if there is no exclusion. As soon as one considers that all human beings are included by reason of their human rights, one has to ask under what conditions, even if they are only conceptual, any kind of exclusion might operate. Once one ceases to consider citizenship as a quality, as something one has and can stop having, and when it comes to be a property of human beings, someone can only be excluded if he or she is considered to be not human, and thus does not therefore have *human* rights. A second consequence of the blurring of the inclusion/exclusion difference is that, if all human beings are included in the polity in question, any criterion that makes it possible to differentiate between included and excluded and distinguish between collectivities would have been eliminated. When any criterion is discarded out of principle, the result is that there will only be individuals as such and not members of a polity. When membership is universal, it means that there is no relevant membership. Accordingly, if one wished to draw a new inclusion/exclusion line, the criterion would be between 'my skin' and outside it. This would be a situation of generalised exclusion or, to put it in other words, of the supremacy of the private domain. If one is to uphold any idea of the non-private, or of what is held in common, one would have to go back to human rights, which takes one back to the starting point and to the aggregation of private interests. In this case, one sees, too, that the exclusion would be twofold: on the one hand, universal and generalised exclusion of anything that is not one's 'own' and 'private' and, on the other, exclusion of all those who have nothing to defend as private except their intimacy, the people who are normally referred to as the poor. To the question of how to make people respect this new line between inclusion and exclusion, which is to say, what government, which would have to be a world government, could enforce this line, what kind of authority would be necessary to see that it is respected, one can conclude by recalling Arendt's dictum when she discussed this question in *The Origins of Totalitarianism*:

The presently popular liberal notion of a World Government is based, like all liberal notions of political power, on the same concept of individuals submitting to a central authority which 'overawes them all', except that nations are now taking the place of individuals. The World Government is to overcome and eliminate authentic politics, that is, different peoples getting along with each other in the full force of their power.[59]

We cannot know yet whether the institutions currently built at a world level will conform to this prospect, but the blurring of all political differences between collectivities only reinforces the liberal understanding of the political as the order instituted to protect the free interaction of individuals, which is the only ideology that can sustain a cosmopolitan global order.

Notes

1. See, for example, John Darwin, *After Tamerlane: The Rise and Fall of Global Empires, 1400–2000* (New York: Bloomsbury, 2008), and Christopher Alan Bayly, *The Birth of the Modern World, 1780–1914: Global Connections and Comparisons* (Oxford: Blackwell, 2004).
2. For an exhaustive critical analysis of the different theories of cosmopolitanism, see Gerard Delanty, *The Cosmopolitan Imagination: The Renewal of Critical Social Theory* (Cambridge: Cambridge University Press, 2010).
3. This chapter does not address theories of freedom in relation to the constitution of a people. I am only interested in the question of whether or not the notion of democracy as autonomy entails a plurality of collectivities. The discussion on what a democratic collective entity consists of, how borders between some people and other people are to be democratically understood, what their possible justifications are, how they are legitimately established and how one should deal with them is a task that needs the length of a book to be properly addressed.
4. In philosophical terms, 'When paradoxes arise in describing a phenomenon, we must assume that the description proceeds from inappropriate premises, that is, it employs inadequate categorical means.' Ernst Tugendhat, *Self-Consciousness and Self-Determination* (Cambridge, MA: MIT Press, 1989), p. 3.
5. See Joan Wallach Scott, *Only Paradoxes to Offer: French Feminists and the Rights of Man* (Cambridge, MA: Harvard University Press, 1996), pp. 4–5; Chantal Mouffe, *The Democratic Paradox* (London: Verso, 2000), p. 4; Martin Hartmann and Axel Honneth, 'Paradoxes of Capitalism', *Constellations*, 13, no. 1 (2006): 47: 'A contradiction is paradoxical when, precisely through the attempt to realize such an intention, the probability of realizing it is decreased.' However, the use of the concept by Hartmann and Honneth, though it avoids the

problems of the concept of ideology, presupposes the idea of two spheres with their own proper 'logics': the economic, represented by neoliberal capitalism, and the 'normative', represented by the welfare state. While recognising that capitalism also contains normative principles, they conceptualise them as radically different from those that shape our sociocultural life. I prefer to interpret the concept of paradox without the need of assuming a priori differentiated functional logics and compartmentalised normative principles, and thinking it synchronically rather than diachronically; as the occurrence at the *same time and place* of phenomena allegedly commonly *thought* as mutually exclusive, and not as the contradictory effect derived from the elapsed time between an intention and its negation occurred in its implementation. To some extent, the sociological concept of 'unintended consequence' or 'perverse effect' and the economic concept of 'negative externalities' have the same assumptions as Hartmann and Honneth's use of 'paradox'. The introduction of the time factor in the analysis, in my opinion, makes difficult the use of the concept of paradox when comparing different moments in time and overall, if one wants to consider human beings also as actors.

6. See Andrew Linklater, *The Transformation of Political Community* (Cambridge: Polity, 1998), pp. 32–4, for the interplay between globalisation and fragmentation.

7. See Hannah Arendt, *The Human Condition* (Chicago: University of Chicago Press 1998), pp. 190–2. I concur with Etienne Tassin's interpretation on this point in his book *Un monde commun: Pour une cosmo-politique des conflits* (Paris: Seuil, 2003), p. 117ff.

8. See the Amnesty International report on the European borders with Ceuta and Melilla, *Spain and Morocco: Failure to Protect the Rights of Migrants – One Year On*, 2006, http://www.amnesty.org/en/library/asset/EUR41/009/2006/en/725e1555-d3e6-11dd-8743-d305bea2b2c7/eur410092006en.pdf (last accessed 29 December 2014). See also Wendy Brown, *Walled States: Waning Sovereignty* (New York: Zone Books, 2010).

9. See Mahmood Mamdani, *Saviors and Survivors: Darfur, Politics, and the War on Terror* (New York: Pantheon, 2009), on the United States' intervention in Sudan and how this way of understanding human rights and conflict resolution only reinforces a postcolonial situation. For the history of human rights, see Samuel Moyn, *The Last Utopia: Human Rights in History* (Cambridge: The Belknap Press of Harvard University Press, 2010).

10. Michael Mann, *The Dark Side of Democracy: Explaining Ethnic Cleansing* (Cambridge: Cambridge University Press, 2005), p. 21: 'In civil society theory, democracy, peace, and tolerance are said to result when individuals are engaged in vibrant, dense social relations provided by voluntary institutions, which protect them from the manipulations of state elites [. . .] This is naïve. Radical ethnonationalists often succeed precisely because their civil society networks are denser and

more mobilizing than those of their more moderate rivals [. . .] *Civil society may be evil*' (italics mine).

11. See Nathalie Karagiannis in this volume.

12. See Andreas Kalyvas in this volume.

13. Whether or not these are real democracies, is a discussion that is well beyond the scope of this analysis.

14. Edward Hallet Carr, *The Twenty Years' Crisis 1919–1939: An Introduction to the Study of International Relations* (London: Papermac, 1981), pp. 26–8.

15. Empires have always been justified on such grounds.

16. Hannah Arendt, *On Violence* (New York: Harcourt, Brace & World, 1970), p. 10.

17. Brad R. Roth, 'Anti-Sovereigntism, Liberal Messianism, and Excesses in the Drive against Impunity', in Martti Koskenniemi, *Finnish Yearbook of International Law Volume XXII 2001* (Leiden: Martinus Nijhoff Publishers, 2003), p. 17: 'The old political messianism saw the realisation of freedom only in the pursuit and attainment of an absolute collective purpose, the new political messianism sees freedom in the negation of collective purpose'.

18. Margaret Moore, 'The Ethics of Secession and a Normative Theory of Nationalism', *Canadian Journal of Law & Jurisprudence*, 13 (2005): 225: 'This is dubious because the state does not "own" the territory. Territory simply refers to the domain of jurisdictional authority, to the geographical area in which self-government operates.' For a critical approach on deterritorialisation, see Michael Hardt and Antonio Negri, *Empire* (Cambridge, MA: Harvard University Press, 2000), p. xii: 'Empire establishes no territorial centre of power and does not rely on fixed boundaries or barriers. It is a decentred and deterritorializing apparatus of rule that progressively incorporates the entire global realm within its open, expanding frontiers.' For the idea of territory as an inescapable condition, see Carr, *The Twenty Years' Crisis*, p. 229; and for a vigorous defence of the relationship, almost one of identity, between people and territory in the international sphere, see Carl Schmitt, *The Nomos of the Earth in the International Law of the Jus Publicum Europaeum* (New York: Telos, 2006), ch. 4.

19. The principle of universal jurisdiction included in the legislation of many states would entail an internal deconstruction of the bond between law and territory. However, when the principle of universal jurisdiction is linked with supra-state and a-territorial entities beyond the reach of democratic control, the International Criminal Court, for example, the risk that it could become an organ used by some polities to hold sway over others is very great. See Chandra Lekha Sriram, 'Externalisation of Justice: What Does It Mean and What Is at Stake?', in Koskenniemi, *Finnish Yearbook*, pp. 47–71; and Mahmood, *Saviors and Survivors*, pp. 282–8.

20. Carr, *The Twenty Years' Crisis*, p. 230; and Hannah Arendt, *The*

Origins of Totalitarianism [1951] (New York and London: Harvest Books, 1973), p. 270ff.

21. Isaiah Berlin, *Liberty*, ed. Henry Hardy (Oxford: Oxford University Press, 2002), p. 181ff. Michael Walzer offers a critique of this metaphor in his book *Spheres of Justice: A Defense of Pluralism and Equality* (Oxford: Basil Blackwell, 1983), p. 39: 'to tear down the walls of the state is not [. . .] to create a world without walls, but to create a thousand petty fortresses'.

22. Tzvetan Todorov, *The Fear of Barbarians: Beyond the Clash of Civilizations* (Chicago: University of Chicago Press, 2010), p. 52: 'These days, in Western countries, collective identity no longer enjoys a good press. It is viewed with suspicion: the suspicion that it is a sort of conspiracy against individual freedom. When it comes to finding a specifically human trait, people prefer to lay the emphasis on the capacity that each person has of opposing all definition from outside, all physical or cultural heredity.'

23. For an understanding of the connection between locality and globality as different dimensions of space, not mediated by global institutions, see Saskia Sassen, *Territory, authority, rights: from medieval to global assemblages* (Princeton, NJ: Princeton University Press, 2008), pp. 365–75.

24. Diogenes Laertius, *Lives of Eminent Philosophers* (Cambridge, MA: Harvard University Press, 1925), p. 64. Diogenes was, in fact, a citizen of Sinope, a Greek *polis*, but had to seek exile in Athens, where it is said that he chose to live outside society in a large jar, after committing the crime of 'defacement of the currency'.

25. Aristotle, *Politics* (London: Harvard University Press, 1944), p. 1253a.

26. See Anatoly M. Khazanov, *Nomads and the Outside World* (Madison, WI: University of Wisconsin Press, 1994), in particular ch. 5, in which he clearly shows the different ways in which nomads constitute differentiated polities, both in relation to other nomad collectivities and to 'sedentary' collectivities.

27. Thomas Hobbes, *On the Citizen* (Cambridge: Cambridge University Press, 1998), pp. 21–2.

28. For the connection between this axiom and the assumptions of political science, see Peter Wagner, *Modernity as Experience and Interpretation: A New Sociology of Modernity* (Cambridge: Polity, 2008), p. 240ff.; and Peter Wagner, *Theorizing Modernity* (London: Sage, 2001), p. 23ff. For the link between the European understanding of the New World and State of Nature hypothesis, see Enrique Dussel, *Politics of Liberation: A Critical Global History* (Norwich: SCM Press, 2011), §8.

29. A clear formulation of this idea may be found in Nigel Rapport, 'Emancipatory Cosmopolitanism: A Vision of the Individual Free from Culture, Custom and Community', in G. Delanty (ed.), *Routledge Handbook of Cosmopolitanism Studies* (New York: Routledge, 2012), p. 101: 'One states that individual human beings might enjoy an existence beyond the bounds of collectivities, their norms, conventional

practices and traditions classifying the world [. . .] According to this vision, individuals are the constituents units of humanity – humankind is a collection of individual I's – and the individual life is a thing-in-itself which cannot be treated as means to any ends besides those it itself has construed.' Martha Nussbaum, 'Patriotism and Cosmopolitanism', in Martha Nussbaum and Joshua Cohen, *For Love of Country?* (Boston: Beacon Press, 1996), offers a less individualist version of this idea.

30. Francis Fukuyama would be the best-known representative of this view.

31. John Darwin, *After Tamerlane: The Rise and Fall of Global Empires, 1400–2000*, pp. 6–7; and Christopher Alan Bayly, 'Introduction', in *The Birth of the Modern World, 1780–1914: Global Connections and Comparisons*, pp. 1–19.

32. 'Just as the family and its property were replaced by class membership and national territory, so mankind now begins to replace nationally bound societies, and the earth replaces the limited state territory' – Arendt, *The Human Condition*, p. 257.

33. For the distinction between mondialisation and globalisation, see Jacques Derrida, 'Globalisation, Peace, and Cosmopolitanism', in Derrida, *Negotiations: Interventions and Interviews, 1971–2001*, ed. and trans. Elisabeth Rottenberg (Redwood City, CA: Stanford University Press, 2002), pp. 371–86; and Jean-Luc Nancy, *The Creation of the World or Globalization* (Albany, NY: State University of New York Press, 2007). For an approximation that does not assume from the outset the principle common to both mondialisation and globalisation, and that contemplates the possibility of the co-existence of different worlds, see Nathalie Karagiannis and Peter Wagner (eds), *Varieties of World-Making: Beyond Globalization* (Liverpool: Liverpool University Press, 2007).

34. The growing importance of the individual is also related to the treatment of soldiers in wars between states in the nineteenth century. See Amy Ross, 'Geographies of Justice: International Law, National Sovereignty and Human Rights', in Koskenniemi, *Finnish Yearbook*.

35. John Hobson, *The Eurocentric Conception of World Politics: Western International Theory, 1760–2010* (Cambridge: Cambridge University Press, 2012), p. 185; and Carr, *The Twenty Years' Crisis*, p. 225. South Africa is the obvious exception. As for implicit theories, the question is more complex.

36. Martti Koskenniemi, *The Gentle Civilizer of Nations: The Rise and Fall of International Law 1870–1960* (Cambridge: Cambridge University Press, 2002).

37. See, for example, Martti Koskenniemi's comment on Hans Morgenthau's work in Koskenniemi, *The Gentle Civilizer of Nations*, p. 437: 'Morgenthau's 1951 book was a critique of American foreign policy but also an end-of-an-era analysis. The Second World War, Morgenthau wrote, had made the destructive effects of three "revolutions of our age" fully plain. A political change had led to "the end of the state system which has existed since the sixteenth century in the Western world".'

38. For critical references to the post-Westphalian order, see Wendy Brown, *Walled States, Waning Sovereignty* and Allan Buchanan, 'Rawls's Law of Peoples: Rules for a Vanished Westphalian World', *Ethics*, 110, no. 4 (2000): 697–721; and for the disappearance of the internal/external division in the international order, see James N. Rosenau, *Along the Domestic-Foreign Frontier: Exploring Governance in a Turbulent World* (Cambridge: Cambridge University Press, 1997) and Hidemi Suganami, *The Domestic Analogy and World Order Proposals* (Cambridge: Cambridge University Press, 1989). We would like to point out that, in historical terms, the Westphalian model was not a direct consequence of the creation of the United Nations, but more a result of the movements for decolonisation and national liberation that gained momentum with the independence of India in 1947.

39. Hardt and Negri, *Empire*, p. 7; and Hedley Bull, *The Anarchical Society: A Study of Order in World Politics* (New York: Columbia University Press), p. 44.

40. It is curious to see how many interpreters of Rawls, for example Thomas Pogge, continue to point out what, in their eyes, would be an inconsistency of Rawls himself in his book *The Law of Peoples: The Idea of Public Reason Revisited* (Cambridge, MA: Harvard University Press, 1999), which would contradict the basic principles of his 1971 *A Theory of Justice*. According to this critique, *A Theory of Justice* would deny any notion of collectivity prior to the formation of the polity in question, because the principles of justice would offer no conception as to what or who the people is, unless they are free and equal individuals. Nevertheless, Rawls's account of peoples as subjects of *ius gentium*, which, although he laments it, is not to be reduced to the sum of individuals comprising the peoples, would be, as far as his adherents are concerned, an inconsistency in his thinking. See Andreas Føllesdal and Thomas Winfried Menko Pogge, 'Introduction', in Andreas Føllesdal and Thomas Winfried Menko Pogge (eds), *Real World Justice: Grounds, Principles, Human Rights, and Social Institutions* (Berlin: Springer, 2005) and Allan Buchanan, 'Rawls's Law of Peoples'.

41. Jürgen Habermas, *El Derecho internacional en la transición hacia un escenario posnacional* (Barcelona: Katz, 2008), p. 10.

42. See Claude Lefort, *The Political Forms of Modern Society: Bureaucracy, Democracy, Totalitarianism* (Cambridge, MA: MIT Press, 1986), pp. 239–73; for a critique of the a-historical and anti-political metaphysics lying behind this conception of human rights. For a critical account of Western epistemological assumptions in the hegemonic discourse on human rights, even while upholding the idea of linking them to individuals, see Boaventura de Sousa Santos, drawing from the work of Raimon Pannikar on diatopical hermeneutics, 'Human Rights as an Emancipatory Script?', in Boaventura de Sousa Santos (ed.), *Another Knowledge is Possible: Beyond Northern Epistemologies* (London: Verso, 2008); and for a moral approach to political affairs as a way of confronting the new global challenges, see Tracy B. Strong in this volume.

43. Giorgio Agamben, *State of Exception* (Chicago: University of Chicago Press, 2005). For a critique of Agamben's position, a subsidiary of Carl Schmitt's, with regard to international affairs and from the historical point of view with numerous counter-examples, see Lauren Benton, *A Search for Sovereignty: Law and Geography in European Empires, 1400–1900* (Cambridge: Cambridge University Press, 2010), ch. 6: 'Neither Schmitt nor Agamben, it must be said, reveals a particular interest in, or knowledge of, the world outside Europe.'

44. See Bull, *The Anarchical Society*, for a critique of the notion that states are in a state of nature vis-à-vis each other, which would imply the absence of order in the relationship. The contractualist paradigm associates order with law as coercion. The federal tradition has its origins in other political assumptions and does not regard the phenomenon of war as the key political element in the international order. See Andreas Kalyvas in this volume for a theoretical contrast between the two approaches.

45. Bull, *The Anarchical Society*, p. 49: 'Because international society is no more than one of the basic elements at work in modern international politics, and is always in competition with the elements of a state of war and of transnational solidarity or conflict, it is always erroneous to interpret international events as if international society were the sole or the dominant element.'

46. The contrary implies affirming that every kind of domination is felt or experienced as unjust or imposed by external coercion, which is manifestly false unless reality is only interpreted on the basis of concepts of ideology and alienation, or normative principles that exclude any kind of relation of domination. 'So far as it is not derived merely from fear or from motives of expediency, a willingness to submit to an order imposed by one man or a small group always implies a belief in the legitimate authority (*Herrschaftsgewalt*) of the source imposing it' – Max Weber, *Economy and Society: An Outline of Interpretive Sociology*, eds Guenther Roth and Claus Wittich (Berkeley: University of California Press, 1978), p. 37.

47. See Àngela L. Fuster Peiró and Gerard Rosich, 'The Limits of Recognition: History, Otherness and Autonomy', in Peter Wagner (ed.), *African, American and European Trajectories of Modernity: Past Oppression, Future Justice? Annual of European and Global Studies vol. 2* (Edinburgh: Edinburgh University Press, 2015), p. 46.

48. David Armitage, *The Declaration of Independence: A Global History* (Cambridge, MA: Harvard University Press, 2007), p. 3: 'Now, more than two centuries since 1776, over half the countries of the world have their own declarations of independence.' It should be borne in mind, as Armitage points out on p. 19, that as of the 1776 Declaration of Independence, declarations had as their prime goal: 'The Declaration affirmed the existence of a population ("one People") and implied a form of government, but it did not define a territory.' Certainly, in the particular case of America, the fact that the territory is not mentioned is related

to the situation that the origins of those concerned lay in migration, in particular because they considered that the continent was *vacuum domicilium* or *terra nullius*. Historically speaking, the 'territorial' construction of the United States was accompanied by extermination and the conquest of other populations that did not belong to 'the one People'. See Mann, *The Dark Side of Democracy*, pp. 83–98, for a description of the way in which this twofold process was constituted and legitimated as the democracy-conquest foundations of the United States. Indeed, historically speaking, it is only after the 1791 Haitian revolution that we can speak (with any rigour) of independence from a colonial power. The British colonies in America were formed by European immigrants.

49. Spinoza's re-interpretation of *causa sui* as an immanent and temporal process of *becoming*, and Fichte's interpretation of Kant's philosophy of autonomy as requiring *Selbständigkeit* and his practical interpretation in the *Discourse to the German Nation*, are key moments of this intellectual history.

50. See in particular Martin Ostwald, *Autonomia: Its Genesis and Early History* (Chicago: Scholars Press, 1982) and Kurt Raaflaub, *The Discovery of Freedom in Ancient Greece* (Chicago: University of Chicago Press, 2004), ch. 4.

51. Rosemarie Pohlman, 'Autonomie', in Günther Bien, Joachim Ritter, Karlfried Gründer and Rudolf Eisler (eds), *Historisches Wörterbuch der Philosophie A–K* (Basel: Schwabe, 1971).

52. See Gerard Rosich, *Autonomy in and between Polities: A Political Philosophy of Modernity*, PhD thesis (University of Barcelona, 2015).

53. Jean-Luc Nancy, *The Experience of Freedom* (Redwood City, CA: Stanford University Press, 1993), p. 171: 'To depend on nothing – to give oneself one's own law – to be the opening of a beginning: in our discourse we cannot escape this triple determination of freedom, in which everything is held (and holds for both a *we* and an *I*).'

54. This harks back to the Stoic tradition's justification of suicide, or Christianity's notion of passing on to another world free of the slavery entailed in being an earthly being; or in contemporary times, to suicide attacks as an extreme defence of claims to absolute and radical independence.

55. This, in other types of discourse, is referred to as the question of alterity or the constitutive Other. See Fuster Peiró and Rosich, 'The Limits of Recognition'.

56. See Wagner, *Modernity as Experience and Interpretation*, p. 2; Cornelius Castoriadis, *World in Fragments: Writings on Politics, Society, Psychoanalysis, and the Imagination*, ed. and trans. David Curtis (Redwood City, CA: Stanford University Press, 1997), p. 332; and Jean-Luc Nancy, *The Experience of Freedom*, pp. 171–2. For a partial criticism of the assumptions of this definition of autonomy because it would entail a strong teleological content, see Jacques Derrida, *Rogues: Two Essays on Reason* (Redwood City, CA: Stanford University Press, 2005), pp. 10–12.

57. I use the concept of disentangling following Peter Wagner's disentangling of the concept of modernity in 'Multiple Trajectories of Modernity: Why Social Theory Needs Historical Sociology', *Thesis Eleven* 100 (2010): 53–60.

58. Nancy, *The Creation of the World*, p. 104: 'A people are always their own invention. But it can also invent itself by giving itself a sovereign and by giving itself to a sovereign or even by giving the sovereignty to itself.'

59. Arendt, *The Origins of Totalitarianism*, p. 142. To continue with Arendt's line of thinking with regard to the risks deriving from associating membership with the defence of private interests, see Peter Wagner, 'Die westliche Demokratie und die Möglichkeit des Totalitarismus', in Antonia Grunenberg (ed.), *Totalitäre Herrschaft und republikanische Demokratie: Fünfzig Jahre The Origins of Totalitarianism von Hannah Arendt* (Frankfurt: Peter Lang, 2003), pp. 131–45.

3 Rethinking 'Modern' Democracy: Political Modernity and Constituent Power

Andreas Kalyvas

La Souveraineté est du tout inseparable de l'État [. . .] La souveraineté est la forme qui donne l'être à l'État.

Charles Loyseau[1]

Politics is the art of associating men for the purpose of establishing, cultivating, and conserving social life among them. Whence it is called symbiotics.

Johannes Althusius[2]

It is commonly assumed that the democratic passage to political modernity coincides with a transfer of sovereignty from the king to the people, from the One to the Many.[3] According to this canonical and highly influential view, the historical birth of modern democracy occurs during the two great eighteenth-century revolutions in North America and France, whereby sovereign power was subtracted from monarchy and illicitly seized by its subjects to be relocated in the people as the ultimate foundation of the newly erected constitutional 'sister' republics.[4] By appropriating the king's supreme prerogatives, the people wore his sovereign mantle, sat on his vacant throne, and replaced him as the highest legitimate authority.[5] In this passage, democratic sovereignty marks a reversal that turns upside down the sources of political authority without, however, breaking away from the monarchical paradigm. Thus, with the modern advent of democracy, sovereignty changed hands but essentially it remained the same.

This dominant narrative has some far-reaching historical, theoretical, political and normative implications. Let me briefly mention the most important, which I will address in the following sections of this chapter.

To begin with, democratic modernity is understood in terms of the regal paradigm of power. The conceptual and political structure of popular sovereignty indicates the historical continuity of monarchical rule and its quantitative extension. As Judith Shklar succinctly put it, 'The word sovereignty has scarcely any meaning at all apart from absolute monarchy.'[6] One can speak of modern democracy as a post-monarchical regime in so far as the abolition of kingship does not entail the elimination of monarchical sovereignty as such but only the replacement of one carrier/subject of supreme power with another. With popular sovereignty, power changes hands but its essence and logic remain intact. Broadly speaking, political modernity represents a reconfiguration and rearrangement that reproduces at its core a pre-democratic mode of power.[7]

Secondly, modern democracy is reduced to and absorbed by the state-form, which was co-original with monarchical sovereignty.[8] The doctrine of the democratic (national) state is but a theory about the gradual democratisation of the absolutist state and how it became increasingly inclusive, national and popular. Democracy in its modern manifestation exists only in and through the centralised and hierarchical form of the state. As Bernard Bosanquet wrote,

> If, for example, we speak of the 'sovereignty of the people' in a sense opposed to the sovereignty of the state – as if there were any such thing as 'people' over and above the organised means of expressing and adjusting the will of the community – we are saying what is, strictly speaking, meaningless.[9]

Consequently, popular (national) sovereignty turns out to be identical with state sovereignty, and democracy and statehood become indistinguishable from each other.[10]

Thirdly, according to this dominant paradigm, the modern theory of constitutionalism emerges as a liberal doctrine of the limitations and constraints placed on popular sovereignty in order to curb the absolutist (monarchical) tendencies of the people (as the nation) expressed through majoritarian rule. Constitutional government is a government limited by law, internally divided into separated powers and branches that check, balance and control each other, aiming to restrain the excesses and arbitrariness of the sovereign people, treated as a direct threat to individual rights and minorities.[11]

Furthermore, as an outcome of the political transfer of regal sovereignty, democracy consists of those theological and transcendent residues that were constitutive of and foundational to the powers of the kings and their divine right to rule.[12] The modern democratic revolutions have reaffirmed and renewed the indissoluble link between religion and politics by replacing God with the People, that is, by deifying the latter: *vox populi, vox dei* – the voice of the people is the voice of God.[13] As Tocqueville powerfully put it while commenting on popular sovereignty in the United States, 'The people reign over the American political world as God rules over the universe. It is the cause and the end of all things; everything rises out of it and is absorbed back into it.'[14] Hence, the political theology of sovereignty becomes a political theology of democracy.[15]

Finally, the modern theory and practice of state sovereignty was invented and grew out of a larger Eurocentric political, legal and economic international world system.[16] The making of modern democracy becomes intelligible within the broader geopolitical framework of the history of European imperial expansion, transnational markets and colonialism.[17] In fact, the Western democratic state appears as an effect of the colonial encounter, complicit and deeply implicated in the historical and spatial movement of capital that appropriated, unified, partitioned and exploited the globe.[18]

My contribution seeks to refute this grand narrative and its implications that continue to dominate existing scholarship on political modernity, democracy, sovereignty and the state. The main argument is quite straightforward. I claim that the rediscovery of democracy cannot and must not be understood as a mere transfer of sovereignty from the king to the people, unfolding immanently within the uninterrupted continuity of the statist paradigm. Simply put, this prevailing historiographical narrative is flawed. Instead, I argue, the democratic imaginary corresponds to a very different experience of sovereignty which is not only distinct from, prior and external to the regal paradigm but, at times, opposed and antagonistic to it. The question of democracy does not pertain solely to *where* sovereignty lies and *who* possesses it but mainly to *what* sovereignty is and *how* it is manifested and enacted. My approach, therefore, redefines political modernity as a series of struggles between two distinct ontologies of power and forms of sovereignty, irreducible and external to each other, the democratic and the monarchical, which have always ended with the victory of the latter over the former.

I proceed in four steps. First, I present the canonical theory of sovereignty to highlight its monarchical, statist, absolutist, imperial and theological attributes. This is the celebrated theory of sovereign power as supreme command that became paradigmatic of political modernity (Section One). Second, I trace the first formative episodes of the conceptual and historical invention of popular sovereignty as constituent power and describe its rise in opposition to the regal model (Sections Two and Three). Third, I examine the basic principles of this alternative paradigm that account for its distinct political content and normative orientation. The central claim is that the concept of constituent power discloses the radical truth of democratic sovereignty, which is worldly and egalitarian, revolutionary and emancipatory, federative and constitutional (Section Four). Finally, by way of conclusion, I briefly explore some implications of my reading in relation to political modernity. In particular, I consider whether a revival of democracy *qua* constituent power might entail a radical departure, that is, a democratic exit from the modern (Section Five).

Sovereignty as command

In 1576, Jean Bodin famously defined sovereign power (*puissance souveraine*) as a 'power of command', which he qualified as 'the most high, absolute, and perpetual power [. . .] over the citizens and subjects in a commonwealth'.[19] With this concept of sovereignty, he arrived at the fundamental political distinction between 'him who commands' and 'him who owes obedience', that is, between he who makes laws and he who obeys them.[20] For Bodin, the sovereign is one who commands without being subject to the commands of another, one whose will is not subject to the will of someone else.[21] Hence, his sovereign is a sort of 'uncommanded' commander.[22] He described the sovereign right of commanding as unitary, absolute, inalienable and perpetual, the exclusive source of juridical norms and their implementation, unbound by laws, set above them, grounded on divine right and justified by a transcendent source of authority. Internally, it cannot be divided or shared; externally, it should not be surpassed or downgraded.

For a human association to be political, Bodin went on to argue, there must exist a recognised sovereign with a monopoly of the unlimited power of command, that is, a single coercive instance of final legal jurisdiction in a political community with the effective ability to command obedience and secure internal order. Such a political association is the state (*l'état*). Bodin introduced the seminal distinction between sovereignty and forms of government by elevating the former to a logically necessary feature of state organisation.[23] His concept shaped the modern language of state, its authority and unity by supplying all the key traits associated with statehood.[24] Thus, in the last quarter of the sixteenth century, he set the theoretical foundations for what will become the paradigmatic modern theory of state sovereignty and positive jurisprudence in Western political theory and European public law. It offered the general principles for a centralised legal and administrative organisation of rule, based on a single supreme political and legislative authority, independent from all other polities.

Bodin's definition was so successful that it spread into different political and juridical traditions, appearing regularly in subsequent modern thinkers of the state theory, from Thomas Hobbes, who concurred that 'Sovereign Power' is 'this Right to give Commands' to Samuel Pufendorf to Emer de Vattel's definition that 'sovereignty is that public authority which commands in civil society, and orders and directs what each citizen is to perform, to obtain the end of its institution', and from Jeremy Bentham to John Austin.[25] The achievement of Bodin's theory can be attested by the fact that it spilled over to non-statist political philosophy. For instance, even Baruch Spinoza, who is credited with a theory of absolute democracy, asserted that the sovereign is he who 'has the sovereign right of imposing any commands he pleases'.[26] This broadening influence and hegemonic standing also resounds in Jean-Jacques Rousseau's failure to break with the state paradigm because of his absolutist, unitary notion of sovereignty as the general will of a collective being.[27] Thus, it is customary to regard Bodin as the founder of modern state theory and his definition as the first systematic statement of modern sovereignty, according to which within every political community there is a supreme political and legal authority, a determinate, undivided absolute power of command, which is not itself subject in any way to the superior commands of another, both internally and externally.[28]

In fact, Bodin's sovereign discourse anticipated and strongly shaped the formation of modern international law and the European interstate system through the constitutive idea that the institution of the state is sovereign over its own territory (the exclusivity principle or external sovereignty) and has absolute control over its subjects (the internal hierarchy principle or internal sovereignty).[29] The Peace of Westphalia (1648) codified the criterion of non-intervention by one state in the affairs of another and sanctioned the supreme authority of the power to command as the primary norm of modern international relations among sovereign states.

This sovereign claim to command reasserted itself proudly in the beginning of the twentieth century, in Max Weber's famous definition of the modern state as that entity 'which lays claim to the monopoly of legitimate physical violence within a certain territory', the sole possessor of the exclusive rights of jurisdiction and control over a particular people.[30] Weber elevated the state to the supreme impersonal rational-legal authority, 'usually defined as the right or power to issue obligating commands'.[31] While the modern form of the state depersonalises further and fully formalises Bodin's sovereign, it operated within the same paradigm by taking up the supreme power of command as its defining mark. Sovereignty becomes a legal-rational power of coercion and domination, a formal, proce-

dural authority, immanent to the centralised bureaucratic organisation of the modern state. In Weber's expositions, bureaucracy
seems to bear the true marks of sovereignty and legality is its chief
tool. As mechanised sovereignty, one of the main tasks bureaucracy
performs is the rational and legal organisation of domination, that
is, to realistically estimate and efficiently increase 'the probability
that a command with a given specific content will be obeyed by a
given group of persons'.[32] By being the most effective instrument of
domination, bureaucracy must also be the supreme political power,
the real procedural sovereign. Two further observations are relevant
in this context. The first pertains to the imperial origins of Bodin's
concept of sovereignty as supreme command. The other relates to its
theological content and transcendent foundations.

With respect to the first observation, it is interesting to note that the
theoretical and conceptual sources of Bodin's theory of the sovereign
command lie elsewhere, further back in history. It was born on the
battlegrounds of the Roman imperial armies and can be traced in
the military title of the imperatore, who, as a supreme general, was
the chief holder of the higher command on the field.[33] The noun *imperium* originally meant 'command', either as a specific command or
as the power to give commands in general.[34] Gradually, for the Romans,
imperium came to mean a plenitude of power (*plenitudo potestatis*) to
take any necessary measure in the name of public utility, invested in
several public magistracies.[35] This power that empowered its holder 'to
investigate, to punish, to administer justice, and make (legal) decision'
was deemed personalistic, hierarchical and repressive.[36] In the end, it
became identical to the ultimate executive prerogative of the Roman
emperor to decide in the last instance and progressively blended into a
centralised imperial authority.[37] In fact, the Roman Emperor is the first
sovereign figure in Western political history.[38]

After the collapse of the Roman Empire, the concept of *imperium*
as supreme command encountered Christian theology and during
the Middle Ages became an indispensable property of the Kaiser
of the Holy Roman Empire, who proudly claimed the *imperium
mundi* of a Roman emperor, sanctioned by the Pope, and thus
asserting a near-absolute and universal dominion over his Christian
subjects under the omnipotence of God.[39] It is this higher instance
of command that resurfaced anew in Bodin's absolutist theory in
terms of *summum imperium* after a protracted struggle among kings,
princes, emperors and popes over the appropriation of sovereign
power.[40] This time, however, it was deprived of its formal imperial
title, de-personalised, kind of territorialised and detached from the
authority of the Church. Hence, Bodin's modern concept of sovereignty has Roman and republican imperial origins.[41]

This Roman ancestry of the modern theory of sovereignty as command resonates indirectly but tellingly in Hans Kelsen's critical description of what he labelled the 'exclusive quality' of state sovereignty. Because of its claim to supreme power and the unconditional priority it assigns to its national legal order, Kelsen asserted that 'the sovereignty of one State excludes the sovereignty of every other State'.[42] The sovereign cannot accommodate rivals and contenders. Who is supreme is by logical necessity higher than everybody else and can have neither superiors above nor equals alongside. War is the only relation it can entertain with them. Its power of command must remain undivided and unlimited. It cannot be challenged, shared or divided. Its right to war is inviolable. This 'dogma of sovereignty', Kelsen added with great insight, anticipating recent arguments by Antonio Negri and Michael Hardt on the imperial nature of sovereignty, is 'the main instrument of imperialistic ideology directed against international law'.[43] For Kelsen, the sovereign nation-state is a predator, envious of all other states, and possessed by solipsistic fantasies of total domination and absolute command. It seeks constant expansion, as it cannot tolerate the presence of an equal, perceived as a threat and an enemy to its monopoly of command. Expansion is a necessity of survival for the state. Sovereignty, Jacques Derrida concurred, 'can only tend toward imperial hegemony'.[44] The political destiny of modern sovereignty as command is imperial.[45]

In addition to its imperial derivation and disposition, Bodin's sovereign also has strong theological connotations. Either as a human simulacrum of the divine command or as founded on or sanctioned by God, his conception of sovereign power is impossible to separate from his religious views.[46] It is often easily forgotten that Bodin was deeply preoccupied with religion and wrote prolifically on theological matters; his writings abound with references to mystical entities and supernatural forces, and his political works directly appeal to divine law and cosmic order.[47] The influence of the Hebrew Bible is as strong as is his fondness for neo-Platonism.[48] Bodin's monotheism permeates his entire political theory in such a way that his concept of sovereignty becomes unintelligible outside his religious worldview, such as his metaphysical belief in the immorality of the soul, his faith in revelation, in the freedom of the will and in a divinely ordered universe. The state is a manifestation of God and a segment of his unquestionable universal omnipotence and omnipresence. The explicit analogy between God and sovereignty is so clear in Bodin that one can unreservedly speak of a political theology of sovereignty, whereby politics becomes inseparable from religion:

Just as God, the great sovereign, cannot make a God equal to Himself because He is infinite and by logical necessity two infinites cannot exist, so we can say that the prince, whom we have taken as the image of God, cannot make a subject equal to himself without annihilation of his power.[49]

Likewise, although sovereignty is free from all positive legal norms, it remains bound by and subordinated to the Law of God, which provides the ultimate invisible limit to political power and endows the sovereign command with its normatively just content:

For if justice is the end of law, law the work of the prince, and the prince is the image of God; then by this reasoning, the law of the prince must be modelled on the law of God.[50]

A failure to abide by divine law, or its secular universal equivalent, the law of nature, turns the sovereign into a transgressor of God's commandments and exposes him to absolute punishment.[51] Thus, for Bodin, the tyrant, redefined in theological terms as a sovereign lacking 'a special calling from God', never must be resisted by his subjects, but he always remains subject to divine justice and retribution:[52]

For just as the great God of nature, very wise and just, commands over the angels, so the angels command over human beings, human beings over beasts, the soul over the body, heaven over the earth, and reason over the appetites [. . .] But contrarily, if it happens that the appetites are disobedient to reason, individuals to magistrates, magistrates to princes, and princes to God, then we see that God moves to avenge his injuries and to secure the execution of the eternal laws established by him.[53]

If one tries to eliminate from Bodin's political theory all his references to God, divine and natural law, and to sovereigns as the lieutenants of God, the whole structure of his argumentation falls instantly.[54] Perhaps for this very reason, his theology of modern sovereignty persists as a necessary but unacknowledged premise in subsequent allegedly secular political and legal doctrines of the state. For instance, Hobbes, following Bodin, described the sovereign as a 'Mortall God, to which wee owe, under the Immortal God, our peace and defence'.[55] As Schmitt perceptively noted, 'In the theory of the state in the seventeenth century, the monarch is identified with God and has a position exactly analogous to that attributed to God in the Cartesian system of the world.'[56] This political-theological discourse, grounded on transcendent foundations and sacred beliefs, will persist

in explicit forms well into the eighteenth century and the beginning
of the nineteenth in most theories of sovereignty, reaching an apex
in the writings of Joseph de Maistre and Hegel. The theological
presence in modern theories of sovereignty that sacralises order and
sanctifies the state challenges and subverts grand narratives and their
modernist certainties that portray political modernity as a secular
age, purified of all theological content and thus superior, either diachronically, to a religious and irrational past, or synchronically, to
less modernised and 'underdeveloped' societies.[57]

At the end of these long, laborious conceptual passages, the sovereign power of emperors passed on from kings to peoples, to their
presidents, their representative assemblies, and to state administration.[58] Sovereignty became the name for the modern state, usually
embodied in personal executive powers and prerogatives, but still
carrying the traces of its martial and theological origins, acknowledging no human superior and not subject to anything and anybody,
stubbornly seeking to enforce obedience over a particular people.
These attributes find their best expression in Hobbes's theory, where
the sovereign 'is not Subject to the Civill Lawes [. . .] Nor is possible
for any person to be bound to himselfe, because he that can bind,
can release; and therefore he that is bound to himselfe onely, is not
bound'.[59] A similar meaning informs John Austin's emphasis on the
sovereign nexus of command and obedience. The relation between
the sovereign and its subjects is purely that of 'sovereignty and
subjection', in which all the members of a society are 'dependent'
and 'subject' to the supreme free will of the sovereign. This reaf-
firms Austin's debt to Bodin and Hobbes's doctrines, according to
which the basic principle that '"sovereign power is incapable of legal
limitation"[. . .] hold[s] universally or without exception'.[60]

Bodin's theory of sovereignty successfully dominated modern
political theory and practice, shaping prevailing understandings of
modernity, democracy and international relations. Its commitment
to the primacy of coercive command suggests a statist conception of
sovereignty that consists of a repressive force, emanating from the
top, hierarchical and unitary, supported by a centralised administration and in need of external checks and balances. Michel Foucault
described accurately this juridical model of sovereignty as 'anti-
energy [. . .] a power that only has the force of the negative on its
side, a power to say no; in no condition to produce, capable only of
posing limits'.[61]

It is exactly these same attributes of state sovereignty that Hannah
Arendt deplored deeply and vocally condemned. For, it divides
between superiors and inferiors whose 'very essence is obviously to
command and be obeyed'.[62] Her normative denunciation of sover-

eignty became one of the central pillars of her critique of political modernity and its chief actor, the state. She warned against the homogenising drive of sovereignty that destroys the constitutive multiplicity, the very plurality, of the public space.[63] Sovereignty for Arendt is theological and anti-political, 'because [. . .] [its] ideal of uncompromising self-sufficiency and mastership, is contradictory to the very condition of plurality'.[64] Arendt's critique uncovers the statist strategies of control and domination lurking in the paradigm of sovereign command and evokes the violence generated by its vertical form of ruling.[65] She abhorred in particular the democratic, popular version of absolute sovereignty, which she traced back to a theological theory of the will, a new 'mortal god', the secular people, 'one supernatural body driven by one superhuman, irresistible "general will"'.[66]

In what follows, I seek to recover an alternative theory of sovereignty as constituent power that radically departs from the canonical paradigm of command in order to investigate its democratic implications. The conceptual and political history of constituent power speaks directly against this master narrative of command and subjection.[67] It illuminates important but neglected dimensions of the democratic experience and discloses another understanding of sovereignty. Negatively put, the modern advent of democracy cannot and should not be treated as a mere transfer of sovereignty from the king to the people, unfolding within the statist, theological and imperial paradigm of the supreme command. In positive terms, popular sovereignty *qua* constituent power discloses a different imaginary of sovereign power, not only historically prior but also analytically and ontologically distinct from the regal model: democratic, egalitarian, federative, constitutional, emancipatory and revolutionary.

Popular sovereignty as constituent power

Two hundred and fifty years before Bodin announced his theory of state sovereignty, as early as the first quarter of the fourteenth century, Marsilius of Padua laid the foundations of a new concept of political power that inaugurated the radical doctrine of popular sovereignty.[68] He wrote during the turbulent conflict over the locus of power between the Holy Roman Emperor Louis IV and Pope John XXII that had led to a temporary breakdown of political authority, creating a fissure from within which popular sovereignty came into being. Marsilius claimed that none of the two were sovereign because they did not have the superior power to appoint either oneself or the other. Since neither the Emperor nor the Pope could settle their quarrel, he asserted, a supreme authority had to decide the matter. It was the multitude, he claimed, that had the final right to appoint secular and spiritual rulers. In the space separating the two higher institutions of medieval politics, in the void opened up by their struggle for supremacy, a new political subject made its appearance: the sovereign people. In his most renowned and controversial text, *Defensor Pacis*, completed in 1324, Marsilius announced that

> The efficient power to establish or elect the ruler belongs to the legislator or the whole body of the citizens [. . .] And to the legislator similarly belongs the power to make any correction of the ruler and even to depose him, if this is expedient for the common benefit. For this is one of the more important matters in the polity; and such matters pertain to the entire multitude of the citizens.[69]

Marsilius's intervention, however, does not stop here. Not only did he recognise the multitude as the real and true subject with the supreme authority to appoint its rulers; he also extended its scope to include the formation of government, the establishment of its fundamental laws and the creation of public offices. For, he asserted, 'it pertains to the legislator [i.e. the multitude] to correct governments or to change them completely, just as to establish them'.[70] Marsilius, in fact, transforms the act of appointment to an act of founding, thus introducing the idea of sovereignty in terms of a productive multitude, 'a universal active causality' that 'forms', 'establishes', and 'differentiates' the parts of the political association (*civitas* or *regnum*).[71] He defined this sovereign power, which resides in 'the whole body of citizens or of its weightier part', as an originary and creative 'power to generate' (*generare formam*) new legal forms and political institutions:

> Since, therefore, it pertains to the whole body of the citizens to generate the form, that is, the law, according to which all civil acts must be regulated, it will be seen that it pertains to the same whole body to determine this form's matter, that is, the ruler, whose function is to order, according to this form, the civil acts of men [. . .] For to whomever pertains to generate some form, it also pertains to determine the subject of that form.[72]

This singular formulation of the sovereign power of the multitude as form-giving suggests an extra-institutional force that institutes political authority, determines the form of government and establishes a just constituted order.[73]

It is noteworthy to observe here that Marsilius's theory of popular sovereignty departs from the theological imaginary of the Middle Ages. His incipient invention of democratic sovereignty breaks away from those metaphysical and transcendent medieval notions of power and politics that survived in Bodin's doctrine of sovereignty as command. His intervention situates the beginnings of the post-classical reinvention of democracy apart from the religious monotheistic imaginary of Judeo-Christianity. Instead of relying on the logic of transcendence and the model of a demiurgic divine figure as an external ordering power, he turned to ancient materialist traditions with a strong biological orientation.[74] Blending creatively Aristotle's text *On Animals* (*De partibus animalium*) and Galen's treatise *On the Formation of the Foetus* (*De formatione foetus*), Marsilius described the power to constitute in terms of physical natality and compared the creative sovereign act to that of animal birth.[75] The political constitution of a community is similar, 'in an analogous manner', to the organic constitution of the animal.[76] The sovereign action, he argued, 'in appropriately establishing the civil form and its parts was proportionate, therefore, to the action of nature in perfectly forming the animal'.[77] His incipient theory of the constituent power of the multitude is informed by a physico-biological materialism and grounded on a naturalistic reasoning, devoid of any transcendentalism, successfully displacing the theological and mystical Pauline metaphor of the sacred body politic. In a bold gesture, he described the institution of political community in terms of animal anatomy and physical desire, thus initiating the most ambitious de-sacralisation and de-theologisation of the political in the context of medieval philosophy.[78] The political body through the animal metaphor expresses its immanence to the material and mortal world of living beings and their physical relationships. Marsilius's theory of popular sovereignty operates strictly on the plane of immanence. It is an affirmation of the powers of this world that dispenses with external causation. He understood constituent politics as 'those methods of establishing governments which are affected by the human will'.[79] The existence of political associations is not divinely ordained, nor does it rest on ideas of sin and biblical transgression; rather, it emanates materially from the actual social activity of the multitude, the '*legislator humanus*' who desires a free, peaceful and sufficient life.[80] With Marsilius, the second historical advent of democracy results from a profane, anti-religious theory of politics and is carried out by means of a materialist method.

With these two major innovations, in the late Middle Ages, Marsilius introduced the general idea of popular sovereignty as constituent power. He was the first author to define sovereignty in terms of the power of the multitude to constitute. It is important, therefore, to clarify these novel elements that remain present in the subsequent trajectories of the concept.

Marsilius's originality rests first of all on the appropriation of the ancient figure of the Legislator (νομοθέτης), in order to rework it in the direction, not of a mythical lawgiver and individual founder of cities, but of an actual community, 'the multitude of the needy', the 'assembled multitude'.[81] The 'primary legislator' (*principatus institutor*) is a 'primary authority', and the multitude is always the legislator because it has the supreme power to establish and abolish its governments and depose its rulers.[82] Correspondingly, the laws derive their authority from the legislator, that is, from the multitude. With this synthesis he brought together the legislator, the sovereign and the multitude in the new formulation of a collective power of the many to constitute their political world. The many, the plural, the poor and the '*vulgus*' are names he interchangeably used to describe the sovereign as a collective founder who can decide the political apart form of its common existence either in a primary assembly of all through majority rule or by its elected representatives.[83]

Moreover, by expanding the faculty to constitute as to include the power to form and establish governments, Marsilius suggested a crucial distinction, differentiating between two separate acts: the act of making laws and the act that institutes a government. The latter designates a founding moment, temporarily and ontologically prior to any specific government. It is the source of authority, the legitimacy of ordinary laws and the final judge. The distinction between the legislator and the government points at a differentiated binary concept of power divided between the '*universitas civium*' of the multitude and the '*pars principans*' of the government. It is in this way that Marsilius anticipates the key distinction between a constituting community and the constituted commonwealth, which will become central in later doctrines of modern constitutionalism as *pouvoir constituant/pouvoir constituée*.[84]

Marsilius, furthermore, asserted the superiority of those who participate in the establishment of a government over those who rule and command within a given institutional framework.[85] The act of establishing/forming is superior to the act of commanding. One important reason is that the common life of the multitude neither emanates from nor depends on the rulers or the government. It is a shared life that proceeds immanently and self-sufficiently from the many, that is, autonomously from the government. There is a dimension of externality of the multitude in relation to its institutions as it is recognised as a political subject that can exist outside positive law, that is, from the supreme coercive command. While the many can exist apart from the government, the government cannot live apart from them. Additionally, ruling depends on and is inferior to constituting because, as Marsilius stated by deploying Aristotelian categories of causality, the former is subordinate to the latter in the same way that a cause is always prior and superior to the effects it generates. Moreover, the supremacy of the many over the few is supported by the logic that 'every whole [. . .] is greater in mass and in virtue than any part of it taken separately'.[86] Finally, he also echoed Aristotle's theory of collective intelligence when he claimed that the multitude is also superior in terms of its wisdom, better than of any part taken separately.[87] In this elaborate defence of the principle of popular sovereignty, the many are treated as supreme because they are antecedent to all constituted authorities, self-sufficient, capable of virtue and wisdom and for this reason, the authors of their political forms.

Sovereign acts of resistance

Two centuries and a half after Marsilius's 'discovery' of the constituent power, in a time of another intense crisis, at the aftermath of the 1572 St Bartholomew's Day massacre, several French Huguenot writers known as the Monarchomachs ('those who fight kings'), renewed this democratic discourse of popular sovereignty in order to defend their radical doctrine of tyrannicide.[88] By radicalising aspects of Marsilius's philosophy, they brought together active resistance and constituent power to advance their doctrines of sovereignty, and eventually laid the foundations for later theories of rebellion, revolt, insurrection and revolution.[89] With the Monarchomachs, the constituent power becomes revolutionary. Active, even violent resistance is treated as a legitimate extra-legal force of political change, rightfully exercised by the people or their representatives in exceptional cases of necessity and self-defence. Relying on Marsilius's suggestion that the multitude can depose unjust rulers and suspend the law in times of crisis, the Monarchomachs went further to explore the disobedient and seditious effects of constituent politics and to rethink the conflictual and revolutionary nature of popular sovereignty.

In fact, their rethinking anticipates the right of democratic revolution. The right of a people to disobey, resist, depose or kill their (tyrannical) rulers derives from their sovereign power to constitute the political forms of their common life.[90] Resistance against tyrannical rule is a manifestation of constituent politics and an affirmation of popular sovereignty.[91] The Monarchomachs, in fact, put forward a new justification, based on the democratic logic that 'those who *constitute* one Form, may *abrogate* it', that is, on the principle of popular sovereignty, according to which the people as constituent power are prior and superior to the forms they constitute, including kings.[92] This collective right that trumps monarchical legality rests on the power of the many to constitute. It offers normative and political validity to the exceptional recourse to legitimate resistance on the part of the people. For the Monarchomachs, it is the sovereign people who decide on the extreme situation of tyrannicide. In this way, they can rightly be credited with inventing the first modern democratic theory of resistance in moments of crisis and emergency.

The emphasis on the revolutionary excess of the constituent power carries a double meaning. On the one hand, it reveals the conditional and authorised existence of all constituted powers. It therefore puts limits on the subjects' duty of obedience, which is a conditional obligation that depends on the ruler's performance.[93] Political forms are de-naturalised to the extent that they are regarded as human historical creations, the result of collective action, reversible and revocable, to be amended, transformed and/or replaced. On the other hand, it argues for an extra-constitutional check on the constituted authorities, a just device for maintaining the reign of law and limiting the dangers of arbitrariness and tyranny. Thus, rulers are subject to limitations and constraints established by the many in their constituent capacity. The first traces of modern constitutionalism are already visible in this seditious attempt to determine the limits of power and to set up political safeguards against the transgressions of the constituted order. Here, the notion of a limited government ruled by law appears internal to the democratic doctrine of active resistance, that is, intrinsic to the power to constitute.[94]

In 1573, François Hotman asserted 'that the People reserved to themselves all the power not only of *creating*, but also of *abdicating* their Kings'.[95] One year later, the French protestant Théodore de Bèze (in Latin: Beza) proclaimed the first principle of his new doctrine of legitimate (violent) resistance: 'they who have the power to *create* a king, have the power to *depose* him', as they have also 'the power to *judge* him'.[96] This supreme power to judge and overthrow rulers belongs solely to the people because 'peoples do not come from the rulers [. . .] and that peoples accordingly, are not created for their rulers, but rulers rather for their peoples'.[97] Politically speaking, the people are above the monarch.[98] The right to disobey and resist that the many possess results from the primacy of the constituent subject over the constituted order. It is because the people constitute their rulers that they have the right to resist and depose them. According to Bèze, a people can disobey and rebel against an unjust ruler because they have constituted him. It is the power of constituting that confers on the people the sovereign right to resist.[99]

His principle is unequivocal: those who constitute have the right to disobey.

Five years later, in the *Vindiciae contra tyrannos*, Junius Brutus the Celt appealed to the same principle by further accentuating the elements of self-determination and externality in popular sovereignty.[100] He succinctly asserted, following Marsilius and Beza, that 'a people can exist of itself, and is prior in time to a king'.[101] Their collective existence is superior to and does not depend on the state, because they give rather than receive.[102] In fact, the life of the people proceeds immanently from themselves, as they are capable of living apart from the state. By recognising the people's political externality to the instituted forms of government, Brutus exposed their autonomous, extra-institutional life as the sovereignty of the '*populus constituens*'.[103] He reached the conclusion that:

> as kings are *constituted* by the people, it seems definitely to follow that the people is more powerful than the king. For such is the force of the word: one who is *constituted* by another is held to be lesser; and one who receives his authority from another is inferior to his appointer.[104]

Brutus, like other Monarchomachs, treated the right to remove and depose any constituted authority and even to kill unjust rulers as derivative, emanating from the sovereign power of the people to constitute. He also anticipated the idea of the constitutional convention when he acknowledged the exceptional 'proviso' according to which established rules and procedures of the normal order are suspended because, 'should the need arise, either the whole people, or else a kind of epitome of the whole people, would be convened in extraordinary assembly'.[105]

A few decades later the great Calvinist jurist, Johannes Althusius, relying on the Monarchomachs' doctrines, affirmed the same principle of popular sovereignty *qua* constituent power and provided the clearest formulation yet.[106] In *Politica Methodice Digesta*, published in 1603, he defended active resistance on the grounds that:

> It cannot be denied that the greater is that which *constitutes* the other and is immortal in its foundation, and that this is the people [. . .] By nature and circumstance, the people is prior to, more important than, and superior to its governors, just as every *constituting body* is prior and superior to what is *constituted* by it.[107]

For Althusius, 'the right of sovereignty [. . .] does not belong to individual members, but to all members joined together and to the entire associated body of the realm'.[108] Sovereign power, therefore, when properly understood as the power to constitute, cannot conceivably reside in any individual or group of individuals less than the whole people. Moreover, as a power that founds/grounds a political and constitutional order, it remains irreducible to and heterogeneous from that order. It is this collective sovereign right that justifies the removal, deposition and overthrow by the people of the constituted authorities when these become unjust and tyrannical.[109] The exercise of the right of resistance pertains to the people in their sovereign capacity as constituent power, or to their representatives. Althusius, like the Monarchomachs, formulated a democratic theory of resistance based on the primacy of the sovereign power of the many to constitute, that is, their autonomous power of associating 'for the purpose of establishing, cultivating, and conserving social life among them'.[110]

It is crucial to notice here that from a historical and political point of view Bodin's famous concept of sovereignty as command was formulated in response to the theory and politics of popular sovereignty as constituent power. It was explicitly invented and deployed against the Monarchomachs in an attempt to preserve and strengthen the authority of monarchy by repudiating the claims of disobedience and resistance in the name of a hierarchical order and a monarchical peace.[111] In other words, the early theory of modern state sovereignty developed as a polemical reaction to incipient formulations of democratic sovereignty deemed unruly and anarchic. The discourse of the sovereign state emerged to refute the rebellious claims and the self-assertion of the many against the few, with the explicit purpose of imposing obedience through the coercive command of a centralised state power.

In this confrontational context, Althusius's work stands out. His theoretical intervention represents a crucial moment in the development of popular sovereignty. He sought to defend the distinction between the practice of constituting a political association (*consociatio politica*) and the act of commanding against Bodin's absolute sovereign power of the king by rejecting altogether the state-form in the name of an alternative political organisation, proper to the constituent power: the federation.[112] Within this polemical exchange between constituent power and command, Althusius introduced the first modern theory of federative association.[113] In doing so, his work brought the theory of popular sovereignty to its ultimate political logic by providing for the first time the appropriate constitutional form fitting to popular sovereignty.[114] With Althusius, democracy finds in the federative principle its own singular organisational and governmental structure beyond the centralised and unitary abstract state. His refutation of Bodin in the name of popular sovereignty *qua* constituent power not only challenges the monarchical paradigm of sovereignty, it also questions the legitimacy of modern statehood. In fact, the development of sovereignty as the power to form and establish governments passes through the rediscovery of the federation as a superior alternative to the absolute and indivisible authority of the state. Althusius is both a thinker of the constituent power of the sovereign people and the first modern proponent of federalism, understood as the mutual binding of families, villages, communities, guilds, cities and provinces that freely associate together through mutual promises into a compound federative body (*universalis publica consociatio*).[115] With Althusius, therefore, the federation becomes the most natural and rational expression of constituent politics; the state, by contrast, appears as its greatest rival and enemy.

Democratic sovereignty

The early theoretical and historical development of popular sovereignty suggests a clear distinction between state sovereignty as command and democratic sovereignty as the power to constitute. Their differences are substantial, as they are separated by distinct histories, ontologies, normative orientations and political objectives.

As Martin Loughlin has correctly pointed out, 'Constituent power as a "power to" is different from "power over".'[116] Very different, indeed. In the state paradigm the emphasis is on the moment of (coercive) command, while the constituent version privileges the acts of establishing and instituting. The one is repressive when contrasted to the dynamic and productive dimension of the other. Consequently, whereas the principle of command is based on the model of *ruling*, that of constituting evokes a *founding* event. The sovereign is not a ruler but a lawgiver and a founder. Instead, then, of fixating on a superior command emanating from the *top*, the notion of the constituent sovereign redirects attention to the underlying sources of the instituted reality located at the *bottom*. The first relies on a vertical structure while the second operates horizontally; the first is unbound and absolute, the second exists through binding mutual promises. In addition, the model of command aims at securing order and stability; the constituent power, by contrast, provokes change and alteration. Moreover, contrary to the paradigm of the sovereign command that invites personification – from the ancient *imperatore* to the king to the modern executive – the constituent power conveys the collective and impersonal attributes of sovereignty, its associative public dimension and its federative inclinations. All these contrasts illustrate how popular sovereignty re-imagined democracy against the regal paradigm of command.

In fact, popular sovereignty indicates a collective practice, involving a plurality of actors coming together to co-*institute*, to establish jointly.[117] Two crucial aspects are involved in the semantic composition of sovereignty as the power to constitute, indicative of two democratic principles.

First, there is equality. An emphasis on the prefix co- presents the concept descriptively: on the one hand, as a negation, that is, the impossibility that one could ever *co*-institute anything by oneself; on the other, positively, prescribing that if one wants to *co*-institute, one has to do it in *co*-operation with others. Acting together, in concert, means to 'do certain common acts as a society, which are acts not of a certain part but of the whole'.[118] These acts point at a federative and associative structure of public authority. They are egalitarian to the degree that the coming together is articulated in terms of equal participation. In all theories of the constituent power, the politics of new foundations are undertaken jointly and voluntarily, free from asymmetrical power relations and arbitrary interferences; that is, free of inequality, in true *co*-operation. Sidney accurately grasped this egalitarian presence when he claimed that:

> every number of men, agreeing together and framing a society, became a compleat body, having all power in themselves over themselves, subject to no other human law than their own. All those that compose the society, being equally free to enter it or not, no man could have any prerogative above others.[119]

This egalitarian meaning indicates that the sovereign act of constituting is performed among peers by mutual association.

Second, popular sovereignty consists also of a generative principle.[120] By underlining the second component of the verb to co-*institute*, theories of the constituent power saw in sovereignty a creative form-giving power.[121] Popular sovereignty is presented in its instituting capacity, with the faculty to 'instaure' new political orders, to bring into being novel constitutional forms, to enact new beginnings. Sovereignty establishes political and legal orders and determines constitutional forms.[122] In a word, it is a productive power, often portrayed as the extra-legal source of all legality. This positing aspect of the constituent sovereign is fully captured by Schmitt's definition of sovereignty as a 'founding power' (*die begründende Gewalt*).[123] The second principle is positive and generative, creative and instituting.

Correspondingly, the sovereign power to constitute pertains to relations of mutual association and self-constitution. The subject of the constituent power is not prior or external to the act of constituting. Rather, it constitutes itself as it constitutes for itself.[124] By framing the political forms of its collective existence, it also produces its own public identity.[125] This process of self-formation is immanent to the degree that the constituent power makes both the subject and the object of politics in the absence of an antecedent, external causality. It is best captured by Althusius's definition of constituent politics as 'symbiotics', that is, as a horizontal practice of freely associating and dissociating with others, the forming of a commonality through reciprocal promises and pledges for the sake of 'mutual communication of whatever is useful and necessary for the harmonious exercise of social life'.[126] The constituent subject is not a pre-formed agent, a natural homogeneous unity credited with an organic collective selfhood, antecedent to the sovereign act of constituting. Rather, it consists of a plurality in the making, an artificial compound body formed during the constituting activity, outside the instituted commonwealth.

Popular sovereignty consists also of a revolutionary principle.[127] It is forged during extreme situations of crisis, conflict and transformation, designed for resistance and revolution, expressing an exhortation to rebel.[128] This is the principle of disruption: self-authorised, unruly, against the fixity and permanence of the statist *nomos*. There is here a strong 'desire for alteration'.[129] The concept indicates discontinuities and ruptures in the constitution of the political; it ponders alterity and otherness against legal closure, and is attentive to accelerated temporalities with sudden unpredictable and contingent outcomes. Theories of constituent power expand the boundaries of politics as to include its own foundations and beginnings. Since Marsilius's original formulation, the people arrive at the moment of a rupture, staging a dispute, in times of exception, to constitute anew their political existence and to renew their constitutional identity.[130] In this post-classical invention of democracy, popular sovereignty is revolutionary.[131]

As surprising as it may sound to some, this revolutionary principle of sovereignty comes into being and co-exists with constitutionalism.[132] Democratic revolutions are constitutional, that is, moments of popular sovereignty and genuine constitutional making. The constituent power is certainly one of the main foundations of modern constitutionalism and public law.[133] It consistently treats politics in terms of constitutional politics; the constitution is understood politically and politics, in turn, is analysed constitutionally, bridging thereby the unconvincing and politically suspicious distinction between politics as the field of factual power and the constitution as the realm of pure normativity. Any meaningful and compelling distinction between higher and ordinary laws in fact presupposes the constituent power of the people. This distinction, which corresponds to one of the main principles of modern constitutionalism, emanates from popular sovereignty: the people are sovereign by virtue of their power to constitute.[134] The fundamental constitutional law, 'the law of lawmaking', enjoys higher and greater legitimacy than normal legislation because it is a sovereign expression of constituent power.[135] This is the modern idea of democratic legitimacy and the democratic foundations of constitutional government.[136]

'Democratic theory', Schmitt argued, 'knows as a legitimate constitution only the one which rests on the constituent power of the people.'[137] Karl Marx had already expressed this view in prescient terms. 'Democracy is the solved *riddle* of all constitutions,' he claimed, because,

> Here, not merely *implicitly* and in essence but *existing* in reality, the core of constitution is constantly brought back to its actual basis, the *actual human being*, the *actual people*, and established as the people's own work. The constitution appears as what it is, a free creation of man.[138]

In a democratic regime, the legitimacy depends on how inclusive, free and equal participation is during constitutional politics. Precisely because this concept of sovereignty recalls at the centre of modern democratic theory the normative ideal of political autonomy, it points at a distinctive theory of political legitimacy. Actual participation in the founding defines the experience of democracy. It is this primacy of participation over obedience that demands from the subjects of a political order to *co*-institute it. Popular sovereignty as constituent power evokes the general value of political liberty: to be free is to live under one's own laws. It re-invents the ancient democratic principle of self-government. In Cornelius Castoriadis's apt formulation, it is the explicit, lucid self-institution of society.[139]

At the same time, the relationship between sovereignty and constitutionalism, democracy and law, is dialectical to the degree that the constituent power supersedes the constitutional universality of the instituted society. As Marx insisted, the 'constitution is no longer equivalent to the whole' and does not monopolise the political because it corresponds to 'only *one* facet of the people'.[140] With democracy, there is an irreducible political outside to the formal organisation of power. As the constituent power cannot be absorbed or consumed by the order of the constitution, democratic politics escapes its total constitutionalisation and full juridical 'objectification'.[141] It remains both below and next to the constituted powers as a force of innovation, alterity, contingency and most importantly, as a democratic presence.[142] The idea of the constituent power as the excess of constitutionalism is a reminder that politics cannot be reduced to abstract legality and that democracy exceeds its constitutional forms.[143]

Equally important, the incipient reinvention of democracy in the late Middle Ages prior to and independent from the colonial history of the modern Western state points at the anti-imperial content of popular sovereignty. Not only because it predates the age of conquests but also because it challenges normatively and analytically any attempt to impose a form of government on those who never participated in its establishment. Hence, besides simply describing a specific political act of a plurality of actors who engage with each other, acting in concert, to erect and set up something new, the concept of popular sovereignty *qua* constituent power, also prescribes who should perform this act and how it must be carried out.[144] It contains, in addition to its descriptive meaning, a specific normative injunction. This injunction has the form of an 'ought' statement. It consists of a norm that excludes that one might constitute something by oneself for another. If one wants to constitute a new political and legal association, one ought to co-institute it, to institute jointly with others. This norm is intrinsic to popular constituent sovereignty and indicates the 'who', that is, the concrete identity that is competent to legitimately create such an association. It is, in short, a general authorising norm because it confers upon someone a certain extra-legal competence, namely the right to participate in the enactment of new political forms of constituted authority. It confers a norm-creating power in the absence of positive rules. In its formal expression, the political norm of authorisation immanent to the sovereign act of constituting both describes and prescribes that the first constitution is/ought to be jointly created and that the founding of a new political association must evenly involve all those who will be included in it. The constituent principle of popular sovereignty suggests that not any practice can claim to be constituent and not any actor can contend to be a founder, even if the actor and the act have been successful, that is, effective in creating a new political and juridical order. Should a person or group appropriate the power to constitute at the exclusion of all those who will be its addressees, the ensuing political form should be regarded as imposed, thus, invalid and illegitimate, the result of an act of usurpation. Such an act would not be democratic but rather a repressive command, an expression of coercive imposition.[145] Institution by conquest, thus, amounts to such a tyrannical act. For this reason, sovereignty as constituent power is inherently democratic and anti-colonial, since it consists of the predicates of equality, inclusion, participation and reciprocity, that is, of the norms of self-determination and autonomy.

A democratic theory of the constituent power, in fact, provides a critical lens to evaluate different foundings and to distinguish between democratic new beginnings and imperial conquests. Constituent democracy offers principles of political founding, in accordance with which we can recognise, measure and assess the legitimacy of existing practices of political and legal new beginnings in relation to whether and how much they approximate or depart from its participatory and inclusive attributes. Especially when it comes to the making of the modern age through the Western imperial attempts over the last five centuries to appropriate space and subjugate peoples, the theory of popular sovereignty offers a powerful critical discourse that exposes and opposes the democratic deficit of such imperial discretionary attempts at global command. It is in this strong sense that the doctrine of the constituent sovereignty of the people is inherently anti-imperial and anti-colonial.

Finally, popular sovereignty enacts a rupture with theological and transcendent notions of power, politics and subjectivity and questions the alleged theological provenance of popular sovereignty, powerfully captured by Carl Schmitt's influential claim that it is merely another secularised theological concept of the modern state theory.[146] A principle of immanence that dispenses with external causation is present in the constituent power. For instance, this concept has always been placed underneath the civil and legal edifice, emanating from the bottom, from the many, those who compose a genuine collectivity. The various names that designate it – 'the community', 'civil society', 'the multitude', 'the poor', 'the plebs', 'the commons', 'the demos', 'the people' – suggest that, in the last instance, the many are the ultimate foundation of the political, the utter social limit of any politics that survives the dissolution of governments, the disruption of legal systems and the collapse of instituted powers.[147] This persistent constitutional externality is due to the immanence of constituent power to social life. It is internal to concrete relations of mutual association, formed by actual pledges and promises; in exchanges, agreements, covenants and contacts; in corporations, alliances and federations.[148] Popular sovereignty is relational and plural and operates strictly on the plane of historicity and immanence. It is profane and material, the affirmation of the powers of this world, of change and contingency, of beginnings and ends, and the recognition that the political world is made by its participants.[149]

Although it is true that during its long history this worldly concept was periodically tainted by elements of political theology, these have remained extraneous, later additions, which never coalesced with the conceptual core to become a constitutive part. By the third quarter of the eighteenth century, Hamilton could proclaim in the opening lines of the *Federalist Papers*, that it seems to have been preserved to the people of this country, by their conduct and example, to decide the important question, whether societies of men are really capable or not of establishing good government from reflection and choice, or whether they are forever destined to depend for the political constitutions on accident and force.[150]

Political authority, the grounds of ruling, the government itself, are not inaccessible, beyond judgement and contestation; instead, they are relativised and de-centred, regarded as human, that is, mortal artefacts, without extra-social support, lacking banners of truth or markers of certainty, open to questioning and thus provisional and revocable, conditional and frail.[151]

Popular sovereignty possesses its own unique logic that clearly differentiates it from the competing statist paradigm of command. Its defining principles describe the democratic content of the sovereign power of the many, which is both revolutionary and constitutional. This reorientation of modern democratic theory towards the power to constitute initiates a shift from the logic of determination to the principle of self-determination, from immobility to movement, from order to change, from the One to the Many, from the transcendent to the immanent, from heteronomy to autonomy.[152] It is a shift that marks the second, post-classical birth of the democratic project and the political imaginary of autonomy.[153] With the constituent power, democracy exists in the radical event of its self-alteration.[154] It is a politics of becoming and freedom, the movement of political transformation and constitutional change.[155] Hannah Arendt, following Machiavelli, described this constituent politics as the 'augmentation of foundations [. . .] this notion of a coincidence of foundation and preservation by virtue of augmentation'.[156] The constituent power inaugurates a fascinating, unprecedented exploration into the radical nature of democratic politics, that is, a politics that revisits its foundations and politicises its origins.[157] Democracy, in short, begins democratically.[158]

A democratic exit from statocentric modernity?

I would like to conclude with some preliminary and tentative reflections on the relationship between democracy and political modernity. Certainly, everything depends on how one defines the latter. And as far as definitions go, there are plenty. The one I have tried to suggest throughout this chapter is rather minimal, and although quite conventional, it is often overlooked. My approach stresses the central role of the modern state and its animating principle of sovereignty as command in the political constitution of modernity. As Skinner notes, 'By the beginning of the seventeenth century the concept of the State – its nature, its powers, its right to command obedience – had come to be regarded as the most important object of analysis in European political thought.'[159] Indeed, the state, as a fact and as a norm, as discourse and as practice, has become an indispensable attribute of the modern condition, displacing communes, cities, leagues and federations as alternative models of political community.[160] The emergence of the state and the emergence of modernity constitute two facets of one and the same reality. With an uninterrupted history of several centuries, constantly on the offensive, expanding well beyond its original European space, presently spread across the entire surface of the globe, the state is the most enduring political achievement of the modern age, the driving force of the modernising project, and the pivotal concept of modern political and legal theorising. It still remains today the sole institutional model of political association and the only legitimate actor recognised by international law. Thus, 'although one speaks of the "modern state" strictly speaking the adjective "modern" is pleonastic'.[161] With the advent of sovereignty as command, the state has become one of the basic attributes of the modern grammar of politics. The geopolitical and symbolic configuration of modernity is clearly statocentric.[162]

In this context, the pressing question to ask is whether democracy and popular sovereignty as constituent power are possible at all in a modern world that came to be shaped and universally dominated by the Eurocentric state-form, that is, by sovereignty as supreme command. As I have suggested throughout this chapter, the answer must be negative. From a historical, conceptual and normative point of view, the post-classical democratic project that began to emerge in the early fourteenth century seems at odds with the organisational logic of statist politics and its centralised apparatus of domination. After all, it must not be forgotten, as the genealogy of the sovereign command clearly indicates, that the theory and practice of the state grew out of reaction to the rebellious aspirations of popular sovereignty and asserted itself against the egalitarian and emancipatory claims of disobedient multitudes.[163] Bodin's 'discovery' of the sovereignty of the supreme command was motivated by the radical theories of the Monarchomarchs, which he deemed destructive to order and peace; Althusius retorted with his federalist model, which was formulated in response to the rise of centralised states and to the theory of sovereignty that came to support them, provoking multiple polemical reactions from Hobbes to Pufendorf, who reaffirmed the unitary and absolutist qualities of state sovereignty as the only guarantee of stability and security and argued against the right to rebel;

George Lawson and John Locke took up the task to defend and further develop the idea of popular sovereignty as constituent power and resistance against the discretionary and authoritarian powers of the supreme command and its repressive prerogatives. This antagonistic relationship continued throughout the eighteenth century and all the way into the twentieth, from the anti-colonial struggles that shook the western hemisphere from north to south to the Soviet revolution, when Lenin dissolved the Constituent Assembly and usurped the revolutionary powers of the soviets in order to strengthen the party-state. All these struggles, and those that followed them, ended with the ultimate victory of the state in one form or another.

Thus, against existing orthodoxies that speak of the modern age as inherently democratic, I have suggested that, in fact, the modern political experience of democracy has been in a perpetual conflict with its rival paradigm of command and its logic of domination and subjection. These struggles have resulted in historical defeats and unrealised aspirations that have been so pervasive as to empty the idea of democracy of its radical constituent popular content, transforming it into a ruling ideology, an administrative and police discourse, a nationalist creed and an imperial instrument of global governance. The idea of a democratic state appears as an oxymoron because democracy and state represent two different and conflicting experiences of the political, two irreconcilable imaginaries that tend to cancel each other out. From such a revisionist perspective, therefore, political modernity represents at best the neutralisation of democracy and at worst its evacuation. In fact, the entire development of modern political thought and the fortunes of modern political history can be rewritten afresh from the perspective of this long, recurrent antagonism between two sovereign projects that have always ended with the total triumph of the sovereign command and its universal consolidation as the sole organisational model of political association.

To rethink democracy today, in short, means to radically question the primacy of the state form and its sovereign command. It also means that the modern age is deeply undemocratic despite its own pretentious, self-professed claims. And what's more, it indicates the pressing need to think beyond the statocentrism of political modernity. Let's recall that democratic constituent politics is the explicit, lucid self-institution of society, whereby the members come freely together as equals and jointly become the authors of their constitutional and political identity in such a way that they all affirm their fundamental equality to practise their political freedoms. Democracy is the only politics we know of that promises to the addressees of the law that they will be as well the revolutionary authors of the law.

The constituent sovereign powerfully evokes concrete practices of collective autonomy and mutual association among a plurality of equals that are incompatible with the vertical and unitary organisation of state structure. This structure reduces politics to a relationship between rulers and ruled, that is, between the few who command and the many who consent to obey. Popular sovereignty envisions a federative and associative structure of public powers that defies centralisation, hierarchy and monopoly of coercion. Respectively, democracy *qua* the constituent power exists in horizontal, reciprocal and diffused relations of power that combine self-rule and shared rule. In this case, I have argued, popular sovereignty as the self-constitution of federal communities remains in opposition to political modernity in such a way that any future revival of democracy might well entail an exit from the modern.

Notes

1. 'Sovereignty is entirely inseparable from the state [. . .] Sovereignty is the form that gives existence to the state' – Charles Loyseau, *Traité de Seigneuries* (Paris: Abel l'Angelier, 1614), Book II.4: 25.
2. Johannes Althusius, *Politica Methodice Digesta*, ed. and trans. Frederick S. Carney (Indianapolis, IN: Liberty Fund, 1995), I.1: 14.
3. For two emblematic versions of this thesis, see Alexis de Tocqueville, *The Ancient Regime and the Revolution* [1856], eds François Furet and Françoise Melonio, trans. Alan S. Kahan (Chicago: University of Chicago Press, 2004); Alexis de Tocqueville, *Democracy in America* [1835, 1840], trans. Phillips Bradley (London: Vintage Books, 1990); Hannah Arendt, *On Revolution* (New York: Penguin Books, 1963).
4. Edmund S. Morgan, *Inventing the People: The Rise of Popular Sovereignty in England and America* (New York: W. W. Norton and Company, 1988), pp. 36–7; R. R. Palmer, *The Age of the Democratic Revolution, vol. 1: The Challenge* (Princeton, NJ: Princeton University Press, 1959); Patrice Higonnet, *Sister Republics: The Origin of French and American Republicanism* (Cambridge, MA: Harvard University Press, 1988).
5. Reinhard Bendix, *Kings or People* (Berkeley: University of California Press, 1978), pp. 4–10; F. H. Hinsley, *Sovereignty* (Cambridge: Cambridge University Press, 1989), pp. 132–7.
6. Judith N. Shklar, *Men and Citizens: A Study of Rousseau's Social Theory* (Cambridge: Cambridge University Press, 1969), p. 168; Hannah Arendt, *The Human Condition* (Chicago: University of Chicago Press, 1958), pp. 234–5. 'The doctrine of sovereignty', according to L. H. A. Hart, 'asserts that in every human society, where there is law, there is ultimately to be found latent beneath the variety

of political forms, in a democracy as much as in an absolute monarchy, this simple relationship between subjects rendering obedience and a sovereign who renders obedience to no one. This vertical structure composed of sovereign and subjects is, according to the theory, as essential a part of a society which possesses law, as a backbone is of a man.' L. H. A. Hart, *The Concept of Law* (Oxford: Oxford University Press, 2012), p. 50.

7. Arendt, *On Revolution*, p. 156.

8. Gianfranco Poggi, *The State: Its Nature, Development, and Prospects* (Redwood City, CA: Stanford University Press, 1990), pp. 34–68; Quentin Skinner, *The Foundations of Modern Political Thought*, vol. II (Cambridge: Cambridge University Press, 1978), p. 351 and p. 358; Anthony Giddens, *The Nation-State and Violence* (Berkeley: University of California Press, 1987), pp. 83–121 and pp. 172–97; Hendrik Spruyt, *The Sovereign State and its Competitors* (Princeton, NJ: Princeton University Press, 1994), pp. 77–106 and pp. 153–80.

9. Bernard Bosanquet, *The Philosophical Theory of the State* (London: Macmillan, 1899), p. 282.

10. Charles E. Merriam, *History of the Theory of Sovereignty since Rousseau* (New York: Columbia University Press, 1900), pp. 85–129; Michael Ross Fowler and Julie Marie Bunck, *Law, Power, and the Sovereign State: The Evolution and Application of the Concept of Sovereignty* (Philadelphia: Pennsylvania State University Press, 1995), p. 157 and p. 163.

11. For two classical versions of this view, see Montesquieu, *The Spirit of the Laws* [1748], ed. and trans. Anne M. Cohler, Basia Carolyn Miller and Harold Samuel Stone (Cambridge: Cambridge University Press, 1992), Book II: pp. 1–6 and pp. 154–66; Alexander Hamilton, James Madison and John Jay, *The Federalist Papers* (New York: The Modern Library, 1938), No. 10: p. 47, p. 51, pp. 54–62, pp. 312–20 and pp. 335–40.

12. Claude Lefort, 'The Permanence of the Theologico-Political?', in Lefort, *Democracy and Political Theory*, trans. David Macey (Minneapolis: University of Minnesota Press, 1988), pp. 213–55.

13. Ann Norton, 'Democracy and the Divine', *Theory & Event* 13:2 (2010).

14. Tocqueville, *Democracy in America*, vol. I, ch. 4, p. 58. Also see Carl Schmitt, *Constitutional Theory* [1928], trans. Jeffrey Seitzer with a foreword by Ellen Kennedy (Durham, NC: Duke University Press, 2004), ch. 17, p. 267.

15. Carl Schmitt, *Political Theology: Four Chapters on the Concept of Sovereignty* [1922], trans. George Schwab (Cambridge, MA: MIT Press, 1988); Jacques Derrida, *Rogues: Two Essays on Reason*, trans. Pascale-Anne Brault and Michael Naas (Redwood City, CA: Stanford University Press, 2005), pp. 100–1; Miguel Vatter, 'Introduction: Crediting God with Sovereignty', in Vatter (ed.), *Crediting God: Sovereignty and Religion in the Age of Global Capitalism* (Bronx:

Fordham University Press, 2010), pp. 1–28; Eric L. Santner, *The Royal Remains: The People's Two Bodies and the Endgame of Sovereignty* (Chicago: University of Chicago Press, 2011); Simon Critchley, *The Faith of the Faithless* (New York: Verso, 2012).

16. Carl Schmitt, *The Nomos of the Earth*, trans. Garry Ulmen (New York: Telos Press, 2003), pp. 80–3, pp. 126–38 and pp. 140–51; Immanuel Wallerstein, *The Modern World-System*, vol. 1 (London and New York: Academic Press, 1974), pp. 132–63 and pp. 165–221; Michael Mann, *The Sources of Social Power*, vol. 1 (Cambridge: Cambridge University Press, 2012), pp. 472–99 and pp. 510–15; Martti Koskenniemi, *The Gentle Civilizer of Nations: The Rise and Fall of International Law 1870–1960* (Cambridge: Cambridge University Press, 2001), pp. 98–178 and pp. 413–509; Anthony Anghie, *Imperialism, Sovereignty, and the Making of International Law* (Cambridge: Cambridge University Press, 2005), pp. 6–7, pp. 10–11 and pp. 310–20.

17. Neve Gordon, 'Democracy and Colonialism', *Theory & Event* 13:2 (2010).

18. Vladimir I. Lenin, *Imperialism: The Highest Stage of Capitalism* [1916] (New York: International Publishers, 1997); Immanuel Wallerstein, 'The Rise of the States-System: Sovereign Nation-States, Colonies, and the Interstate System', in Wallerstein, *World-Systems Analysis: An Introduction* (Durham, NC: Duke University Press, 2005), pp. 42–58; Antonio Negri and Michael Hardt, *Empire* (Cambridge, MA: Harvard University Press, 2000), pp. 114–59 and pp. 183–204.

19. Bodin, *On Sovereignty*, trans. Julian Franklin (Cambridge: Cambridge University Press, 1992), Book I.8: 1.

20. Ibid., Book I.10: 49, 51.

21. Skinner, *The Foundations of Modern Political Thought*, vol. II: p. 287.

22. Bodin, *On Sovereignty*, Book I.8: 11.

23. Martin Loughlin, *The Idea of Public Law* (Oxford: Oxford University Press, 2003), pp. 73–7.

24. Within four years of its initial publication, Bodin's treatise was reprinted eight times. Sixteen reprints appeared during the next two decades. It became known and read all over Europe, acquired the status of a classic, and was made into a textbook in European universities. See also Otto Gierke, *Natural Law and the Theory of Society 1500–1800* (Boston: Beacon Press, 1957), p. 40; Giddens, *The Nation-State and Violence*, pp. 93–4.

25. Thomas Hobbes, *On the Citizen* [1642], eds Richard Tuck and Michael Silverthorne (Cambridge: Cambridge University Press, 1998), ch. 4, p. 11 and p. 73; Samuel Pufendorf, *Of the Law of Nature and Nations* [1672], trans. Basil Kennett (Clark: The Lawbook Exchange, 1729), Book VII.3: 654–60; Emer de Vattel, *The Law of Nations* [1758], eds Béla Kapossy and Richard Watmore (Indianapolis, IN: Liberty Fund, 2008), Book I.4: 38, 97; Jeremy Bentham, *A Fragment on Government* (Oxford: Oxford Clarendon Press, 1891), ch. 1, pp.

131–63; John Austin, *The Province of Jurisprudence Determined and the Uses of the Study of Jurisprudence* (Indianapolis, IN: Hackett Publishing Company, 1998), Lecture VI, pp. 191–361.

26. Benedict de Spinoza, *A Theologico-Political Treatise*, trans. R. H. M. Elwes (New York: Dover Publications, 1951), p. 207.

27. Jean-Jacques Rousseau, *On the Social Contract, or Principles of Political Right* [1762], trans. Maurice Craston (London: Penguin Books, 1968), Book II: 1–5.

28. Hans Kelsen, *Das Problem der Souveränität und die Theorie des Völkerrechts: Beitrag zu einer Reinen Rechstslehre* (Tübigen: Mohr, 1920), pp. 2–5; Julian Franklin, 'Sovereignty and the Mixed Constitution: Bodin and his Critics', in J. H. Burns (ed.), *The Cambridge History of Political Thought 1450–1700* (Cambridge: Cambridge University Press, 1994), p. 307; Robert Jackson, *Sovereignty* (Cambridge: Polity, 2007), pp. 47–8; John William Allen, *A History of Political Thought in the Sixteenth Century* (Lanham, MD: Roman and Littlefield, 1928), pp. 407–25. Harold Laski has concisely summarised the principle of state sovereignty: 'The modern theory of sovereignty is [. . .] a theory of political organisation. It insists that there must be in every social order some single centre of ultimate reference, some power that is able to resolve disputes by saying a last word that will be obeyed' – Harold J. Laski, *Studies in the Problem of Sovereignty* [1917] (New York: Fertig, 1968), p. 44.

29. Jules Basdevant, *Contribution de Jean Bodin à la formation du droit international moderne* (Paris: Librarie du recueil Sirey, 1946); Stanley Benn, 'Sovereignty', in Paul Edwards (ed.), *The Encyclopedia of Philosophy* (New York: Macmillan, 1967), vols 7–8, pp. 501–5; Hans J. Morgenthau, 'The Problem of Sovereignty Reconsidered', *Columbia Law Review* 48, no. 3 (1948): 341–65.

30. Max Weber, 'The Profession and Vocation of Politics', *Max Weber: Political Writings*, ed. Peter Lassman, trans. Robert Speirs (Cambridge: Cambridge University Press, 1994), pp. 310–11.

31. Hans Kelsen, *General Theory of Law and State* (Cambridge, MA: Harvard University Press, 1945), p. 383.

32. Max Weber, *Economy and Society: An Outline of Interpretive Sociology*, vol. 1, ed. Guenther Roth and Claus Wittich (Berkeley: University of California Press, 1978), p. 53.

33. Tacitus, *The Annals*, trans. John Jackson (Cambridge, MA: Harvard University Press, 2005), Book 3.69, pp. 632–3; J. S. Richardson, 'Imperium Romanum: Empire and the Language of Power', *The Journal of Roman Studies* 81 (1991): 1–9; Andrew Lintott, *Imperium Romanum: Politics and Administration* (London: Routledge, 1993), p. 22.

34. Andrew Lintott, *The Constitution of the Roman Republic* (Oxford: Oxford University Press, 1999), pp. 96–7.

35. Caesar, *The Civil Wars*, trans. A. G. Peskett (Cambridge, MA: Harvard University Press, 1914), Book 3.51, pp. 268–9; Cicero,

The Laws (Cambridge, MA: Harvard University Press, 1928), Book III.3.8: 464–6.

36. *The Digest of Justinian*, vol. 1, ed. and trans. Alan Watson (Philadelphia: University of Pennsylvania Press, 1985), Book II.1: 40; M. H. Crawford, *Roman Statutes*, vol. 1 (London: University of London Institute of Classical Studies, 1995), no. 12; Claude Nicolet, *Rome et la conquête du monde méditerranéen*, vol. 1 (Paris: PUF, 1979), pp. 394–6.

37. *The Digest of Justinian*, vol. 1, Book I.2–4: 5, 13, 14–15.

38. C. H. McIlwain, 'A Fragment on Sovereignty', *Political Science Quarterly* 48:1 (1933): 96.

39. For the conceptual overlapping of emperor, king and sovereign, see Otto Gierke, *Political Theories of the Middle Age*, trans. F. W. Maitland (Cambridge: Cambridge University Press, 1958), pp. 14–21 and pp. 30–7; Walter Ullmann, 'The Development of the Medieval Idea of Sovereignty', *The English Historical Review* 64 (1949): 1–33; Gaines Post, *Studies in Medieval Legal Thought* (Princeton, NJ: Princeton University Press, 1964), pp. 453–81; Marcel David, *La souveraineté du people* (Paris: PUF, 1996), pp. 8–12.

40. Antony Black, *Political Thought in Europe 1250–1450* (Cambridge: Cambridge University Press, 1992), pp. 113–14. It is not a coincidence that Bodin's first work on public authority and sovereign majesty was titled *De imperio*, written during his stay at the Law School of Toulouse (Bodin, *On Sovereignty*, Book I:8, 88). This early work has not survived, probably because he requested that it be destroyed when he died. See also Merriam, *History of the Theory of Sovereignty since Rousseau*, pp. 11–12; David Held, *Democracy and the Global Order: From the Modern State to Cosmopolitan Governance* (Redwood City, CA: Stanford University Press, 1995), p. 38.

41. Bodin, *On Sovereignty*, Book I:10, 55.

42. Kelsen, *General Theory of Law and State*, p. 386.

43. Hans Kelsen, *Introduction to the Problems of Legal Theory*, trans. Bonnie Litschewski Paulson and Stanley L. Paulson (Oxford: Clarendon Press, 1992), p. 124; Hardt and Negri, *Empire*, pp. 67–204.

44. Derrida, *Rogues*, p. 102.

45. Michael Hardt and Antonio Negri, 'Sovereignty', in Antonio Negri, *Reflections on Empire*, trans. Ed Emery (Cambridge: Polity, 2008), pp. 50–3; Ann Stoler, 'On Degrees of Imperial Sovereignty', *Public Culture* 18, no. 1 (2006): 125–46.

46. Bodin, *On Sovereignty*, Book I.10, 8, 46, 45. See also Allen, *A History of Political Thought in the Sixteenth Century*, pp. 400–2; Christopher R. Baxter, 'Jean Bodin's Daemon and His Conversion to Judaism', in Julian H. Franklin (ed.), *Jean Bodin* (London: Ashgate, 2006), pp. 294–8; Paul Lawrence Rose, *Bodin and the Great God of Nature: The Moral and Religious Universe of a Judaiser* (Geneva: Droz, 1980), pp. 1–15.

47. Jean Bodin, *De la démonomanie des sorciers* [1580] (London: Nabu

Press, 2011); Jean Bodin, *Universae Naturae Theatrum* [1595] (Whitefish, MT: Kessinger Publishing, 2011); Jean Bodin, *Colloquium of the Seven about Secrets of the Sublime* [1593], trans. Marion Leathers Kuntz (Philadelphia: Pennsylvania University Press, 2008); Julian H. Franklin, 'Introduction', in Franklin (ed.), *Jean Bodin*, pp. xv–xvi; Daniel Engster, *Divine Sovereignty: The Origins of Modern State Power* (Chicago: Northern Illinois University Press, 2001), p. 11, p. 53 and p. 56.

48. Maryanne Cline Horowitz, 'Bodin and Judaism', *Il Pensiero Politico* 30 (1997): 205–16.

49. Bodin, *On Sovereignty*, Book I: 10, 50.

50. Ibid., Book I.8: 45.

51. Baxter, 'Jean Bodin's Daemon', pp. 298–300.

52. Bodin, *On Sovereignty*, Book II: 5, 110.

53. Bodin, 'Préface', *Les six livres de la République* (Paris: Le Livre de Poche, 1993), p. 9.

54. Engster, *Divine Sovereignty*, pp. 70–1.

55. Hobbes, *Leviathan*, ed. Richard Tuck (Cambridge: Cambridge University Press, 1996), Part II.17: 120. For the theological aspects of Hobbes's political thought, see F. C. Hood, *The Divine Politics of Thomas Hobbes: An Interpretation of 'Leviathan'* (Oxford: Clarendon Press, 1964); Tracy Strong, 'How to Write Scripture: Words, Authority, and Politics in Thomas Hobbes', *Critical Inquiry* 20 (1993): 128–59; Joshua Mitchell, 'Hobbes and the Equality of All under One', *Political Theory* 21 (1993): 78–100; A. P. Martinich, *The Two Gods of 'Leviathan': Thomas Hobbes on Religion and Politics* (Cambridge: Cambridge University Press, 1992).

56. Schmitt, *Political Theology*, p. 46. For the importance of religious beliefs in the development of the modern state theory, also see Paul Monod, *The Power of the Kings: Monarchy and Religion in Europe 1589–1715* (New Haven, CT: Yale University Press, 1999); Jean Bethke Elshtain, *Sovereignty: God, State, and Self* (New York: Basic Books, 2008).

57. For a powerful and informed statement of this argument, see Kathleen Davis, *Periodization and Sovereignty: How Ideas of Feudalism and Secularization Govern the Politics of Time* (Philadelphia: University of Pennsylvania Press, 2008). For the sacralisation of order and unity in theories of state sovereignty, see Laski, *Studies in the Problem of Sovereignty*, pp. 1–26.

58. Ullmann, 'The Development of the Medieval Idea of Sovereignty', p. 19.

59. Hobbes, *Leviathan*, Part I.26: 184.

60. John Austin, *The Province of Jurisprudence Determined*, p. 254.

61. Michel Foucault, *The History of Sexuality: An Introduction*, vol. 1, trans. Robert Hurley (New York: Vintage Books, 1990), p. 85; Hannah Arendt, 'What is Freedom?', in Arendt, *Between Past and Future* (London: Penguin Books, 1993), p. 152 and p. 164.

62. Arendt, 'What is Freedom?', p. 159; Hannah Arendt, 'On Violence', in Arendt, *Crises of the Republic* (New York and London: Harvest/ HBJ, 1972), p. 139. Also see Hardt and Negri, 'Sovereignty', p. 49.

63. Arendt, *The Human Condition*, p. 57 and pp. 234–5; Arendt, *On Revolution*, pp. 6–7.

64. Arendt, *The Human Condition*, p. 234.

65. Arendt, 'What is Freedom?', p. 164.

66. Hannah Arendt, *The Origins of Totalitarianism* [1951] (New York and London: Harvest Books, 1978), pp. 465–6; Arendt, *On Revolution*, p. 60, pp. 76–7.

67. Antonio Negri, *Insurgencies, Constituent Power and the Modern State*, trans. Maurizia Boscagli (Minneapolis: University of Minnesota Press, 1999), p. 332; Antonio Negri, 'Political Subjects: On the Multitude and Constituent Power', in Negri, *Reflections on Empire*, p. 103.

68. Friedrich von Bezlod, 'Die Lehre von der Volkssouveranität während des Mittelalters', *Historische Zeitschrift* 36 (1876), p. 46; Ewart Lewis, *Medieval Political Ideas*, vol. 1 (London: Routledge and Kegan Paul, 1954), p. 30; Walter Ullmann, *Principles of Government and Politics in the Middle Ages* [1961] (London: Routledge, 2010), pp. 268–79; Quentin Skinner, *The Foundations of Modern Political Thought, vol. 1: The Renaissance* (Cambridge: Cambridge University Press, 1978), pp. 62–5.

69. Marsilius, *Defensor Pacis*, ed. and trans. Alan Gewirth (Toronto: University of Toronto Press, 1956), Book I: 15, 61.

70. Marsilius, *Defensor Pacis*, Book I: 18, 87.

71. Ibid., Book I: 8, 15, 26, 63–4.

72. Ibid., Book I: 15, 62, 64, 65.

73. Alan Gewirth, *Marsilius of Padua: The Defender of Peace* (New York: Columbia University Press, 1951), pp. 167–225.

74. Ibid., pp. 50–6.

75. Marsilius, *Defensor Pacis*, Book I: 8, 15, 27, 63; Gierke, *Political Theories of the Middle Age*, pp. 24–6; C. J. Nederman, 'Character and Community in the *Defensor Pacis*: Marsiglio of Padua's adaptation of Aristotelian Moral Psychology', *History of Political Thought* 13, no. 3 (1992): 384–5; Francesco Maiolo, *Medieval Sovereignty: Marsilius of Padua and Bartolus of Saxoferrato* (Delft: Eburon, 2007), pp. 202–3 and p. 210.

76. Marsilius, *Defensor Pacis*, Book I: 15, 64. Takashi Shogimen, 'Medicine and the Body Politic in Marsilius of Padua's *Defensor Pacis*', in Gerson Moreno-Riaño and Cary J. Nederman (eds), *A Companion to Marsilius of Padova* (Leiden: Brill, 2011).

77. Marsilius, *Defensor Pacis*, Book I: 15, 62.

78. Ibid., Book I: 8, 27. Gewirth, *Marsilius of Padua*, pp. 39–44; Gerson Moreno-Riaño and Cary J. Nederman, 'Marsilius of Padua's Principles of Secular Politics', in Moreno-Riaño and Nederman (eds), *A Companion to Marsilius of Padova*.

79. Marsilius, *Defensor Pacis*, Book I: 9, 10, 12, 29, 36, 44, 46.
80. Ibid., Book I: 19, 89–97.
81. Ibid., Book I: 8, 13, 27–8, 52, 53, 54–5. On the idea of the constitu-
    ent power in Marsilius's theory of popular sovereignty see Gierke,
    Political Theories of the Middle Age, pp. 46–7; Charles Howard
    McIlwain, *The Growth of Political Thought in the West: From the
    Greeks to the End of the Middle Ages* (London: Macmillan Company,
    1932), pp. 305–6; Alexander Passarin D'Entreves, *The Medieval
    Contribution to Political Thought* (Oxford: Oxford University Press,
    1939), pp. 54–5 and p. 59; Gewirth, *Marsilius of Padua*, p. 169.
82. Marsilius, *Defensor Pacis*, Book I: 12, 15, 18, 45, 48, 64, 87–8. Also
    see Gewirth, *Marsilius of Padua*, p. 172 and p. 183.
83. Marsilius, *Defensor Pacis*, Book I: 12, 45–6. Marsilius also anticipates
    the revolutionary idea of the constitutional convention.
84. Respectively, Marsilius relegated the power of command to an infe-
    rior status even within the instituted order, thus minimising its politi-
    cal significance. In his differentiated hierarchy of powers, command is
    secondary to legislation, which itself is inferior to the act of constitut-
    ing. The latter belongs exclusively to the entire community, which also
    retains its legislative powers while the right of command is granted to
    the constituted structure of government in its administrative capacity
    and remains subordinated to the sovereign authority of the multitude.
    See Ullmann, *Principles of Government and Politics in the Middle
    Ages*, pp. 272–6.
85. Gewirth, *Marsilius of Padua*, pp. 167–225.
86. Ibid., Book I: 12, 46.
87. Ibid., I: 13, 49–55; Janet Coleman, *A History of Political Thought:
    From The Middle Ages to the Renaissance* (Oxford: Blackwell
    Publishing, 2000), pp. 153–6.
88. The Scottish Catholic jurist William Barclay coined the name 'monar-
    chomach' in his polemical pamphlet, *De Regno et Regali Potestate
    adversus Buchanum, Brutum, Boucherium et reliquios monarchoma-
    cos* (Paris: G. Chaudière, 1600). See J. W. Allen, *A History of Political
    Thought in the Sixteenth Century* [1922] (Lanham, MD: Rowman
    and Littlefield, 1977), pp. 306–8; William A. Cummings, 'The
    Monarchomachs: Theories of Popular Sovereignty in the Sixteenth
    Century', *Political Science Quarterly* 19: 2 (1904): 277–301; Oscar
    Jászi and John D. Lewis, *Against the Tyrant: The Tradition and
    Theory of Tyrannicide* (New York: The Free Press, 1957), pp. 59–74;
    W. J. Stankiewicz, *Politics and Religion in Seventeenth-Century
    France: A Study of Political Ideas from the Monarchomachs to Bayle,
    as Reflected in the Toleration Controversy* (Berkeley: University
    of California Press, 1960); Ralph E. Giesey, 'The Monarchomach
    Triumvirs: Hotman, Beza, and Mornay', *Bibliothèque d'Humanisme
    et Renaissance* 32, no. 1 (1970): 41–56.
89. Julian Franklin, 'Introduction', in Franklin (ed.), *Constitutionalism
    and Resistance in the Sixteenth Century* (Cambridge: Pegasus, 1969),

pp. 11–12; Pauline Maier, *From Resistance to Revolution: Colonial Radicals and the Development of American Opposition to Britain, 1765–1776* (New York: Alfred A. Knopf, 1972), pp. 3–49; Antonio Negri, 'From the Right to Resistance to Constituent Power', in Negri, *The Porcelain Workshop: For a New Grammar of Politics*, trans. Noura Wedell (Los Angeles: Semiotext(e), 2008), pp. 109–26.

90. Carl J. Friedrich, *Constitutional Government and Democracy: Theory and Practice in Europe and America* (Boston: Ginn and Company, 1950), pp. 129–31.

91. Julian Franklin, *Jean Bodin and the Rise of Absolutist Theory* (Cambridge: Cambridge University Press, 2009), pp. 47–53.

92. This is Sidney's classical version, almost a century later, which exemplifies the normative meaning of popular sovereignty based on the power to constitute. It also testifies to its discursive permanence beyond and after the Monarchomachs. Algernon Sidney, *Discourses Concerning Government* [1680], ed. Thomas G. West (Indianapolis, IN: Liberty Fund, 1996), ch. 1:6, p. 20; Gierke, *Natural Law and the Theory of Society*, pp. 256–7; Franklin, *Jean Bodin and the Rise of Absolutist Theory*, pp. 43–8.

93. Allen, *A History of Political Thought in the Sixteenth Century*, pp. 311–12 and pp. 316–18; Jászi and Lewis, *Against the Tyrant*, p. 52.

94. Franklin, 'Introduction', p. 37 and pp. 42–5.

95. François Hotman, *Franco-Gallia: Or an Account of the Ancient Free State of France* [1573] (Charleston: BiblioBazaar, 2007), X: 82 (emphasis added).

96. Théodore de Bèze, 'Rights of Magistrates [1574]', in Franklin (ed.), *Constitutionalism and Resistance in the Sixteenth Century*, p. 124 and p. 126 (emphasis added).

97. Ibid., 104.

98. Franklin, 'Introduction', p. 33.

99. Théodore de Bèze, *Rights of Magistrates*, p. 106.

100. Junius Brutus, the Celt (most probably Philippe du Plessis-Mornay), *Vindiciae, contra tyrannos or, concerning the legitimate power of a prince over the people, and of the people over a prince* [1579], III.1, ed. George Garnett (Cambridge: Cambridge University Press, 1994), pp. 68–76; Gierke, *Natural Law and the Theory of Society*, pp. 44–8; Franklin, 'Introduction', pp. 39–44.

101. Brutus, *Vindiciae, contra tyrannos*, p. 71 and p. 156.

102. Ibid., pp. 99–102.

103. Ibid., p. 75 and p. 169.

104. Ibid., p. 74 (emphasis added), pp. 68–74, p. 92, p. 94 and p. 130.

105. Ibid., p. 78 and p. 82.

106. Gierke, *Natural Law and the Theory of Society*, p. 241, p. 244 and p. 257.

107. Althusius, *Politica*, IX: pp. 72–3 (emphasis added), XVIII: p. 93, pp. 96–7 and pp. 110–11. For Althusius's theory of active resistance and tyrannicide see *Politica*, XXXVIII: pp. 191–200.

108. Ibid., IX: p. 70.

109. Ibid., IX: pp. 72–3.

110. Ibid., I: p. 17. See also Gierke, *Natural Law and the Theory of Society*, pp. 1–2.

111. Bodin, *On Sovereignty*, Book II: 5, 110–26; Franklin, *Jean Bodin and the Rise of Absolutist Theory*, p. vii, pp. 49–51 and pp. 93–4; Franklin, 'Sovereignty and the Mixed Constitution', pp. 307–9; Skinner, *The Foundations of Modern Political Thought*, vol. 2, pp. 285–6; John Hearsey McMillan Salmon, 'Bodin and the Monarchomachs', in Horst Denzer (ed.), *Jean Bodin: Verhandlungen der internationalen Bodin Tagung in München* (Munich: Beck, 1973), pp. 359–78; S. Rufus Davis, *The Federal Principle: A Journey through Time in Quest of Meaning* (Berkeley: University of California Press, 1978), p. 43; Ellen Meiksins Wood, *Liberty and Property: A Social History of Western Political Thought from the Renaissance to Enlightenment* (New York: Verso, 2012), p. 161 and p. 164.

112. Althusius, *Politica*, pp. 6–7, Book IX: 71–2 and Book XVIII: 104–5; Gierke, *Natural Law and the Theory of Society*, p. 70; Carl J. Friedrich, *Trends of Federalism in Theory and Practice* (Westport, CT: Praeger Publishers, 1968), pp. 12–13; Brian Tierney, *Religion, Law, and the Growth of Constitutional Law 1150–1650* (Cambridge: Cambridge University Press, 1982), pp. 73–4; Daniel J. Elazar, *Exploring Federalism* (Tuscaloosa, AL: The University of Alabama Press, 1987), pp. 129–30.

113. Daniel J. Elazar, 'Federalism', in *International Encyclopedia of the Social Sciences*, vol. V (New York: Macmillan, 1968), p. 363.

114. Howell A. Lloyd, 'Constitutionalism', in *The Cambridge History of Political Thought 1450–1700* (Cambridge: Cambridge University Press, 1988), pp. 289–91.

115. Gierke, *Natural Law and the Theory of Society*, pp. 73–4.

116. Loughlin, *The Idea of Public Law*, p. 112.

117. For a discussion of the etymological and semantic content of the concept of constituent power, see Andreas Kalyvas, 'Popular Sovereignty, Democracy, and the Constituent Power', *Constellations* 12, no. 2 (2005): 235–7.

118. Lawson, *Politica Sacra et Civilis* [1660], ed. Conal Condren (Cambridge: Cambridge University Press, 1992), p. 24.

119. Sidney, *Discourses Concerning Government*, 1.5: 99.

120. For the most systematic treatment of the power to institute as pouvoir instituant, see Cornelius Castoriadis, *The Imaginary Institution of Society*, trans. Kathleen Blamey (Cambridge: Polity, 1987), pp. 369–73; Cornelius Castoriadis, 'The First Institution of Society and Second-Order Institutions', *Free Associations* 12 (1988): 39–51; Cornelius Castoriadis, 'Power, Politics, Autonomy', in Castoriadis, *Philosophy, Politics, Autonomy: Essays in Political Philosophy*, ed. and trans. David Ames Curtis (Oxford: Oxford University Press, 1991), pp. 143–75; Cornelius Castoriadis, 'Radical Imagination

and the Social Instituting Imaginary', in David Ames Curtis (ed. and trans.), *The Castoriadis Reader* (Oxford: Blackwell Publishers, 1997), pp. 319–38; Cornelius Castoriadis, 'The Imaginary: Creation in the Social-Historical Domain', in Castoriadis, *World in Fragments: Writings on Politics, Society, Psychoanalysis, and the Imagination*, ed. and trans. David Curtis (Redwood City, CA: Stanford University Press, 1997), pp. 3–18.

121. Negri, *Insurgencies, Constituent Power and the Modern State*, p. 22 and pp. 305–7.

122. Schmitt, *Constitutional Theory*, p. 125. Olivier Beaud proposes the following formulation: 'Constituent sovereignty signifies that, in contemporary states, the Sovereign is he who makes the constitution' – Olivier Beaud, *La puissance de l'état* (Paris: PUF, 1994), p. 208.

123. Carl Schmitt, *Die Diktatur* (Berlin: Duncker und Humblot, 1921), p. 134 and pp. 137–8; Carl Schmitt, *Über die drei Arten des rechtswissenschaftlichen Denkens* [1933] (Berlin: Duncker und Humblot, 1993), p. 21, pp. 23–4. Accordingly, the French constitutional scholar Maurice Hauriou has described the constituent power as 'a founding legislative power' – Maurice Hauriou, *Précis de droit constitutionnel* (Paris: Sirey, 1929), p. 246.

124. Paine, *The American Crisis*, III: p. 124; Paine, *Rights of Man*, pp. 464–8 and pp. 551–8, both in Eric Fonner (ed.), *Thomas Paine: Collected Writings* (New York: The Library of America, 1995); Sheldon Wolin, 'Collective Identity and Constitutional Power', in Wolin, *The Presence of the Past: Essays on the State and the Constitution* (Baltimore, MD: The Johns Hopkins University Press, 1990), pp. 8–31.

125. Negri, 'Political Subjects: On the Multitude and Constituent Power', pp. 109–10.

126. Althusius, *Politica*, Book I: 17.

127. Thomas Paine, *Common Sense* [1776], in Fonner (ed.), *Thomas Paine: Collected Writings*, p. 42 and p. 52; Thomas Paine, *The Last Crisis, XIII* [1783], in Fonner, *Thomas Paine: Collected Writings*, pp. 348–54; Paine, *Rights of Man*, pp. 512–13, pp. 536–40, pp. 547–51 and pp. 572–9; Thomas Jefferson, *Letter to James Madison*, 30 January 1787, in Joyce Appleby and Terence Ball (eds), *Jefferson: Political Writings* (Cambridge: Cambridge University Press, 1999), 107–11; Arendt, *On Revolution*, pp. 141–214; Andrew Arato, *Civil Society, Constitution, and Legitimacy* (London: Rowman and Littlefield, 2000), ch. 7; Beaud, *La puissance de l'état*, pp. 359–76; Miguel Abensour, 'De la démocratie insurgeante', in Abensour, *La Démocratie contre l'Etat* (Paris: Félin, 2004), pp. 5–19.

128. For the relationship between constituent power and crisis, see Negri, *Insurgencies, Constituent Power and the Modern State*, pp. 1–36 and p. 319; Jon Elster, 'Forces and Mechanisms in the Constitution-Making Process', *Duke Law Journal* 45 (1995): 370, 375.

129. Lawson, *Politica Sacra et Civilis*, p. 227.

130. Even contemporary liberal thinkers have come to realise that dem-

ocratic legitimacy presupposes a break with the inherited legality. John Rawls, for instance, has acknowledged that the 'constituent power of the people sets up a framework to regulate ordinary power, and it comes into play only when the existing regime has been dissolved' – John Rawls, 'The Idea of Public Reason', in Rawls, *Political Liberalism* (New York: Columbia University Press, 1993), p. 23.

131. Pierre Rosanvallon, 'Revolutionary Democracy', in Rosanvallon, *Democracy Past and Future*, ed. Sam Moyn (New York: Columbia University Press, 2007), pp. 79–97; Wolin, 'Norm and Form: The Constitutionalizing of Democracy', p. 29, p. 37, p. 41, pp. 47–8 and pp. 53–7; Ulrich Preuss, 'Constitutional-Making and the Foundation of a New Polity', in Preuss, *Constitutional Revolution: The Link between Constitutionalism and Progress*, trans. Deborah Schneider (New York: Prometheus Books, 1994), pp. 2–3.

132. Loughlin, *The Idea of Public Law*, p. 110 and p. 113.

133. Ibid., pp. 99–113.

134. For a detailed distinction of this point, see Raymond Carré de Malberg, *La Loi, expression de la volonté générale* [1920, 1922] (Paris: Economica, 1984), pp. 103–39.

135. For the concept of 'the law of lawmaking', see Frank Michelman, *Brennan and Democracy* (Princeton, NJ: Princeton University Press, 1999), p. 48.

136. According to Maurice Duverger, 'It is the constitution that derives its authority from the constituent power and not the constituent power that derives its authority from the constitution' – Maurice Duverger, 'Légitimité des gouvernements de fait', *Revue du Droit Publique* (1948): 78.

137. Schmitt, *Constitutional Theory*, p. 112, pp. 120–1, pp. 136–9, p. 143 and pp. 255–67.

138. Karl Marx, 'Critique of Hegel's Doctrine of the State', in Marx, *Early Writings* (London: Penguin Books, 1975), p. 87.

139. Castoriadis, *The Imaginary Institution of Society*, pp. 369–74; Cornelius Castoriadis, 'The Greek Polis and the Creation of Democracy', in Castoriadis, *Philosophy, Politics, Autonomy*, pp. 81–123; Castoriadis, 'Radical Imagination and the Social Instituting Imaginary'.

140. Marx, 'Critique of Hegel's Doctrine of the State', p. 87 and p. 88.

141. Ibid., p. 80 and p. 90.

142. Schmitt, *Constitutional Theory*, pp. 268–79. Also see Andreas Kalyvas, 'Carl Schmitt and the Three Moments of Democracy', *Cardozo Law Review* 21, nos 5–6 (2000): 1,525–67.

143. Cornelius Castoriadis, *Philosophy, Politics, Autonomy*, pp. 152–3; Sheldon Wolin, 'Transgression, Equality, and Voice', in Joshua Ober and C. Hedrick (eds), *Demokratia: A Conversation on Democracies Ancient and Modern* (Princeton, NJ: Princeton University Press, 1996), p. 64.

144. For a detailed discussion of the normative democratic content of

the concept of constituent power, see Andreas Kalyvas, 'The Basic Norm and Democracy in Hans Kelsen's Legal and Political Theory', *Philosophy and Social Criticism* 32:5 (2006): 573–99.

145. Arendt, *On Revolution*, p. 146; Schmitt, *Constitutional Theory*, pp. 104–5.

146. Schmitt, *Political Theology*, p. 36 and p. 51; Schmitt, *Constitutional Theory*, pp. 126–8. Also see Ulrich Preuss, 'Constitutional Powermaking for the New Polity: Some Deliberations on the Relations between Constituent Power and the Constitution', in Michael Rosenfeld (ed.), *Constitutionalism, Identity, Difference, and Legitimacy: Theoretical Perspectives* (Durham, NC: Duke University Press, 1994), pp. 144–5.

147. Negri, *Insurgencies: Constituent Power and the Modern State*, p. 13.

148. Karl Marx, 'Preface', in Marx, *A Contribution to the Critique of Political Economy* [1859] (New York: International Publishers, 1970), pp. 20–1; Arendt, *The Human Condition*, pp. 243–7; Arendt, *On Revolution*, pp. 165–78.

149. Preuss, 'Constitutional-Making and the Foundation of a New Polity', p. 4.

150. Alexander Hamilton, *The Federalist*, no. 1, p. 3. Madison concurred and explained 'the improvement made by America on the ancient mode of preparing and establishing regular plans of government' as 'a revolution by the intervention of a deliberative body of citizens' (James Madison, *The Federalist*, no. 38, p. 234 and p. 235); Paine, *The American Crisis*, V [1778], p. 169; Paine, *Rights of Man*, p. 668; Arendt, *On Revolution*, pp. 46–7. From the seventeenth century on, the term *constitutio* came to designate a written document and a set of explicit superior, higher, fundamental legal norms and procedures instituted by human beings in opposition both to customs or conventions and to a transcendental natural law. See Gerald Stourzh, 'Constitution: Changing Meanings of the Term from the Early Seventeenth to the Late Eighteenth Century', in Terence Ball and J. G. A. Pocock (eds), *Conceptual Change and the Constitution* (Lawrence, KS: University Press of Kansas, 1988), pp. 43–4.

151. Georges Burdeau, *Traité de Science Politique*, vol. IV (Paris: Librarie Générale de Droit et de Jurisprudence, 1983), pp. 172–3; Arato, *Civil Society, Constitution, and Legitimacy*, pp. 170–5; Cornelius Castoriadis, 'Institution of Society and Religion', in Castoriadis, *World in Fragments*, pp. 311–30.

152. Karl Marx, 'Economic and Philosophical Manuscripts of 1844' [1927], p. 348, p. 366; Marx, 'Critique of Hegel's Doctrine of the State', pp. 118–20; both in Marx, *Early Writings* (London: Penguin Books, 1975).

153. Castoriadis, *The Imaginary Institution of Society*, pp. 135–59 and pp. 353–68.

154. Stathis Gourgouris, 'On Self-Alteration', *Parrhesia* 9 (2010): 1–17.

155. Marx, 'Critique of Hegel's Doctrine of the State', p. 80, pp. 87–8,

p. 90, p. 98 and pp. 117–19; Abensour, *La Démocratie contre l'Etat*, p. 105 and pp. 112–13.

156. Arendt, *On Revolution*, p. 201 and p. 202.
157. Marx, 'Critique of Hegel's Doctrine of the State', p. 80, p. 85, p. 87; Karl Marx, 'The Civil Wars in France', in Robert C. Tucker (ed.), *The Marx-Engels Reader* (New York: W. W. Norton, 1978), p. 628 and p. 633; Abensour, *La Démocratie contre l'Etat*, pp. 106–7, pp. 109–10, pp. 127–30 and pp. 140–2.
158. As Friedrich correctly observed, 'To make the constitutional decision genuine it is also necessary that it be participated in by some of those who are being governed as contrasted with those who do the governing. This differentiates such a constituent act from a coup d'état' – Friedrich, *Constitutional Government and Democracy*, p. 128. Also see Arendt, *On Revolution*, p. 146; Schmitt, *Constitutional Theory*, pp. 104–5.
159. Skinner, *The Foundations of Modern Political Thought*, vol. 2, p. 349.
160. Spruyt, *The Sovereign State and Its Competitors*, pp. 153–80.
161. Poggi, *The State: Its Nature, Development, and Prospects*, p. 25.
162. Thus, despite a widely shared belief that the age of globalisation has provoked a crisis of the state, a quick look at the geopolitical map of the contemporary world indicates a different situation. Not only is the number of states on the rise but, moreover, many secessionist movements seek to form their own states. In addition, the current global economic financial crisis seems to have caused a reaction characterised by statist and nationalist responses against the arbitrariness of world markets. Contrary to many widespread predictions that the twenty-first century will mark the end of the state, there is a proliferation and strengthening of this modern political form as it is adapting to new conditions.
163. Quentin Skinner, 'The State', in Terence Ball, James Farr, and Russell L. Hanson (eds), *Political Innovation and Conceptual Change* (Cambridge: Cambridge University Press, 1989), pp. 121–2.

4 Democratic Surplus and Democracy-in-Failing: On Ancient and Modern Self-Cancellation of Democracy

Nathalie Karagiannis

Democracy contains in itself the seeds of its own destruction. This is a conviction that is widespread in the history of political thought, from its origins in ancient Greece to contemporary political science. True, there are numerous historical examples of the downfall of democracies, and many of the highly varied attempts at conceptualising the reasons for such occurrences contain fruitful insights. However, is it really appropriate to identify the causes for the cancellation of democracy in its 'self', its nature? This chapter will argue that it is more useful to underline the possible persistence of a democratic spirit, or culture, even in the face of a cancellation of the institutional underpinnings of democracy. To see democracy as a tragic regime means to recognise the ever-present risk of its cancellation, but it also means to emphasise the anti-democratic nature of such cancellation, thus its incompatibility with democracy.[1]

The following reflections can be read in two different ways, one conceptual and the other historical, and maybe best as a combination of these two. On the one hand, conceptually, this chapter will provide a counterpart to the notion of the democratic paradox, widely evoked recently in politico-philosophical debates about the conceptual origins of liberal democracies. In one version, the notion of paradox refers to two distinct and not consistently connected political traditions at the core of our political self-understandings, namely liberalism and democracy. To use Chantal Mouffe's words:

> We are dealing with a new political form of society whose specificity comes from the articulation between two different traditions. On one side we have the liberal tradition constituted by the rule of law, the defence of human rights and the respect of individual liberty; on the other the democratic tradition whose main ideas are those of equality, identity between governing and governed and popular sovereignty. There is no necessary

relation between those two distinct traditions but only a contingent historical articulation.[2]

More generally, the paradox refers to the question of the origins of liberal democracy: democracy is the self-government by the people. However, the people as a political collectivity does not exist before its self-government. It is only brought about by democracy. In this form, the paradox has been discussed with regard to the performative character of the declaration 'We the People . . .'[3] The following reflections form a counterpart to these observations because they do not concern the origins of democracy, but the paradox of its end: how can we think of democracy as popular self-government being terminated by the people themselves?

Historically, on the other hand, this chapter is a reflection on the remarkable combination of fragility and vitality of ancient Greek, in particular Athenian, democracy, and maybe more particularly a reflection on Thucydides' consideration of the end of democracy in Athens in 411 BCE, namely that:

> it was no light matter to deprive the Athenian people of its freedom, almost a hundred years after the deposition of the tyrants, when it had been not only not subject to any during the whole of that period, but accustomed during more than half of it to rule over subjects of its own'.[4]

In the course of the Peloponnesian War, democracy was replaced in Athens twice by an oligarchy, in 411 and 404 – a political transformation brought about by the people – but it was also reinstalled shortly after. Thus, democracy can be put to an end by the people themselves, but it also tends to persist in the spirit of the people.

Preliminary conceptual reflections

Historians as well as political philosophers face enormous difficulties when discussing ancient Greek political concepts because our current terminology differs considerably from that of the ancients.[5] Significantly, the ancients made a distinction between the political, which included all concerns of the *polis*, and the personal, which included not only current 'private' matters but also economic ones,[6] but they did not have a distinction between politics and society – or, as one may prefer, avoiding reification: the political and the social. The reason why such a distinction is important even for the analysis of ancient Greece, in which it was absent, is that 'the discovery of politics',[7] and the institution of democracy in particular, precisely means the distanciation of ways of dealing with common matters of the *polis* from other relations between residents of the city. Thus, in our reflections on democracy, we will take the political to consist in those relations among people and among institutions within the *polis* that aim at deciding about the *polis*'s fate. And we will take the social to be those relations among people and among institutions within the *polis* to which such decisions about the *polis*'s fate apply and which they create. Doing so, we can recognise in democracy a tension between the political and the social, which produces change. If democracy is understood as tension between the two, then the relation between those who decide and those who are subjects of the decision is never entirely pacified, never crystallised – hence, always contested and in need of specification. This tension does not mean that there is no coincidence, in democracy, between those who decide and those to whom the decisions apply, as in the standard definition of democracy as the rule by the people for the people. Rather, it means that, despite and even because of this coincidence, it is possible to contest the roles, contents, and equilibria played out practically in this coincidence. The significance of this clarification takes on its full meaning when democracy is related to democracy's self-cancellation, as is the main concern of this chapter. When the political is firmly tied to the social, namely, we are facing non-democratic situations in one way or another.

The central argument here will be that democracy is incompatible with democracy's self-cancellation, which is, as the expression suggests, the putting-an-end to democracy from within democracy itself. The term itself has been used as early as the late eighteenth century, by Christoph Martin Wieland, who saw democracy's 'tendency towards self-cancellation' as residing in the fact that in democracy, 'the rulers are at the same time the ruled, and the ruled are the sovereign itself'.[8] In our terminology, Wieland sees the democratic constellation as tension-ridden, and the resulting tendency is the one of getting rid of the tension by cancelling the very democratic constellation. The argument developed here will suggest that, true, there is a fundamental feature of democracy that leads to fragility, but that an eventual cancellation of democracy cannot for that reason be attributed to democracy itself.

The paradoxical-sounding argument will draw occasionally on contemporary readings of the ancient Greek experience, and centrally on Cornelius Castoriadis's notion of 'democracy as a tragic regime'.[9] By this expression, Castoriadis formulated what he saw as most characteristic of democracy: the epitome of the indeterminacy that, he believed, characterises the political – that is, he defined democracy as something that has no grounding outside itself. As a consequence, Castoriadis pointed at the risk inherent in democracy, the risk that always accompanies a situation in which not everything is under control but, to the contrary, everything can be questioned. Pushed to its limit, this interpretation extends to the risk that democracy runs of revoking or cancelling itself.

The idea underlying the present use of 'democracy as a tragic regime' is that, countering treatments of democracy as a system of election and procedures, it points at democracy as a 'political culture' – which, translated in the terms above, is a culture of tension between the political and the social.[10] The cancellation of this 'culture' occurs when this tension is brought to an end. Centrally arguing for the incompatibility (or radical separability) between democracy and democracy's self-cancellation, this chapter grapples with the ambiguity that arises in the relation between such a notion and democracy's inherent risk.

The cancellation of democracy in ancient Greece and in current political thought

Has democracy's cancellation not been treated before? Among classical scholars, the replacement of democracy by oligarchy in Athens – the case to which this chapter limits itself – in 411 and 404 as well as the externally imposed and long-lasting end of democracy under Macedonian and later Roman domination are obviously well known.[11] However, the conceptual attention has most often, and understandably, been on the political innovations of ancient Greece and their possible import for world history, and the cancellation of democracy, in turn, tends to be treated as a historical process from which significant conceptual conclusions cannot be drawn in the same way.

In ancient Athens, though, there was no scarcity of conceptual criticism of democracy, often indeed suggesting the unsustainability of democratic regimes. The authors whom current political philosophers regard as having inaugurated the genre of political philosophy, most importantly Plato and Aristotle, are better understood as observers of democratic practices, past and present, and as developing their critical views contextually on the basis of experiences with democracy. Significantly, Plato can be read as having, at least in one text, *The Republic*, argued for the end of democracy and suggested an alternative: the reign of philosophers. Aristotle, in turn, weighed various experiences with democracy and saw the likelihood of successive regime changes away from democracy and back towards it.[12] These arguments were drawn upon when, closer to our time, the question of democracy returned to the political agenda at the end of the eighteenth century. At this moment, though, debate was not about the end of democracy but about reasons why democratic experiments should not be started again at all.[13]

In current social and political theory, arguments as to the mortal perils that democracy faces take new conceptual shape. Briefly, we can distinguish three strands of such argumentation. The first strand runs along the lines of 'democracy is not good enough'. This is an argument that can be found both on the right and on the left: on the right it will tend to take on the colours of lack of freedom, suggesting that all-inclusive collective self-determination limits individual autonomy, while on the left it will tend to bemoan inequalities and discrimination, suggesting that formal political equality is insufficient for true collective self-determination in contexts of high social inequality. In more complex versions, like Castoriadis's, it will tend to regret the lack of both collective and individual autonomy by resorting to *topoi* such as generalised conformism and populism.[14] Recent French debates, to provide another example, identify a degeneration of democracy in the course of the democratic experiences of the last decades – and in particular in the social experiences of democracy. Thus, Pierre Rosanvallon's trilogy on the current democratic condition and Jacques Rancière's incisive short book on the 'hatred of democracy' have aimed at understanding recent disaffection with democracy or even 'anti-democratic' waves.[15] These analyses expose the ambiguity of much of the recent criticism of democracy, as it at once bemoans the progressive 'equalisation' of conditions because of their populist or vulgar character and applauds wars conducted in the name of democracy. The understanding of what exactly the alleged 'excesses' of democratic life are change across space (from the USA to France) and across time (from the 1980s to the 2000s). Significantly, Rancière himself concludes: 'A good democratic government is one that is capable of mastering an evil that is simply called democratic life.'[16]

The second strand argues that 'democracy is not effective enough'. This is a straightforwardly conservative argument, even if it comes from people who consider themselves to be social democrats, such as Giandomenico Majone or Fritz Scharpf.[17] This argument tends to prefer efficiency, technicality and quickness of decision over debate. Though it has found some echoes among political scientists and bureaucrats, this type of argument neglects the foundations of what democracy means in that it restricts the decision-takers to a very small minority and may, at times, not even insist on representation, but rather focus on expertise.

The third strand is also straightforwardly conservative: it aims at braking change. Albert Hirschman has distinguished three *topoi* of the argumentation against democratic change: perversity, futility and jeopardy:

> According to the perversity thesis, any purportive action to improve some feature of the political, social or economic order only serves to exacerbate the condition one wishes to remedy. The futility thesis holds that attempts at social transformation will be unavailing, that they will simply fail to 'make a dent'. Finally, the jeopardy thesis argues that the cost of the proposed change or reform is too high as it endangers some previous, precious accomplishment.[18]

These are highly different ways of aiming at the same target: impeding change. All three reasonings implicitly address democracy's end. The first two say societies cannot change through conscious action – thus cancelling the fundamental idea of democracy, collective self-determination. The third effectively argues for the cancellation of democracy by insisting that willed change, which is inherent in democracy, endangers democracy.

In the terms introduced above, all of these ways of thinking detect the cancellation of democracy in arresting the tension between the political and the social. In the last case, most clearly, the social has its own dynamics which is recalcitrant to any attempt at change by action within the realm of the political. In the second case, in apparent contrast, only effective political steering based on expert knowledge will satisfy the demands arising from the social even if those were not explicitly voiced as such. Here, too, though, the ambiguous openness of the relation between the political and the social is replaced by a concise concept of political intervention into the social. In the first case, the most complex because of its internal variety, existing social structures within 'the people' as subject of law undermine the political promise of collective self-determination of 'the people' as maker of law.

These reasonings are recognisable in ancient critiques of democracy, too. The 'technocratic' argument that the holders of superior knowledge should govern the city has been read into Plato's *Republic*. Considerations of 'the social' conditioning 'the political' can be found, for instance, in Aristotle's double use of the term 'demos', sometimes referring to all citizens and sometimes to the multitude. And Solon's reforms can be seen as creating more distance between 'political' institutions for rule-making and 'social' relations within the polity. One should not exaggerate the proximity between the ancient and the current debates about democracy, though. The latter is informed by the conceptual distinction between the social and the political, going back to the Renaissance and becoming prominent during the nineteenth century, which is unknown to the former. For that reason, the risk of democracy's self-cancellation was diagnosed differently in ancient and current debates, and a contrasting look can be instructive for current purposes. In the remainder of this chapter I will first explore the notion of democracy as a tragic regime as a key to the ancient understanding, and then discuss the two exemplary forms of democratic self-cancellation in our time – the state of exception and totalitarianism – as a contrast. This brief comparison will lead to concluding reflections about democracy's potential to outlast its self-cancellation.

Democracy as a tragic regime

Acknowledging the explicitness and originality of his reflections on the matter, our brief discussion of democracy and tragedy will focus on Cornelius Castoriadis's work.[19] Castoriadis saw tragedy as democratic and democracy as tragic. Of the first relation, we need only retain two elements for present purposes:[20] the first is the presentation, by tragedy, of the limits of human action, most of all of '*monōs phronein*', 'to be wise alone', that is, of reasoning, arriving at an opinion and a decision on one's own, not collectively.[21] Tragedy, Castoriadis argues, 'shows' its audience, by default, that the best decisions are those that are arrived at together. The consequence that can be drawn here is that the best decisions or laws are those where the maker and the subject of the law coincide, which is proper of a democratic situation. *Monōs phronein* would thus take place when the maker of the law is other than the demos.

The second significant element is the particularity of the concept of hubris in Castoriadis's understanding, a particularity which is very useful for an understanding of the end of democracy. Indeed, the ethical and ontological aspects of hubris are at the centre of the relation between tragedy and the political/democracy established by this thinker. Although hubris – human excess – is one of the most common exegetical concepts of the Greek worldview, Castoriadis's insistence on the absence of borders accompanying hubris renders his version very distinct. Indeed, in the common understanding of hubristic action, humans arrogantly transgress their humanness, which distinguishes them from gods.[22] In Castoriadis's version, that which is central is that humans do not *know* where the borders are that should not be transgressed. It is in this sense that hubris is different from sin: 'no one knows in which moment hubris begins, and

nevertheless there is a moment in which one finds oneself in hubris'.[23]
One finds oneself in hubris suddenly.

Demonstrating the consequences of *monōs phronein* and hubris,
tragedy is democratic for Castoriadis, but democracy is also tragic.
Democracy is the explicit political form of the autonomous polity.[24]
Democracy is a regime that does not know any norms that come from
the outside; it has to set its own norms, and it has to set them without
the support of another norm. In other words, there is no grounding of
democracy outside itself. Giving oneself one's own laws – the fulfilment, as it were, of this indeterminacy – represents a risk, since nothing
other than democracy itself – nobody but the demos – can decide about
that which it is to become. There is no other law, no higher law than
the one that originates in the subject of law, the subject that is hence
the maker of the law, too. Thus, democracy is the political regime of
autonomy. But autonomy necessarily also means auto-limitation:

> In democracy, the people *can* do anything – and it has to know that it
> *should not* do anything. Democracy is the regime of auto-limitation;
> therefore it is also the historical regime of risk – another way of saying
> that it is the regime of freedom – and a tragic regime.[25]

Castoriadis goes on to give the example of the defeat of Athens in
the Peloponnesian War as a result of the hubris of the Athenians. At
the limit, thus, this means that democracy may decide to cancel itself.

Democratic autonomy is both individual and collective. Collective
autonomy, that is, participation in making the *polis*'s law and in
defining the common good, is that which makes democracy a regime
rather than just a sum of procedures. In Athenian practice, there is
no opposition between individual and collective autonomy; together
they form the self-understanding of the city. The relation can be out
of balance, however. Josiah Ober reminds us that

> the Athenian democratic ideology construed the threat to public order,
> the prime suspect of 'paranomic' activity, as the hubristic individual [. . .]
> [T]he powerful hubristic individual was imagined as seeking to establish
> hierarchical relations within the *polis* on his own terms by demonstrat-
> ing his capacity to humiliate, by outrageously insulting weaker persons
> by speech or deed [. . .] and by seeking to do so with impunity. And if he
> (or the class of powerful persons he represented) were successful in estab-
> lishing a secure 'personal' hierarchy within the *polis*, a social space free
> from the legal authority of the democratic state, it would clearly mean
> the end of the effective rule of the demos; this is why a successfully perpe-
> trated, unchastised act of hubris would be characterised as signifying 'the
> overthrow of democracy'.

Here we recognise in practice the problem of the *monōs phronein* mentioned earlier.[26]

Qualifying autonomy, a further tragic feature of democracy is its explicitness. The element of explicitness is significant because it points to acknowledged self-institution: there is self-reflexivity in the instituting process; we are, therefore, again in a situation where the subjects of the political give themselves their own law and, in addition, *know* that they are doing this and *express* this (through *logos*): the element of explicitness is then evidently closely related to *doxa*, opinion. It is this interpretation of the political as democracy that leads to an understanding of politics as not an *epistēmē* or a *technē* but a *doxa*. Consequently, the knowing and the expressing leave open the space for debate. It clearly follows that any law thus enacted can be cancelled – and transposing this at the very general level of democracy itself, the regime itself can be cancelled.[27]

The self-cancellation of democracy (I): the state of exception

Moving from the ancient situation to the modern one, among the many possible cancellations of democracy I consider now two cases that are usually thought to be self-cancellations: the state of exception and totalitarianism. The first represents the temporary, the second the permanent self-cancellation of democracy. My main argument will be that, contrary to what is commonly assumed, both these situations break with a linear continuation of the democratic phenomenon: they are due to a displacement that is akin to the hubristic displacement in Castoriadis ('there is a moment in which one finds oneself in hubris').

According to Castoriadis, as we have seen, democracy knows no norm outside of itself – is the state of exception an exception to this rule? Democracy's temporary self-cancellation obliges us to confront again the democratic paradox, that is, the idea that none other than the demos decides who the demos is. The circularity inherent here is theoretically useful in that it prevents us from taking any starting assumption on the democratic origins for granted. Thus, not only is there a moment before democracy which is not democratic but brings democracy about, and that is the moment of origins; this original arbitrariness will also keep leaving an imprint on decisions about membership and citizenship. Surreptitiously, the idea of a fundamental and lasting imperfection of democracy is introduced here.

How, one may now want to ask, is the issue of the paradoxical origins of democracy connected to democracy's end, its self-cancellation? The answer is: through law. It is one of the merits of post-structuralism to have touched legal theory, which found a renewed interest in the liminal case of the origins of law.[28] The state of exception is the illustration of this liminality. In the state of exception, all legality – all legal normality – is withdrawn in favour of a para-legal situation, a situation that is managed outside the law. The state of exception itself, however, is decreed legally – even though the mere call for something outside the law can never entirely fall under the law. Reminiscent of the questions that declarations of independence pose, the state of exception is both in and out of the law.

The state of exception has explicitly been discussed in social and political theory from the onset of fully inclusive democracy, most clearly marked by the granting of equal universal suffrage in many countries around or after the First World War. A first 'debate' was led between Carl Schmitt and Walter Benjamin,[29] and the topic has recently been re-addressed by Giorgio Agamben – the following brief exploration limits itself to these thinkers.

Schmitt's original formulation of the state of exception justifies it in terms of the exceptionality of the situations it addresses: according to Schmitt, because there is a gap in the law, which can therefore not address a given exceptional situation, the state of exception intervenes. By contrast, Benjamin's[30] much-discussed text draws a distinction between the false, fascist 'state of emergency' and the 'real state of emergency' which should be brought about 'to improve our position in the struggle against Fascism'.[31] Agamben writes against the background of these two famous works on the state of exception, but tries to reverse the terms of the debate. Throughout his work he has been interested in limits and limit-situations and thus naturally drawn to the question of the state of exception. He aims to emphasise the marginality of 'inherited' distinctions such as those between friend and enemy, also advanced by Schmitt in his definition of the political, and others such as inclusion versus exclusion or exception versus norm.[32] Rather than siding with those who believe nation-state necessity to be above the law and thus argue that, in situations of emergency, there is a lack of law that the 'state of exception' fills, Agamben claims that the state of exception itself creates the lack that it fills and that, by doing so, it consolidates the position of the norm. Like Benjamin, and in contrast to Schmitt, Agamben claims that we are in a permanent state of exception and that the norm has become the state of exception: 'there is no possible return to the state bound by the rule of law from the effective state of exception in which we live'.[33] Unlike the messianic, revolutionary promise of Benjamin, however, Agamben does not advocate a 'real' state of exception for the future.[34]

Without discussing this diagnosis of the present in more detail, I intend to underline a conceptual feature of this debate that is most disturbing for our own purposes: all thought and texts around 'the state of exception' seem to focus on law and the political, thus failing to examine democracy and its relation to the making of law. As we noted early on, democracy can fruitfully be seen as that political form that is based on a specific tension between the political and the social, not as the subordination of the one under the other. In the assembly democracy of ancient Athens, the people as maker of the law was in such immediacy to the people as subject of the law that rules that did not emerge from that constellation were almost unthinkable. For that reason, ancient democratic Athens did not know a state of exception or any equivalent measures.[35] The only known and noteworthy rule concerning situations of political disorder is the famous Solonian law on stasis, which obliged every citizen to side with one of the fighting parties.[36] Rather than a weakness or a lack of sophistication in the foundation of ancient democracy,[37] one may see in this absence the sign of a radical incompatibility between democracy and state of exception.

Thus, an examination of the state of exception – of democracy's temporary self-cancellation – in the light of a definition of democracy that comprises both the political and the social becomes, on the one hand, more complete and, on the other hand, thornier. We may reconsider in this light the time-diagnostic question that interested Schmitt, Benjamin and today Agamben: 'are we living in democracies?' If the answer is no – no, we do not live in democracies but under oligarchic regimes, as among others also Castoriadis and Rancière maintain[38] – then the state of exception poses no particular problem: the oligarchs decree the state of exception, that is, they who have made the law decree that the norm is no longer applicable to the polity's population, who are subjected to the law. If the norm ceases to be applicable to the population, the population stops being a subject of law, as in the agential meaning of 'subject', and becomes subjected to it. The relation between the oligarch and the former subject of law becomes one of unmediated power – perhaps Agamben's 'bare life' – and the former subject of law loses its discursive specificity; that is, it loses any possibility of being articulate.

Before going on to examine what analysis would be suitable – in case the answer to our question 'are we living in democracies?' were yes – the expression that I have now used several times, 'the subject of law', needs further discussion. Under oligarchy, the subject of law – in other words, those whom the law subjects – can be called 'a population', a term intended, without political connotation, to designate those who live in a polity. This population corresponds to the biggest part of society. Under oligarchy, in the ancient understanding, those who make the law are the group of the *oligoi* (the few). They correspond *both* to a much smaller part of society and to the whole of the political – they, the few, are the body politic, to the exclusion of the many or the masses or, as we have neutrally called them, the population. How is this apportioning of power revisited under current forms of democracy?

If the answer to our question is 'yes, we do live in democracies', then the sovereign who decides the state of exception is the demos, in the sense of all citizens. But if the demos decides a state of exception, in effect it decides that democratic norms are not applicable to the demos. Contrary to what happens in the oligarchy we just discussed, in democracy the maker and the subject of law coincide – the logical consequence is that if the demos as maker of the law decided the state of exception, the law would stop being applicable to the demos as subject of the law. The demos as subject of law would cease to exist. The mechanism would be the same as under oligarchies: there would be no subject of law anymore but something inarticulate at the mercy of raw power. However, what is equally worth noting here is that this action would at the same time transform the demos as maker of the law into a non-democratic sovereign, that is, it would transform the demos into what the sovereign is under any other regime, an autocratic figure.[39] In other words, the tension between the political meaning of the demos and its social meaning would vanish; the two meanings would collapse into each other. In this precise sense, the abolition of the tension between the political and the social, a polity ceases to be a democracy and becomes an autocracy when the state of exception is decreed by a democracy. This is what can be called democracy's temporary self-cancellation.

If we now recall Castoriadis's reflections on democracy, it will be clear that the reason why democracy has space for self-cancellation is its commitment to autonomy and its rejection of all externally set norms. Democracy is a situation of initial and recurring openness that needs to be filled by autonomous and auto-limiting decisions, in the context of a tension between the political meaning of the people (the maker of the law) and its social meaning (the subject of the law). The absence of external norms, that is, autonomy in a radical sense, creates the possibility for democratic auto-limitation to fail; in other words, it is possible for a democracy to cancel itself, for the democratic tension between the political and the social to cause democracy's own vanishing. In current political thought, as briefly described above, the renunciation of attempts at changing society as futile or dangerous or the emphasis on efficient rather than democratic government are ways of conceptually limiting autonomy and thus reducing the risk of self-cancellation. Because they are limiting autonomy, however, these critiques of democracy have themselves anti-democratic implications.

At this point, we may conclude that it is misleading to say that we live in a continuing state of exception in our current polities. We witness limitations of autonomy and elements of oligarchy, but we do not witness the collapse of the social into the political. Furthermore, such a claim, unless it adopts the messianic vision of the revolution, would be bound to lead nowhere: whose voice can be raised, or heard, against the permanent state of exception?[40] It is much more fruitful to say that we live in democracies-in-failing, that is, democracies that contain risks of self-cancellation, such as that of the state of exception, but democracies that nevertheless remain democracies, and this means, democracies which denounce anti- or un-democratic situations, such as the state of exception. I will come back to the exact place of the state of exception in such democracies-in-failing at the end of this chapter.

The self-cancellation of democracy (II): totalitarianism

The state of exception has historical links to totalitarianism, which we will take here to represent democracy's full or permanent self-cancellation. To put it briefly in the light of the earlier reasoning: we will need to see now how the situation in Athens in 411 BCE, when a democracy abdicated in favour of a narrow oligarchy, resembles, or not, the one in Germany in 1933, when an electoral majority inaugurated the totalitarian regime of Nazism.

To proceed with our argument, Claude Lefort's vision of totalitarianism seems at once the most complex and the most convincing:[41] under totalitarianism, Lefort claims, the state collapses into society (in other words, state violence is imposed on all society in detail and everywhere) on the one hand, and on the other hand, the various divisions within society collapse into one another. This double movement occurs under the aegis of radical novelty, of the creation of an absolutely novel society and of the new human being, both of which are completely transparent to themselves, about both of whom perfect knowledge exists (there is thus a collapse of the symbolic orders of power, law and knowledge onto one another). For Lefort, these symbolic aspects of totalitarianism (the fixed history, the absolute novelty, the creation of the new man) erupt 'against the background of modern democracy itself'. They find their direct source in modern democracy.[42] And indeed nothing similar occurs in ancient Greece, in which the overthrow of democracy was not accompanied – neither in reasoning nor in practice – by the abolition of the cleavages in society. Rather, the overthrow of democracy was a return to an allegedly more viable or desirable political form for the same society.

In the contrasting light of our own definition of democracy, thus, totalitarianism can be viewed as the regime that abolishes the democratic tension between the social and the political, which is a tension that produces change. Thus, the translation of Lefort's thought is that if state power, or the political, is collapsed into society, if all plurality vanishes, then all possibility of tension is erased. However, to follow Lefort fully would mean not only accepting totalitarianism as the permanent cancellation of democracy but also as a possible consequence of the latter, that is, a *self*-cancellation.[43] The nuance in Lefort's work deserves high praise but the fact remains that on the one hand there is, theoretically, no space left for the resistance needed against totalitarianism in such a conceptualisation, and on the other hand there is no admission of the fundamental aporia that the jump from one to the other state represents – that is, all that cannot be covered by the idea of some continuities between the two.

As with the state of exception, it is perhaps more useful to assume that though there is inherent in democracy the risk of its cancellation (precisely because it lacks the authoritarian instruments of total control), the transformation of the democratic regime into totalitarianism nevertheless always comes about on a different plane, as it were, where democracy has ceased to be the space in which the relation between the social and the political deploys itself – where, quite simply, this space is abolished, even though, in parallel, other democratic spaces may not have ceased to be alive for a certain period.

Thus it seems that insisting on the gap or radical separability between democracy and its cancellation presents one important advantage: it leaves us enough space for thinking about the possibility of the return of democracy. Putting, inspired by Castoriadis, an accent on the *hubristic way* in which democracy is transformed into something else, on the jump that is then effectuated when moving from democracy to totalitarianism instead of on the logical continuity between the two, allows us to visualise what is and what is not democracy as happening in different spaces.[44] Some concluding observations will be devoted to further exploring this avenue.

Democracy's surplus and democracy-in-failing

How can it be argued both that democracy can cancel itself, in other words, that it contains the risk of its end, *and* that democracy's cancellation is radically separable from democracy? To enable us to do so, I have tried to suggest that there is no linearity between democracy and its self-cancellation. That means that there is no legitimacy to be found in democracy for undemocratic procedures – the temporary or permanent self-cancellation of democracy is not something that is a natural continuation of democracy, even though democracy contains the tendency towards this self-cancellation. The self-cancellation of democracy is something which is not democratic anymore. This is more than a paradox: practically, it means, first, that the level on which the self-cancellation takes place is a level that is unreachable for democracy – if I may insist on this imagery, it can be pictured as a parallel space that has no common points with democracy; at that level, the democratic procedure, the democratic rule and decision are not effective. There is nothing to be done. It is the level of the Castoriadian hubristic displacement. This is a situation that bears resemblances to the question of the democratic origins, but it is more aporetic than the democratic paradox: for what becomes of the demos? Can the demos ever want to cancel itself?

Second, the hubristic displacement also means that, at some other, 'regular' level, democracy (the symbolism and effectivity of a law, a knowledge, a power, which are separate from each other) does not cease to exist. We can call this the democratic surplus or excess, and it is what ensures resistance to anti-democratic rule, even under totalitarianism. In some sense, one may say that, once democracy has existed, this surplus can never be eradicated – it will always emerge as that which counters raw power. As Thucydides suggested, 'it was no light matter to deprive the Athenian people of its freedom'; and this deprivation is never final. From the viewpoint of the temporary self-cancellation, it is the notion of democracy-in-failing that becomes the mirror image of democratic excess. Just as even under totalitarianism, there are elements of democratic resistance, so we have accepted that the state of exception can happen next to spaces which remain democratic. A democracy-in-failing to which a state of exception has happened, so to speak, is not a permanent state of exception, not a perfectly successful democracy and not an oligarchy: it is a democracy which has entirely lost a part of itself (that to which the state of exception applies), but which can draw on other parts to denounce this loss and resist its cancellation. The idea is that democracy is as much what it does as what it does not do; it is as much that to which it aspires as that which it fails to achieve. And that by being so, democracy allows both denunciation and emancipation.[45]

In his latest book, Josiah Ober accompanies the Athenian citizen Theogenes on a fictional tour of democratic Athens.[46] At some point, just before climbing the hill of Ares, Theogenes reads an inscription according to which:

> Areopagites were forbidden by Eukrates's *nomos* from ascending the hill [of Ares] if and when 'the demos and the democracy were overthrown' [. . .] The law explicitly acknowledges the possibility of political conflict in the community, conflict that could lead to the revolutionary overthrow of the democracy and thus the suspension of the political authority of the demos. One might suppose that if the democracy were overthrown, its laws would be nullified and that they would thereby lose (inter alia) their capacity to allow or forbid Theogenes to climb the hill [. . .] Democratic Athenian law [however] claims a persistent moral authority that transcends the institutional authority of the demos itself.

Ober adds that if Areopagites happened to respect the law under non-democratic regimes, then those regimes would lack the legitimacy needed to perdure and would therefore prove ephemeral. Thus, he concludes, if 'Theogenes [. . .] chooses to obey the law, *democracy will survive – even if overthrown*'.[47] This, I think, is a perfect illustration of the possibility of resistance, a possibility which is inscribed so strongly in democracy that even when democracy is cancelled, the possibility remains.[48]

Notes

1. I would like to thank Kurt Raaflaub for detailed comments on an earlier version of this chapter.
2. Chantal Mouffe, *The Democratic Paradox* (London: Verso, 2000), pp. 2–3.
3. Jacques Derrida, 'Declarations of Independence', *New Political Science* 7, no. 1 (1986): 7–15; Bonnie Honig, 'Declarations of Independence. Arendt and Derrida on the Problem of Founding a Republic', *American Political Science Review* 85, no. 1 (1991): 97–113.
4. Thucydides, *History of the Peloponnesian War*, Book 8.68.
5. See for some discussion also Nathalie Karagiannis and Peter Wagner, 'Towards a Theory of Synagonism', *The Journal of Political Philosophy* 13 (2005): 235–62; and 'Imagination and Tragic Democracy', *Critical Horizons* 13, no. 1 (2012): 12–28.
6. Christian Meier, *The Greek Discovery of Politics*, trans. David McLintock (Cambridge, MA: Harvard University Press, 1990), ch. 2, pp. 20–9.
7. Ibid.
8. Quoted after Koselleck, in Werner Conze, Hans Maier, Christian Meier, Reinhart Koselleck and Hans Leo Reimann, 'Demokratie', in Otto

Brunner, Werner Conze and Reinhart Koselleck (eds), *Geschichtliche Grundbegriffe: Historisches Lexikon zur politisch-sozialen Sprache in Deutschland*, vol. 1 (Stuttgart: Klett-Cotta, 1972), p. 849.

9. Cornelius Castoriadis, 'La polis grecque et la création de la démocratie', in Cornelius Castoriadis, *Domaines de l'homme: Les carrefours du labyrinthe, II* (Paris: Seuil, 1977), pp. 296–7; Cornelius Castoriadis, *La montée de l'insignifiance: Les carrefours du labyrinthe, IV* (Paris: Seuil, 1996), p. 168. I have discussed this notion first in Nathalie Karagiannis, 'Democracy as a Tragic Regime: Democracy and Its Cancellation', *Critical Horizons* 11, no. 1 (2010): 35–49, of which this chapter provides further elaboration.

10. The expression of democracy as a 'political culture' stems from Josiah Ober, *Athenian Legacies: Essays on the Politics of Going On Together* (Princeton, NJ: Princeton University Press, 2005), p. 1 and passim; it should not be interpreted as signifying that, in the initial absence of such a culture, there is no possibility for democracy to emerge but, rather, that the self-understanding of current democracies can only be valid if they cultivate such a tension. For a related argument about the formation of a culture of freedom in Europe with reference to ancient Greece, see now Christian Meier, *Kultur, um der Freiheit willen* (Munich: Siedler Verlag, 2009).

11. Martin Ostwald, *From Popular Sovereignty to the Sovereignty of Law: Law, Society, and Politics in Fifth-Century Athens* (Berkeley: University of California Press, 1986); Mark Munn, *The School of History: Athens in the Age of Socrates* (Berkeley: University of California Press, 2000).

12. For detailed discussion, see Josiah Ober, *Political Dissent in Democratic Athens: Intellectual Critics of Popular Rule* (Princeton, NJ: Princeton University Press, 1998).

13. See Jennifer T. Roberts, *Athens on Trial: The Antidemocratic Tradition in Western Thought* (Princeton, NJ: Princeton University Press, 1994); and Peter Wagner, 'Transformations of Democracy', in Johann Arnason, Kurt Raaflaub and Peter Wagner (eds), *The Greek Polis and the Invention of Democracy: A Politico-Cultural Transformation and its Interpretations* (Malden, MA: Wiley-Blackwell, 2013).

14. Cornelius Castoriadis, 'Le délabrement de l'Occident' and 'La montée de l'insignifiance', in Castoriadis, *La montée de l'insignifiance*.

15. Pierre Rosanvallon, *La contre-démocratie: La politique à l'age de la défiance* (Paris: Seuil, 2006); *La légitimité démocratique: impartialité, réflexivité, proximité* (Paris: Seuil, 2008); *La société des égaux* (Paris: Seuil, 2011); and Jacques Rancière, *La haine de la démocratie* (Paris: Fabrique, 2005), p. 10.

16. Rancière, *La haine de la démocratie*.

17. Giandomenico Majone, *Regulating Europe* (London: Routledge, 2002); Fritz Scharpf, *Governing in Europe: Effective and Democratic* (Oxford: Oxford University Press, 1999).

18. Albert Hirschman, *The Rhetoric of Reaction: Perversity, Futility, Jeopardy* (Cambridge, MA: Harvard University Press, 1991), p. 7.

19. For further analyses on tragedy and ancient politics see, among others, Christian Meier, *The Political Art of Greek Tragedy*, trans. Andrew Webber (Baltimore, MD: Johns Hopkins University Press, 1993); and Suzanne Saïd, 'Tragedy and Politics', in Deborah Dickmann Boedeker and Kurt A. Raaflaub (eds), *Democracy, Empire, and the Arts in Fifth-Century Athens* (Cambridge, MA: Harvard University Press, 1998).

20. For more detail on Castoriadis's vision of tragedy, see Nathalie Karagiannis, 'The Tragic and the Political: A Parallel Reading of Kostas Papaioannou and Cornelius Castoriadis', *Critical Horizons* 7 (2009): 303–19; and for his view of the relation between tragedy and democracy, see Karagiannis and Wagner, 'Imagination and tragic democracy'.

21. Sophocles, *Antigone*, 707–9; Cornelius Castoriadis, 'La polis grecque et la création de la démocratie', p. 303.

22. See exemplarily Sophocles, *Antigone*, 332–72. 'Antigone is in my eyes [. . .] *the* tragedy of democracy' – Cornelius Castoriadis, *La montée de l'insignifiance*, p. 191.

23. Cornelius Castoriadis, 'Imaginaire politique grec et moderne', in Castoriadis, *Domaines de l'homme*, p. 173; Engl. tr. NK.

24. See most concisely Cornelius Castoriadis, 'Pouvoir, politique, autonomie', in Castoriadis, *Le monde morcelé: Les carrefours du labyrinthe, III* (Paris: Seuil, 1990), pp. 113–39.

25. Cornelius Castoriadis, 'La polis grecque et la création de la démocratie', pp. 296–7.

26. Josiah Ober, 'Quasi-Rights: Participatory Citizenship and Negative Liberties in Democratic Athens', *Social Philosophy and Policy*, 17 (2000): 27–61. We should, however, be attentive to Ober's more conventional use of hubris, which is at odds with Castoriadis's and the one used here.

27. Cornelius Castoriadis, 'Institution première de la société et institutions secondes', in Castoriadis, *Figures du pensable: Les carrefours du labyrinthe, VI* (Paris: Seuil. 1999), pp. 115–26. On page 121 he makes explicit mention of 'the end of form', indeed referring to the end of Athenian democracy, but never looks at it in a sustained way.

28. Drucilla Cornell, Michel Rosenfeld and David Gray Gralson (eds), *Deconstruction and the Possibility of Justice* (London: Routledge, 1992).

29. Carl Schmitt, *Political Theology* [1922], trans. George Schwab (Chicago: University of Chicago Press, 2005).

30. Walter Benjamin, 'On the concept of history' [1940], in H. Eiland and M. W. Jennings (eds), *Selected Writings*, vol. 4, trans E. Jephcott, H. Eiland, M. P. Bullock, M. W. Jennings, G. Smith and R. Livingstone (Cambridge, MA: Harvard University Press, 2003).

31. Agamben cites Theodor Reinach's 1885 book *De l'Etat de siège: Etude historique et juridique* (reprint: Whitefish, MT: Kessinger, 2010) as the origin of the Schmitt–Benjamin controversy.

32. Carl Schmitt, *The Concept of the Political* [1932], trans. George Schwab (Chicago: Chicago University Press, 2007).

33. Giorgio Agamben, *Lo stato d'eccezione* (Turin: Bollati Boringhieri, 2003), p. 111.
34. In a review of Agamben's book, Antonio Negri ('Il frutto maturo della redenzione', *Il manifesto*, 26 July 2003) registers what he calls 'the imperial' line of the argument where state of exception and constituting power are one and the same. In such a conception, Negri rightly observes, the very possibility of antagonism disappears. The conclusions Negri himself draws from this criticism are, however, problematic too, since he not only considers that we live under a state of exception but also sees in this the sign of an ongoing 'civil war'.
35. In the late Roman Republic the Senate introduced an emergency measure that essentially declared a state of exception: the *senatus consultum ultimum* ('ultimate senate decree') that empowered all magistrates to do whatever it took to restore order and prevent the state from suffering harm. See Jürgen von Ungern-Sternberg, *Untersuchungen zum spätrepublikanischen Notstandsrecht* (Munich: Vestigia 11, 1970).
36. For a recent discussion, see Andreas Kalyvas, 'Solonian Citizenship: Democracy, Conflict, Participation', paper presented at the TRAMOD conference on 'Political modernity in the 21st century', University of Barcelona, February 2012.
37. The historical invention of the state of exception is, as Giorgio Agamben puts it, referring to the Revolution's 'état de siège', 'the history of its progressive emancipation from the war situation to which it was originally linked, to be used as the extra-ordinary police measure to confront disorder and internal strife, and thus turning from being effective and military to fictitious and political. It is in any case important not to forget that the modern state of exception is a creation of the democratic-revolutionary and not of the absolutist tradition.' This ultimate phrase is one of the rare links established by Agamben between democracy, rather than the political, and the state of exception. Agamben, *Lo stato d'eccezione*, p. 14.
38. Castoriadis, 'Le délabrement de l'Occident', pp. 68–9; and Rancière, *La haine de la démocratie*, p. 58.
39. Assuming that the demos remains at the centre of the political, thus does not explicitly hand over power to a tyrant/monarch or an oligarchy, as happened in Athens in 411. Similarly, I do not refer here to the situation known as 'demos tyrannos' in which the people (in the sense of the many, not in the sense of all citizens) rule over the few in their own interest. On this situation, see Kathryn Morgan (ed.), *Popular Tyranny: Sovereignty and Its Discontents in Ancient Greece* (Austin: University of Texas Press, 2003).
40. The prison camp at Guantanamo with its tortures and human-rights violations has been referred to as an indication of a state of exception, and it may rightly be seen as a consequence of it. However, the same authority which has decreed the state of exception keeps up a rhetoric of democracy. And this may be so because, despite it indicating a state of exception, like all states of exception, Guantanamo reflects the norm

that it has abolished (as Agamben would originally argue) – and that is why it is not part of a continuing state of exception.

41. Even though it rests on and is developed against the background of a long tradition. See Enzo Traverso (ed.), *Le totalitarisme: Le XXe siècle en débat* (Paris: Points Essais, 2001) for an overview of the important texts that have explored the phenomenon.

42. Claude Lefort, 'La logique totalitaire', in Traverso, *Le totalitarisme*. On page 728 (and similarly earlier, on page 726), he writes: 'At the basis of such a [totalitarian] system, we have to recognize the key representations that form its ideological matrix. In one sense they are not new as they derive from the experience of a world that modern democracy has inaugurated, but they cease to be latent, they find themselves charged with the affirmation power of the being of the social that gives them an entirely new efficacy and makes thus a new destiny visible.'

43. Let me open a short parenthesis here to say that, usually, Claude Lefort's thought on totalitarianism is presented as exposing the latter's radical opposition not only to the political but also to democracy (e.g., Traverso, *Le totalitarisme*, p. 711; or Claude Habib, Claude Mouchard and Pierre Pachet, 'Présentation', in Claude Habib, Claude Mouchard and Pierre Pachet, *La démocratie à l'oeuvre – Autour de Claude Lefort* (Paris: Éditions Esprit, 1993), p. 9. In the latter volume, however, Miguel Abensour ('Les deux interprétations du totalitarisme chez Lefort', p. 124ff.) gives a much more nuanced contribution, clearly tracing the thought that links democracy and totalitarianism. This observation has been used by the historian François Furet in his analysis of the French Revolution, *Penser la révolution française* (Paris: Gallimard, 1979), and it is on these grounds that Rancière attacks it: 'The image of democracy that [the new anti-democratic discourse] provides is made of features that once were associated with totalitarianism' – Rancière, *La haine de la démocratie*, pp. 19–20. By contrast, Hannah Arendt, *The Origins of Totalitarianism* (New York and London: Harvest Books, 1978) or Raymond Aron, *Democracy and Totalitarianism* (London: Weidenfeld & Nicolson, 1970), opposed totalitarianism to democracy in a more conventional way.

44. It is clear that the propaganda, theatricality, mise-en-scène of both temporary and permanent self-cancellations of democracy aim at precisely that: separating the spaces and if possible the times of the experience of democracy and non-democracy. Guantanamo is the current example *par excellence*.

45. For an elaboration of the need to hold denunciation and emancipation together, see Karagiannis, 'Democracy as a Tragic Regime'.

46. Ober, *Athenian Legacies*, pp. 21–2.

47. Ibid., first emphasis added.

48. Just as totalitarianism is, of course, totalitarianism-in-failing: the experience of disorder always erupts against the striving for order. See on this a brief note in Lefort, 'La logique totalitaire', p. 731.

5 Setbacks of Women's Emancipation (Condition, Consequence, Measure and Ruse)

Geneviève Fraisse

One does not easily escape a linear representation of history. The figure of emancipation suffers from the image of progress, the sense of assured conquest, the idea of access as a continuous path. This linearity affects the thought of emancipation with a modern, democratic value, that of the new history of freedom and equality.[1]

However, the affirmation of emancipation is always illuminated by a precise moment, the passage from one state to another, a temporal rupture. This passage can appear natural, as the passage from child to adult. It is, however, socially structured by the fixed legal, civic or sexual age. Citizenship, criminal responsibility, marriage age, sexual orientation, all of these potential individual states have variable age thresholds depending on the country, and may vary as well inside each country. But a threshold there is. Images of progressive continuity on one hand, and fixed thresholds on the other, are thus the two somewhat opposed markers of a spontaneous representation of emancipation. Admittedly, we know now that we must add, by necessity, the idea of democratic incompletion, the bitter taste of incomplete conquests, of fragile, even reversible, rights. However, the idea of emancipation merits, again and always, to be understood in all of its primary force. When it appears that the notion of progress is old-fashioned, the idea of democratic incompletion has lost the strength of its conviction; what remains is the importance of emancipation, and its subtext, the image of rupture.

Contemporary political emancipation has therefore been patterned on the model of individual emancipation, borrowing from it the corollaries of progress and transformation. The times to come will always be the best; a particular moment, a passage, threshold or rupture, will often be necessary. Examples include the emancipation of peoples and the future revolution (or 'grand Soir') to prepare, or the emancipation of nations and the colonies' proclamation of independence, or national revolution. The emancipation of women is the third component of the trilogy 'people, race, sex' (or 'nation, race, sex') which structures the contemporary era; emancipation and liberation being stackable distinguishable terms. This trilogy can be related to Kant's *Anthropology*, which clearly demarcates this triple distinction, ushering in discussions from the nineteenth century on, now discussed by the term 'intersectionality'. Indeed, in identifying the anthropological categories of modern society, we also open political discussion: the categories of sex, race and people (later indicating nation, then class) will be affected by the republican or revolutionary dynamic. Placed on the same level, they would necessarily intersect, in thought and history. One notes, in passing, that these categories, anthropological and at the same time political, are from the outset considered as outside of natural perspective; they are, thus, strictly speaking, historical.[2]

And yet, one must, first of all, distinguish the emancipation of women from other dynamics, because the rupture to come, the point of no return, the revolution is rather irrelevant to gender relations ('rapports de sexe'). One thinks of the end of slavery, of apartheid, of colonisation; but the end of masculine domination? The thought of radical rupture (notably feminist revolution) is very rarely a theoretically constructed political project. When this rupture is evoked, it remains imaginary – such as the takeover of the Amazons, or closer to us in time, Monique Wittig's 1969 *Les Guerillères*, who want to desert the social contract of heterosexuality. The dream of rupture would thus also be thought of in an inverted manner: like an imaginary rupture, that of a reversal of relationships, male servitude and female takeover. Whence comes, in banal political language, the scarecrow of sex reversal to curb women's liberation. Whence comes, as well, the difficulty of integrating women as actresses in the historical process, and the facility of keeping them at a distance. So, blocking women's evolution rather than deploying their historicity is at work in every narrative of exceptionality (heroines, crimes, etc.). The history of women maintains a specific relationship to political temporality.

Late or early

Then the emancipation of women follows a unique pattern: one thinks of it as progressive by providing it a spontaneous and naturalistic temporality: then it would be understood, in fact, that as Western democracy advances, women's rights advance along with it. One thinks about it thus without 'passage' or threshold, without revolution or sudden overthrow. False confidence in progress, or is it rather lucidity about an illusory end of male domination? The imprecision of representations illustrating the emancipation of women is troubling. The political layout is neither a programmed and progressive movement, nor a dialectic settled between dominant and dominated, as were other emancipatory theories, ends of colonial states, the abolition of slavery or apartheid. The disappearance of male domination, which some pretend to believe in, is obviously not going to happen tomorrow. Not only because linear progression is non-existent, but also because historical analysis remains problematic. Thus, the trouble is explained by a double lack of representation: women's history remains to be elaborated in theoretical thought as in political action; to think of a future unconflicted relationship between the sexes obviously seems unreal.

Hence the interest (for example) of the title of the 'altermondialist' feminist workshop in Florence, in November 2002: 'A Necessary Conflict for a Common Future'. A necessary conflict between the sexes expresses the idea that the 'war' between the sexes must be translated into political practice, a recognition of tension; the common future indicates the utopia of a resolution of this conflict, shared between women and men. The emancipation of women could therefore be a story like all stories, a political history, and it could have a goal, like all utopias.

We must now emphasise that this emancipation is necessarily integrated with other emancipations, all the while being held at a distance, like a symptom, or a corollary. We will momentarily leave aside the work of the actor, more precisely the actress, on the path of social or national emancipation. Agreed, women are subjects of history, full-fledged subjects in their own right; and they are more and more so. However, some regularly sing the praises of the 'role' of women, in a war of liberation for example, or in a political insurrection. This singing is to unearth the forgotten history of women's participation or to colour the history of great men with feminine hues. This is a way to leave women on the sidelines. What is even more difficult is to know which path the emancipation of women must take as a political objective. Rarely thought about alone, it is attached to other emancipations, people, race, nation, class; but at an angle.

The polemic on the contempt which taints feminist demands in general, devaluing their sense, will not be brought up again here. It will be noticed that the polemic between the specificity of the 'women's struggle' or the necessity to link it to other political battles is recurrent, and, in fact, repetitive. This dispute arose at the time of the French Revolution. And in the space of a single generation, I believe I have attended two highlights of this paradoxical polemic, in the 1970s (class/sex) and in the 2000s (race/gender). The question, therefore, is structural: the category 'women' is a different category from all the others (one half of humanity) and simultaneously, 'women', in the history of Western thought, are never thought of alone (the child, the servant, the crazy person, the slave, the proletariat, the colonised). This epistemological, and consequently political paradox must be thought out. First of all, we must broaden our view of the problem, outside of the contemporary historical period: the other categories which 'neighbour' women vary according to the time and thought at work. Aristotle, in designating the family, sees the child and the servant alongside the woman; Spinoza, expressing concern about reason, puts the child and the crazy person in company of 'la bavarde'.[3]

This is why I have decided to leave the question of political-anthropological categories aside in favour of an inquiry into historicity and its difficulties. With this purpose in mind, therefore, we will look at how the emancipatory dynamic works. Several positions clash from the nineteenth century on. The classic formula, of women viewed as late arrivals by the pioneers of democracy, along with the necessity of their education to access emancipation, leaves them at the gate of history in the making. They will become citizens, for example, once they have ceased to live under religious influence, or once they have been sufficiently educated. Historical time hangs on their transformation; their participation in history must be deserved. They must win a place in the republic in order to be fully recognised. The second formula, according to which the social revolution or national revolution will result in a de facto change in the lives of women, is an illustration of the Marxist affirmation which emphasises the hierarchy of the contradictions of the capitalist system. Class relations are a primary contradiction, gender relations are a secondary contradiction. The emancipation of women, the resolution of male domination, is a result of the outcome of the main contradiction, capitalism and class struggle. There, it is no longer a question of earning/deserving an entrance into history; one must instead patiently await the rewards of history.

If women are assigned a latecomer's place, they remain at the edge of the path of emancipatory history. But if they are assured of receiving equality in the basket of revolution, they are guests of a historical process that surpasses them. In the first case, history is not waiting for them, and in the second, history makes them wait. Late or early, they are never at the right moment of historical development. Yet, in both cases, late or early, one is willing to imagine a future; but never a present intertwined with the others present. It is a default of historicity. It will be noted that this problem of historicity is found in other categories of political anthropology. 'People without history' were often spoken of, in earlier times. Furthermore, it's always the 'wrong moment' to emancipate oneself, a well-known argument of the dominant. Let us underline, however, that for women, the stakes are original because, no matter the political moment, it is always problematic. Even right in the middle of modernity, a little underhanded interrogation on the right of women to stand fully in history will always remain.

A condition

In the preceding two centuries there has been abundant discussion of the problems of the temporality of emancipation. But, other, rarer, layouts are also a part of history. Beginning in the nineteenth century, for example, Charles Fourier formulates a utopia of a new society by posing the emancipation of women as the condition of the subversion and freedom of all people. Not beside history due to delay, or thanked by history after the Revolution to come, women are included at the heart of the new time: 'Social progress and changes of historical period are brought about as a result of the progress of women towards liberty: and the decline of social orders is brought about as a result of the diminution of the liberty of women.'[4] Fourier, socialist thinker of utopia, includes his dream of freedom in the materiality of history. Witness the famous Fourier thesis, summarised a few lines later: 'the extension of the privileges of women is the basic principle of all social progress'.[5] There will not be a path of emancipation, of freedom and utopia, if women as a social category, able to dream of gender equality, are placed aside or marginalised. They are at the heart of the process of emancipation; they are even necessary to it. The radicalness of this thesis is the recognition of this necessity. But, even more, this theory implies, consequently, a perspective of historicity between the sexes. History is written, says Charles Fourier, in and with the relations between the sexes. This position doubly diverts from the two preceding representations: women are necessary to the freedom of peoples; the sexes, also, write history, together and separately. Fourier clearly states, and unambiguously assumes, that it is men that need women's freedom, that men's well-being, and the well-being of nations, depends on it. An instrumental analysis of this figure of emancipation is required. Man would need the emancipation of women for his own emancipation. Is this interpretation problematic? This is not certain.

Before answering this question, it is interesting to read a current version, perhaps less utopian, and certainly more pragmatic than

Fourier's, yet just as radical. The Indian economist Amartya Sen places women at the centre of possible development in the world's poorest countries. Referring to the feminist writings of Mary Wollstonecraft in 1792, he points out the twofold aspect of women's rights, when they are 'patients', eligible for rights, on the one hand, and when they are 'agents', situated to be actresses of development, on the other. With this dual signification, he places women at the centre of the developmental dynamic in poor countries: 'women are increasingly seen, by men as well as women, as active agents of change: the dynamic promoters of social transformations that can alter the lives of *both* women and men'.[6] Amartya Sen reaches this conclusion after a lengthy demonstration, from book to book, and from the perspective of an analysis focusing on income inequality and the inequality of 'capabilities', the capability of well-being, health, education, etc.; because only unequal capabilities can account for the high amount of social disparity between men and women, can explain, for example, the phenomenon of 'missing women', meaning the disproportionate mortality among women compared with men in certain countries. More clearly than Fourier, he speaks in terms of social efficiency, giving women a role that is, at the same time, for themselves and for others; the simplest example is that of the children, the first beneficiaries of the women's well-being. It is a lucid instrumentalisation of women and their emancipation. 'Nothing, arguably, is as important today in the political economy of development as an adequate recognition of political, economic and social participation and leadership of women. This is indeed a crucial aspect of "development as freedom".'[7] This instrumentalisation requires recognition of women as 'agents', he states – subjects and actresses of history, we would say. The relations between the sexes thus takes on a political, therefore historical sense; and women themselves are in history, contemporaries in history in the making.

The utopian philosopher Charles Fourier and development economist Amartya Sen are very close, two centuries apart. They express an uncommon idea of the history of the sexes, an idea which includes the emancipation of women at the heart of all history in the making. They also recognise the active character of women's participation in history. For today's economist, it is about women's right to be capable to act for their own well-being. For Charles Fourier, that meant that the already emancipated women ought to serve the emancipation of all women: 'Women should have been producing liberators, not writers, political leaders like Spartacus, geniuses who could plan ways of leading their sex out of degradation.'[8] Like an avantgarde, some enlightened women would change the course of history. But they do not, he states at the beginning of the nineteenth century, as if ignoring the regression imposed on women in the aftermath of the French Revolution.

Today no one ought to doubt the importance of women as actresses and subjects of their own history and history in the making. It remains to be understood how they act, how emancipatory thought has become theirs, how they have appropriated it. One of the theses of the sociologist Pierre Bourdieu, in his book on male domination, is to understand how tradition has produced a dishistoricised representation of this domination, how, precisely, it masked this historicity. My agreement with this thesis is due to its allowance for a historical thinking of the emancipation of women. It was stated above how much this emancipation could be thought of as outside of history, implicitly invalidating it in so doing. But Pierre Bourdieu's explanation suffers from a strange facility in the treatment of the agents of change, precisely, women. His brief remarks on feminism, on the history of feminism, testify to a sort of refusal to involve historical subjects in his explanation. Pierre Bourdieu often places himself above it all, as an outside analyst. The observation, 'Thanks, in particular, to the immense critical effort of the feminist movement' – which he conjugates in the past tense – is used as a substitute for an analysis in itself. Yet this quote shows little curiosity concerning the contents of this critical work. And once more, at the cost of a damaging approximation (feminism has been concerned with domestic issues more than those of education or state), he invites feminism, no longer to the past, but to the future: 'then a vast field of action is opened up for feminist struggles, which are thus called upon to take a distinctive and decisive place within political struggles against all forms of domination'.[9] Once again, women find themselves in a historical setback: they belong to the past, or to the future; but never to the present. The sociologist provides them with instruction on work and action from a global point of view. His position as a scientist doubles as a political mastermind. The historicity of male domination is dissociated de facto from a very historical reality of feminist thought.

Feminist struggles are convoked in the past for their critical production, and in the future for their upcoming action. They are not active in the present, within the sociologist's analysis, which always leaves feminists on the sidelines, alongside the explanation. How can we believe in a demonstration and a desire to reconstruct the historicity of women's history when we see how far it is from taking into account the content of the critical work of feminism, its theoretical contribution and the impact of its actions? Evoking these contributions and this participation is insufficient; simply, abstractly evoking this work as if it were an external element, separate from the theoretical explanation, is to deny its relevance, its historical function.

Politics of temporality

We are far from knowing the path to emancipation for women. The examples recalled here show their limits, and testify, above all, to the difficulty of thinking about how they are tied, historically, to the emancipation of women. Placing this emancipation at the heart of a society's transformation and affirming the quality of women as agents of this transformation are two principles established by Charles Fourier and Amartya Sen. Some would argue that these principles are obvious. However, the patterns they are confronted with, that of making up for lost time, and that of the assured result, still persist today. Pierre Bourdieu's difficulty in including the theoretical and practical content of feminism into reflection – precisely in a thought as aware as his of the difficulties of historicising the conflict between the sexes – can be attributed to the fragility of the thought of the emancipation of women, generally depreciated and delegitimised.

Furthermore, it has not escaped us that the inclusion of women at the heart of the historical process always reveals an instrumental usage of their participation. Without women, no happiness or well-being is possible, conclude Charles Fourier and Amartya Sen. Subjects of their emancipation, women are also the means, the tool of the emancipation of others. Impossible, thus, to avoid the question posed earlier: is this instrumentalisation problematic, does it obscure the hope of gender equality? Does the price of emancipation require that women must be both the end and the means of an emancipatory dynamic? It is troubling that their own goal, the purpose of their freedom, is always accompanied by arguments concerning others more than themselves.

This question is essential, but the solution seems improbable. Is the freedom of women a conquest for themselves, or a necessity for the good of others? Apart from Amartya Sen's reflections, international institutions have taken over his findings, and metaphors abound in their descriptions of future development: women are the 'motor', the 'source', are the determining factor. The remarkable journal *Equilibres et Populations* unhesitantly writes, citing Kofi Annan, at that time Secretary General of the UN: 'the equality of the sexes is not a goal in itself but it is indispensable to the attainment of other goals, and no strategy of development can be effective if it does not accord women a role at the forefront'.[10] And yet it must be stressed that, yes, the equality of the sexes, and women's freedom is an end in itself!

Instrument or purpose, the emancipation of women is fundamentally concerned by this issue. One can laud the radicalness of the remarks of Charles Fourier or Amartya Sen, one can delve into the manner in which women could be included in the fabric of history, but the question remains. Women are for themselves and for something else, they are an end and a means – currency, or rather a means of exchange, in political history as much as historical theory. Our task, mine and others', is to develop women's historicity given this thought of women as objects, this thought which resists any thought of emancipation and subversion, including thinking about becoming a subject of history and of her own history.[11]

Returning to my opening statement: it is difficult for the emancipation of women to be contemporary with other movements in global history. It is required as a condition of participation in the exercise of democracy; or it is seen as a consequence of a revolutionary process. Before or after the historical moment itself, it is eventually assigned a role, a function of service to general history. Why not? Before going further, let us emphasise that women seem to remain eternal 'guests' of a global process, never quite on time, always positioned to justify themselves.

From this we must conclude, or rather offer a perspective familiar to feminist history for the past two centuries: the temporality of feminist thought and action is not always in synchrony with the ensemble of political movements. More precisely, these moments are simultaneously contemporary and disjoint, seemingly able to share a dynamic and yet ignoring each other. Here again comes the issue of comparison with other dominated categories. Are there not other contrary temporalities in decolonised, postcolonial and neocolonial thought? Probably. But if we must define the specificity of the gender issue, it is, once again, by its situation of globality, being half of the human species. Whence comes a reversal of stakes. An example in the domain of social life: women want to work, to have paid employment while at the same time we witness dreams and declamations about the end of work, denunciations of alienation, as well as demand of free time. If women have a desire to be employed, it is clearly because economic self-sufficiency is at stake. Example in the domain of thought: the construction of the female subject has been claimed at the height of criticism on the Western subject, at the same time as reflections on 'the death of Man'. Anachronism or paradox? More of a setback: times are not always right, not always the same for everyone. Belonging to one's time is an inadequate image for the history of women's emancipation.

Another more current example: the first European Treaty, signed at Rome in 1957, states in its Article 119 that there must be equal pay for women and men. This represents remarkable progress compared with various national constitutions. We can even be proud of it, while recognising that directives relevant to economic male-female equality were not given until 1975 and 1976. But above all, the introduction of this Article 119 must be commented upon, and in two ways. First of all, one can consider the irony of the fact that this equality arose to prevent wage competition, obviously unfair given the inegalitarian state between women and men in the world economy. Paid far less, women can serve as 'scabs' during a strike, for example. It is thus due to an economic system, one of competition, that the goal of gender equality appeared for the first time in Europe. An irony of history, somehow. Let me remind you, furthermore, that the European Convention of Human Rights, dated 1950, only postulates equality negatively, with the enumeration 'without distinction of'.[12] I note, in passing, that economic equality is the inescapable support of all gender equality. My next and second commentary is that we will not turn our back on this surreptitious entrance of the crucial mention of gender equality. Whatever the origin, the cause, the purpose of this reference, Article 119 was placed in the service of a political objective, that of equality. Historical ruse? Enter through the back door to come out through the front? This is also historicity: to be caught in a political dynamic, far from moral transparency where one would like to confine 'women's issues'.

This last example simply illustrates the purpose of this text, a reflection on the temporality of the emancipation of women. If the sexes also write history, to see this emancipation as a simple addition of a time (in action, in writing) to other historical times, a confluence and synchronicity of movements and projects, would be an illusion. The setback is, it seems to me, the image closest to the usual and repetitive distortions often seen when it comes to the historicity of the gender issue. A setback is unexpected and untimely. Feminism is certainly inopportune, and that always renders it fragile in the face of other struggles. But here I want to say more. A setback is not only an instant or accident; it has a duration, a temporality that is uncoincidental with other durations, the gap between them is large or small. Measuring it ought to allow the inclusion of this specific temporality into universal history.

Notes

1. Parts of this text were published in *La philosophie et l'emancipation de l'humanité, Journée de la philosophie à l'Unesco* (Paris: Unesco, 2004); then in Geneviève Fraisse, *A côté du genre, sexe et philosophie de l'égalité* (Bordeaux: Éditions Le Bord de l'Eau, 2010). This is an extended version, translated from French by Marianne Choquet.
2. On historical temporality, see Reinhart Koselleck, *The Practice of*

Conceptual History: Timing History, Spacing Concepts (Redwood City, CA: Stanford University Press, 2002); Françoise Proust, *L'Histoire à contretemps, le temps historique chez Walter Benjamin* (Paris: Éditions du Cerf, 1994); and Peter Wagner, *Modernity: Understanding the Present* (Cambridge: Polity, 2012).

3. See Geneviève Fraisse, 'Les amis de nos amis', in Geneviève Fraisse, *A côté du genre, sexe et philosophie de l'égalité*.

4. Charles Fourier, *Fourier: The Theory of the Four Movements: Cambridge Texts in the History of Political Thought*, eds Gareth Stedman Jones and Ian Patterson (Cambridge: Cambridge University Press, 1996), p. 132.

5. Ibid.

6. Amartya Sen, *Development as Freedom* (New York: Anchor Books, 2000), p. 189.

7. Ibid., p. 203.

8. Fourier, *Fourier: The Theory of the Four Movements*, p. 148.

9. Pierre Bourdieu, *Masculine Domination* (Redwood City, CA: Stanford University Press, 2001), p. 4.

10. *Equilibres et populations*, 85 (April–May 2003): 2.

11. See Geneviève Fraisse, 'Le devenir sujet et la permanence de l'objet', in Fraisse, *A côté du genre, sexe et philosophie de l'égalité*.

12. See Geneviève Fraisse, 'Inscrire les droits des femmes, expliciter les droits de l'homme', in Fraisse, *A côté du genre, sexe et philosophie de l'égalité*.

6 Political Modernity, Democracy and State–Society Relations in Latin America: A New Socio-Historical Problématique?

Manuel A. Garretón

Does Latin America exist?

When dealing with modernity and the political in Latin America, in the sense given to both terms in this book, an initial question is related to the concept of the region under consideration. For some observers, the process of globalisation led to very different forms of insertion into it and answers to it, so that it is not possible to speak of Latin America in general and we should instead distinguish between the Southern cone countries, Brazil being the central and fundamental one there; the Central American countries; Mexico, more tied to the North American pole; and the Andean countries that have lived most intensely the problems of destruction and recomposition of the matrix of the national-popular state, to which I will refer later.[1] In such a view, these countries cannot be seen today as affected by a single common problématique and, consequently, 'Latin America' would disappear as a historic expression with a 'real' content, beyond the purely rhetorical or imaginary.

Here, instead, we will insist on the idea of Latin America, without entering into the eternal discussion, coming from the international organisations, about which countries or types of countries to include or not under this label. The reason to defend, in a globalised world, the idea of countries, societies, nations or national and multinational states, and the idea of Latin America, is not only affective or historical. It is based on the insight that it is impossible to conceive of the insertion in the globalisation processes by each country separately. Beyond all the vicissitudes Europe is currently experiencing, a very strong message or signal emerges from there: the affirmation that globalisation and this century's world will develop in a complex game of nation-states and supranational blocks, in which there is no destiny for countries that do not enter into a block – with the exception of those few countries that comprise each such a large share of the world population that they can avoid block formation.

Latin American societies, beyond the rhetoric of regional integration, are facing hard decisions in issues such as energy, environment, knowledge society, new strategic branches of the economy, in all of which a substantial leap in the process of autonomous insertion is necessary if the countries do not want to be condemned to the periphery. Certainly there are temptations in some countries to avoid the question by saying that our major partner, the United States of America, is in our block, or by seeing oneself as similar in magnitude to the United States and thus capable of isolated development, as happened during certain times with Brazil. But let us recall that current globalisation at its origins had two characteristics that are not essential parts of every process of globalisation and have changed today, but reflected the real power situation in the world at the time. The first is geopolitical: it consisted in the unilateral hegemony of the United States though weakened in the following years. The second is ideological as well as socio-economic and was based in the hegemony of the neoliberal model. Given these two features it was impossible that single countries could integrate themselves into the globalisation dynamic without a growing process of fragmentation and loss of identity and cohesion. The condition for an autonomous integration into the global world is, as the Europeans have shown us, some kind of unity through big blocks or spaces consisting of several state-nations, including the idea of multinational states. In the light of current structural transformations, and in contrast with the experiences in earlier centuries, these blocks will be more pronouncedly models of cultural modernity than of a geopolitical dimension based on military power or even a geo-economic dimension based on markets.[2]

So, there is no future for Latin American societies without the constitution of a solid block among their states and nations. Important advances have been made during past years in trying to organise the region in more political terms, less based on pure economic trade agreements. But still the main problem is the lack of a general vision that combines the necessary reinforcement of each national state capacity with the acceptance of the common destiny of all these societies. Thus, we affirm that it is possible to speak of Latin America, in a constant tension between a differentiated empirical reality and a common or collective project, and we will affirm the possibility of thinking a socio-historical problématique, which shows specificities for each country, but which connects with the 'political'[3] common to all of Latin America. In analytical terms, this means that we pursue something akin to an ideal-type analysis, which neither considers single countries nor elaborates intra-regional typologies, but emphasises features common across Latin America, even though with different degrees of development or different temporal sequences.

The classic state–society relations in the twentieth century

The classical model of relations between state and society – what we have called, in ideal type terms, state-national-popular socio-political matrix[4] – prevailed in most of the more developed Latin American countries, though not in all, from roughly the 1930s to the 1960s/1970s. The main features of this matrix were: its socio-economic base was import-substituting industrialisation, in which the state, defined as 'state of compromise'[5] (including contradictory interests of competing sectors like oligarchy, bourgeoisie, middle and organised working classes, and excluding peasants and urban poor), had a leading role and was not only the main development agent, but also the main reference of the collective action of the masses that were incorporated into the national life. At the political level, what some authors have called a hybrid formula prevailed: sometimes authoritarian, sometimes formally democratic with cycles of authoritarianism and democracy, or authoritarian elements within democratic regimes, or democratic components within rather authoritarian regimes. This socio-political matrix existed in a historical-structural context characterised by the contradicting confluence of nationalist, developmental, modernising processes, at the same time as an industrialisation oriented towards the internal market with a central role of the state, a leading presence with oligarchic and middle-class components, and intense processes of popular mobilisation in which politics constituted the main axis.

During this period Latin American societies developed, in various forms, a relationship of fusion, imbrications and subordination between the state, the system of representation and the social actors. In some countries, the fusion between these elements was achieved through the figure of the populist leader, in others through the identification between state and political party or upon the articulation between social organisation and political-party leadership. There was also the case where the party system fused all the social fractions or the corporate organisations captured the totality of collective action without leaving room for autonomous political life.

In this classical matrix, as we said, the state was the point of reference for all collective action, be it development, social mobility and mobilisation, redistribution, the integration of popular sectors. But it was a state with a weak autonomy from society and upon which weighed all the pressures and demands, both internal and external. This interpenetration between state and society gave to politics a central role. Aside from exceptional cases, it was more a mobilising than a representational politics, and the institutions of representation were, in general, the weakest part of the matrix. The 'statist' principle present in the whole of society was not always accompanied by an institutional autonomy of the state and its effective capacity for action.

These so-called national-popular regimes[6] showed more populist expressions in some countries and more partisan expressions in others, but they all reached breaking point during the 1960s through revolutionary radicalisation, on one side, and on the other, through the military or authoritarian responses coming from the dominant national sectors and the USA; and they collapsed precisely with the triumph of authoritarian alternatives through the Southern-cone military dictatorships or the authoritarian hardening where no actual military dictatorships were put in place.

The revolutionary movements of the1960s criticised the dependent capitalism, the mesocratic hegemony and the inability of this model to satisfy popular interests. The military regimes that began in Brazil in 1964 sought to eliminate the popular mobilisation in its reformist, populist or revolutionary dimensions and to recompose capitalism in a kind of repressive counter-revolution from above based in an alliance between the military, dominant societal sectors and the political right from inside and from the USA.[7] In the 1980s and 1990s, the processes of political democratisation and of structural adjustments and economic reforms, in turn, coincided with the recognition of the void left by the disarticulation of the old matrix. It had not been replaced by another stable and coherent configuration of the relations between state and society. Different substitutes tended to install themselves in this void, making impossible the strengthening, autonomy and complementarity between the components of the matrix (state, regime and political actors, social actors or civil society), either eliminating one or two of them, or subordinating them, or emphasising exclusively only one of them.

Changes at the end of the century

Four main changes occurred in the last decades of the twentieth century in Latin America, in different moments and degrees across the region. The first was the dominance of political-institutional models of consensus and conflict that tend to replace the dictatorships, civil wars and revolutionary modalities of previous decades. The second was the exhaustion both of the model of 'inward development', and of its replacement with formulas of adjustment and stabilisation, based on the so-called 'Washington consensus', a set of policies that seek new forms of insertion into the world economy, characterised by phenomena of globalisation and transnationalisation of the market forces.[8] The third was the transformation of the social structure, with an increment in inequality, poverty and marginality and the precariousness of the educational and labour systems, even after new educational reforms, but also important policies to overcome some of these deficits. All this has produced a recomposition of the system of social actors and a questioning of the traditional forms of collective action. Finally, the model of modernity associated with Western modernisation and the North American mass culture that was predominant in our societies or at least among the leading elites, entered into crisis, and in response indigenous and hybrid formulas of modernity were proposed.

A more profound change that affects the entire world, and in a specific way the Latin American societies, lies behind these transformations. The phenomena of globalisation and expansion of the principles of identity and citizenship, among others, produced a disarticulation of what was the predominant societal type, the national-state industrial society, although with different degrees of development according to the concrete historical societies.[9] This type was organised around labour and politics (in Latin America, especially the latter) and around processes of social change defined as modernisation, industrialisation and development, and its fundamental social actors were classes, parties and social movements.

Latin American societies, in different degrees and forms, can indeed be said to have never completely achieved such national-state industrial society, but although being less defined by that structure, they saw themselves as moving towards this society of reference in a process called development and social integration. These societies were always torn between their national-state industrial society project and a fragmented, hybrid blend of different civilisational worlds within each society and the permanent exclusions of indigenous and poor sectors. Today, without being an integrated national-state industrial society, that is, a particular historicalcultural variant of this type of society, Latin American societies face the challenge to become also a historical-culturally specific and original combination between that type and the post-industrial globalised societal type. This transformation redefines the roles of politics and states, the central actors of social change and the concept itself of development, as different theories and institutions have been proposing.[10]

All these changes point towards a transformation of the matrix of constitution of society, or the socio-political matrix, in Latin America. In fact, there is a dislocation of society related to, evidently, the processes of globalisation and the shift from a socio-economic model of development based on industrialisation and the leading role of state to a model which will emphasise mainly the insertion in global markets, the financial dimension and the central role of transnational markets, usually accompanied by extreme ideologies such as neoliberalism. But at this point no new model of development was built, because what happened was the disarticulation of the previous model without its replacement by a new one in any coherent way. This change in the development model, from the developmentalist projects of popular national states to much more liberal or neoliberal models, and then the search for a new one that overcomes inequalities and replaces neoliberalism, was accompanied by a cultural transformation with the raising of gender, ethnic and regional identities among others, but also individualistic tendencies.[11]

The changing role of politics

At least two important socio-cultural transformations that pervade societies all over the world affect the role of politics which has been so crucial in the constitution of Latin American societies.[12] In the first place, new forms of capitalism, both in the production and in its development models, have produced a dissociation between economy, politics, culture and social organisation, where each one of these dimensions acquires its own dynamic in relation, in part, to diverse forms of globalisation. This apparently leaves the society without a 'centre' (as was the national state) or without a 'cement' (as was politics) that co-ordinated or articulated the different dimensions. Consequently the society as a political community, as a *polis*, is weakened, and various partial 'centres', especially de facto powers, appear competing with the national state or reducing its role and space.

On a psycho-social and cultural level, secondly, we live in a time in which we produce and will continue to produce an expansion of subjectivity as a principle and reference of social life, with the search for meaning and happiness acquiring predominant roles. This implies, on the one hand, the de-institutionalisation of social life, which can be seen, among other dimensions, in the deep transformations and diversification of the family institution. This is accompanied by the de-normativisation of individual behaviours and the personalisation and intersubjectivation of ethics. On the other hand, ideological movements that united individual and group projects with the collective destiny of society and that provided utopias and a complete architecture for it seem to have disappeared. It is not that the ideologies or the utopias themselves disappeared, just that they lose their all-encompassing nature and move on to being tentative and partial principles to manage change and to seek more human forms of personal and collective life.[13]

All of this necessarily influences the redefinition of politics in Latin America. In the classical socio-political matrix, politics played a decisive role, as we stated. Politics as a means of access to goods and services of the modern society, politics understood in its representative or clientelistic elements, in its dimension of vindication and satisfaction of interests and access to state, whether for employment, education, housing, social security or health; but also politics in its dimension of collective project and source of meaning, i.e., its ideological or cultural dimension. The source of meaning for collective action was found less in identities or individual aspirations, as seems to be the case nowadays, than in ideologies that sought not only to represent but also to mobilise around the idea of a project, of a future that could be reached through struggle and conflict. Politics thus understood was somehow the cultural cement of society. Where capitalism was unable to provide a complete rationality for the co-existence of different modes of production, where other dimensions, even the cultural one, were unable to provide for the unity of the national state, there was politics.

To put it simply, during the 1960s and 1970s the view was common that the world could be 'changed', and changed through politics. In this sense, in the society of national-popular states, the emblematic actor – sometimes empirically real, sometimes imaginary – was *el pueblo* (the people), originally incarnated as the working class and its political expressions, but when it was felt that the working class was incorporated into the system, it was replaced by other actors such as peasants or, in some cases, the student movement or the party organisation itself, especially at the time when the leftist parties were militarised and transformed in guerrilla movements. In contrast, in the latter part of the twentieth century, the idea that became dominant is that the world cannot be changed, at least not through politics. And this has to do, on one hand, with the expansion of subjectivity and also individualism, the appearance of new cleavages and the emergence of identities from other sources than politics, the weakening of the role of the state as provider of goods and collective meaning, new forms of sociability and communications, and on the other hand, with the disappearance of what might be called a central social movement, a movement that aims at the transformation of society and that defines its basic conflict from the point of view of a project of society.[14] Thus, the key question is not the discrediting of politics that indeed exists but has been overemphasised by the media, but the change of the meaning of politics in society, how it affects the political actors and the particular process of decomposition or recomposition of political parties or party systems in some countries.

Success and deficits of political democratisation

Historically, democratic practice and thought in Latin America were characterised by the contamination between political democracy and social democratisation. The military dictatorships in the Southern Cone and, in other places, the authoritarian components of regimes that could not be defined as properly military, are a landmark that provoked a mutation in the political life and the theoretical reflection on the matter. Human rights and democracy, the latter seen as the political order able to consecrate the former and avoid the rise of any power to suppress them, became a goal in itself and crucial object of social struggles.

The processes to replace military dictatorships or authoritarian regimes ended more than two decades ago and are not the central political processes any more.[15] In other words, the great crises of formal authoritarian regression seem to be controlled, with very few exceptions. But this does not mean that the political democratisation processes have been completely successful. Their pending tasks will have to be fulfilled in the context of social and political processes that cannot be reduced to classic political institutions.

The record of political democratisation, thus, has two very different dimensions. On the one hand, and with a few significant exceptions, electoral democracy is working and the acceptance of democracy as the best political regime in which to live prevails – and this is an entirely new reality in Latin American societies.[16] On the other hand, frustration about the capacity of democracy to effectively change the power relations in society led to severe criticism of what is called the 'political class' and to the search for new formulae like participatory or direct democracy and mobilisations that express real democratic exercise.[17]

Beyond the analysis of democratisation processes, what the Latin American case shows is the weakness and troubles of democratic theory in some historical contexts. Such theory was classically thought for one type of society, for a *polis*. And a *polis*-society is a space where an economic system, a political organisation, a model of identity and cultural diversity and a social structure co-exist, even if in contradictory ways. Today, this *polis* finds itself exploded by processes that have to do with globalisation, local and ethnic identities, public spaces that overflow the limits of a country, among others, which diminish the margins for manoeuvre of national states, conditioning them and penetrating societies. And this accounts for what we will call the new Latin American socio-historical problématique, namely the reconstruction of the political community or of new relations between state and society.

New actors and social movements

During the national-populist period, populism was the predominant form of collective action; and the cultural orientations were of mesocratic-popular, nationalist and developmentalist kinds. In the classical matrix, the social actors exert pressure on the state via political action, be it class-based or populist or mediated by parties or corporations or in a personalised way. The central social actor can be defined as the National-Popular Movement, and it identified itself as part of *el pueblo*,[18] the latter being the only subject of history. The paradigmatic social actor or movement of the National-Popular Movement was generally the workers' movement, but in various periods this leadership was questioned and replaced by referring to different actors, such as the peasants or the students or the vanguard parties.

The military dictatorships of the 1980s entailed profound consequences for the social actors and the forms of collective action.[19] On the one side, there was the search for the reconstruction of the social fabric that had been destroyed by the authoritarianism and the economic reforms; on the other side, during authoritarian regimes until their very end, the orientation of collective actions, even sectorial and not particularly political ones, had become politicised. Owing to the repressive character of the dictatorships, the main collective actions were social mobilisations that tended to emphasise the symbolic over the claiming and instrumental dimension. In this sense, the leading symbolic role of the Human Rights Movement is telling. It was the seed of what we can call the central social movement of the period of rupture with the national-popular matrix under the authoritarian regimes: the democratic movement.[20]

The processes of political democratisation tended to separate collective action according to three logics that pervaded all particular social actors. The first one is the political logic orientated towards establishing a consolidated democracy as a precondition for any other kind of claim. The second one is the particular logic of each single actor oriented towards concrete benefits in social democratisation as a precondition for actively supporting the new democratic regime. The third logic criticises the insufficient nature of the institutional changes and conceives democracy as a more profound social change extended to other dimensions of society.

The existence of unresolved ethical questions during the transitions or democratisations, in particular the violation of human rights during the dictatorships, sustained the importance of the human rights movements at the onset of the new democracies. But these movements saw their activities severely limited by restrictions emanating from other authoritarian enclaves, be those of institutional kind or by powerful social actors (the military, business, paramilitary groups), in particular because of the risk of authoritarian regression and economic crises. These risks gave political actors, both in government and in opposition, the key roles in social action, thus subordinating the principles of other actors to their own logic. In turn, the tasks connected with the consolidation process privileged at the beginning the necessities and requirements of economic adjustment and stabilisation over collective action that was thought of as putting at risk this process.

The socio-economic transformations after the democratisation or transition processes and the concomitant political and cultural changes profoundly modified the landscape of social actors. Classical actors lost part of their social significance, while those that emerged around the new post-authoritarian issues did not succeed in constituting themselves as stable actors or as a corpus of citizens, appearing rather as contingent publics or pressure groups. Thus, earlier forms of recurrent social action tended to be replaced, on the one hand, by sporadic mobilisations and fragmentary and defensive actions, sometimes in the shape of social networks, significant but with a low political institutionalisation and representation, sometimes as consumerist reactions against neoliberal measures. On the other hand, the scene is taken by the aggregation of individuals through the phenomenon of public opinion, measured through polls and mediated by the mass media, not by mobilising or representative organisations.

The dismantling of the classical matrix at the end of the democratic transitions generated a situation in which a unifying principle of social action had disappeared and in which, on the contrary, principles diversify and in some cases even enter in contradiction (environment versus growth, to name just one example), each one of them expressing itself in different actors. This meant the disappearance of the central social movement and the inability to replace it by any other, but rather by a multiplicity of movements. The historic role played by the popular movements – the working class or peasantry

in some countries or, in other cases, the student movement or the
pobladores – found no equivalent in the new situation, which was
marked on the one hand by new social movements of an identitarian
type, and on the other by collective initiatives and mobilisations that
are defined generically as citizen movements.

With regard to the latter, the concept of citizenship has undergone
a process of reinvention, for it covers almost any claim or demand
in a normative sense.[21] Currently it maintains an individual basis,
not linked to a collective subject, society being seen as an aggregate
of individual rights. Thus, any claim to a right is made without a
counterpart in the concept of 'citizenry', where rights are derived
from membership in the *polis* and belonging to a collective body,
accompanied by duties. The new understanding of 'citizen' tends
to abandon the concept of 'pueblo', the 'citizenry' dimension, and
leaves only the individual, the 'citizenship' dimension, in its place.
The processes of globalisation, neoliberal reform, and new technologies of communication are undermining the idea of *polis*, namely a
territorial space in which there is an economy, polity, culture, social
structure with one centre of decision which is called the state, and a
relationship between the people and the state which is called politics. So the idea of the citizen tends to be reduced to the status of
an individual, holder or owner of all rights, without duties or other
links than the constant demand for such rights. Undoubtedly, there
is an extremely positive element in the revaluation of the citizenship
concept, where intermediate actors such as parties and social movements tend to weaken, but there is an individualistic residue that
tends to be transferred and used by the mass media and the informat-
ics network that becomes the public space, where the figure of the
citizen tends to be reduced to the figure of the consumer, or of a par-
ticipant in the networks or public opinion, partly created by the same
mass media.[22] The citizen is thus defined in Macphersonian terms of
possessive individualism, in which even the definition of rights is a
definition in terms of property or ownership.[23]

Thus, the expansion and strengthening of citizenship accompanied by the weakening of the *polis* constitutes a paradox, which is
expressed through the relative loss of the functions of the state as a
regulator, leader and provider, and the weakening of the major social
categories – working class, middle class, students, etc., all of them
segmented and fragmented – and the replacement of the concepts of
equality and social justice by the concept of equity, and the transformation of social movements, especially of the identitarian type, into
collective bearers of demands, not necessarily assuming the *polis* as
the place where they all come from and to which they all relate.

The new situation nevertheless contains a potential for a

redefinition of citizenship and a new way of conceiving collective action. The panorama of collective action during the last decade shows that the citizen dimension has been one of the main constitutive elements of such action and of the social actors in the region, reaching from the ethnic movements to the new features of the *pobladores* movements, the claims by the poor urban sectors, the neighbourhood organisations and the regional movements, youth movements, environmental mobilizations as well as movements against company closures. The strong irruption of the so-called 'civil society' in almost all areas of the globe during the last two decades appears to demonstrate that organisation around specific and concrete demands, but also for rights and identities, can be more effective in reaching solutions for the great social problems than political parties and the traditional channels of representation.[24]

In this sense, the identitarian orientation searches for more than rights claims, namely the affirmation of a social and political subject, of a 'we' based on an attribute, generally with an adscriptive character. Thus, the horizon opens towards the activities of movements that can convert themselves into vectors of wider and more urgent demands (such as in the case of the Bolivian coca-growers, student movements or environmental movements). The mobilisations in the street are an expression of this situation.

In the background of the anti-neoliberal mobilisations of a predominantly economic nature and tied to consumption, therefore, one can detect a refoundational dimension in the identitarian expressions linked to the constitution of a subject, in the citizen struggles for rights, often related to changes of government or in the defence of governments that are threatened by the de facto powers.[25] We see here the effects of the transformations that originated in the processes of globalisation, democratisation, the neoliberal reforms as well as other structural and cultural changes in the world, which have had profound impacts on the national-popular state matrix by fragmenting the state–society relations and by the economy gaining autonomy from politics in the neoliberal moment. Thus emerges a new historical problématique that we will address in what follows: the recomposition of state–society relations. This refoundational dimension, in sum, is centred in struggles over a model of modernity.[26] This is probably the most innovative dimension of collective action in Latin America over the past years, most visible in the new forms of indigenous action, in the mobilisations that led to new constitutions and even new forms of state, as in Bolivia, but also in the Chilean student movements of 2006 and 2011, whose refounding elements address not only the educational system but the relations between the political and the social.[27]

A Latin American model of modernity?

By modernity, we understand the way in which a society constitutes its subjects. Modernity is the affirmation of subjects, individual or collective, builders of their own history; it is another way of talking about the self-determination and autonomy that is being emphasised in this book. Thus, the modernity of a society refers to the way in which social subjects are constituted, which in general tends to be a combination of rationality, subjectivity and historical-memory. Modernisation should be defined as the process by which each society constitutes its own modernity, without committing the mistake of identifying it with the processes of rationalisation, technologisation and secularisation particular to Western modernity in its European and North American varieties. In other words, modernisation, except for some historical models, is not necessarily determined by the rupture with tradition, nor by the productive system or the use of determined objects and instruments. It is not adequate to speak of 'modernity', but rather 'modernities' or 'models of modernity'. We cannot speak of 'the' modernisation, but of different processes that can fit, or not, within known modernisations.

The particular form of Latin American modernity around what we have called the national-popular state matrix is in crisis, and the aspiration to the model of modernity identified with specific processes of modernisation in developed countries, with a special emphasis on the North American consumption and mass culture model, appears as a counter-project. Opposing this, one can identify the vision of a Latin American modernity either with a 'deep' Latin America, based on its indigenous root, or on a social base that is racially mixed ('mestizaje') or with a particular subject that is the Catholic Church.[28] Indeed, the Latin American model of modernity, if it existed, combined embryonically several features: the construction of societies by the state; the domination or exclusion of the 'ethnic nation' by the 'civic nation',[29] an aspect that today is dramatically changing; the deficit of instrumental rationality; the crucial role of politics as the cohesive element of society; the vocation of social integration with a permanent memory of exclusion; the communitarian and egalitarian-democratic ethos subordinating the liberal one; the capacity of absorbing Western cultures and blending it with original elements, among others. Certain historical landmarks cross all Latin American societies, even with different chronological sequences and timing, such as: reaching independence with the exclusion of indigenous people; the creation of a national state without incorporating the entire society; the incorporation of a segmented working and middle class through cycles of democratisation and authoritarianism;

the search and failure of anti-imperialist and anti-capitalist revolutions; military dictatorship, neoliberalism, and transitions to democracy that consecrated democratic regimes all over the region.

As mentioned above, contemporary societies, and among them the Latin American ones, are going through transformations, to different extents, from a model of modernity based on the national-state industrial society to a societal type that combines the previous model with dimensions of globalised post-industrial society through the filter of cultural identities and historical memory that constitute them as national communities. While economic development no longer depends only on social and resource mobilisation on the part of the national state and actors organised around it, but also on the forces of transnational markets, at the same time, the notion of development as a process of transformation of a given society ceases to identify itself with the economic growth and includes all other dimensions of society, where the concept of quality of life, among others, exemplifies this complexity.

Therefore, modernity can no longer be defined by identifying it with historical models of modernisation or with one only of its variants, be it the most rationalist or instrumental one, the most subjective one, or only the historical memory of a national identity. Each society combines these three dimensions in a different way and 'invents' its own modernity. The question for Latin American societies is whether or not they will be able to construct their models of modernity, at the level of individual countries and the whole region, in order to enter autonomously into the globalised world.

During the commemorations of the bicentennials of independence we have witnessed contradictory celebrations between those who see in the post-independence history the affirmation of national identities and wills, and those who, instead, see no reason to celebrate because such history has been one of domination and imposition of wills by external and domestic powers. The first vision is related to the processes of modernisation, development, revolution, social and political democratisation. The large deficit in the construction of these societies as socio-economic and political communities is behind the other vision, the best synthesis of which is the idea, mentioned above, that the ethnic nation was subjugated by the civic one.

We can find here again the debate about models of modernity, supported also by the social sciences. Since the birth of the social sciences as academic disciplines in the region, in fact, a concern for Latin American society has prevailed over the search for general theories of society and collective behaviour. The social sciences – especially sociology, which was the predominant discipline for a couple of decades – were dominated by an analysis of social change in which development and modernisation were specific forms of social change in Latin America. The response to structural-functionalist approaches to this problem, theoretically expressed mainly in Marxism and analytically in the dependency approach, is a critical variant of a paradigm which emphasises the structural and political processes, analyses progress and failures, makes evaluations of what our societies have become, which in some cases turn out to be positive ones, and in others more negative ones.[30]

In a second paradigm, which has an anthropological and cultural root rather than a sociological or political one, the colonial reality was never overcome by these societies. Even social actors who express the gender, territorial, ethnic-cultural, or civil-society dimensions have always been oppressed by men, race, the metropolis, military or institutionalised politics, including the populist and leftist versions.[31] The emphasis here is not on the analysis of structures and processes, but on a vision of the fragmentations, the tears and the search of subjects, i.e., it is nearer to formulations of the 'multiple modernities' approach than the modernisation models. Here there are no evaluations, whether frustrated or optimistic, but the rejection of the history that is celebrated in the bicentennials.

Even in its most democratic and integrated moments or versions, Latin American modernity was, in fact, always marred by sectors that were excluded from the capacity to be a subject. Thus, this modernity did not merely create underdeveloped societies, but what in different moments and sometimes from contradictory points of view have been called, among other definitions, dual and structurally heterogeneous, disarticulated, colonial, dependent, hybrid societies.[32] The persistence of oligarchic forms and the socially partial democratisations, which were masking the reality of internal and external domination, impeded consistent and generalised processes of self-determination. We will now examine the hypothesis that today we are facing a new socio-historical problématique in which the convergence of the two visions mentioned above is possible.

The new Latin American socio-historical problématique

The existence of a common problématique to all Latin America, which is expressed differently by each country, is an idea that has been questioned in recent times. The processes of globalisation, interpenetration of financial and communication markets, disarticulation of national communities and the weakening and, at the same time, strengthening of some state issues seem to stress the idea that we are not in front of societies – in the classical sense of the term – but of processes, flows, networks, which define the contemporary world in a different way than the mainstream of the last two centuries: the national-state industrial society, whether capitalist or socialist.[33] In an opposite way, behind the idea of a socio-historical problématique of Latin America or of a specific country lies the affirmation – which looks, on the face of it, banal – that societies and countries prevail in spite of the existence of processes of globalisation. Then these societies or these countries can be defined not only in terms of a set of multiple axes of different problems and issues, but it is possible to find a core unit, a certain axis around which other axes can be ordered. That is the idea of a socio-historical problématique, which also implies a structural element that goes beyond a moment, situation or crisis, which some have called the medium or long duration. In this sense Latin American society today is less defined in terms of crisis, i.e., is less in the presence of a great conjuncture or short-term crisis, but rather faces a profound transformation in the socio-historical problématique of its countries.

When we speak of the transformation of a socio-historical problématique, we have in mind situations analogous to other profound historical transformations. In the nineteenth century, the problématique of these countries was the construction of independent national states. Later, the problématique of many countries in the 1920s and 1930s was the building of an inward model of development and the integration of the popular masses and the middle class, and the state playing the main role in the industrialisation processes after the debacle of the oligarchic order. The development problem in the 1950s and 1960s was radicalised since the Cuban revolution in terms of the problématique of the revolution, i.e., development no longer as modernisation but as the shift from a dependent capitalist society to a socialist society.[34] In recent decades, such transformation concerns the rise of democracy against dictatorships or the reinsertion into the globalised world, in which the role of the state is challenged by the transnational forces of markets.

The current Latin American socio-historical problématique includes, of course, development issues or the question of the construction of viable democratic regimes. But behind the persistently present issues of the last thirty or forty years there is a relatively new situation, which perhaps does not find the same expression in different countries but applies in some way to all of them. At the core of this new situation resides the issue of what ECLAC has called social cohesion and, in its 2010 report, equality.[35] And behind this issue lies the reorganisation of the bond between citizens and subjects members of the *polis*, between state and society, that is, the construction of a new socio-political matrix replacing the national popular and the neoliberal ones.

Ensuring the cohesion of a society means rebuilding relations between state and society, which were dismantled by the neoliberal processes, military dictatorships and the process of globalisation. The most dramatic expression of this is found in the Bolivian case, in which we are clearly in the presence of a refoundation of the nation-state. In Bolivia, unlike other cases, the new nation-state project is not identified with and must not be confused with the leader's personal project, even though it needs him. Beyond the emblematic cases, in each of our countries – be it the restructuring of the relationship between state and regions or provinces, a new constitution, inter- ethnic relations, new production systems to face globalisation, overcoming poverty that affects nearly half the population, demands for deliberative democracy and participation that complements representative democracy, legitimacy of the state across its territory, to name a few real and symbolic examples – we face the same issue of restructuring the relations between state and society in a globalised world and the generation of a new socio-political matrix or a new foundation of the nation-state.[36] This process does not exhaust itself, as we used to think in the past, with development processes or democracy, nor with economic reforms, even if it requires all of these dimensions.

This central problem has at least three levels: the local, the national-state and the supra-national level, the last one referring to Latin America as a regional block, as mentioned above, that will facilitate access to the globalised world for national societies. In terms of content, this reorganisation involves at least another three major dimensions. First, an ethical nucleus, without which no social cohesion or sense of belonging to the community can exist. This core or foundational ethical consensus is not subjected to the game of majorities or minorities; rather it constitutes what some call the common heritage or moral cohesion of society. It is not an ideology or a sealed package created to prevent cultural diversity, religious or otherwise, that may not be universal in society, but a set of principles, guidelines, orientations, aspirations that society has decided through history, which mark the horizon of meaning and the project of a country, so important that without it a country would not be more than a territory with a population. Today, this idea has universal roots – such as human rights – but also contains the learning processes by which society creates its tradition and history. This core is not the same across countries, although in the case of Latin America human rights issues, recognition and valuation of native peoples, appraisal of democracy, and the pursuit of equality and solidarity seems always to be present, although in different formulations and intensities. In their declarative parts the constitutions of the modern world often enshrined these principles and also created institutions that respect and promote them. In our view, this was a deficient element in our history as countries, perhaps because there was an elite enforcement, involving very deep divisions and exclusions. Today the force of democracy, weak as it is, has made it possible to develop processes of construction and generalisation to the whole society of its shared ethical nucleus.

A second dimension is that of change in the structural and institutional foundations of a socio-economic community that prevent the co-existence of several countries inside one. This is, in short, the theme of equality and the role of the state to guarantee it. Equality means the establishment of a minimum and reasonable distance, always fluctuating, between the members of a society. This goes far beyond the vision that reduces the issue of equality in society to equal opportunities or equity. Indeed, equity does suppose a basic floor, a starting point and an individual basis. Equality and social justice do have a minimum and a maximum (a floor and a ceiling), and refer to social categories, and therefore the concept of equality requires redistribution of power and wealth and the intervention of an entity that makes the distribution: the state. As we have stated elsewhere,[37] if the absence of equity destroys individual lives, the absence of equality destroys the life of societies, creating different and juxtaposed worlds that cannot be recognised as part of a space or common project.[38] On one hand, this implies a redefinition of the production model, but on the other it requires the implementation of a redistributive formula in which the state plays a key role as a legitimate agent of redistribution. If equality is not part of the ethical nucleus to which we referred above, the legitimacy of a redistributive and protective state will be very weak.

Thirdly, the moral and structural reconstruction of society requires the reconstruction of the political community that is behind the political reforms that make representative democracy more accountable. New forms of participatory democracy must be developed to enable citizenship to control a necessarily intervening state.[39]

The models at play

It is possible to analyse some political processes in Latin America at the start of the twenty-first century in the light of the new socio-historical problématique that we have outlined.[40]

We refer here to the emergence of leftist governments in the last decade. If the central hypothesis of this work proves to be true, we could say that we are facing a non-conservative socio-historical issue; something more akin to tradition, actors and leftist sensibilities. The leftist governments are in office, in part, because they were the political forces that did not support the neoliberal transformations, but presented criticism and proposed solutions and corrective mechanisms of the socio-economic model after the 'Washington consensus'.[41] It is uncertain how much of this alternative economic model, either in its more leftist variant or in the particular version of social democracy,[42] will be viable for the future. Voters can change their preferences, and in important countries like Mexico, Colombia and Chile in 2010, the right-wing parties won national elections.[43] The leftist governments try to overcome the neoliberal crisis and to expand social rights and social participation and diminish poverty. Their success depends not only on the answers to the demands of a population increasingly aware of their rights but, above all, on the deepening of democracy and, within this framework, the refounding of state–society relations.

Within this left turn in Latin America during the last decade, we witness different ways of coping with the new socio-historical problématique and the emergence of a probably new central social movement or subject. Each of these models tends to privilege one main subject of collective action: the leader, the party, a specific social (ethnic) movement, street citizenry, or the state.[44]

One of these models is based principally on politics, with two variants: one through more personalised or populist politics (Venezuela, Ecuador in the 2000s, Argentina at the beginning of the century) at the possible expense of institutions and some authoritarian inclination; the other through the party system (Uruguay and Chile in the 1990s, the latter only in its dimension of democratisation because other aspects of the jump to new state–society relations have hardly existed) at the possible expense of social actors and social movements.

Another model is the recomposition of the political community from the angle of society, of which there are also two variants. On the one hand, there is Bolivia in the middle of the 2000s where this reconstruction is done from a communitarian 'we', basically though not exclusively defined in ethnic terms, and where the problem emerges in the integration of the sectors that do not identify themselves with the ethnic 'we', but identify themselves with the idea of a country. On the other hand, and more as a trend experienced in many countries and actors without having a national case that specially fits with this variant, we find the prospect of Social Forums, in which society is reconstructed from civil society and from social movements and organisations that reject and distrust politics. Hence, it is weak to establish itself as a viable project, despite its great international influence.

Finally, there is also the reshaping made by international organisations and national elites of Washington consensus, mixing what was called the first wave of neoliberal economic reforms with concepts of civil society and citizenship taken from the criticism of such reforms. Here, the reconstruction of countries is based on state-regulated markets, through public policies that respond to specific sectorial demands formulated on the basis of expert knowledge, which in the end replace politics. This is what we might call the technocratic model, which has been the influence of the World Bank and the IBD and developed by parties and governments that today constitute the new right.

Some of these models arose at a moment of a severe national crisis, either economic or political, and generated initially large consensus; some of them deteriorated either because of authoritarian excesses or because of the distance from existing institutions. All of them combine in different ways the political (parties and leadership), social (civil society and movements) and technocratic (state and expertise) dimensions, but mostly privilege one of them at the expense of the others. Lula's Brazil and Morales's Bolivia were the cases that combined all of them. We also always find again some of the aspects that characterised the classic national-popular modernity, like populism or fusion between different elements of the socio-political matrix.

In contrast to what the media and international organisations often suggest, what is currently at stake in Latin America is the reconstruction of political communities. That is why political and cultural components of the transformation dominate over the economic and market dimensions. At the same time, the historical attempts of recomposition, mentioned above as examples, do not necessarily mean successful refoundations; they can fail or lead to decompositions, authoritarian or conservative reactions, as the crisis of the beginning of the 2010 decade shows for some of them.

Concluding remarks

The political and politics, both dimensions tied together along the twentieth century, have been the seal of the Latin American struggle for modernity. This is to say that political modernity is 'the' modernity in Latin America, the core of all modernity. This modernity has been expressed in specific stages or types of state–society relations, and it has been a torn modernity based on a dependent capitalism with strong inequalities and exclusions. The common model of modernity has for a long time been what we called the national-popular state matrix. The different expressions of this political modernity were linked in some way to the Western problématique of development, modernisation or revolution. This entailed that the majoritarian centre or leftist orientations, including the more radical or revolutionary ones, did not express any search for other varieties of modernity coming from ethnic, regional or, later, gender dimensions that challenged the main vision including the one coming from the more radical left. The civic nation prevailed over the ethnic or 'deep' nation. Military dictatorships and a wave of authoritarianism disarticulated this model of modernity, trying to impose a more repressive version subordinated to the new tendencies of world capitalism and markets. Transitions and political democratisations consecrated democracy, for the first time in regional history, as the unique political regime in all the countries. In the context of this reality and of processes of globalisation, of neoliberal reforms and attempts to correct them, and of identitarian and also individualistic and citizen irruptions, four main tendencies seem to become predominant. Firstly is the rupture, indeed relative, between the political and politics which, secondly, leads to more cultural than economic or political ways to constitute subjects and actors. Thirdly, these new subjects are not necessarily linked to the classical variants of modernity in Latin America and tend to redefine development in terms of equality and better collective life, which implies new relations between state and society. Fourthly, this recomposition has today as its locus not only the local and national or multinational territories but also the region as a block, able to incorporate all these countries in the process of globalisation with voice, not exit, and without subordination to transnational powers.

As we have explored in other works, in the same way in which the main social actors in other epochs configured themselves around a determined historical problématique such as those of development, revolution or democracy, that marked all collective action and all orientations of the actors, so one can say today that collective action and the configuration of actors originates, in terms of its historicity, in the new problématique of reconstruction of the *polis*.[45] This problématique constitutes the central social movement, the main actors of which vary from country to country. In terms of the life-world (*lebenswelt*) and subjectivity, in turn, we witness a diversification of problématiques and sectorial demands that, beyond being new in the new structural and cultural context, do not acquire the classical forms of mediation and organisation known from the national-popular state matrix. If one considers the instrumental dimension in its organisational expression, we witness at the same time a weakening of the party-political linkage and the predominance of communitarian forms of citizen or corporate association, while in its institutional expression, jointly with the respect for given institutional frames, one observes the search for new forms of participation and expression that go beyond the former ones but point towards their institutionalisation.

We are participating in a recomposition of social forces. The initially isolated collective action typical of the 1990s gains progressively in density. In other words, the actors pass gradually from the levels of the life-world (cultural) and the instrumentalities of organisations and institutions (economic and social) towards a 'hybrid' orientation into which a political dimension is incorporated. These changes affect the scope and the temporality of collective action and of organisational forms.

In the course of these processes the meaning of politics gets redefined, accompanied by criticism of, and distrust in, institutional politics. Much of the criticism directed at the democracies in the region expresses a profound questioning of the classical forms of politics.[46] But it would be a great error to interpret this distancing of important sectors of the population as the disappearance or the end of politics and as the predominance of extra-institutional or insurrectional action. In contrast to other periods, the refoundational dimension of collective action situates itself within the frame of acceptance of democratic institutionality, be it to question or even replace the same government that one had elected or mainly to modify the institutions radically. There is a search for new relations between politics and collective action: either through processes of relegitimation of politics in its classical party forms, or through the construction of new parties that express social movements, or through more autonomous expressions of civil society or more complex penetrations of the political apparatuses by the movements – with the evident risk of loss of autonomy for the latter.

In the new scenario generated by the social, structural and cultural transformations to which we have referred and which decompose the unity of society and *polis*, of society and nation-state, the exclusive centrality of politics as the expression of collective action tends to disappear. But politics acquires a new, more abstract centrality as it takes on the task of approaching and framing the various spheres of social life without destroying the latter's autonomy. Thus, there is a demand for 'meaning' in politics, which the market forces, the mediatic universe, the particularities and identities or the mere calculations of individual or corporate interest are unable to provide.

The redefinition of the relations between politics and society, both as meaning of collective action and as institutional and organisational arrangements, constitutes the nucleus of the struggle over modernity in Latin America today and in the future.

Notes

1. On the concept of the socio-political matrix and its transformation in Latin America, see Manuel Antonio Garretón, Marcelo Cavarozzi, Peter Cleaves, Gary Gereffi and Jonathan Hartlyn, *Latin America in the 21st Century: Toward a New Sociopolitical Matrix* (Miami, FL: The North South Centre Press, 2003). In elaborating the following chapter I have drawn on several of my own works, mainly Manuel Antonio Garretón, *La Sociedad en que vivi(re)mos: Introducción sociológica al cambio de siglo* (Santiago: LOM Ediciones, 2001); *Incomplete Democracy: Political Democratization in Chile and Latin America* (Chapel Hill: The University of North Carolina Press, 2003); 'Las dimensiones de la acción colectiva en América Latina', in Jaime Llambías Wolff (ed.), *Los nuevos desafíos para América Latina: Economía, equidad, participación y desarrollo* (Santiago: RIL, 2013).
2. On geocultural modernity, see Manuel Antonio Garretón, Jesús Martin Barbero, Marcelo Cavarozzi, Nestor García Canclini, Guadalupe Ruiz-Jimenez and Rodolfo Stavenhagen, *El espacio cultural latinoamericano: Bases para una política cultural de integración* (Santiago: Fondo de Cultura Económica, 2003).
3. See the discussion about 'political modernity' in the Introduction to this volume and also in Garretón, *La Sociedad en que vivi(re)mos*, and Garretón, *Incomplete Democracy*.
4. See Garretón et al., *Latin America in the 21st Century*.
5. On this concept, see Jorge Graciarena and Rolando Franco, *Formaciones sociales y estructuras de poder en América Latina* (Madrid: Centro de Investigaciones Sociológicas, 1981).
6. Gino Germani, *Política y sociedad en una época de transición. De la sociedad tradicional a la sociedad de masas* (Buenos Aires: Paidós, 1965); Alain Touraine, *La parole et le sang. Politique et société en Amérique Latine* (Paris: Odile Jacob, 1988).
7. On authoritarian and military regimes in the last part of the twentieth century in Latin America, see Guillermo O'Donnell, 'Reflections on the Patterns of Change in the Bureaucratic-Authoritarian State', *Latin American Research Review* 13, 1 (1978), and *El Estado burocrático autoritario* (Buenos Aires: Editorial de Belgrano, 1982).
8. On the Washington consensus, see John Williamson, 'What Washington Means by Policy Reform', in John Williamson (ed.), *Latin American Adjustment: How Much Has Happened?* (Washington, DC: Institute for International Economics, 1990). On its meaning as the installation of neoliberalism in Latin America, see José Antonio Ocampo, *Más allá del Consenso de Washington: una agenda de desarrollo para América latina* (México DF: CEPAL, 2005).

9. We have referred to these transformations in Garretón, *La Sociedad en que vivi(re)mos* and Garretón, *Incomplete Democracy*.

10. The concepts of human development by the United Nations Development Programme, alter globalisation by the Social Forums and 'buen vivir' by Bolivian and Ecuatorian Constitutions are some examples of these new visions of development in Latin America.

11. See Garretón et al., *El espacio cultural latinoamericano*.

12. Garretón, *Incomplete Democracy*.

13. Wallerstein has called this 'utopistic' instead of 'utopian'. See Immanuel Wallerstein, *Utopística. O las Opciones Históricas del Siglo XXI* (Madrid-México: Siglo XXI Editores and IIS-UNAM, 1998).

14. On the idea of a central movement that embodies the 'central conflict' or problématique of society, see Alain Touraine, *La voix et le regard* (Paris: Seuil, 1978) and *Pourrons nous vivre ensemble? Égaux et different?* (Paris: Fayard, 1997); and Manuel Antonio Garretón, 'Social Movements and the Process of Democratisation. A General Framework', *International Review of Sociology*, vol. 6, 1 (1996) and 'Las dimensiones de la acción colectiva en América Latina'.

15. On the transitions and democratisations processes in Latin America, see Carlos Barba, José Luis Barros and Javier Hurtado, *Transiciones a la Democracia en Europa y América Latina* (México DF: Miguel Angel Porrúa, 1991); and an overview in Garretón, *Incomplete Democracy*.

16. PNUD, *La democracia en América Latina. Hacia una democracia de ciudadanas y ciudadanos* (Buenos Aires: PNUD, 2004).

17. On mobilisations and non-institutional forms of participation, see Isidoro Cheresky (ed.), *Ciudadanía, sociedad civil y participación política* (Buenos Aires: Miño y Dávila Ediciones, 2006); and on participatory democracy experiences, see Maxwell Cameron, Eric Hershberg and Kenneth E. Sharpe, *New Institutions for Participatory Democracy in Latin America: Voice and Consequence* (London: Palgrave Macmillan, 2012).

18. Indeed 'the people', based on individuals, does not reflect well the idea of 'pueblo', a collectivity in the society with a common destiny based on poor and working sectors, which is the essence of the nation. For a very influential concept of populism, see Ernesto Laclau, *La razón populista* (Buenos Aires: Fondo de Cultura Económica, 2004). On diverse experiences of populism, see Jean François Prud'homme, Guy Hermet and Soledad Loaeza (eds), *Del populismo de los antiguos al populismo de los modernos* (México DF: El Colegio de México, 2002).

19. For movements and actors under the dictatorships, democratic transitions and post transtions, see Susan Eckstein, *Power and Popular Protest: Latin American Social Movements* (Berkeley: University of California Press, 1998).

20. For the meaning of human rights violations under military dictatorships and their consequences see Luis Roniger and Mario Sznajder, *The Legacy of Human Rights Violations in the Southern Cone: Argentina, Chile, and Uruguay* (Oxford: Oxford University Press, 1999). For

human rights movements, see Elizabeth Jelin and Eric Hershberg (eds), *Constructing Democracy: Human Rights, Citizenship and Society in Latin America* (Boulder, CO: Westview Press, 1996).

21. See the discussion of citizenship in Isidoro Cheresky, *Ciudadanía y legitimidad democrática en América Latina* (Buenos Aires: CLACSO-Prometeo Editores, 2011).

22. For an extensive discussion of the distortions produced by the media logic see Manuel Castells, *Comunicación y poder* (Madrid: Alianza, 2009).

23. Crawford Macpherson, *The Political Theory of Possessive Individualism: Hobbes to Locke* (Oxford: Oxford University Press, 2011).

24. On civil society, see Aldo Panfichi (ed.), *Sociedad civil, esfera pública y democratización en América Latina* (México DF: Fondo de Cultura Económica, 2003) and Evelina Dagno, Alberto Olvera and Aldo Panfichi (eds), *La disputa por la construcción democrática en América Latina* (México DF: Fondo de Cultura Económica, 2006).

25. We have addressed these themes more extensively in Garretón, 'Las dimensiones de la acción colectiva en América Latina'.

26. On the discussion of modernity, see Garretón, *La sociedad en que vivi(re)mos.*

27. About the 2001–12 student mobilisations in Chile, see Fernando Atria, *La mala educación Ideas que inspiran al movimiento estudiantil chileno* (Santiago: Catalonia, 2012); Sergio Gonzalez Rodriguez and Jorge Montealegre (eds), *Ciudadanía en marcha. Educación superior y movimiento estudiantil 2011: curso y lecciones de un conflicto* (Santiago: Editorial USACH, 2012); Jorge Rojas, *Sociedad bloqueada. Movimiento estudiantil, desigualdad y despertar de la sociedad chilena* (Concepción: RIL Editores, 2012). For my own views on 2006 and 2011 mobilisations, see Manuel Antonio Garretón, *Del post pinochetismo a la sociedad democrática. Globalización y Política en el Bicentenario* (Santiago: Random House-Mondadori, 2007) and 'El movimiento estudiantil chileno', *Observatorio del conflicto social* (http://observatoridelconflictesocial.org; last accessed 27 June 2015) respectively. These mobilisations differ from the Brazilian 2013 events that can be seen more as a response to the foundational deficit of the Lula governments.

28. For a sociological approach of this vision, see Pedro Morandé, *Cultura y modernización en América Latina* (Santiago de Chile: Cuadernos del Instituto de Sociología Universidad Católica de Chile, 1984). For a complete discussion on the different definitions of Latin American modernity, see Jorge Larraín, *Modernidad, razón e identidad en América Latina* (Santiago de Chile: Editorial Andrés Bello, 1996).

29. Rodolfo Stavenhagen, *Ethnic Conflict and the Nation-State* (London: Macmillan, 1996).

30. A synthesis of these perspectives of the social sciences can be found in Helgio Trindade, Gerónimo de Sierra, Manuel Antonio Garretón,

Miguel Murmis and José Luis Reyna, *Las Ciencias Sociales en América Latina en perspectiva comparada* (Mexico DF: Siglo XXI, 2007).

31. Expressions of this paradigm can be found in Alberto Bialakosky and Pablo Gentilli (eds), *Latin American Critical Thought: Theory and Practice* (Buenos Aires: CLACSO, 2012).

32. See for each one of these perspectives on structural heterogeneity, CEPAL, *El pensamiento de la CEPAL* (Santiago de Chile: Editorial Universitaria, 1969) and CEPAL, *Cincuenta años de pensamiento de la CEPAL* (México DF: Fondo de Cultura Económic, 1998); on disarticulation, Alain Touraine, *Les sociétés dépendantes* (Paris: Duculot, 1976); on colonialism, Pablo González Casanova, *Sociología de la Explotación* (México DF: Siglo XXI, 1969); Anibal Quijano, 'Colonialidad del poder, eurocentrismo y América Latina', in Edgardo Lander (ed.), *Eurocentrismo y Ciencias Sociales: Perspectivas Latinoamericanas* (Buenos Aires: Ediciones Faces/UCV, 2000); on dependency, Fernando Henrique Cardoso and Enzo Faletto, *Dependencia y Desarrollo en América Latina* (México DF: Siglo XXI, 1969); on hybrid cultures, Néstor García Canclini, *Hybrid Cultures: Strategies for Entering and Leaving Modernity* (Minneapolis: University of Minnesota Press, 1995).

33. A discussion on the decline of the concept of society can be found in Alain Touraine, *La fin des sociétés* (Paris: Seuil, 1996).

34. For a complete review of all these periods, see Tulio Halperin Donghi, *Historia contemporánea de América Latina* (Madrid: Alianza Editorial, 1997).

35. ECLAC, *Cohesión social: inclusión y sentido de pertenencia en América Latina y el Caribe* (ECLAC, 2006); ECLAC, *La hora de la igualdad. Brechas por cerrar, caminos por abrir. Trigésimo Tercer Período de Sesiones* (ECLAC, 2009).

36. Garretón et al., *Latin America in the 21st Century*. It is possible to argue that this new socio-historical problématique was announced by the Zapatista Movement at Chiapas in January 1994.

37. See Garretón, *Incomplete Democracy*.

38. For a current discussion on the issues of justice and equality, see Amartya Sen, *The Idea of Justice* (Cambridge, MA: Harvard University Press, 2011).

39. About different experiences and possibilities of participatory democracy and its relationship with the representative one, see Maxwell Cameron, Eric Hershberg and Sharpe, *New Institutions for Participatory Democracy in Latin America* and Cheresky, *Ciudadanía y legitimidad democrática*.

40. I developed this analysis in Garretón, *Del post pinochetismo a la sociedad democrática*.

41. Francisco Panizza, *Contemporary Latin America: Development and Democracy beyond the Washington Consensus* (New York: Zed Books, 2009).

42. Jorge Lanzaro, 'La social democracia criolla', *Revista Nueva Sociedad* 217, Septiembre–Octubre (2008).

43. There are several volumes of journals and books devoted to this phenomenon – see for example *Revista Nueva Sociedad* 205, Septiembre–Octubre (2006); Isidoro Cheresky (ed.), *Elecciones presidenciales y giro político en América Latina* (Buenos Aires: Ediciones Manantial SRL Argentina, 2007); Cynthia Arnson, Catalina Smulovitz, Gastón Chillier and Enrique Peruzzotti, *La nueva izquierda en América Latina: Derechos humanos, participación política y sociedad civil* (Washington, DC: Woodrow Wilson International Centre for Scholars, 2009); Steven Levitsky and Kenneth Roberts, *The Resurgence of the Latin American Left* (Baltimore, MD: The Johns Hopkins University Press, 2013); and Kurt Weyland, Raúl Madrid and Wendy Hunter (eds), *Leftist Governments in Latin America: Successes and Shortcomings* (Cambridge: Cambridge University Press, 2010).

44. For a balance of the experiences, see CLACSO, *Contrapuntos en torno a los nuevos gobiernos progresistas de América Latina* (Rosario: Revista Temas y Debates, 2013) and Cheresky, *Ciudadanía y legitimidad democrática en América Latina*.

45. Garretón, *Del post pinochetismo a la sociedad democrática*.

46. An overview of such criticism just a decade ago can be found in PNUD, *La democracia en América Latina*.

7 Communitarian Cosmopolitanism: Argentina's Recuperated Factories, Neoliberal Globalisation and Democratic Citizenship. An Arendtian Perspective

Carlos A. Forment

When I asked Ricardo why he and some of his co-workers at Ghelco, a food processing plant with fifty or so workers, had decided in early May 2002 in the midst of Argentina's worst socio-economic debacle, to 'recuperate' their factory after the owner had filed for bankruptcy and terminated them, he responded:

> if we had not done so, we would have been unemployed, and at our age [late 40s to late 50s] it would have been impossible to find another job [. . .] Anyone who is jobless is treated like garbage; look at the Piqueteros [. . .] Restarting the factory enabled me to regain my dignity.[1,2]

After pressing Ricardo several times to clarify the meaning of this last phrase, he replied:

> Whenever I talk to the Piqueteros in my neighborhood, they always tell me that they should have stayed put and recuperated their factory [. . .] All of them are now receiving Planes (welfare relief) from the government, but this makes them feel like shit, like real nobodies [. . .] They lost their place (in public life) the moment they abandoned their factory.[3]

Many of the workers that I interviewed used strikingly similar terms rooted in civic recognition and political belonging to describe their own situation as well as the plight of unemployed *Piqueteros* who had been stripped of their 'right to have rights', to borrow from Hannah Arendt. They were as fearful of losing their jobs as they were of losing their 'place in the world which is what makes opinions significant and actions effective'.[4]

After the interview I spent the remainder of the afternoon strolling through the neighbourhood of Barracas, where Ghelco is located, on the city's southern edge. Prior to the debacle this area had been one of the most economically vibrant and productive in the country, home to hundreds of workshops and medium-sized factories which provided countless skilled workers with stable, well-remunerated jobs and their children with a sense of security, knowing that someday they would follow in their parents' footsteps.[5] This was not to be. Barracas now displayed all the familiar signs of deindustrialisation: abandoned, rusted warehouses surrounded by mounds of rubbish and shattered glass. As I walked along a blighted side street not far from where Ricardo was raised and which he had described somewhat nostalgically as a cohesive and staunchly Peronist community, I became keenly aware of the ethico-political chasm that now separated the Barracas of his youth from the wasteland that it had become. It also dawned on me that Roberto, along with the thousands of other workers who had restarted their factories, had played a pivotal role in replacing neoliberal notions of citizenship rooted in 'property rights' with a democratic alternative based on the 'common good'.

This chapter seeks to understand from an Arendtian perspective how Buenos Aires's recuperated factory workers, in the course of engaging in participatory and representative forms of democracy in daily life across the domestic and transnational domain, generated the socio-economic, political, legal and narrative resources they needed to transform themselves from superfluous pariahs into really existing citizens.[6] In tracking these practices across various microsites I have accentuated the ways these workers recycled the material and symbolic resources of neoliberalism rooted in exchange value into use value, thereby creating new forms of democratic life. Current scholarship on globalisation continues to downplay or ignore them, granting primacy and centrality to other aspects, including: media, financial and technological flows; politics of the governed; global cities; graduated sovereignty; international migrations; transnational governance; anti-'mondial' forums and movements; as well as to the idiom and discourse of human rights, cosmopolitanism and transparency, the lingua franca of the UN and other international organisations.[7] My work on recuperated factory workers is also in dialogue with the two best books that have been published on them from a localist perspective: by Gabriel Fajn (on 'opportunity structures and social movements') and by Julian Rebón (on 'class consciousness and vanguard leadership') respectively.[8]

My chapter is in five parts. In the first I discuss Hannah Arendt's tripartite and hierarchical ordering of rights ('civic', 'human' and 'a right to have rights') in light of the experience of Buenos Aires's factory workers. The second examines how Argentina's democratic

institutions invisibilised and transformed these workers into superfluous pariahs. The next section studies the communitarian practices
these factory workers instituted across civil and economic society,
and how this enabled them to regain their place in public life. The
fourth analyses the ways in which workers practised their right to
have rights in political society and in the process persuaded fellow
citizens to recognise them as equals, as members of the 'demos'.
Section Five focuses on the transnational ties that Buenos Aires's
workers forged with the European Union (EU) and the Bolivarian
Alternative for the Americas (ALBA). In my closing remarks I move
beyond this case study to explore the subterranean connections
between democratic life and globalisation in order to shed new light
on Arendt's gloomy remarks on 'neototalitarianism', the 'crisis of
our century'.

Citizenship and globalisation: some Arendtian reflections

Arendt's Delphic remarks on rights have launched a thousand scholarly articles. I will be brief.[9] On her account, the civic rights that
nation-states provide to citizens remain a far more significant guarantee than the human rights that international organisations, including the UN, extend to stateless peoples but rarely can enforce.
Human rights, for Arendt, are a dangerous chimera. Cosmopolitans
disagree; transnational organisations have now developed the legal,
organisational and military capacity to protect the rights of stateless
and minority peoples. Liberals recognise this as well, however, they
continue to side with Arendt: nation-states remain unmatched in
their capacity for protecting the rights of citizens.

Cosmopolitan and liberal interpretations predominate; however,
a small but growing group of scholars, mainly among political theorists, are shifting the terms of the debate towards a right to have
rights. Although Arendt privileged it over civil and human rights, her
discussion of a right to have rights remains truncated and opaque,
making it difficult even for those who recognise its foundational
character to make sense of it. Her discussion of a right to have rights
appears in Chapter 9 of *The Origins of Totalitarianism*:

> Something much more fundamental than freedom and justice, which are
> rights of citizens, is at stake when *belonging to a community* into which
> one is born is no longer a matter of course and not belonging is no longer
> a matter of choice [. . .] They are deprived not of the right to freedom, but
> of the right to action.

We became aware of the existence of a right to have rights (and that means to live in a framework where one is *judged by one's actions and opinions*) and a right to *belong to some kind of organised community*, only when millions of people emerged who had lost and could not regain these rights. [my italics]

We are not born equal [. . .] we become equal as members of a group on the strength of *our decision to guarantee ourselves mutually* equal right. [my italics][10]

Arendt associates a right to have rights with 'belonging' and 'recognition'. In the passage above, her references to the former are explicit (*'belonging to a community'*; *'belong to some kind of organised community'*); her references to the latter remain allusive (*'judged by one's actions and opinions'*; *'decision to guarantee ourselves mutually'*). Both have generated much discussion.

For Etienne Balibar, among others, these terms are inextricably related to direct forms of political participation (not representational) and are a public expression of 'equaliberty', to use his well-known portmanteau.[11] Balibar's argument is compelling and attractive. And yet, when Buenos Aires factory workers sought to regain a right to have rights in daily life (belonging and recognition) they relied on the material and symbolic resources in their community, not universal principles. On my account, a right to have rights is a complex, practical and paradoxical blend of elements from political practices (participatory and representative) and communitarian life, understood in Arendt's sense: 'the entire social texture into which they (citizens) are born'.[12]

A right to have rights approach, in any of the versions currently available, differs in numerous aspects from the cosmopolitan and liberal perspective. I will list only three of them: first, while the former approach anchors rights in 'organised communities of belonging', cosmopolitans and liberals ground them in one or another state apparatus or international organisation. Second: scholars identified with a right to have rights focus on the horizontal, inter-subjective practices of recognition among citizens in daily life (self-rule), whereas cosmopolitans and liberals construe rights in juridical terms and focus on the vertical ties and legal duties between citizens and officials.[13] Third and last: in contrast to the 'thick' conception of democratic life that underlies a right to have rights, cosmopolitans and liberals offer a 'thin' version of it. In the words of Craig Calhoun:

The new cosmopolitans retain one of the weaknesses of older forms of liberalism. They offer no strong account of social solidarity nor the role of culture in constituting human life [. . .] Indeed, belonging is a matter of social constraint from which individuals ought to escape [. . .] Claims of special loyalty or responsibility to nations, communities or ethnic groups, thus, are subordinated or fall under suspicion of illegitimacy.[14]

The differences between a right to have rights and these two other accounts are, indeed, significant.

Adopting a right to have rights perspective, however, also generates a problem for an Arendtian conception of citizenship. Briefly stated: how can unemployed workers and other pariahs practise a right to have rights if fellow citizens construe their public actions and statements as nonsensical, irrational or, worse, a menace to democratic life? In other words, if the 'demos' has decided to silence, ignore or vanish certain pariah groups from public life, how can they gain recognition from the same citizens who were responsible for depriving them of a place in the world? This intractable problem is directly related to Arendt's understanding of citizenship: true citizens (*homo politicus*) have been 'liberated from the necessities of life' and can therefore serve the common good; unemployed workers and other pariahs (*animal laborans*) are 'determined' by and remain beholden to private, socio-economic needs, making it impossible for them to act and speak as true citizens. In naturalising this distinction, Arendt drains rights of any socio-economic content and also depoliticises the institutional boundaries between the public and private domains.[15]

In studying Buenos Aires's factory workers my underlying concern is to rethink certain aspects of Arendt's argument in relation to neoliberalism today: 'thought itself arises out of incidents of living experience and must remain bound to them as the only guideposts by which to take its bearings'.[16] In order to accomplish this we need to immerse ourselves in the 'living experiences' of factory workers.

Creating a market-centred society and invisibilising citizens

Beginning in the mid-1980s, the Argentine democratic state, under intense and sustained pressure from the International Monetary Fund (IMF) and World Bank (WB), implemented a series of wide-ranging and radical policies aimed at transforming the country into a market-centred society. It accomplished this more thoroughly and in less time than any other South American country, including Chile under the dictatorship of General Augusto Pinochet.

Buenos Aires's factory workers were among the first to experience the full force of neoliberalism.[17] Their economic expulsion and political invisibilisation from public life could not have been accomplished without support from the judiciary, labour unions, political parties and newspapers – in other words, without the assistance of key democratic institutions across political society, civil society, economic society and the public sphere. In democratic societies these institutions are stewards of the public good and are responsible for protecting the rights of citizens, especially the most vulnerable; however, in Argentina these institutions contributed to organising and unleashing on society a neoliberal 'enclosure' movement, to recall Karl Polanyi's argument.[18]

In 1995, Domingo Cavallo, Minister of Economics under President Menem, secured congressional approval for his 'Law of Insolvency and Bankruptcy' (Law 24.522), signalling to international investors and agencies that the Argentine government now had the legal mechanism, in addition to the political will and economic tools, to turn the country into a market-centred society.[19] Pedro Kesselman, who participated in reforming the national constitution after the end of military dictatorship, summarised the meaning and consequences of Law 24.522 (hereafter, 'new Law'):

> [. . .] civil and commercial judges are concerned solely with property rights; they view them as sacrosanct, as if the rights of creditors are the only ones that are worthy of defending. These judges ignore the rights of workers who, after all, have suffered the most from when their factories become bankrupt or insolvent.'[20]

Neoliberal notions based on property rights now became the language of juridical life, requiring judges, lawyers, factory workers and businessmen, among others, to speak in these terms.

IMF and WB experts described the 'cram-down clause' as the most 'innovative' aspect of the new Law; it was supposed to restructure property relations in Argentina and serve as a model for other countries across the global South that were scheduled to undergo 'structural adjustment'.[21] Under the terms of this clause, businessmen were granted a two-year moratorium on their debt and allowed to retain ownership of their factories; in return, they were required to turn over their firms to commercial judges who appointed a trustee to manage them (see below). If at the end of the period the factory remained insolvent, then the judge embargoed and auctioned it and used the funds generated to compensate creditors.[22]

The purpose of cram-down was to enable distressed owners to retain their factories; however, many of them used it to hasten their own bankruptcy. Prior to surrendering their factories to the courts, owners transferred all their assets to a newly created 'phantom' or 'offshore' firm. On the day of the auction, a frontman representing the owner would bid and regain the embargoed factory that trustees sold at below market value in order to entice buyers. Between 1994 and 1996, the years prior to and after the new Law was implemented, the annual number of bankruptcy and insolvency cases soared from 1,400 to 2,450; during the next decade, the number of cases per year continued to climb, though not as steeply as before.[23] Instead of 'creative destruction', in Schumpeter's sense, cram-down generated a 'habitus of impunity' across public life and contributed to the further pauperisation of working families across Buenos Aires.

Under neoliberalism the judiciary, like all the other wings of the state, slashed its budget and reduced its personnel, requiring commercial judges to outsource and privatise the task of dispensing justice. Judges hired professional accountants from private firms to serve as trustees. In addition to managing embargoed factories, trustees were responsible for maintaining a detailed inventory of the machinery, tools and stock in each plant (in the event it was auctioned). The WB sent a team of experts to evaluate their performance; they concluded:

> The sharpest criticism was directed against the 1995 bankruptcy law for having privatised insolvency proceedings and allowing [. . .] persons (trustees) from outside the judiciary to administer them [. . .] (M)any creditors complained [. . .] that trustees often acted in collusion with debtors.[24]

Businessmen routinely bribed trustees so that they would omit from their inventory stock and equipment from the embargoed factory. Prior to the auction, trustees allowed owners to enter and ransack their ex-factories under cover of night. The new Law atrophied the state's diminished capacity to protect the social and property rights of all its citizens, especially unemployed workers.

Prior to the debacle, Buenos Aires's workers had a long history of acting and speaking as citizens both inside and outside their factories.[25] In Argentina more than in any other salaried society across the globalised South, populist unions had been relatively successful (until the military dictatorship of 1976–83) in ensuring that workers enjoyed all the civil, social and political rights that the 1947 constitution accorded them. During the crisis the country's most important labour confederation, the CGT (Confederación General de Trabajadores), under pressure from the Minister of Labour, instructed shop stewards to discourage rank and file from recuperating factories and to also negotiate privately and accept whatever compensation the owners offered them.[26] At street marches and demonstrations, recuperated factory workers often chanted slogans and displayed banners denouncing the CGT.

Workers in recuperated factories were also expelled from the political field. In the upper and lower chambers of Congress, the three most important national parties – Front for Victory (FPV, *Frente para la victoria*), Peronists (PJ, *Justicialistas*) and Civic Radicals (UCR, *Unión Cívica Radical*), refused to sponsor or support any bills in support of the factories. The Governors of Buenos Aires, Felipe Solá (PJ) and Daniel Scioli (FPV) also blocked any legislation that favoured the factories.[27] During the early years of the crisis, Paul O'Neill and other high-ranking IMF officials visited Argentina and warned the government that if it revoked the new Law the country would not receive the additional thirteen million dollars in credit that it had requested.[28] As with many other factory workers, Damián Giordano, a metallurgist from Constituyentes, followed the month-long negotiation between the Argentine government and the IMF, and concluded:

> Instead of spending their day reading faxes from the IMF [. . .] our legislators should convene all (the recuperated) factories so that we can begin to discuss how we can salvage them.[29]

Factory workers now accused the Argentine government of representing the IMF instead of its citizens, and petitioned the judiciary to issue a warrant for the arrest of O'Neill on charges of conspiring to subvert national sovereignty.

Leftist parties depicted recuperated factories in Leninist terms as the vanguard of the labour movement, 'poised to lead the national struggle against capital and the state'.[30] At the very outset, these parties sent their most experienced militants to colonise Brukman (textile), Sasetru (food processing), Unidos por el Calzado (footwear) and a few more factories.[31] Roberto Salcedo, an electrician at the metallurgical plant Gip, recalls:

> When we began several political parties came by and offered us assistance; we accepted it, but when we realised that they were using our factory as a war trophy we told them to leave.[32]

By 2002 few factories had any contact with leftist parties. Nevertheless, the conservative media (radio, television, newspapers, magazines) continued to exaggerate their influence, provoking considerable panic in the business community and beyond.

The country's most prestigious daily, *La Nación*, used Manichean images from the recent past in its editorials, portraying recuperated factory workers as 'occupiers' and 'usurpers', and describing factories as 'soviets', 'a menace to the constitutional order' and so on:

> The occupation and control of these factories by workers is a violation of property rights, and annuls one of the central precepts enshrined in our constitution. The right of workers to make demands on their employees and on our government must never be allowed to prevail over the right to private property.[33]

These terms and phrases were mnemonic devices to remind readers that the last time factories had been occupied, this had 'provoked' the armed forces into imposing a bloody dictatorship and brought about the 'disappearance' of 30,000 citizens. *La Nación*'s editorials and 'news' coverage were so biased that Lavaca, an independent news agency staffed by professional journalists, brought formal charges against the daily before the Inter-American Commission on Human Rights.[34]

La Nación's middle- and upper-class readers began to use a 'reactionary rhetoric', borrowing a term from Albert Hirschman, in talk shows, public forums and in their informal gatherings, generating a hostile 'climate of opinion' against the factories.[35] Commercial and criminal judges, who are not immune from the influence of public opinion, routinely ordered the special anti-riot police squad to retake the factories. This 'criminalisation' of the workers continued until 2004 when several human rights groups and distinguished jurists, including Supreme Court magistrate Raúl Zaffaroni, denounced the raids as anti-constitutional, a violation of the right of workers to strike and protest.[36]

As stewards of the public good, Argentina's democratic institutions had the legal responsibility of protecting the 'commons' – however, during the crisis they colluded with neoliberal poachers and privatised its resources. These institutions prepared the way for the neoliberal enclosure movement that would soon transform the country into a market-centred society like never before.

Communitarian practices in the factories and across civil society

Although Argentina's factory workers had been stripped of a right to have rights and deprived of a place in the world, they restarted approximately 280 shuttered factories across the country between 2000 and 2009. Nearly all of them were organised prior to 2005, the worst years of the crisis. The vast majority of these factories were either small or medium-sized firms (5 to 20 workers) in the industrial (metallurgical, food processing), manufacturing (textile) and service sectors (tourism, printing) of the economy.[37] By 2009, roughly 90 per cent of these factories remained profitable, providing their workers with salaries equivalent to what many of their counterparts earned in privately owned firms.[38]

No one, including researchers in the Ministry of Labour, knows with any degree of certainty the number of workers in these factories; the most recent and credible estimate puts them at 22,000.[39] These workers are, typically, family men and women between the ages of 46 and 65; somewhat skilled, having completed several years of secondary or technical school; and without any significant experience of activism in labour unions, political parties or social movements.[40] In addition to providing for their own spouses and children, most of them are financially responsible for their aged parents, their in-laws and, increasingly, their (fatherless) grandchildren, adding another 154,000 persons to the list whose livelihood is linked to these factories, thus bringing the grand total to 176,000.

Eighty per cent of all factories are concentrated in the greater metropolitan region of Buenos Aires (see Map I), the most urbanised, populated and industrialised area in the country. This was also the hardest hit area during the governments of Presidents Carlos Menem (Peronist: conservative, 1989–95, 1995–9); Fernando de la Rúa (Civic Radical: social democratic, 1999–2001); Eduardo Duhalde (Peronist: centrist, 2002–3); Nestor Kirchner (FPV: populist, 2003–7) and Cristina Fernández (FPV: populist, 2007–11, 2011–present).[41]

Recuperated factories have provided unemployed workers with a place in the world and have provided citizens from all walks of life with an alternative vision of democratic life.

Mutual recognition, risk and uncertainty

When the recuperations started, 60 per cent of workers followed the advice of their shop stewards and abandoned their factories; the remaining 40 per cent decided to remain in the plants and restart production.[42] Bourdieu's account of neoliberalism's corrosive effects on social relations remains useful for understanding the actions of the first group:

> Job insecurity is now everywhere, in the private and in the public sector [. . .] In all these areas it produces more or less identical effects, which become particularly visible in the extreme case of the unemployed: the destructuring of existence [. . .] and the whole relationship to the world [. . .] Casualisation profoundly affects the person who suffers it by making the whole future seem uncertain; it prevents all rational anticipation.[43]

In taking the 'exit' option, these workers unwittingly transformed their sense of collective uncertainty into personal insecurity. In privatising their anguish many of them became 'disaffiliated', in Robert Castel's sense, from family members, friends and neighbours, and transformed themselves, ironically, into 'possessive individualists', thereby contributing to the spread of neoliberal forms of subjectivisation.[44]

How can we account for the remaining 40 per cent of the workers who stayed put and restarted their factories despite the fact that many of them experienced the same degree of despair as their counterparts? Bourdieu's rationalist account is inadequate for making sense of this second group.[45] An alternative interpretation emerged in the course of interviewing Anibal and several other metallurgists from Unión y Fuerza:

> [Prior to recuperating the plant] we never had much to do with each other; we came to work, did our job and went home [...] We spent eight or ten hours daily, but we hardly knew each other [...] When we heard that the owner was about to close the plant we began to meet and talk amongst ourselves about the situation [...] We were scared shitless [...] We visited several recuperated factories; their workers encouraged us to do the same. After months of discussion, we restarted our factory; most of us didn't believe that we would be able to pull it off [...] We lived from day to day without knowing what would happen next [...] We kept returning to the plant, day after day, although we really did not think that we would be able to keep this going.[46]

From whence did Anibal, his colleagues and other recuperated factory workers get their motivation to recuperate their factory? Family relations, I discovered, played a crucial, albeit indirect, role in motivating workers to develop ties of trust with each other. Enrique, a printer at Chilavert, described his experience and those of his co-workers:

> Our families supported us; this was very important [...] [During the recuperation] they brought us food, and when we went home to rest every few days they recharged our batteries [...] Seeing each other's family in the plant and visiting each other [at home and while attending neighbourhood events] made us realize that we were in this together; there was no turning back [...] because this was not only about us, the factory or even a job; this was primarily about our family, about all our families, and their future as well as our own futures.[47]

Arendt's overly romantic conception of family life as a 'haven in a heartless world' might still be relevant for understanding certain aspects of bourgeois life; however, it remains inadequate for making sense of family life among the working poor and unemployed. No matter, Arendt's insight on the nature of social trust remains relevant for understanding how factory workers projected their current self into a future self:

> [I]nterdependence shows in the mutual give and take in which people live together. The attitude of individuals toward each other is characterised here by belief [. . .] as distinguished from real or potential knowledge. We comprehend [. . .] human and temporal acts by believing – which means by trusting, but never by understanding. This belief in the other is the belief that he will prove himself in our common future. Yet this belief that arises from our mutual interdependence precedes any possible proof.[48]

Arendt's understanding of social trust is reminiscent of T. S. Eliot's definition of fiction: 'willing suspension of disbelief'. As their families became acquainted with each other, factory workers began to transform their sense of individual uncertainty into collective risk. In the course of socialising risk these workers were able to distribute it amongst themselves and make it slightly more bearable.[49]

Restarting the factory

From the perspective of workers, the single greatest challenge was to find a way of remaining in the plant without violating the property rights of the owner. In cases where this had occurred, judges had been known to send the anti-riot police to evict and arrest them. In the courtroom, workers used neoliberal terms in order to justify their continued presence in the factory. They described themselves as 'permanent guards' who were there to enforce the new Law and prevent ex-owners from pilfering factories. This phrase had taken on special meaning in Buenos Aires after the national, provincial and city governments had slashed their budgets for police protection; businessmen were forced to hire security guards to protect their factories and homes. During the worst years of the debacle, the number of private security firms, robberies and other types of crimes against property spiked and was closely correlated with the unravelling of the state and the pauperisation of society. Despite their scepticism, judges agreed to allow workers to guard their plants if for no other reason than that this would discourage owners and trustees from plundering them.[50]

Recall that 60 per cent of all workers, under pressure from their shop stewards and the ex-owners, had abandoned their factories; all of them had to be replaced by the workers who had restarted the plant. But hiring such a large number of workers in a short period of time threatened to undermine factory life from within; the majority of the workers were not committed to self-management.[51] Many factories resolved this dilemma in the only way that they could: recruiting family members (nuclear, consanguineal, affinal), friends, acquaintances and neighbours. Roughly 45 per cent of all new hires were of this type; nearly all of them were unskilled.[52] This approach might seem clannish, exclusionary and anti-democratic, an atavistic residue from the past – however, it was a modern communitarian response to the state's inability to provide its citizens with a place in the world.

There were additional reasons for adopting this hiring practice. After President Menem privatised public education and closed hundreds of technical schools, an entire generation of working youth, including the children, nieces, nephews and grandchildren of factory workers, was left without the opportunity to acquire skills and learn a trade.[53] A significant number of these youths, moreover, had been raised in broken homes where one or both parents, or the guardian, were 'structurally unemployed' and disaffiliated. Many of Buenos Aires's working youth had never experienced the 'culture of work'.[54] Older factory workers mentored newcomers, transmitting to them technical knowledge, a work ethic and an appreciation for self-management. When these young workers returned to their neighbourhoods at the end of the day, they disseminated what they had learned in the factory among their own circle of friends, encouraging them to find a job in the same or another recuperated factory. Young factory workers played a key role in revitalising working-class neighbourhoods across Buenos Aires.

Recuperated factories also hired a sizeable number of skilled and experienced workers; most of them had few, if any, personal ties with older workers. These skilled newcomers eroded patron-client ties among friends and family members and instilled the older workers with a sense of meritocracy and efficiency. At the same time older workers took it upon themselves to train new hires in the practice of self-management. These changes in socio-personal relations generated considerable strain and tension among all the workers, regardless of age, skill and experience. But because the job market had collapsed, this encouraged them to discuss and resolve their differences during the factory's assembly.

Resignifying the meanings of 'labour', 'worker' and 'salary'

Recuperated factory workers redefined the meaning of productive labour. During the early years of the movement, workers spent a portion of the work week participating in public protests, meeting with judges in their court chambers, lobbying politicians and state officials in their offices and so on. A survey done in the city of Buenos Aires among 150 workers distributed across 17 factories indicates that prior to 2004, roughly 80 per cent had taken part in one or more acts of public protests.[55] During their weekly meetings, factory workers debated whether or not to recognise and remunerate political activism in the same way as productive labour. Scores of factories voted in support of this proposal, eroding further Arendt's distinction between *animal laborans* and *homo politicus*.

Factory workers also altered the rhythm and meaning of work. When the firm was privately owned, after completing their task, workers 'walked the dog' (loafed); they hid in the bathroom or another secluded area to chat, smoke and drink tea (mate):

> Before [recuperating the factory], after completing your task you 'walked the dog'; why work more if at the end of the month I was always paid the same [amount] [. . .] [Now that we are in charge of production] 'dead time' does not exist anymore [. . .] if you complete your task, you look around and find someone to help. All of us now earn the same; our 'withdrawals' depend on our level of production; if this declines, then so does our withdrawal.[56]

Workers developed an 'integrated-holistic' conception of production, and assisted each other in completing their tasks and in monitoring each other's productivity. In almost all the factories, workers used the term 'withdrawal' when discussing 'salaries', suggesting that for them the factory was similar to a joint bank account; each worker was responsible for 'depositing' and 'withdrawing' funds from it.

Businessmen, bank officers, court magistrates and state officials often referred to factory workers as 'blackies' (*negritos*; slang for ignorant simpletons), and told them that they would never succeed in managing these factories.[57] Daniel, a woodcutter from the Maderera Cordoba lumber yard, recalls his transformation from a 'blackie' to a bona fide 'laburante':[58]

> Our old administrator [before the factory was recuperated] called our suppliers when we needed to renew our stock; our accountant paid our salary on time; our salesmen sold our products and found us new customers. And the owner was the brain behind the entire operation [. . .] Now

we do everything ourselves [. . .] We have no one to blame. Running your factory is risky; when you do things right everyone wins, but when you do them wrong everyone loses [. . .] Some of my co-workers pretend to be '*laburantes*' but they are still blackies.[59]

Factory workers now used the term 'blackie' to describe their own co-workers who arrived late to work and left early; came 'tipsy' to the factory; left their tools scattered about on the shop floor; rarely cleaned their work area; and so on.

Most recuperated factories have maintained an egalitarian salary structure. Every worker – from the maintenance person responsible for sweeping the floor, to the bookkeeper in charge of ordering stock and balancing the books – earns roughly the same amount. Seventy-five per cent of the factories have a relatively 'flat' salary structure; income differences in the remaining 25 per cent are insignificant. Reducing salary inequalities was more than just a way of efficiently distributing limited resources; it was a way for workers to practise recognition on the factory shop floor.[60] The examples discussed in this section go beyond Arendt's dichotomy, based as it is on an overly simple and binary distinction between social need and political freedom.

Self-rule on the shop floor

When a firm was privately owned, authority and power was distributed hierarchically and unevenly; managers at the top were responsible for making all the decisions, while workers at the bottom were required to follow orders. After recuperation, workers replaced this Taylorist model with self-management. Each worker considered himself or herself equal to the rest, compelling all of them to discuss and resolve their differences publicly at factory assemblies that were held twice a month.

Workers established a two-tiered system of governance composed of an executive council (responsible for defining general policies pertaining to financial and production matters and also representing the firm in commercial courts and in the factories dealing with government officials) and a legislative assembly (responsible for attending to the daily problems related to shop floor life and personnel matters – hiring, terminations and so forth).[61] A study of 214 workers in 32 factories (five in the city of Buenos Aires, the others from across the province) indicates that 75 per cent of them participated often in factory assemblies; the remaining 25 per cent rarely participated.[62] At these meetings, workers combined socio-economic needs and political concerns in ways that Arendt might have found puzzling.

Moral economy and associative networks among factories

Buenos Aires's recuperated factories lacked juridical status, and were therefore unable to secure credit from any private bank. In October 2001, state officials from the National Institute of Social and Associative Economy (INAES), a government agency responsible for providing legal and socio-economic assistance (and monitoring) to popular movements, including the *Piqueteros*, met with all the factories and offered to assist them. The workers declined the offer, claiming that the INAES was trying to turn them into clients of the Peronist party-state.[63] The factories agreed to meet again and to organise their own 'credit system'.

In the course of these discussions, the factories organised two networks: National Movement of Recuperated Enterprises (MNER, *Movimiento Nacional de Empresas Recuperadas*) and National Movement of Recuperated Factories (MNFR, *Movimiento Nacional de Fábricas Recuperadas*). Factory delegates from each network usually meet bimonthly to discuss political and financial concerns. Each factory pays membership dues (roughly 300–400 pesos annually), a portion of which the networks use to provide loans to newly restarted factories who need to pay the utility bills left behind by ex-owners, purchase raw materials and repair old machinery. As soon as a new factory begins generating profit, it begins paying dues as well, so that the next generation of factories will have access to MNER and MNFR loans. This Maussian gift-giving strengthened the socio-organisational and ethico-political ties among factories in each network.[64] As of 2005, approximately 75 per cent of all the factories in Buenos Aires were affiliated to the MNER (centre left) or the MNFR (centre).[65]

In public life the two networks assist each other whenever one of their factories is under siege by the police or from commercial courts. However, inside each factory MNER and MNFR delegates compete fiercely for influence and control over shop-floor life. In 2005 a bitter and prolonged feud broke out between the delegates, rank and file and leadership of MNER and MNFR over control of Metallurgical and Plastic Industry of Argentina (IMPA, *Industria Metalúrgica y Plástica de Argentina*), the largest metallurgical plant in the city of Buenos Aires. This conflict provoked a large number of factories in both networks to break away from MNER and MNFR and create a third network: Co-operative Federation of Self-Managed

Workers (FACTA, *Federación de Cooperativas de Trabajadores Autogestionados*). In contrast to previous networks, the internal socio-organisational structure of FACTA is relatively decentralised and based on economic specialisation-function. For example, seven of the largest printing presses in the city of Buenos Aires organised a 'node' (*Red Gráfica*).[66] Each press in the node provides the rest with technical and administrative advice and limited use of their machinery; they also negotiate price schedules; share customer lists; order paper, ink and other supplies from the same wholesalers; and so on. These measures have contributed to making the presses in the node increasingly efficient and profitable.[67] In 2007, FACTA and several of its factories signed various major contracts with Venezuelan state-owned firms (see below), signalling the globalisation of this network.

Socio-institutional relations with the community

Recuperated factories were also committed to repairing the social fabric in poor neighbourhoods throughout Buenos Aires, which had unravelled due to the corrosive influence of neoliberalism. Dozens of factories established adult education, high school and outreach programmes for local residents. In 2006, there were a total of 1000 'high-risk' students taking courses at the three largest factory-based schools in IMPA, Maderera de Córdoba, a lumber yard, and Cooperativa Patricios, a printing shop.[68] In addition to courses from the state-approved curriculum (i.e. Spanish, history, mathematics), factory-staffed schools offered courses such as the 'History of popular and community struggles in Argentina' to encourage students to become activists (organic intellectuals).[69]

After touring me through Yaguané, South America's largest slaughterhouse, located in Virrey del Pino (La Matanza), the poorest district in the province, its director Roberto invited me to the plant's library. This was a single-storey, three-room building on the far side of the complex. When I visited it there were roughly twenty boys and girls ranging in age from eight to seventeen, and three tutors (university students) assisting them with schoolwork in maths, English and Spanish at several computer stations.[70] The community library is open daily on weekdays from 9 a.m. to 7 p.m.; it provides breakfast and an afternoon snack daily to roughly 200 students.[71] Yaguané's workers also donate cheap cuts of meat each week to several communal kitchens that service thousands of poor and indigent families in the region.

In the town of Saavedra, Pigüé's textile workers signed an agreement in 2006 with the director of a medium-security penitentiary in order to provide training to inmates who had completed most of their jail sentence. After completing the course, inmates worked part of the week in Pigüé alongside its workers, producing sports clothes; in the first year, they manufactured and sold 25,000 pairs of sneakers and 1,600 jogging suits. This money facilitated their integration into the community. Once they had completed their sentence and were released, Pigüé's hired the most reliable and skilled ex-inmates.[72]

With a full-time staff of 120 workers, Bauen, a fourteen-storey, eighty-nine-room hotel with a restaurant and fitness centre, provides discount rates to low-income families from the provinces who are visiting Buenos Aires in order to resolve some medical, family or legal issue. Bauen also offers discounted rates to dissident unions, political parties and social movements who need to use its auditorium for rallies, meetings and special events.[73]

Chilavert Graphics established a 'Centre for Documentation on Recuperated Factories' in their plant. Staffed by ten part-time students from the University of Buenos Aires, the Centre collects primary documents (petitions, flyers, newspapers articles), audiovisual materials (CDs, taped interviews) and secondary sources (journal articles, academic theses, conference papers, books) on the factories so that journalists, students, public intellectuals and scholars will have access to information not readily available in 'mainstream' media. In the transition from lived experience to historical memory, the role of the Centre is to ensure that factory workers are able to 'represent' themselves rather than the way that they have been portrayed in the mass media, including *La Nación*.[74] The communitarian practices that workers generated on the shop floor, among factories, in working-class neighbourhoods as well as with a variety of groups across civil society indicate that socio-economic needs and political freedom are reconcilable in ways not fully understood by Arendt and some of her followers.

Enacting citizenship across political society

Buenos Aires's factory workers were successful in translating the idiom and practices of communitarianism from inside the factory and across economic and civil society into different arenas of political society. They relied on both participatory (street marches, demonstrations, lobbying) and representative (court hearings, elections) forms of democratic life to achieve this. In the process, factory workers gained visibility in public life and acquired recognition from fellow citizens.

Judicial politics, property rights and popular protests

Instead of individualising and depoliticising the conflict, judicial contestation encouraged workers and businessmen to mobilise 'public opinion' in support of their own cause. This had the unintended effect of publicising the debate over property and social rights and attracting the attention of citizens from all walks of life.

Although commercial judges framed the legal discussion over factory ownership in terms of property rights, they also relied on their own judgement in order to reconcile juridical doctrine and socio-political reality.[75] Magistrates who favoured a 'jurispathic' approach were keenly aware that 'legal interpretations always take place in the shadow of coercion'; those who adopted a 'jurisgenerative' approach understood that any 'legal precept is generated through social activity that falls outside the boundaries of the law itself'.[76] These alternative interpretations, along with public opinion, framed the debate over the legality of recuperated factories.

Businessmen and factory workers adopted different strategies for winning over public opinion. Businessmen enlisted the support of *La Nación*. During my interview with Marcela of Mayorista. com, a leading wholesaler and Bauen's main purveyor, she described the role of newspapers in fomenting moral panics in the business community:

> Each time the Bauen makes headlines – because of a street march or because the judge has threatened them with eviction – my boss became exceedingly tense; he would summon me into his office and ask me about their [Bauen's] account. I would also get calls from clients and colleagues [. . .] They advised me to stop doing business with Bauen, that its staff was incompetent and dishonest and that sooner or later I would lose money. In our line of business, everyone knows each other; we always take care of our own.[77]

In addition, businessmen, journalists and judges also met at professional gatherings, trade fairs, cocktail parties, working lunches and other social events that served as opportunities to discuss the growing threat of recuperated factories.

Factory workers relied on street marches and demonstrations to influence judges and public opinion. And who better to explain this elusive relationship than the editors of *La Nación*:

> The [socio-political] pressure that is exerted on judges often leads them to favour solutions that decompress the situation at hand, however, in doing so they are also tolerating acts of usurpation [by factory workers]. This

solution is untenable and in the long run it will undermine the norms of conviviality that enable us to live together.[78]

Businessmen and factory workers tried, each in their own ways, to shape the 'climate of opinion' in the knowledge that commercial judges would be influenced by it.

Given the sheer number and complexity of factory-led protests in Buenos Aires, it is impossible to analyse them in a few pages; for example, between mid-June and mid-December 2005 the *Hotel Bauen* alone organised nineteen street marches and rallies.[79] In the following paragraphs I discuss two examples: Hotel Bauen in the city of Buenos Aires, and Yaguané in La Matanza, deep in the province. Neither of these cases is, strictly speaking, representative of the rest; however, each of them is illustrative of a different style that workers used to mobilise public opinion and make themselves visible.

The Hotel Bauen is located on the corner of a busy intersection (Callao and Corrientes) in the middle of Buenos Aires's financial, commercial and theatre district, making it an ideal place for its workers to broadcast their cause. During rush hour and at other times of the day, the Hotel's staff move furniture from the lobby to the middle of the street and invite pedestrians to join them on 'stage' for a discussion of their situation.[80] The Bauen also hosts public rallies and rock concerts in front of the hotel and invites celebrities, such as Nobel Prize winner Adolfo Pérez Esquivel, the human rights organisation Abuelas de Plaza de Mayo (Grandmothers of the Plaza de Mayo), the film director 'Pino' Solanas and León Gieco (Argentina's answer to Bob Dylan) to these events, drawing crowds of up to 4,000, mainly passers-by.

The Hotel's staff also organises street marches to the courthouse located six blocks away whenever the judge summons them in order to convince the court that Bauen has the support of the community and is a force for public good. During the past fifteen years the Hotel's workers have won as many cases as they have lost against Marcelo Iurcovich, the Hotel's ex-owner and an influential member of the political establishment. That the Hotel is still in litigation after fifteen years underscores the considerable influence that public opinion has on judicial life.

Yaguané's workers in La Matanza, the poorest district in the province, routinely organise marches and demonstrations in order to bring public attention to their cause. However, because this slaughterhouse is located in the hinterlands in an area where socio-political conditions are most unfavourable (thin and dispersed population; lack of independent media; absence of press coverage; limited access to courts; *caudillo*-style politics; police corruption, and so on),

Yaguané's meat workers have tended to rely on 'rougher' tactics than their urban counterparts in order to influence public opinion. After waiting for nearly four years for the judge to decide their case, the workers decided to take matters into their own hands; they removed their bloodstained aprons, sheathed their carving knives and organised a caravan with 250 workers (another 250 remained working in the slaughterhouse in order to meet their production quota) to the municipal courthouse in San Justo, the district capital.[81]

When the meat workers arrived at the courthouse, they surrounded the building and parked their trucks directly in front of each entrance. They then stacked rubber tires along the building's perimeter and set them ablaze, covering the area in thick clouds of black smoke; a worker described the scene as 'hellish'.[82] The following day the workers lifted their siege after the mayor of San Justo agreed to intervene on their behalf. Soon after their meeting, the judge responsible for resolving Yaguané's case resigned and a new judge was appointed. It took him under a month to review the evidence and to deliver his judgement, in this case, in favour of the meat-cutters.

Social rights, legislative politics and lobbying

Beginning in 2003, workers launched a major lobbying campaign to persuade municipal and provincial legislators to declare recuperated factories 'a common good' – similar to when the state invokes eminent domain when it needs to construct a highway or park on privately-owned land.[83] In Argentina, cases of this type are considered to be 'political' (as opposed to judicial) and are, therefore, voted on by legislators (not judges). In invoking a pre-existing law, factory workers were doing more than just relying on established norms and principles to make their case; they were enlarging the scope, nature and meaning of the common good, and in doing so, re-interpreting the law.

Factory workers and businessmen lobbied members of Buenos Aires's municipal and provincial legislature, presenting them with divergent interpretations of the phrase 'common good'. Workers argued that factories provided them with a 'living wage'; this also benefited the state and taxpayers, as it meant that public funds did not have to be used to provide welfare relief. In any case, the national constitution guaranteed citizens the right to a salaried job, and the state should act in accordance with the law.[84] The business community disagreed; recuperated factories benefited only a small number of workers. Businessmen defined the common good in numerical terms, and used political arithmetic to determine whether the benefits accrued to workers was less than, equal to or greater than the benefits that would otherwise accrue to all the other citizens in the region. Workers were, clearly, a numerical minority; their factories were not a common good.

Factory workers from dozens of plants spent countless hours during many months visiting the offices of, and lobbying with, municipal and provincial legislators. One of the most energetic and steadfast lobbyists for the worker was Jorge, a trucker from Rabbione, a moving firm with a fleet of seventy vehicles in the city of Buenos Aires:

> We lived day and night [*internados*] in the municipality for three months. We spent most of our days in meetings with legislators in their offices, one at a time. At these audiences, we had to present them with an evaluation of our business plans. And once they had approved them, then we had to start all over again and do the same in front of several different legislative committees (municipal budget, economic development and so on) so that their members could evaluate our petition and decide whether our company was viable or not. It was difficult to convince them. However, in the end the legislature voted: twenty-eight in favour, eighteen against, and one abstention. The judge had already announced that our factory would be auctioned on the next day; he had already condemned us and tied a noose around our necks; we were simply waiting to be hung.[85]

As part of their lobbying campaign, workers invited legislators to their factory and had *asados* (barbecues) in their honour so that they would be able to have direct contact with their families and appreciate the 'human' and 'private' side of their struggle, contrary to what Arendt would have advocated. In mid-2004, the Buenos Aires city legislature decreed that 80 per cent of the recuperated factories were of 'public interest' and a common good.[86]

But a problem remained: in order for a recuperated factory to achieve this status, workers had to spend a large part of their working hours lobbying legislators and leading street marches rather than on the shop floor attending to production, thereby undermining their chances of economic survival. Workers now confronted the classic dilemma that is faced sooner or later by most popular movements: whether to practise solidarity, or adopt an individualist strategy. The city of Buenos Aires's recuperated factories resolved this dilemma by drafting a bill that would allow them to present 'class action' suits. Diego Kravetz, who had been legal counsel for the factories and was now a legislator in the municipal government presented the bill; it was approved in November 2004 (Law 1529, Kravetz's Law).[87]

On the day that the bill was to be discussed and voted in the municipal legislature, hundreds of workers descended on the Buenos Aires city hall; some packed the visitors' gallery and the rest gathered outside. A journalist described the scene:

> It resembled a football championship match with Boca fans (MNER) on one side and River fans (MNFR) on the opposite bleacher [. . .] nevertheless, this time all of them were cheering for the same team [factories] [. . .] As the legislators took their seats in the hall on the main floor directly below the visitors' gallery where all the workers were seated, they gesticulated to them, encouraging those legislators they knew to vote in support of the bill. Then the workers began chanting in unison a [familiar football tune]: 'Let the legislators know, that from our factories we will never leave. Our factories were closed, but now we restarted them [. . .] Olé, olé, olé [. . .] we will never abandon them, Olé [. . .]

> After tallying and announcing the results of the election, the workers in the gallery leaped from their seats and cheered; tears of joys streamed down their faces. Several of them hurried to the railing and dumped white, shredded paper on the legislators below; it resembled a snowstorm [. . .] At the end of the session, a large group of workers rushed the main floor, and hugged and kissed the legislators [. . .] In the streets adjacent to city hall, groups of workers began banging on their drums and setting off fireworks.[88]

This and other legal and political cases, along with the different practices discussed in the previous sections, contributed to shifting the language of public life from property rights to social rights.[89]

Manoeuvering across the electoral field

Julio Abelli, machinist and leader of the MNER, explained the reason that factory workers had decided to enter the electoral field:

> We need to [enter the electoral field to] persuade [our fellow citizens] to support our social democratic agenda: we want a just distribution of wealth as in the 1950s and 1960s when workers' salaries accounted for half of the gross national product. We do not have the power or capacity to achieve this yet [. . .] however, our aim is to organize a party similar to the Worker's Party in Brasil [which brought President Luis 'Lula' da Silva to power].[90]

In August 2003 the factory movement participated for the first time in electoral politics; they put forward a slate of ten candidates for a

variety of offices including those of governor, provincial and municipal legislator, and city mayor.[91] Two of their candidates won: Diego
Kravetz (sponsor of Kravetz's Law) was elected to the city of Buenos
Aires legislature; Francisco Gutiérrez was elected twice to serve in the
Buenos Aires provincial congress, and was also voted twice to serve
as mayor of the city of Quilmes. The workers' relative success in
the electoral field has to be evaluated in light of the representational
crisis under way, which had pulverised the party system and made
it possible for the workers' candidates to bypass all the traditional
parties and rely on the 'mass media' and community organisations to
create a constituency for themselves.[92]

As MNER's legal counsel, Kravetz had broad support among
factory workers, but he remained unknown to most other voters. In
order to acquire visibility and enlarge his electoral base, Kravetz joined
the Democratic Revolution Party (PRD), led by the well-known left-
of-centre journalist and public intellectual, Miguel Bonasso.[93] The
PRD inaugurated its political campaign in the metallurgical factory
IMPA; Kravetz had spent the previous two years serving as its legal
counsel (as well as the MNER's).[94] At this and all subsequent rallies
Kravetz appeared on stage alongside Bonasso, who promoted his
candidacy and introduced him to his own supporters.[95] In addition,
Página 12, the most widely read social democratic daily, provided
extensive coverage of the campaign, transforming Kravetz overnight
into a political celebrity.

Kravetz's electoral victory was also due to his own ability to reach
middle-class voters. He used the idiom of community in order to
create a symbolic and imaginary bridge between their grandparents, many of whom had been immigrant '*laburantes*' and factory
workers.[96] At public rallies, in radio and television programmes, and
in newspaper articles Kravetz associated factory workers with the
generation of immigrants who had made Argentina a 'modern and
developed' country. Kravetz's campaign provided factory workers
with the visibility and recognition they sought from other citizens. In
the words of Arendt:

> The process of representation does not blindly adopt the actual view of
> those who stand somewhere else [. . .] but of being and thinking in my
> own identity where actually I am not [. . .] the better I can imagine how I
> would feel and think if I were in their place, the stronger will be my capac-
> ity for representative thinking.[97]

A random survey of 600 citizens from across Buenos Aires that was
completed in 2007 revealed that 80 per cent of the respondents had
a 'favourable' view of factories, indicating that the factory workers

had now been incorporated into the 'imagined community' of the demos.[98] This was accomplished, in part, through the communitarian idiom of kinship and memory rather than any lofty political principle or act of representative thinking, as Arendt maintains.

After taking office in November 2003 Kravetz broke with Bonasso's PRD, which had brought him to power, joined the ruling party of President Nestor Kirchner, FPV ('Front for Victory') and was made its 'bench-leader' in the City of Buenos Aires legislature. Soon afterwards, Kravetz resigned from the MNER; workers accused him of using their factories in order to feed his political ambitions and advance his career.[99] Experienced journalists have portrayed him in similar terms, as an 'operator', a virtuoso of 'liquid politics', and an 'acrobat'.[100] Like many other political outsiders, Kravetz made and broke alliances without having to adhere to party discipline or political doctrine.

A leader of the local dissident branch of the metallurgical worker's union UOM (Unión Obrera Metalúrgica), Francisco Gutiérrez had broad support among the rank and file in the southern districts of Quilmes, Florencio Varela and Berazategui. When they began recuperating factories, Gutiérrez joined them and resigned from the UOM. Along with Luis Farinello, a longtime activist, Catholic priest and head of the poorest parish in the area, Nuestra Señora de Luján, Gutiérrez organised a political coalition, Polo Social.[101] With its base of support among the poor and unemployed, Polo recruited voters in soup kitchens, day-care centres, alcohol and drug rehabilitation centres and other church-run establishments. Despite intense opposition from Presidents Kirchner and Fernández's government-party apparatus (FPV), Gutiérrez defeated their candidates and went on to serve in the provincial congress and twice as mayor of the city of Quilmes.[102] Unlike Kravetz, Gutiérrez had a strong and broad electoral base.[103]

Buenos Aires's factory workers developed a relatively 'thin' idiom and set of representational practices, to borrow from Michael Walzer, as they manoeuvered among various institutional sites (courtrooms, electoral field, lobbying, street marches, public demonstrations) throughout political society. These thin, site-specific idioms and practices, however, remained in dialogue with 'thick' forms of communitarianism and were eventually transformed by them in ways that remain unarticulated in Walzer's accounts.[104] In the course of engaging in participatory and representative politics in daily life (including civil disobedience), Buenos Aires's factory workers gained recognition from fellow citizens who had previously invisibilised them.

Cosmopolitanism and transnational networks

Buenos Aires's factory workers forged ties with both the EU and ALBA in order to secure material and symbolic resources that had been denied to them by the majority of public institutions in Argentina. In the course of manoeuvering across the transnational terrain, these workers practised cosmopolitanism in three ways: socio-culturally, they learned from strangers new ways of organising economic life, developing their own type of 'gaucho specialisation' (inspired by Italian 'flexible specialisation'); politically, they practised the right to have rights and forged alliances with a great many workers, citizens and officials from dozens of foreign countries and also several international agencies and organisations; and socio-psychologically, the majority of Buenos Aires's factory workers had never travelled beyond the province, and though they experienced unease when they came into contact with strangers throughout Europe and Latin America, they remained open-minded and tolerant throughout it all.[105]

Italian co-operatives and flexible specialisation

Between 2002 and 2007, twenty factories from the southern districts of Quilmes, Florencio Varela and Berazategui – among the poorest in the province – in partnership with the EU and several co-operatives from the Emilia-Romagna and Le Marche regions of north-eastern Italy, designed an ambitious development project: 'Network of Factories and People' (hereafter Network). Factory workers across southern Buenos Aires borrowed from and adapted flexible specialisation, the most successful alternative to Fordism and mass production, with the aim of transforming the region into a 'growth pole'.[106] In their final report summarising their accomplishments to the EU, Network's local directors in several of the factories noted that the project had taken nearly five years to complete, had cost roughly 1.171 million Euros and had transformed the lives of no fewer than 960 workers in thirty different factories along with 250 of their family members.

In order to promote the socio-economic development and integration of the region, Network brought together a total of thirteen metallurgical plants from Quilmes (seven), Florencio Varela (three), and Berazategui (three), organising them into a single 'cluster'. Instead of each attending to its own particular needs, all the factories in the cluster agreed to share resources and co-ordinate production schedules and output; this contributed greatly to lowering costs, increasing efficiency, maximising profit and local sources of credit and loan.[107] Gaucho specialisation generated 'backward' and 'forward' linkages among the region's factories as well as 'synergistic' ties with local firms outside the cluster, which served to benefit everyone in the region: producers, consumers and workers.

Network modernised factory production. In collaboration with the University of Quilmes, a public university, Network offered workers courses in 'industrial branding', 'intelligent production', 'customer loyalty' and so on. For example, in the course on intelligent branding workers learned to use Auto-Cad and other software programs. After completing the course, they were given desktop computers and software programs so that they would teach their co-workers what they had learned. During the 2007 academic year, 126 workers from fifteen factories completed this course, and many more workers were tutored in the factory by those who had graduated.[108]

Network's community development programme targeted the spouses and children of factory workers; most of them were structurally unemployed and many suffered from family violence, drug dependency, alcoholism and other symptoms of disaffiliation.[109] Spouses were taught how to organise micro-enterprises (day-care centres, community kitchens, sidewalk shops) and secure 'micro-credit' from the WB and other international agencies. The children of factory workers were offered technical training; the most skilled were offered jobs in local factories. In November 2007 the magazine *Nudos*, written by and for recuperated factory workers, published an interim report summarising two years of activity related to community development: 230 women and 120 working youth had benefited from its programme.[110] In addition to acquiring various skills, these women and young adults had been able to regain their sense of personal dignity and rebuild social ties within their families and in their neighbourhoods.

ALBA and social economy

In October 2005, and again in June 2009, Argentina's factory movement sent a delegation to the Latin American Congress of Recovered Enterprises, held in Caracas under the auspices of the Venezuelan government. The first Congress was attended by 400 workers from 235 factories across Brazil, Bolivia, Ecuador, Peru, Paraguay, Uruguay and Venezuela; the second Congress was slightly smaller. In his inaugural address at the first Congress, President Chávez described recuperated factories as the 'soul' of the social economy that was emerging across Latin America; their workers were the foot soldiers in the economic war against the Washington Consensus. On the last day of the Congress, the workers organised a 'business fair'. The Argentine delegation signed thirty commercial contracts and promissory notes with representatives from factories across the continent, half the total number that were signed at the fair, committing each other to various types of long-term business ventures.[111] In order to assist these firms in forging organisational and economic networks amongst themselves, President Chávez announced the creation of a regional development bank, *Empresur*, and committed five million dollars to it in the first year.[112]

When the Argentine delegation returned to Buenos Aires, MNER circulated a statement criticising one of its own delegates, Eduardo Murúa of IMPA, for acting like a 'revolutionary caudillo' and using the Congress to regain influence among the factories in Buenos Aires. MNER delegates met and expelled him from the network.[113] With Murúa out of the way, several recuperated factories now affiliated with FACTA and the Venezuelan government signed a number of contracts. In January 2006, Venezuela's state-owned oil company (PDVSA) and Astilleros Río Santiago, a recuperated shipyard in the port of Ensenada and the largest of its kind in South America, signed a contract to launch four new oil tankers in an equal number of years; the Minister of Culture singed a contract with Chilavert and a few other printing presses for 10,000 school textbooks; and the Ministry of Tourism signed a multi-year contract with Hotel Bauen to provide lodging at discounted rates for state officials visiting Buenos Aires on official business.[114] Representational conflicts as well as forms of co-operation among factory worker in daily life had a decisive influence in shaping their organisational networks and ties with the EU and ALBA.

Concluding remarks

Buenos Aires's factory workers refused to refashion themselves in the image and likeness of a commodity ('exchange value') and generated, instead, an alternative form of democratic life rooted in a right to have rights based on everyday practices of belonging and recognition ('use value'). In the course of doing so, they transformed themselves from superfluous pariahs into communitarian cosmopolitans. Whether unemployed workers in the remaining 5,000 factories that are shuttered across Argentina will restart them in the coming years remains to be seen. Whether the experience of Buenos Aires's recuperated factory workers can also shed light on similar cases across the globalised South (India, South Africa and People's Republic of China) and definancialised North (Greece, Spain and France's 'indignados') is worth considering.

This study of Buenos Aires's recuperated factory workers is an opportunity to reconsider Arendt's grim account of the crisis of our century. When she wrote her book on totalitarianism, Nazism had been soundly defeated and 'Uncle Joe' Stalin laid on his deathbed. Nevertheless, on Arendt's reckoning the socio-political conditions that had given birth to these regimes remained with us, and would eventually bring forth a purer, less brutal type of neototalitarianism:

> If [. . .] the elements of totalitarianism can be found by retracing the history [of superfluous pariahs] and analyzing the political implications of what we usually call the crisis of our century, then the conclusion is unavoidable [. . .] it will no more disappear with the death of Stalin than it disappeared with the fall of Nazi Germany. It may even be that the true predicaments of our time will assume their authentic form – though not necessarily the cruellest – only when totalitarianism has become a thing of the past.[115]

If Europe's totalitarian regimes of the interwar period had relied on savage techniques to strip citizens of a right to have rights and to 'disappear' them from public life, the emergent neototalitarian regimes would employ relatively diffused, indirect and 'structural' forces to accomplish the same. Arendt's discussion of neototalitarianism might seem fanciful; however, recall that Alexis de Tocqueville, the other great theorist of modern democracy, also discerned an affinity between democracy and despotism.[116]

Instead of 'radical evil', neototalitarian regimes practise 'the banality of evil', in Arendt's sense.[117] The legal and political philosopher Thomas Pogge has pursued some of the ethico-political and empirical implications of her argument in light of our current situation: 'global poverty is the largest crime against humanity ever committed, the death toll of which exceeds [. . .] every three years, that of World War Two, the concentration camps and gulags included'.[118] According to Pogge and other scholars, the dramatic increase in the number of pauperised citizens across the globalised South is directly correlated to the spread of neoliberalism (structural adjustment programmes), and has transformed our world into a 'planet of slums', to borrow from Mike Davis.[119] If one takes seriously Arendt's argument on 'representative thinking' as discussed earlier, and the central role that it plays in the development of democratic life, then our inability to envision human misery on a planetary scale (much less to have any personal contact with it) is itself constitutive of the banality of evil that makes neototalitarianism possible. Might we be like the good and law-abiding citizens of the antebellum South, who never owned slaves but greatly benefited, even if indirectly, from this socio-political and economic arrangement?

Argentina's own experience with neototalitarianism, on my account, began in the mid-1990s, a decade after the country had completed its transition to democracy (the military dictatorship that preceded it was totalitarian). As I noted earlier, the different democratic governments (conservative, centrist, populist, social democratic) that have ruled the country during the last three decades turned Argentina into a market-centred society. The neoliberal policies they implemented, under intense pressure from the IMF and WB, transformed a significant number of citizens into superfluous pariahs and turned Argentina almost overnight into one of the poorest and most unequal countries in the world, alongside those of sub-Saharan Africa. This socio-political and economic debacle deprived many thousands of citizens in Buenos Aires of their right to have rights. Despite the dire conditions that they faced, Buenos Aires factory workers, the *animal laborans* of neoliberalism, have played a crucial role in recuperating democratic life from the grip of neototalitarianism.

Notes

1. Maristella Svampa and Facundo Vega tutored me in Argentine politics. Craig Calhoun, Leon Fink, Stathis Gourgouris, Peter Wagner, Luis Roniger and Mario Sznajder invited me to present earlier versions of this chapter at New York University's Institute for Public Knowledge; University of Illinois's Institute for the Humanities; Columbia University's Heyman Centre for the Humanities; Universitat de Barcelona and the Hebrew University's Institute for Advanced Study, respectively. Emmanuel Guerisoli, Jake Hanin and Iddo Tavory spotted several gaps in my argument. I am grateful to all of them, and also to the Open Society for funding a portion of my research.

2. Personal Interview 8 (hereafter PI). All the interviews with workers (22) and businessmen (12) are numbered; those with public figures are identified as such – Luís Caro, founder of the 'Movimiento nacional de fábricas recuperadas'; Eduardo Murúa, founder of the 'Movimiento nacional de empresas recuperadas'; Dr Horacio Esber, City of Buenos Aires's Public Defender's Office; Diego Kravetz, City of Buenos Aires municipal government. This chapter draws on my new book: *Citizenship and Its Fragments: Democratic Life in Argentina in the Wake of Neoliberal Globalization*.

3. Denis Merklen, *Pobres Ciudadanos: Las clases populares en la era democrática* (Buenos Aires: Editorial Gorla, 2005). *Piqueteros* routinely organise 'monster' marches to demand jobs and welfare from

the state's 'Programme for Unemployed Male and Female Heads of Households' (*Programas de Jefes y Jefas de Hogar*).

4. Hannah Arendt, *The Origins of Totalitarianism* [1951] (New York: Meridian Books, 1971), p. 296.
5. E. H. Puccia, *Barracas: su historia y sus tradiciones* (Buenos Aires: Compañía General Fabril, 1968).
6. Nadia Urbinati, 'Representation as Advocacy', *Political Theory* 28: 6 (December 2006): 759, breaks with the age-old dichotomy – participatory vs representative democracy – by conceiving them 'as related forms of democracy, constituting the *continuum* of political action'. Despite her claims, her argument remains lopsided and reinstates this dichotomy. For a balanced, integrated account see Partha Chatterjee, *The Politics of the Governed* (New York City: Columbia University, 2004) and Pierre Rosanvallon, *Counter-Democracy* (Cambridge: Cambridge University Press, 2008).
7. Arjun Appadurai, *Modernity at Large* (Minneapolis: University of Minnesota Press, 1996); Chatterjee, *The Politics of the Governed*; Saskia Sassen, *The Global City* (Princeton, NJ: Princeton University Press, 2001); Aihwa Ong, *Neoliberalism as Exception* (Durham, NC: Duke University Press, 2006); Stephen Castles and Mark Miller, *The Age of Migration* (London: Guilford Press, 2003); William Fisher, 'Doing Good? The Politics and Anti-Politics of NGO Practices', *Annual Review of Anthropology* 26 (October 1997): 439–64; Walden Bello, *Deglobalization* (London: Zed Books, 2002); Seyla Benhabib, *Another Cosmopolitanism* (New York: Oxford University Press, 2006); Christopher Hood and David Held, *Transparency: The Key to Better Governance?* (Oxford: Oxford University Press, 2006).
8. Gabriel Fajn, *Fábricas y empresas recuperadas* (Buenos Aires: Centro cultural de la cooperación, 2003); Julian Rebón, *La empresa de la autonomía* (Buenos Aires: Colectivo Ediciones, 2007).
9. James D. Ingram, 'What is a Right to Have Rights', *American Political Science Review* 102, no. 4 (November 2008): 401–16 surveys the debate.
10. Arendt, *Origins of Totalitarianism*, p. 293, pp. 296–7 and p. 301.
11. Etienne Balibar, 'Rights of Man' and 'Rights of the Citizen', in Balibar, *Masses, Classes, Ideas: Studies on Politics and Philosophy Before and After Marx* (New York: Routledge, 1994), pp. 9–59.
12. Arendt, *Origins of Totalitarianism*, p. 296.
13. Ingram, 'What is a Right', pp. 409–11.
14. Craig Calhoun, 'Belonging in the Cosmopolitan Imaginary', *Ethnicities* 3 (2003): 535.
15. Richard J. Bernstein, 'Rethinking the Social and the Political', *Philosophical Profiles: Essays in the Pragmatic Mode* (Cambridge: Polity, 1986), pp. 238–59.
16. Hannah Arendt, *Between Past and Future* (New York: Penguin, 1968), p. 14.
17. Instituto Nacional de Estadísticas y Censos, *Encuesta Permanente*

de Hogares (Buenos Aires: 2002, 2003, 2004, 2005). By the end of 2003, 25 per cent of workers were jobless; another 10 per cent were underemployed; 35 per cent of those who had jobs now worked in the informal sector. 60 per cent of citizens were poor; another 27 per cent were indigent. Between 1990 and 2005, real wages plummeted by 50 per cent. Inequality reached record-breaking levels, representing the largest transfer of wealth from the lower to the upper sector of society since the 1970s, when data of this type began to be collected systematically.

18. Karl Polanyi, *The Great Transformation*, foreword R. M. McIver (Boston: Beacon Press, 1968).
19. Santiago Fassi and Marcelo Gebherdt, *Concurso y Quiebra (ley comentada)* (Buenos Aires: Editorial Astrea, 2000) for a technical discussion of the new law, especially articles 48, 190 (cramdown); 189, 197 (firm continuity); and 126, 195, 241 (creditors).
20. Laura Vales, 'Un caso testigo para las recuperadas', *Página 12*, 3 November 2008.
21. World Bank, *Latin American Insolvency Systems: A Comparative Assessment* (Technical Paper, 2007), p. 29; Maria A. Rodriguez, *Argentina: May 2002 Bankruptcy Law Changes* (Working Paper, 2002).
22. PI Horacio Esbers, Public Defenders' Office. Factory workers were rarely compensated because the new law reclassified them as investors. According to the law, workers had agreed freely to sell their labour power to factory owners with the aim of making a profit. Premised on neoliberal notions of property rights, this law did not distinguish between wealthy investors who speculated and took financial risks in order to gain, and a salaried worker compelled to sell his labour in order to survive.
23. Esteban Magnani, *El cambio silencioso* (Buenos Aires: Prometéo, 2003), pp. 36–7.
24. World Bank, *Latin American Insolvency*, p. 29; World Bank, *Argentina, Insolvency and Creditors' Rights System* (Technical Paper, 2002), p. 11.
25. Daniel James, *Resistance and Integration: Peronism and the Argentine Working Class* (Cambridge: Cambridge University Press, 1988). Their practice of citizenship was intertwined with populist elements.
26. Fajn, *Fábricas y empresas*, pp. 23–5.
27. 'Fábricas recuperadas y también legales', *Página 12*, 2 June 2011. After fifteen years of acting and speaking as citizens, President Fernández could no longer ignore the factories and enacted a law in support of them.
28. Armando Vidal and Carlo Eichelbaum, 'Luego de un debate tenso, se aprobó la Ley de Quiebras', *Clarín*, 15 May 2002.
29. Jorge Palomar, 'Capital Humano', *La Nación*, 30 June 2002.
30. Pablo Heller, *Fábricas ocupadas* (Buenos Aires: Ediciones Rumbos, 2005).

31. Avi Lewis and Naomi Klein's international box-office hit, *The Take*, was filmed during the first wave of recuperations; it exaggerates the role of leftist parties.

32. Magnani, *El cambio silencioso*, pp. 165–6.

33. See the following editorials in *La Nación*: 'Usurpaciones protegidas', 24 May 2004; 'El dilema de las fábricas recuperadas', 4 March 2004; 'La propiedad privada en peligro', 23 September 2005; 'Nos alcanzará la epidemia de la acción directa?', 12 June 2005; 'Ocupación de fábricas', 11 September 2008.

34. Lavaca Collective, *Sin Patrón: Stories from Argentina's Worker-Run Factories* (Buenos Aires: Haymarket Books, 2007), p. 112.

35. Albert Hirschman, *The Rhetoric of Reaction: Perversity, Futility, Jeopardy* (Cambridge, MA: Harvard University Press, 1991).

36. E. Raúl Zaffaroni, 'El derecho penal y la criminalización de la protesta social', *Situación de los derechos humanos en Argentina: 2002–2003* (Buenos Aires: Comisión de investigación jurídica, 2003).

37. María Rato, 'En los últimos meses surgieron mas fábricas recuperadas', *La Nación*, 13 June 2009.

38. Graciela Moreno, 'El gobierno nacional asumió compromiso', *Veintitrés*, 29 June 2009.

39. Andrés Ruggeri, *Las empresas recuperadas en la Argentina* (Buenos Aires: Universidad de Buenos Aires, 2010).

40. Rebón, *La empresa de la autonomía*, pp. 63–72. This description is of the rank and file; a few of the leaders, including Murúa and Caro, have a history of militancy.

41. Matías Kulfas, 'El contexto económico', *Empresas Recuperadas, Ciudad de Buenos Aires* (Buenos Aires: Gobierno de la Ciudad, 2003), pp. 9–19.

42. Rebón, *La empresa de la autonomía*, pp. 60–3.

43. Pierre Bourdieu, *Acts of Resistance* (Cambridge: Polity, 1998), pp. 82–3.

44. Robert Castel, *From Manual Workers to Wage Laborers*, trans. Richard Boyd (Rutgers: Transaction Publishers, 2002); C. B. MacPherson, *The Political Theory of Possessive Individualism* (Oxford: Oxford University Press, 1962).

45. PI 3, 5, 6, 7. Some workers admitted to experiencing prolonged periods of depression, excessive drinking and bouts of family violence.

46. PI 7, 15, 18.

47. PI 10, 13. 14.

48. Hannah Arendt, *Love and Saint Augustine*, ed. Joanna Vecchiarelli and Judith Chelius Stark (Chicago: University of Chicago Press, 1996), p. 101.

49. PI 4, 9, 13, 14, 21.

50. PI 2; Alejandro Blanco, 'Fábricas recuperadas: otra cara de la resistencia civil', *La insignia*, 14 December 2002.

51. PI 2, 3, 7, 9.

52. Fajn, *Fábricas y empresas recuperadas*, pp. 185–218.

53. 'Crear el espacio para las nuevas generaciones', *Nudos* I, no. 12 (July 2007): 4–6.

54. Ibid.; Mirta Zaida Lobato, *La vida en la fábricas* (Buenos Aires: Prometéo, 2001).

55. Fajn, *Fábricas y empresas recuperadas*, pp. 185–218; Rebón, *La empresa de la autonomía*, pp. 101–6.

56. Horacio Esbers, *Transiciones liminares, ritual y poder; Un estudio etnográfico de las Fábricas Recuperadas* (Buenos Aires: FLACSO, 2009), p. 123.

57. Hugo Ratier, *El cabecita negra* (Buenos Aires: CELA, 1971). The term 'blackie' began to be used in the postwar period when immigrants from the provinces migrated to Buenos Aires in search of opportunities.

58. Norberto Galasso, *Julián Centeya: el poeta de las musas* (Buenos Aires: Corregidor, 2007). 'Laburante' was first used during the interwar period by the poet Centeya to describe skilled, virtuous workers.

59. PI 13.

60. Fajn, *Fábricas y empresas recuperadas*, p. 162.

61. PI with Caro and Murúa.

62. Amalia Gracia and Sandra Cavaliere, 'Repertorios en fábricas. La experiencia de recuperación fabril en Argentina, 2000–2006', *Estudios Sociológicos*, XXV, no. 73 (2007): 156, 175.

63. PI with Caro and Murúa.

64. Esbers, 'Transiciones liminares', pp. 60–2. Yaguané lent Bragado 830 US dollars; Ghelco received 1,500 dollars from Unión y Fuerza, and so on.

65. Rebón, *La empresa de la autonomía*, pp. 50–180, on ideological differences between MNER and MNFR.

66. Modesto Guerrero, 'Eduardo Murúa y la descomposición en las empresas recuperadas' (25 May 2006), http://www.aporrea.org/internacionales/a22077.html (last accessed 27 June 2015).

67. 'El cooperativismo de trabajo se junta para crecer', *Anter*, 26 May 2008.

68. Miriam Tasat, 'Entrevista', *Mundo Docente* (November 2006).

69. Irina Hauser, 'El saber, otra empresa recuperada', *Página 12*, 23 March 2004.

70. The barbed wire fence around the library was placed after someone broke in and stole several computers.

71. PI 6.

72. Carlos Galván, 'Grupo de presos hará ropa deportiva con máquinas de fábrica recuperada', *Clarín*, 14 November 2006.

73. *Hotel Bauen: Síntesis de su historia* (Buenos Aires: Typescript, 2008).

74. PI 18; Javier Lorca, 'Primer Centro de documentación de empresas recuperadas', *Página 12*, 16 July 2007.

75. For list of court cases: Javier Echaide, *Debate sobre empresas recuperadas: un aporte desde lo legal, lo jurídico y lo político* (Buenos Aires: Centro cultural de la cooperación, 2004); Eduardo Fontenla,

Cooperativas que recuperan empresas y fábricas en crisis (Buenos Aires: Colegio de graduados en cooperativismo, 2007).

76. Robert Cover, 'Nomos and Narrative', *Harvard Law Review* 97, no. 1 (1983): 4–68; and his 'Foreword', *Harvard Law Review* 97, no. 4 (1983–4): 18.

77. PI 13.

78. 'El dilema de las fábricas recuperadas', *La Nación*, 4 March 2004.

79. Zoe Brent, *New Labor Struggles in Argentina* (Berkeley: University of California, Undergraduate Thesis, 2006).

80. Karen Ann Faulk, 'If They Touch One of Us, They Touch All of Us: Cooperativism as a Counterlogic to Neoliberal Capitalism', *Anthropological Quarterly*, 81, no. 3 (Summer, 2008): 579–614.

81. PI 6.

82. PI 9; 'Un juez denunció a obreros por impedir su salida del tribunal', *La Nación*, 30 September 2004.

83. PI Esber.

84. Fontenla, *Cooperativas que recuperan*, p. 34.

85. Vales, 'Un caso testigo para las recuperadas'.

86. 'Se renueva el reclamo por la expropiación de empresas recuperadas', *Anter*, 13 February 2007.

87. 'La legislatura porteña sancionó la ley de expropiación definitiva para empresas recuperadas', *Anter*, 1 December 2004.

88. 'De las empresas recuperadas no nos vamos nunca más', *Lavaca*, 26 November 2004, http://www.lavaca.org/seccion/actualidad/1/1118.shtml (last accessed 28 June 2015; formerly http://www.ensantelmo.com).

89. 'Y el fondo para las expropiaciones', *Nudos*, 2, no. 13 (August 2007): 3–5; 'Se renueva el reclamo por la expropiación de empresas recuperadas en la provincia de Buenos Aires', *Diario Hoy*, 13 February 2007. Kravetz's Law has been overturned because the city legislature failed to compensate factory owners as required. These cases are under review in various circuit courts; one of them is slowly making its way to the Supreme Court.

90. Irina Hauser, 'Las fábricas recuperadas hacen política', *Página 12*, 7 September 2003.

91. Ibid.

92. Bernard Manin, 'The Metamorphoses of Representative Government', *Economy and Society*, 23, no. 2 (May 1994): 133–71.

93. PI Kravetz.

94. Abel Zuriano, 'Miguel Bonasso lanza su candidatura', 30 June 2003, http://argentina.indymedia.org/news/2003/06/118258_comment.php (last accessed 28 June 2015).

95. PI Kravetz.

96. Ibid.

97. Arendt, *Between Past and Future*, p. 241.

98. Roberto Salgado, *Empresas recuperadas por sus trabajadores* (Buenos Aires: Universidad de Buenos Aires, 2010), p. 53.

99. Santiago Rodríguez, 'La línea porteña se fija en Olivos', *Página 12*, 21 November 2008; and 'Huellas de las últimas elecciones', *Página 12*, 16 August 2009.

100. Laura di Marco, 'Los nuevos gerentes K y política sin banderas', *La Nación*, 23 March 2008; 'Los saltimbanquis: Candidatos que saltan de partido en partido', *Clarín*, 30 May 2007. 'Diego Kravetz acusado de estafas', the organisation H.I.J.O.S. (por la identidad y la justicia contra el olvido y el silencio; Buenos Aires, 2006) accused Kravetz (and Murúa) of diverting 500,000 US dollars they lent IMPA to pay for his electoral campaign. At the time of writing, this case is in court.

101. Nati Vaccaro, 'Entrevista al Padre Farinello', http://dilo.ws/notas/ Entrevista%20a%20Farinello.htm (last accessed 2 July 2015).

102. 'Quilmes, el escenario que divide en dos al kirchnerismo', *La Nación*, 6 August 2011.

103. Chatterjee, *The Politics of the Governed*, pp. 53–80. A Foucauldian account based on governmentality is unable to make sense of the civil and political practices of factory workers as I have described them.

104. Michael Walzer, *Thick and Thin: Moral Argument at Home and Abroad* (London: University of Notre Dame Press, 1994), p. 4.

105. Calhoun, 'Belonging in the Cosmopolitan Imaginary', pp. 539–41.

106. J. Rogers Hollingsworth and Robert Boyer, *Contemporary Capitalism: The Embeddedness of Institutions* (Cambridge: Cambridge University Press, 1997). 'Flexible specialisation' relies on small and medium-sized firms to generate reciprocal ties among producers, consumers and public institutions. These practices altered public life in north-western Italy, now referred to as the 'Third Italy', in contrast to the 'First Italy' (fordist/corporativist: Turin, Milan, Genoa) and 'Second Italy' (impoverished/clientelist: Sicily, Calabria, Campania).

107. 'Cuando más compartimos más tenemos', *Nudos* I, no. 1 (June 2006): 3.

108. 'Que cada vez sean más nudos', *Nudos* I, no. 12 (July 2007): 13–14.

109. 'Sale a la cancha el Fondo Capital Semilla', *Nudos*, 2, no. 15 (November 2007): 3–4.

110. 'Crear el espacio', 4–6.

111. Martina Noailles, 'Sin traje, corbata, ni patrón', *Sur capitalino* IV, no. 40 (November 2005).

112. Hugo Chávez, 'Primer encuentro latinoamericano de empresas recuperadas', speech, 27 October 2005, http://www.inti.gov.ar/saber como/sc35/inti2.php (last accessed 2 July 2015).

113. 'El MNER aclara sobre encuentro', *Anter*, 16 October 2005.

114. Marian Aizen, 'El astillero Río Santiago vuelve a trabajar', *Clarín*, 24 January 2006.

115. Arendt, *Origins of Totalitarianism*, p. 461.

116. Alexis de Tocqueville, *Democracy in America*, ed. J. P. Mayer, trans. George Lawrence (Garden City, NY: Doubleday, 1969), pp. 118–29, pp. 430–5, pp. 691–3.

117. Hannah Arendt, *Eichmann in Jerusalem: A Report on the Banality of Evil* (London: Faber and Faber, 1963).
118. Thomas Pogge, 'World Poverty and Human Rights', *Ethics and International Affairs*, 19, no. 1 (2005): 2. For a fuller, richer account, see his *World Poverty and Human Rights* (Cambridge: Polity, 2002).
119. Mike Davis, *Planet of Slums* (London: Verso, 2006), especially pp. 17–69 and pp. 151–98.

8 Middle-Classing in Roodepoort: Unexpected Sites of Post-Apartheid 'Community'

Ivor Chipkin

The last thirty years of capitalist development have, especially in what used to be called the advanced capitalist countries, generated paradoxical, if not contradictory trends. The 'great crisis' of 2008 was rooted in an ideological failure. Marching under the banner of the free markets, writes James K. Galbraith, the state permitted the globalisation of finance; the unrestrained growth of financial derivates, tax havens, regulatory arbitrage and the carry trades.[1] In short, state authorities in the USA, in the UK and elsewhere acted as if the market really was a self-regulating mechanism functioning according to natural laws.[2] The result was the first full-fledged credit collapse and debt deflation since 1930. At the very moment that governments in the West were treating markets as quasi-natural (quasi-religious) systems, capitalist firms themselves were often moving in a different direction. Luc Boltanski and Eve Chiapello have documented how in France, in particular, large corporations took on board the anti-capitalist critique of alienation and bureaucracy to develop new models of management and workplace organisation. The paradox is often not sufficiently noted.[3]

This chapter argues that there was another, no less remarkable, shift in capitalism. During the 1970s, but especially from the 1980s, the bundle of rights associated with private property mutated in many countries to accommodate historically non-capitalist modes of social organisation. This chapter will unfold in three parts. In the first section, it argues that there has been an innovation in the rights of private property, especially in the area of residential property. Starting in the 1960s, though only really coming into its own in the 1980s, the rights of private property have been grafted onto a regime of communal ownership. In the condominium (or sectional title estate), individual property rights are exercised in and through a system of collective control and management. During the very period of capitalist ascendancy, in other words, historically non-capitalist forms of sociability were being elaborated from within the very holy ark of capitalism itself, the relation of private property.

Not only has a novel regime of ownership emerged as a legal instrument, but from the 1980s this legal regime has given rise to massive new social phenomena in the USA and increasingly across Asia, Africa and the Middle East. In the second part of the chapter we will see that the condominium or sectional title estate is transforming the urban landscape, generating novel urban constellations that are frequently imagined and lived as anti-suburbs. In other words, we will see that the growth of townhouses is associated with the decline of the traditional suburb as an urban phenomenon.

In 1971 this hybrid property regime came to South Africa in the form of the Sectional Title Act. In the third part of this chapter, we will see that condominiums (or townhouses under sectional title, as they are called in South Africa) have become important sites of uncanny, post-apartheid community. Using the example of Roodepoort in the Johannesburg region, this chapter argues that Body Corporates are elaborating domains of post-apartheid sociality that are largely unrecognisable and even uncomfortable from the dominant, normative tropes of post-apartheid life: non-racialism, cosmopolitanism, constitutionalism.

In summary, this chapter will defend three claims:

1. Sectional Title constitutes a shift or development in the legal form of capitalism.
2. It is associated with material changes to the urban form and the rise of new urban typologies, neither townships nor suburbs.
3. Sectional title regimes have accommodated qualitatively new post-apartheid communities.

The capitalist collective

There has been considerable attention paid to the macro structure of capitalism over the last several decades, usually under the rubric of 'globalisation'. A lot of this work has been concerned with the effects of new information technologies, of developments in the world financial system, the emergence of new markets and cheaper sites of production. Typically, Giddens notes that:

> globalisation is political, technical and cultural, as well as economic. It is 'new' and 'revolutionary' and is mainly due to the 'massive increase' in financial foreign exchange transactions. This has been facilitated by dra-

matic improvement in communications technology, especially electronic interchange facilitated by personal computers.[4]

Apart from these global transformations, there have been key changes in the micro-organisation of capitalism as well. Luc Boltanski and Eve Chiapello's superb study of the reorganisation of the capitalist firm from the 1970s describes a 'new spirit of capitalism' manifest in the transformation of its operations and mechanisms.[5] Driven by crises of production arising from political and social resistance to capitalism itself – class struggle – firms responded by taking on board elements of the anti-capitalist critique associated with the revolts of 1968. Capitalist firms, they write, were:

> receptive to the critiques of the period that denounced the mechanisa-tion of the world (post-industrial society against industrial society) – the destruction of forms of life conducive to the fulfilment of specifically human potential and, in particular, creativity – and stressed the intoler-able character of the modes of oppression which [. . .] had been exploited by capitalist mechanisms for organising work.[6]

The shift to 'networks', the emphasis on 'visionary leadership', on 'self-organisation' and 'autonomy' reorganised work in response to this 'aesthetic' critique of 'alienation'. In the 1980s this analysis of the capitalist firm was extended to an argument about bureaucracy *per se*, so that its force and ultimately prescriptions were deemed relevant to the public sector as well. I have begun to explore how this post-bureaucratic fashion came to dominate the policy arena in South Africa after 1994, and its effects on the integrity and perfor-mance of government departments individually and collectively.

Less well documented, however, are the changes that have occurred to the content of 'property rights' during the period after the Second World War. This deserves attention. Not only do these changes create the legal framework for the emergence of the townhouse phenomenon in the first place, but they constitute a mutation in the private property relationship itself.

In the 1940s in the USA, notes David Hulchanski, one either rented or owned a house, and there were few options in between.[7] Starting in the 1960s, condominium ownership became possible. We get a sense of the novelty of this arrangement by considering it in his-torical terms. The condominium is a form of what Marshall Tracht calls 'co-ownership' – that is, a legal relationship that makes it pos-sible for two or more people (or legal entities) to have equal rights to the use and enjoyment of a property.[8] Historically, co-ownership has been most common in situations of 'tenancy in common' governing property relationships between married spouses (community of property) or within families (joint tenancy). Joint tenancy, for example, was a feudal right designed to prevent the division of landed estates amongst numerous heirs. It was abolished in England in 1925. In the USA, 'tenancy by the entirety' is recognised in twenty jurisdictions and applies between married couples. In situations where a property is owned jointly by a couple, limitations are placed on the ability of either spouse to alienate their portion of the property without the consent of the other. Ownership in 'indivision' is the common law version of 'tenancy by the entirety'. All the legal forms discussed above are designed for situations arising in the family and between spouses. They are all ancient. The condominium, however, is a recent innovation. It extends the logic of such provisions to relations between strangers.

Starting in Puerto Rico in 1958 and then spreading to the fifty US states by 1968, the condominium is a form of home ownership that makes it possible for an individual to own a housing unit without exclusive ownership of the land on which the structure is built and its surroundings.[9] At its simplest, the condominium allows the unit owner possession of the 'air space' in his or her house, while the real estate is owned in common with the other owners. In effect, what home-buyers own of their unit is very modest, essentially from the middle of the brick inwards. Everything else, including gardens, the driveway, the parking area, the backyard, even the exterior of the house itself, is regarded as common property that is owned and managed by the Body Corporate. It thus combines two regimes of property rights in a hybrid bundle. On the one hand, an individual has unique authority to use, enjoy and alienate the dwelling in question; that is, he or she is an owner of property. On the other hand, he or she shares in the ownership of various common spaces and facilities; that is, he or she is a tenant (in common).

In the residential arena, at least, condominiums or sectional title laws socialise private property. Consider the following hypothetical situation. A home-owner in a traditional suburb is distressed by the way that her neighbour neglects to maintain her property. She is concerned that his neglect will discourage potential buyers to the area and thereby bring down the market value of the units there. A home-owner in a townhouse complex has a similar worry. The owner of a neighbouring unit is failing adequately to maintain her property. There is, though, a major difference in the rights of these respective home-owners. In the traditional suburb, unless the neighbour breaks the law, including by-laws, the home-owner has no formal recourse. She could perhaps bring moral pressure to bear. This is not the case in the sectional title arrangement. There, the owner may appeal to the Body Corporate to intervene to discipline the neighbour in question. In other words, it is not enough that the owner in a townhouse is compliant with the law of the land in the way that he or she disposes and uses this property. In the condominium there is an additional obligation. The owner must use his or her property in a way that is both in accordance with national laws and municipal regulations, and compliant with the rules and norms of the collective. This is the first novelty of the condominium: private ownership is subject to collective social control. This collective control ranges from norms of behaviour in the complex even to the aesthetic form of the house or unit in question.

Secondly, the particularity of this collective deserves further attention. Let us return to the example above. In a traditional suburb there is also a form of collective oversight: it comes, as we mentioned, in the form of laws and by-laws. This is the oversight of the state – a collective, in this instance, of citizens with political rights to define the norms of neighbourliness (via an elected municipal assembly). In the condominium, it is not the state that sets the rules of social conduct. Residents, in other words, do not set the rules of the condominium or townhouse estate as citizens. They do so as property owners. The collective in the townhouse is not, in other words, a political community – it is a community produced by the rules of the condominium itself. Therein lies another element of its originality: the collective originates in the regime of private property itself. We have already noted the novelty of this situation in the area of residential property, but it is worth noting its originality *tout court*.

What are the social forms that, historically, arise from the private property relations? Classes, in the strict sense of social groups whose identity is given by whether they own/do not property and/or own/control property, and various kinds of economic organisations of which the firm and the corporation are the most well-known. There are many social institutions that have a transcendental relation to the property form, including the family and the school. These institutions are, at best, conditions of private property. In the other direction there are collectivities that have emerged to manage the social effects of private property or to resist the institution itself. These include trade unions and political parties, corporatist organs in their various forms, think tanks, research foundations, scientific bodies and so on. There is great variety across time and place. None of them is directly generated by the legal form of private property itself, however. In the condominium, the collective is issued from the private property relation itself, by design.

If we say that private property gives capitalism its particular signature as a social and economic system, then a development in this category of rights is not insignificant. It is suggestive of a development within capitalism itself. At least in the residential field, a collective form of capitalism has made an appearance. In an earlier period, Marxists might have seen in this movement the green shoots of socialism. This development is much more surprising, in that it has coincided with the collapse of the Soviet Union and the reported failure of the project of collective ownership.[10]

Major social phenomenon

For all its importance, this change in the character of property rights, starting in advanced capitalist countries and spreading rapidly around the world, has barely received attention in academic or political circles. Tracht notes, for example, the 'historical patterns of change in co-ownership appear largely unexplored in the legal and economic literature'.[11] In the South African context there is no academic literature that this author could find on the topic at all. Yet the emergence of forms of social ownership within the category of private property is not only of legal or taxonomical interest (in the sense of how we distinguish societies and economies). The condominium as a legal instrument has given rise to condominiums as a major social and urban phenomenon as well. The US case is instructive. Let us recall that prior to 1960 there were no complexes or buildings on mainland America owned and managed through the condominium form. By 1980 there were 2,252,835 units – that is, 2.5 per cent of houses or flats in America were condominiums. By 1990 the number had almost doubled to 4.7 per cent, or 4,847,921 units.[12] In Canada, too, condominium units grew rapidly, from zero in 1965 to more than 170,000 units in 1981; that is, 3.3 per cent of all units in sixteen years[13]. There is very little data for the rest of the world.

In South Africa, this property arrangement first became possible in 1971 (Act 66 of 1971), though sectional title estates only gained momentum after 1986, when the Sectional Title Act of that year cleared up ambiguities in the original legislation. The Act provides for the 'division of buildings into sections and common property and for the acquisition of separate ownership in sections coupled with joint ownership in common property'.[14] Between 1988 and 2011 in Gauteng Province alone, and chiefly in Johannesburg and Pretoria, 32,774 sectional title housing *schemes* were registered. The documents that we have from the Deeds Office do not record how many units have been constructed per complex or collectively. In the absence of a recent census, moreover, we do not have accurate demographic data in this regard. If, however, we work on the basis of a conservative estimate of 20–30 units per development, then we can forecast that in Gauteng alone there are approximately a million units under sectional title. If, moreover, we assume that many units are inhabited by young families or young couples or people living alone, in equal proportion, then we can work on an average household demographic of two people per unit (2.3, more precisely). As a rough indication, two million people in Gauteng or 18 per cent of the population (eleven million) live in sectional title arrangements.

The growth of condominiums or sectional title estates is surprising for another reason as well. Their growth is traditionally attributed to their affordability relative to free-hold property. As the South African arm of the international real-estate agency RE/MAX explains, the attraction of sectional title arrangements is threefold: security, affordability and a communal lifestyle.[15] I will return later to the idea that townhouse complexes are sites of community. For the moment, let us note their financial advantages. Unlike freehold properties, RE/MAX continues, where owners pay for their own home insurance and for the upkeep of the garden and exterior of their homes, owners of sectional title units pay an inclusive monthly levy. The levy includes the costs of insurance premiums, maintenance of the common property, wages and salaries of cleaners, security and other staff involved in maintaining the common property, as well as any water and electricity required for the common property. The cost of maintaining pools, tennis courts, communal park areas and clubhouses in the development is shared.[16] Essentially, sectional title living is a way of exercising private ownership of a property, while sharing the costs of maintenance and of communal infrastructure.

Using the language of economists, we can say that individual housing unit prices are kept down because the costs of the land and facilities in common are externalised – that is, shared with other owners. If the values of the units in the complex increase, however, the benefits accrue individually. Owners who alienate their unit for more than they paid for it keep the surplus for themselves. From a strictly economic perspective, the benefits are self-evident. However, when we consider the social aspects of the condominium or sectional title regime – or, more precisely, the social conditions of this economic relation – its strictly economic advantages become less clear.

From a rational choice perspective, the central economic and legal problem arising is this: how can the conflicting preferences and actions of co-owners be co-ordinated so that some owners do not invest in their own properties in a way that imposes costs on their co-owners, and/or underinvest in projects whose benefits are shared with others?[17] This is the problem of the commons. In cases of the condominium or of sectional title, the law provides an instrument to deal with the problem of externality. It imposes a legal obligation on co-owners to make decisions communally; that is, through the Body Corporate (as it is called in South African law). Rules governing the composition of the Body Corporate and defining the norms of social behaviour in complexes, including granting this committee the right to impose social and economic sanctions on owners, are central to sustaining the property relation. The fact that the officers of the Body Corporate must be elected and that they must take decisions democratically is not intended to serve a democratic purpose. It is designed to maximise co-ordination between owners.

Hulchanski observes that 'by its very nature it [a condominium] involves a communal environment requiring each tenant-owner to yield some individual rights for the sake of achieving harmonious management of the common element and of the project as a whole'.[18] Or as a South African estate agent put it: 'Management, maintenance, co-operative environment, levies and rules all require some level of understanding, acknowledgement and commitment to make a scheme functional and efficient.'[19] Indeed, writes another, 'owning sectional title property can be highly profitable if your Body Corporate is well managed and maintained. There is a direct relationship between the state of affairs of your Body Corporate and the property value of your section.'[20] In this sense the townhouse complex requires a literal social contract between owners; not so much to deliver them from the State of Nature, but to protect the value of their individual and collective assets.[21]

Within the sectional title complex, the market value of residential units is dependent on the quality of the social relations between neighbours. What matters is the ability to make binding collective decisions. When social relations are not harmonious, the value of the property is at stake. The first problem arises when some of the residents in a complex are not owners but tenants; that is, they rent the unit from an owner-tenant. There is a structural conflict between owners and tenants at the best of times. Tenants relate to the property which they rent as a 'use value'; that is, it is a place of shelter and/or a home. It has no exchange value from their point of view. In contrast, for an owner, a property has a use value when he or she lives in it, but it also has an exchange value. The exchange value of a unit is related to its use value in this way: its price on the market is affected by the manner in which it has been maintained, that is, handled as a use value. A tenant only has an interest in maintaining the unit or using it well to the extent that it increases his or her pleasure. He or she does not live in it with a view to its actual or future market value.

Under sectional title, these inherent problems are exacerbated. One of the remedies that an owner has vis-à-vis a tenant is the termination or non-renewal of the contract between them (even if, depending on the jurisdiction, this remedy is more or less difficult to achieve). Yet in the case of a sectional title regime, the risk of a bad tenant is externalised. In other words, somebody else's bad tenant may have a negative effect on the prestige, appearance, orderliness – that is, value – of the complex as a whole. The only remedy that the Body Corporate has in these cases is via the owner of the unit – tenants have no representation there. If, however, the owner, for whatever reason (including being far away or dependent on the rental income) is loath to act, then the costs of the bad tenant are borne by all.

If this is the normal state of affairs, the riskiness of the condominium arrangement is amplified in the South African context (or for that matter, in any context where there has been widespread social conflict). Hence, some writers have reduced townhouse complexes to 'security villages'. In Lindsay Bremner's evocative phrase, Johannesburg has become a 'city of walls'[22] where the image is at once metaphorical and methodological. In her essays on her Johannesburg, the closest we get to these complexes is to the gate. The only residents that we hear of are the security personnel who control access to what is inside. Yet the wall, its electric fences and technologies of surveillance exclude as much as they include. Townhouse complexes – or the vast majority of them, as we have seen – are not luxury estates. They must be distinguished by more than wealth or class. Their relationship to the traditional garden suburb is visibly different.

A new urban geography: townhouses as non-suburbs

What we have in the townhouse complex is a spatial and especially urban form constituted through a particular regime of *governance*. As such, the complex and the landscape that it produces are unlike the traditional suburb. This is why the townhouse or condominium is not a further development of the American Levittown. This phenomenon of post-World War Two America consisted of mass housing schemes intended for American servicemen and their families. After the war, the US government made a subsidy available to former military personnel that incentivised private developers. The most famous of these was the company Levitt and Sons. What was distinct about these developments was that houses were built according to a modular formula to reduce their costs. There were usually only two or three designs from which to choose. In the 1980s, under the auspices of the developer Schachat Cullum, South Africa acquired many Levitt-type suburbs. In Johannesburg, suburbs from Blairgowrie and Bordeaux to Helderkruin and Windsor Park were built on this model:[23] modest houses on their own stands that were available in a limited number of design variations.

This modular or repetitive architectural form is certainly a key aspect of the townhouse phenomenon. Yet there is a difference. Levittowns reproduced a traditional municipal relationship. Home-owners related to the municipality as separate individuals in a bilateral relationship with the city, be it as citizens or as consumers of services. This is precisely the character of the suburb. It is not simply a spatial phenomenon, but a political relationship between citizens (organised through the family) and the state (represented by the municipality). This is the classically liberal social contract.[24] In contrast, the condominium or the sectional title complex instantiates a new kind of social contract. In the first movement there is a collectivisation of individuals and households. In the second movement there are multiple contracts between the collective and sometimes the state (in the form of the municipality), sometimes simply other complexes and a myriad of private companies offering traditionally state services (companies offering policing, developers providing bulk services and road maintenance).[25] This is a landscape that is more uncanny than it is neoliberal. At the moment when the logic of capitalism comes more and more to configure the physical environment and subject social relations to its property regime, it yields not a society of individuals but one organised as communes of a special kind.

Wealthy estates like Featherbrook or Eagle Canyon or Leopard Creek on the West Rand are attempts to recreate an idealised version of the South African suburb of the 1960s. They contain large houses on their own stands, not separated by walls or fences. They are places of idealised domesticity where children are free to roam and explore in safety. In Roodepoort, they are also overwhelmingly 'white' spaces. In Featherbrook, for example, less than 10 per cent of families are black. In this sense, luxury townhouse estates are enclosed suburbs. This is what Benjamin Christopher Stroud calls the suburban promise – 'that home ownership and living close to the land will make you a better person'.[26]

Consider the following discussion with 'P'. She is a resident of Featherbrook Estate, for a long time the benchmark of a security estate. She recalls arriving in Johannesburg from Durban and settling with her husband in Weltevreden Park, an established suburb in the North West of Roodepoort.

We moved to Weltevreden Park [. . .] and we had a lovely home, with beautiful six foot walls all the way around it. The usual [security features]: sparks on the wall and alarm system and the whole trip. I was in this house with my daughter who was only 3–4 years old at the time and 'M' [her husband] travelled. He was away three nights a week. I was a bit of a baby on my own, so I used to lock myself in the bedroom at night with my child, with my daughter and lock the passage doors and switch the alarms on. Then 'C' was born [her second daughter]. I used to have the cam-cords [security cameras] as well in their room.

'P' eventually tells her husband she can no longer live like this. 'I am absolutely petrified on my own,' she admits. They eventually buy a house in Featherbrook. Since then, she says, they have 'never looked back'. They love Featherbrook estate.

Featherbrook fulfils the suburban promise that Weltevreden Park did not. 'I think', she explains, 'that from the point of view of raising children, on an estate you can't compare it to anything. [W]hen I was growing up we used to walk everywhere. We would, after school if we wanted to go the beach, we went to the beach. Or if you wanted to go to movies, you hopped on a bus and you went into town. Children don't have that freedom [today].'

In Featherbrook, however, children 'have a little bit of freedom'. 'They can get on the bus to go and visit their friends, or they can go for a ride. My daughter likes to run. She goes for a run every afternoon and I don't have to panic. I don't have to worry. It's been absolutely amazing for us.'[27]

Therein lies the paradox of the estate. Its artificiality – walls and electric fences, surveillance cameras and regular armed patrols – is seen to permit a more natural life, one oriented towards the outdoors and where family relations are unmediated by fear. Featherbrook and estates like it are contemporary versions of the traditional suburb.

Ongoing ethnographic research by Liezemarie Johannes and Federica Duca finds that social life is overwhelmingly organised around a gendered division of labour. Men are fathers and bread-winners. They leave the estates in the morning and return in the evenings. Women are mothers and homemakers. They look after the children. Given that domestic work is mostly handled by a housekeeper, women are free to participate in the wide selection of activities available for them on the estate; ranging from cooking classes, to 'scrap-booking' to dancing and yoga.[28] Federica Duca has found, furthermore, that woman frequently begin meeting from lunchtime. Drinking (usually white wine) can continue throughout the afternoon.

When Betty Friedan revitalised American feminism in the 1960s with the publication of *The Feminine Mystique*, she described women living in post-war suburbs; probably Levittowns. Expecting to find fulfilment as wives and mothers, they were inexplicably unhappy, burdened with a 'problem that had no name'.[29] In American fiction of the period after the Second World War, especially from the 1970s, the suburb is frequently portrayed as 'perilous': its families are breaking apart, children die, girls are abducted, the streets are not safe.[30] Suburbs are bleak and dangerous, reflecting, Stroud suggests, disillusionment with the suburban promise. Yet it is less perilous than it is duplicitous. It promises genuine family, but delivers something else[31].

It is not surprising, therefore, that the counterpoint to the suburb was, or used to be, the township; at least places where sounds, things and people mixed and intermingled in apparently authentic ways. Descriptions of Sophiatown in the 1950s are exemplary in this regard. It is diverse, from its landscapes (shebeens and slumyards and courtyards) to its cosmopolitan society (workers, rural immigrants, gangsters and liberal whites). It is a place which produces genuine things, from the images of Gerard Sekoto, to marabi music and the tickey-draai, musical genres that were combined to produce the distinctive sound of township jazz.[32]

This is why it is important to distinguish between the luxury estates and the average townhouse development. The complexes that form the object of this report are frequently lived as *non-suburbs*, as urban spaces that are unlike the suburbs in which many of their residents grew up and from which they have recently come. We will see too that their appeal also lies in not being like the township. This is why if we reduce all walled complexes or closed-off streets simply to the phenomenon of 'gated community' or 'security village', we simply cannot see that a new urban geography is emerging in front of our eyes[33].

Middle-classing in Roodepoort

There is another reason, however, to move beyond the complex gate. Not only are townhouses (under sectional title) phenomena of a concession to collectivism in modern capitalism, not only are they new urban constellations that preview a post-suburban landscape, but in the South African context they are also important sites of post-apartheid community – even when these forms of community are not easily recognisable from the promise, say, of non-racialism.

Roodepoort forms the Western edge of the Witwatersrand, a distinctive east–west series of hills and linear ridges with shallow valleys and rolling country to the north. Clive Chipkin notes that the names of Boer farms, often mispronounced by English-speakers, provided a vivid sense of *locale*, many with watercourse or river eye suffixes:

spruit, fontein; some with *koppie, kloof* or *krans* to designate high ground. *Roodepoort*: the gap or portal through the red rock face.[34]

The Main Reef Series, the main line of sedimentary gold, is south of the ridges, nicely parallel in an easterly direction. Here gold mines and compounds with their industrial and labour adjuncts were linked historically by the Main Reef Road – the major communication route for gold production and the creator of urban nodes east and west of Johannesburg.

Following closely the northern edge of the Witwatersrand, the suburbs of Wilgeheuwel and Ruimsig are portions of what was originally the farm Wilgespruit. Until recently they largely consisted of small agricultural estates, nurseries and horticultural plantations.

Over the last decade, especially since 2003, tens of thousands of townhouse units have been built on this land, forming a dense residential wedge between Johannesburg's two main, western axial routes, Hendrik Potgieter Boulevard and Beyers Naude Avenue in the north.

Milky Way was one of the first large-scale townhouse developments in the Roodepoort area. Built and financed by Genesis Projects in 2003, the cluster development consists of thirty-one complexes comprising 957 units. They average thirty units per complex, ranging between nine units and fifty. The director of Genesis is a young man, Charl Fitzgerald, who was formerly an estate agent operating in the Wilgeheuwel and Honeydew areas. His fortune was made on the basis of an acute insight; that there was a large market of young South Africans with little or no savings yet with formal employment. Moreover, they were seeking to leave the suburbs and townships they were born or grew up in, in favour of new, more *modern* settlements. Genesis took advantage of the lax conditions for originating bonds in South Africa to offer units at attractive prices and, best of all, with the option of not having to put down a deposit.[35]

The aerial photograph in Figure 8.1 shows the scale of development in the area between 2000 and 2006. There is a key aspect of these developments: private developers installed much of the urban infrastructure, from roads to storm-water systems and the electrical network. Most of the streets around and between complexes were built and named by the original developer (Genesis Projects), and their current legal status is unclear. They are unmarked, and the Johannesburg Road Agency does not service them. If Milky Way becomes a Home Owners Association in terms of the law, then these streets will be designated private thoroughfares.

In the 2006 image in Figure 8.2 there are site excavations on either side of Nic Diederichs Avenue, where it meets with Hendrik Potgieter Boulevard. Today there are a number of 'warehouse' shops there, mostly dedicated to home improvements and home decoration: Penny

Figure 8.1 An aerial photo, courtesy of the City of Johannesburg, of the area around the intersection of Hendrik Potgieter Boulevard and Nic Diederichs Avenue in 2000.

Pinchers, Timber City, Bathroom Bizarre, @Home, the Lighting Warehouse, Mr Price Home, UFO Furniture. The competition is fierce, yet the market is large. Timber City, a hardware supermarket chain, sells everything from timber roof tresses to three-inch nails. The shop on the corner of Hendrik Potgieter Boulevard and Nic Diederichs Avenue is one of the largest in the country.[36] It supplements an older Timber City store in Roodepoort. A new Penny Pinchers/Timber City combination store has been built along Hendrik Potgieter Boulevard, a few kilometres from the one near Milky Way.

Castra is one of thirty-one complexes that make up the Milky Way constellation.[37] It has twenty-nine units that sell for between R550,000 and R650,000. They vary in size, but even the two-bedroomed units are less than 100m². Fifteen of the units (approximately half) are occupied by tenants, and the remaining fourteen by owner-occupiers. The complex is also socially diverse. In June 2011 (when many of the interviews quoted in this chapter were conducted), almost 50 per cent of units were inhabited by black families, and this number has continued to grow. There was a wide range of languages spoken including English, Afrikaans, Zulu, Tswana, Hausa, Portugese and Ndebele. It was mixed in term of national-

Figure 8.2 An image of the same area in 2006.

ity, and also in terms of South African regions. Some residents came from far afield, including large coastal cities and small inland towns. There were nuclear families and many women living alone or with friends. There were openly gay couples. Some households included practicing Muslims, Christians and Hindus.

It became strikingly clear during the interviews that residents in Castra had very little contact with each other. When asked whether she interacts with her neighbours, a resident named Mrs Khumalo first laughs and then replies, 'No [. . .] In Castra everybody keeps to themselves [. . .] There are boundaries, you know, it's their living space, don't go and intervene [in] people's places.'[38]

All respondents made similar observations about the lack of social life in the complexes. Neo, the wife of a well-known DJ, commented:

> Another thing I've noticed is that the more we stay in areas like Castra, the less we socialise. It's not the same as in Kwa-Thema, where you will know the person staying three streets away from you. It is very different here. You come home and you box yourself in. There is no socialising. Yes, you greet your neighbour every now and then [. . .] I have been here for two years, but I know absolutely nothing about my neighbour or his family.[39]

Gavin and Lauren, a coloured couple from Port Elizabeth, also contrasted the deeply convivial world of their childhoods to their current living environment:

We grew up in Port Elizabeth [. . .] and the culture was so different when we moved to Joburg. I mean we did not have high walls, electric fences and all that [. . .] In Port Elizabeth you make friends so easily, even when you meet on the road people are a lot more open. Here, they are aloof, they connect on a superficial level, not on a deeper level; they are very distrusting [of] each other.[40]

Navarshni, a young Indian woman, represents the extreme of this social isolation. She starts by contrasting Castra to an idyllic elsewhere, this time Durban, from where she has moved recently. She speaks without full stops. 'It's very different because I'm from Durban. There you'll always be meeting people all the time and here the only person that I talk to is my neighbour [. . .] I live alone, so I'm always scared. I'm paranoid. I check my door and windows ten times before I go to bed. And when I read the paper I freak me out when I hear about the things that happen around here.'[41] The fact that she lives so close to others, however, is no comfort to her.

'There is no sense of being so close to other people that you feel more secure. If you shout out people would not hear. I had an incident a couple of months ago. It was about one o'clock in the morning and my alarm went off. My neighbour wasn't around that weekend. I refused to get out of my room. I was trembling.'[42] Eventually Navarshni called the head of the Body Corporate, Madame E., who advised her to call her armed response company.

If residents of Castra report high levels of anonymity between themselves, they all report regular encounters with the head of the Body Corporate, Madame E. Madame E. constitutes the exclusive point of communal interaction in the estate. The context is frequently disciplinary.

Like other complexes, Castra has a set of rules and regulations devised by the Body Corporate. One of the key tasks of Madame E. is to police life in the complex accordingly. It is a role she takes very seriously. Residents are fined for making too much noise – the fine is added directly to their levy. They are penalised for not closing the electric gate immediately after entering. They are fined for any infringements of the communal spaces, including for not maintaining their 'private' gardens.

Madame E. explained:

If somebody complains about your noise level, I will step in. Okay, I will go to you and I will say I had a complaint. Cut down your music, control your guests. Please. I'm not going to come down here again. If I come here again I'm going to switch off your lights, half an hour later, if it's worse, I just switch your lights off.[43]

Every resident we interviewed had a story about this uncompromising regulatory environment. Gavin and Lauren, for example, remembered being fined R500 for allowing their guests to follow them into the estate without first shutting and then re-opening the gate. 'I don't know how she does it but she finds out.' Lauren continued: 'You can't fix your car in the complex, you can't make so much noise. Like animals, *ag* it was Chevonne's rabbit [her daughter's]. We couldn't have a rabbit. They don't allow animals.'[44]

Navarshni recalls her first day in the estate:

> The estate agent gave me a remote control and I came in the complex and the gate wouldn't open when I had to go out [. . .] So I parked my car on the side because I didn't know anything about the rules. I saw this lady and she said, 'What are you doing? If you park your car there you'll get a R500 fine for this.' I said I want to go out but the remote is not working [. . .] She said 'I don't know how you are going to get out because residents of Castra know that [. . .] nobody is allowed to let you out.'[45]

Apart from fining residents for transgressions of the regulations, Madame E. also 'names and shames' them in newsletters. Lauren explains: 'She would put it in a letter that so and so was fined because of this and this or with the noise or [someone] didn't wait for the people to close the gate.'[46]

DJ Talso referred to the 'very strict rules':

> Look, the lady *waka mo* [on this side], the one that's staying behind us, she's the chairperson, and she is very strict with the rules. She tends to think that she owns the place [. . .] I'm sure she is in [her] sixties or late fifties. And we come from a different time you know. And with my background, white people don't make the best impression. So when things start I will always say, hey *wena* [you], *ska bua lenna okare*, you know, 1973 [don't talk to me as if it's 1973][47,48]

It is far from obvious, however, that Madame E.'s enforcement of the regulations is motivated by racism. 'Well,' says Lauren, 'people think somehow she's a racist because of the way she handles things in a situation [. . .] She's not racist. I know she treats everybody like that.'[49]

In 2008 a young, Afrikaans-speaking male, at his wits' end with the disciplinary regime in Castra, played an April Fools' joke on the head of the Body Corporate. At some cost and with much effort, he prepared posters, all in red, which he displayed on the entrance gate to the estate. The first was of a hapless man hanging from the gallows. The second bore an image of a skull and crossbones, with the text 'Warning: Whingers get shot!' underneath. The third poster was a mock official notice. It read: 'Welcome to Castra, You are entering a cemetery, offenders [of the rules] will be made to hug the electric fence for an hour.'

The rigid, even oppressive insistence on communal by-laws and regulations, while apparently petty, is informed by a geopolitical sensibility. Madame E. frequently refers to the *multinational* character of Castra. Discussing Nigerians, for example, she explained: 'The actual thing is that they are a different nation.'[50] When asked if there are other 'nations' in the estate, she replied:

> Uh, there are so many [. . .] I've got Sotho, I've got Zulu, I've got Muslim, Italians, Portuguese, er [. . .] [pauses] staunch Afrikaans, very staunch Afrikaans. Obviously, and then I've got number 16 which is actually [pauses] a Nigerian.'[51]

In this traditional taxonomy, each nation evidences fixed 'national' traits. Nigerians deal drugs. 'When you got a Nigerian living in your complex,' she explains, 'you can scare yourself out of your skin because [the] things they get up to is absolutely pathetic. They will actually do drugs right in front of your doorstep.' Madame E.'s stereotypes are uncompromising. The tenants in the unit in question said they were from Malawi. Madame E. would have none of it, insisting they were Nigerians.

Madame E. is also inclined to invoke the term 'black' to discuss common 'black' behaviours, manifest, irrespective of particular 'national' identity. She describes what she calls 'quite a funny incident':

> We were doing the garden up at the top there and he [a black man] came in with such speed that I just had time to jump out of the road [. . .] Okay he stopped before he could open the door, I opened the door, I grabbed him, I slapped him [. . .] It was hilarious, I will tell you something now, ever since that day I could be anywhere in the street, he will greet me, he will respect me because I stood up to him. *That's where as a white woman, white people you don't show that you are scared of them, even if you are shaking you don't.*[52]

She discussed Afrikaans-speaking residents in equally stereotypical fashion, saying, 'Listen, staunch Afrikaans is Afrikaans okay. Just like a little *boertjie* can be, when I say to you I am Afrikaans I am Afrikaans and I will not speak your language, I will not do anything else.'[53] Madame E.'s national and racial stereotyping serves other purposes besides discrimination or segregation. From her perspective, what makes 'respectful' relations possible under conditions of social diversity is the law; that everyone is subject to the same regime of by-laws and regulations. In this regard, she is uncompromising. This is nothing less than a version of the social contract, not so much between individuals as between nations. Castra is a United Nations of residents.

In Castra, however, the social contract is not a mythical, foundational act of political union. It is sustained on an hourly/daily basis through the predictable, even and transparent enforcement of the regulations. In other words, it is possible because the Body Corporate has sovereign power and is prepared to exercise it, either through the law (fines) or through violence (a 'good *klap*'), if need be. Hence, the function of Madame E.'s racial/national taxonomy is instrumental rather than political. It helps her devise strategies, as a woman, as a white person, to enforce the common law. There is an acute irony in this. Authority, undergirded by a performance of being white, is invoked as a strategy to integrate the complex or subject its residents to a common regime of civility.

The strict disciplinary regime and the lack of social interaction might make Castra sound like an unhappy place to live, yet interviewees uniformly expressed ambivalence about the Body Corporate. On the one hand, it is annoying. On the other, it provides a peaceful and safe living environment. In DJ T.'s terms, it helps people 'learn their boundaries'.

Even when some respondents compare Castra with their convivial place of origin, the distinction is not between *community* and *alienation* or between *warmth* and *coldness*. The strict, regulatory environment makes the estate a peaceful, quite, relatively safe place to live. What Castra makes possible is privacy. In other words, the comparison is between community and *privacy*.

'I love the rules,' Navarshni tells us, 'because I like the peace and quiet and the neatness of the place.'[54] DJ T. says similar things:

> One thing I really liked about [Castra] was that you have your own yard that is not that attached to somebody else. In Ferndale we had a guy above us. Eish, this guy was noisy [. . .] After experiencing that guy, we appreciate that [Castra] is so peaceful and there is no-one around.[55]

Busisiwe has been explaining to the interviewer that she misses Soweto.

> Castra is very restricted [. . .] I feel like I need a place where my kids will be able to play and actually enjoy the play and ride their bikes and, you know, feel like they're at home, so now they're restricted, my son just sits and watches TV.[56]

Then she interrupts herself:

> I can never go back to Soweto. It's fine that I have a home day, but I can never go back and live there [. . .] I think because I'm getting used to the peace, I'm getting used to the quiet, I'm getting used to the cleanliness, I'm getting used to having my own space and privacy.[57,58]

In Soweto,

> everybody knows everybody's business. [When] you buy a new car, everybody knows. It's like you bought a new car and other kids that you grew [up with] don't have cars and they've got three kids and you only have one kid and because you have a car you think you are educated, you are better than others, and so on and so forth and this one is not talking to you, and this one [. . .] says this [. . .] In Soweto when you go to the shop, they know what you going to have tonight, she is buying that and that, that is what they're having tonight [. . .] and when you don't go to the shops, they say you don't go to the shops because she works in Sandton and this and that [. . .] [At least] here I know, I get home, I get into the house, it's my own space and safe.[59]

The search for privacy, here, is not just a personal preference. These testimonies of home as a haven from the world of family and kin are remarkably consistent across all residents of the complexes. They speak to a growing tension in the domestic and social realm. Kate Philips's work on structural unemployment in South Africa shows convincingly that formal economy wages are functioning as a social wage. With such high rates of unemployment, nearly every household has at least one unemployed member. Under such conditions, those with a regular income face constant financial demands from members of their immediate and extended family for support.[60] This is the situation that many of the Roodepoort households are trying to manage. On the one hand, young households are 'middle-classing', that is, trying to live a middle-class standard of living, with all the material and lifestyle choices that this implies. On the other, they are embedded in networks of solidarity that tie them in to responsibilities to parents and siblings, grandparents, uncles, aunts and cousins and distant family. Their ambivalence to the townhouse environment speaks to this tension. On the one hand, they miss the conviviality of township life. On the other hand, the location of the Roodepoort complexes gives households a break from the financial and other claims of extended family, neighbours and community. It allows them to conserve some of their income for savings and for consumption. The townhouse complexes are thus key elements in the process of becoming middle class. They help to situate these respondents in a long, transnational history of middle-class emergence.[61]

Castra does not simply offer privacy, however. The character of the estate as a highly regulated environment (quiet, neat and safe) conforms to a standard of what some interviewees defined as 'respectable'. Respectability is a term used to perform two types of differentiation. In the first place, it allows young, newly married couples to indicate that they have matured into responsible adulthood. In this sense, living in Castra is a generational term. In the second instance it is a term that designates class membership: that the respondent has left, or is not part of, the (noisy, chaotic) working class.

Stacey recalls:

> You have to sign the rules before you are allowed in here. And on the door they stipulate what you are allowed to do and what you aren't allowed to do. So it's basic things like the noise level, your garden. You're not allowed to put Wendy-houses or anything like that.[62]

A Wendy-house is a wooden, prefabricated structure that is sometimes attached to the main building, usually as an additional storeroom.[63] They are common in some estates. In Castra they are strictly forbidden. 'I think that something that worries Madame E. about Wendy-houses,' Gavin explains, 'is that it will be outside and people will be putting their stuff outside.'[64] He, too, favours this arrangement. He likes the fact that Castra is respectable.[65]

That the rules are sometimes onerous should not obscure what they permit. As long as the Body Corporate is sovereign, potential disputes and conflicts between residents are mediated through a legitimate authority via an impersonal set of rules and regulations. Residents are able to negotiate diverse and complex histories of family, of community, of race, of gender in their own space, and in an environment that enables them not to have to full control over each other.

Conclusion

A common social world is emerging in Roodepoort that has paradoxical features. On the one hand, white and black South Africans (terms used here as shorthand for those who formerly had and those who did not have full South African citizenship) are entering a *common world*. On the other hand, racial and ethnic solidarities have not weakened. Entry into a common world is not associated with new patterns of sociability that transcend race or ethnicity.

Racial and ethnic heterogeneity in the Roodepoort complexes, as important as it is, does not adequately capture the significance of this emerging *common world*. Apartheid was not only a system of racial (and class) domination. It was also a system of government and regulation, one that splintered the administration of peoples and things according to hundreds of parallel and overlapping agencies and departments. Even if there were some isolated, mixed social spaces (Hillbrow, Yeoville), there were no mixed institutions of social citizenship. It is this reality that is evoked in political metaphors like Thabo Mbeki's image of 'two nations' and, before that, in theoretical expressions like the 'articulation of modes of production'[66] or, more generally, in images of the 'bifurcated' state.[67]

Relative to this recent past, a common world represents a place where former citizens and former subjects share not simply a common geography, but a space where they are equally subject to a regime of rules. These are post-apartheid spaces, though not postcolonial ones. The term 'postcolonial', that is, has come to be associated with an ironic smile. It suggests that the period chronologically after the colonial one, that is, after the departure of the white/European colonial power, represents not so much a break with the past (an 'after') as the continuation of the colonial present.

The common world in Roodepoort is not one where violence is absent. Far from it: daily life in the townhouse complexes is frequently oppressive, and there are sometimes hostile encounters between residents and officials of the management body. For all that, the violence of the complex is qualitatively different to that associated with apartheid or colonialism more generally. Even if it is regarded as sometimes fierce, the violence of the Body Corporate is the violence of modernity. It is the ally of rules and regulations that are widely accepted as general and legitimate. Residents (mostly) submit to the regulatory environment, not because they have been cowed into submission, but because they desire the rule itself. They might object to the way the rule is applied (unfairly, for example, or inconsistently) but they seldom object to the rule itself. This was not the case with apartheid laws.

The objection to apartheid (except perhaps from apartheid legalists) was *not* that it was implemented unevenly or unfairly. The problem was with the law itself. The law was evil.[68] We might recall the arguments about the legality of Nazi law after the Second World War.[69] In his famous critique of moral positivism in 1958, Fuller argued that the incorporation of evil aims in law undermines its very foundation, namely, the claim to command fidelity to law.

When a system calling itself law is predicated upon a general disregard by judges of the terms of the laws they purport to enforce, when this system habitually cures its legal irregularities, even the grossest, by retroactive statutes, when it has only to resort to forays of terror in the streets, which no one dares challenge, in order to escape even those scant restraints imposed by the pretence of legality – when all these things have become true of a dictatorship, it is not hard for me, at least, to deny to it the name of law.[70]

Unlike apartheid law, which often lacked the character of law, the Body Corporate is a space of legality. In the complex, residents are subject (and subject themselves) to a regime of rules and regulations that have coherence and are logical. They are regulations to the extent that they are publicly announced, that they do not contradict themselves and that they do not require 'forays of terror' to exercise. Even if some Body Corporates implement these rules in an arbitrary way, the rules themselves have what Fuller called a certain 'internal morality'.[71] In this sense, townhouse complexes in Roodepoort are spaces of legality: they subject their residents to a common set of rules as a condition of social order. This is precisely what apartheid law could not achieve. The implementation of apartheid laws worked against the possibility of good social order – their very exercise required bare violence against black South Africans (humiliation, forced removals, censorship, detention without trial, execution, war).

Apartheid laws have since 1994 been progressively repealed. This is not enough to constitute a regime of legality, however. It is not enough for laws and rules and regulations to be issued from duly constituted bodies or agencies for them to be legal. What matters, in addition, is how they are administered. In this regard, in the period since 1994 the exercise of laws and rules and regulations is frequently *ad hoc*, uneven and inconsistent. There are numerous reasons for this, including the limited reach of the South African state itself (aggravated by policy choices at the beginning of the transition and the politicisation of the public service by the ruling party). Taken together, however, the state itself has not realised social order and in some cases generated new forms of disorder. We might say that the South African state is not delivering, and perhaps cannot deliver, post-apartheid modernity.

This study, however, has found post-apartheid modernity in an unlikely place. Township complexes in Roodepoort, organised as condominiums or in terms of the Sectional Title Act, are sites of common place legality or the legality of what I have called *ordinary life*. Townhouse complexes elaborate social order in the day-to-day transactions of their residents. They are thus post-apartheid locations in an ordinary sense.

What has rendered these spaces invisible to academic and official notice is that they have been constituted in unexpected places (Roodepoort!) and through unexpected instruments. They are products of an innovation in capitalist property relations, and not that of the Constitution or that of government policies and actions. Post-apartheid modernity has been elaborated in Roodepoort through the further development of capitalism. Spaces of order have been constituted through a regime of (private) property. For those who looked forward to a post-apartheid society tending towards non-racialism or socialism or participatory democracy, or, at least, subject to the morality of the Constitution, these are surely awkward terrains. They are post-apartheid terrains nonetheless.

Notes

1. James K. Galbraith, 'Introduction to the Paperback Edition', in Galbraith, *The Predator State: How Conservatives Abandoned the Free Market and Why Liberals Should Too* [2008] (New York: Simon & Schuster, 2009), pp. xi–xii.
2. See Paul Krugman, 'How Did Economists Get It So Wrong?', *The New York Times*, 2 September 2009.
3. Luc Boltanski and Eve Chiapello, *The New Spirit of Capitalism* (New York: Verso, 2005).
4. Anthony Giddens, *Runaway World: How Globalisation is Reshaping our Lives* (London: Profile Books, 2002), p. 10.
5. Boltanski and Chiapello, *The New Spirit of Capitalism*, p. 168.
6. Ibid., p. 201.
7. J. David Hulchanski, 'The Evolution of Property Rights and Housing Tenure in Post-War Canada: Implications for Housing Policy', *Urban Law and Policy*, 92 (1988): 135.
8. Marshall E. Tracht, 'Co-ownership and Condominium', in *Encyclopedia of Law and Economics* (Cheltenham: Edward Elgar and University of Ghent, 2000), p. 62.
9. Hulchanski, 'The Evolution of Property Rights', p. 140.
10. The shopping mall, that temple of high capitalist consumerism, also has an unexpected socialist provenance. In 1956 Victor Gruen, an Austrian socialist and former student of the modernist designer Peter Behrens who had moved to the USA in 1938, invented the shopping mall. He designed Southdale Shopping Mall in the USA, to recreate in America the experience of the European arcade. Gruen enclosed shops and department stores in an air-conditioned mall with the intention of realising a utopian experiment in master-planned, mixed-use community, complete with housing, schools, a medical centre, even a park and a lake. People would come together to shop, drink coffee and socialise in otherwise alienated American suburbs. Coffee shops and other com-

munal places would become, he hoped, animated by people discussing the major ideas of the day. See Jeffrey Hardwick, *Mall Maker: Victor Gruen, Architect of an American Dream* (Philadelphia: University of Pennsylvania Press, 2004).

11. Tracht, 'Co-ownership and Condominium', p. 65.
12. US Census Bureau, 1994.
13. Hulchanski, 'The Evolution of Property Rights', p. 142.
14. Sectional Title South Africa, Sectional Title Act and Prescribed Management Rules, http://www.sectionaltitlesa.co.za/2010/08/free-body-corporate-forms/ (last accessed 30 June 2015).
15 15. RE/MAX, 'Sectional Title Versus Freehold Ownership', http://www.remaxonehundred.com/News/Sectional-title-versus-freehold-ownership/504/ (last accessed 8 March 2011; subsequently removed). Similar information can be found at http://igrow.co.za/buying-property-in-a-sectional-title-scheme-2/ (last accessed 2 July 2015).
16. RE/MAX, 'Sectional Title Versus Freehold Ownership'.
17. Tracht, 'Co-ownership and Condominium', p. 63.
18. Hulchanski, 'The Evolution of Property Rights', p. 140.
19. Sayed Iqbal Mohamed, *The Challenges of Sectional Title in the Low-Cost sector*, http://www.academia.edu/10570944/The_challenges_of_sectional_title_in_the_low-cost_sector (last accessed 30 June 2015).
20. Sectional Title South Africa, *Sectional Title Act and Prescribed Management Rules*.
21. We might recall that for Rousseau the social contract was always an instrument designed to protect the integrity and value of property, so that property owners were necessarily the privileged beneficiaries of the political community.
22. Lindsay Bremner, *Writing the City into Being: Essays on Johannesburg 1998–2008* (Johannesburg: Fourthwall Books, 2010), p. 203.
23. Before them were Glenanil and all those suburbs with Glen in the name: Glenvista, Glendower and so on.
24. See Jacques Donzelot, *The Policing of Families* (Baltimore, MD: John Hopkins University Press, 1997).
25. See Federica Duca, 'Good People, Good Weather. Living, Working and Vacationing in a Golf Estate', *PARI Short Essay* (forthcoming).
26. Benjamin Christopher Stroud, *Perilous Landscapes: The Postwar Suburb in Twentieth-Century American Fiction* (Charleston, SC: BiblioBazaar, 2011), p. 6.
27. 'P', personal interview with the author, 7 June 2011.
28. Duca, 'Good People, Good Weather'.
29. Betty Friedan, *The Feminine Mystique* [1963] (New York: W. W. Norton & Company Inc., 1997).
30. Stroud, *Perilous Landscapes*, p. 145.
31. I suspect that this sentiment goes a long way towards explaining why the suburb is barely treated in the South African literature. In *Johannesburg: The Elusive Metropolis* (Durham, NC: Duke University Press, 2008) a collection of essays edited by Achille Mbembe and Sarah

Nuttall on the city that was first published as a special edition of the journal *Public Culture*, the topic scores a brief mention in an essay on literatures of the city. In *Blank: Architecture, Apartheid and After* (Rotterdam: nai010 publishers, 1999), the book edited by Judin Hilton and Ivan Vladislavic associated with the very successful exhibition on South African architecture, there is no discussion of the suburb as an urban form at all. There is no mention, for example, that 'House Martiennsen', built by the architect for himself in 1942 and one of the first major statements of modern movement architecture in South Africa, is situated in Greenside, an area in the northern suburbs of Johannesburg. Yet surely the relationship of the house to the suburb is one of its key tensions?

32. Clive Chipkin, *Johannesburg Transition: Architecture and Society from 1950* (Johannesburg: STE Publishers, 2008), p. 204.
33. We might call them *quarters*, derived from the French 'quartier', to distinguish them from suburbs but also to allude to their more communal organisation.
34. Chipkin, *Johannesburg Transition*.
35. Charl Fitzgerald, personal interview with the author, 17 August 2010.
36. Mr Mare, personal interview with the author, 28 March 2011.
37. The name of the complex has been changed to protect the identities of the inhabitants of the complex. Castra, like the complex's real name, refers to a star in the Capricorn constellation.
38. Mrs Khumalo, personal interview with the author, 23 June 2009.
39. Neo, personal interview with the author, 12 July 2009.
40. Gavin and Lauren, personal interview with the author, 4 July 2009.
41. Navarshni, personal interview with the author, 8 August 2009.
42. Vashni, personal interview with the author, 8 August 2009.
43. Madame E., personal interview with the author, 22 July 2009.
44. Gavin and Lauren, personal interview.
45. Navarshni, personal interview.
46. Gavin and Lauren, personal interview.
47. DJ T., personal interview with the author, 12 June 2009.
48. DJ T., personal interview.
49. Gavin and Lauren, personal interview.
50. Madame E., personal interview with the author, 3 September 2009.
51. Ibid.
52. Ibid.
53. Madame E., personal interview with the author, 22 July 2009.
54. Navarshni, personal interview with the author, 29 July 2009.
55. DJ T., personal interview.
56. Mrs Khumalo, personal interview.
57. Ibid.
58. Ibid.
59. Mrs Radebe, personal interview with the author, 23 June 2009.
60. Kate Philip, *Inequality and Economic Marginalisation: How the*

Structure of the Economy Impacts on Opportunities on the Margins (Pretoria: Trade and Industry Policy Strategies, 2011).

61. Jürgen Kocka, 'The Middle Classes in Europe', *Journal of Modern History*, 67, no. 4 (December 1995): 787.
62. Stacey, personal interview with the author, 6 July 2009.
63. Wendy houses have their own history, beginning as dolls' houses for aristocratic families in Edwardian England. Lutyens created a full, large dolls' house for Queen Mary (wife of King George V), complete with furniture in minute detail, all to scale. Even the doors opened and closed. Rich families called in carpenters to build small but habitable miniature houses in their gardens – called 'Wendy houses' after the character of Wendy in J. M. Barrie's *Peter Pan*. Somewhere in the 1960s or 1970s a local South African firm started making prefabricated dolls' houses that became storerooms for garden equipment and overflow goods. These degenerated into pre-made stores. They still retained the name Wendy house, from the 'age of respectability'.
64. Gavin, personal interview with the author.
65. Ibid.
66. Harold Wolpe, 'Capitalism and Cheap Labour Power: From Segregation to Apartheid', *Economy and Society*, 1, no. 4 (1974).
67. Mahmood Mamdani, *Citizen and Subject: Contemporary Africa and the Legacy of Late Colonialism* (Princeton, NJ: Princeton University Press, 1996).
68. Some qualification is required here. Not every law passed during the apartheid period was an apartheid law in the sense that it was an element of a system of racial domination. In other words, 'apartheid laws' refer to those laws whose basic purpose was racial domination and discrimination. Other laws, including those pertaining to inheritance or contract or public administration, etc., had racial exclusions, though their purpose was not racial domination itself.
69. H. O. Pappe, 'On the Validity of Judicial Decisions in the Nazi Era', *Modern Law Review*, 260 (1960): 263.
70. Lon L. Fuller, 'Positivism and Fidelity to Law', *Harvard Law Review*, vol. 71 (1958).
71. Ibid., p. 645.

9 Democracy and Capitalism in Europe, Brazil and South Africa

Peter Wagner

Economic developments are often seen as following their own logics: driven by scientific-technical innovations, such as in the three 'industrial revolutions'; by market laws of competition and utility, as assumed by the economic sciences; or by profit-seeking expansion and commodification, as maintained by neo-Marxist critical theory. There is a broad consensus today that we have entered a new phase of capitalism since the 1980s, and all three approaches have been employed to understand the recent transformation of capitalism and the specific dynamics of this new phase. To emphasise the inherent logics of an industrial-capitalist-market economy, however, entails downplaying the impact of other social phenomena on economic developments. Such selective emphasis has long been enhanced by disciplinary specialisation in the social sciences and by the assumption that 'modern societies' are functionally differentiated and permit each 'subsystem' to operate on its own terms. Nevertheless it is surprising that such emphasis is maintained in a context in which 'the economy' is marked by dysfunctions, generating crises, poverty, inequality, unemployment and the devastation of the earth, and in which calls for political action to put the economy back on a societally beneficial track are widely voiced. After all, we supposedly live in an era of 'democratisation'; and if democracy means collective self-determination, it should be possible, in principle, to regulate economic action with a view to collective benefit.

As we shall see, current analyses of capitalism and democracy tend to argue that the posture of 'yes we can' is nothing but misplaced political voluntarism and that political claims today are merely another case of 'we want but we cannot', to use a common Spanish expression. This chapter, in contrast, argues that democracy matters and can bring about transformations of capitalism, though not without unintended consequences. It will start, in the first section, from observations on a recent turn in the European – or 'Northern' – analysis of capitalism away from political considerations and back towards the emphasis on the economy alone. A critical discussion of this shift shows that its limitations arise through its temporally and spatially confined perspective. As a remedy, a longer-term historical perspective shows how democracy transformed capitalism (as discussed in the second section); and a global perspective, as discussed in the third section, demonstrates how the current weakening of European democracy was enabled by spatial displacements of production. These displacements, however, do not have the same political consequences across the globe. Looking at the examples of Brazil and South Africa, it will be shown in the fourth section how vibrant democracy co-exists with current capitalism under certain conditions. These observations allow a more systematic comparison in the fifth section of the relations between democracy and capitalism today. The chapter concludes with reflections about the current tension between democracy and capitalism.[1]

From varieties of capitalism back to the logic of capital

Since the late 1980s the question of whether there is an alternative to capitalism has been a central concern of critical analysis. The collapse of existing socialism seemed to confirm Margaret Thatcher's provocative claim that 'there is no alternative'. An important focus of discussion then became the idea that, in the apparent absence of alternatives, there might at least be 'varieties of capitalism', some of them distinguishable from one another also in normative terms. The phrase belongs to David Soskice, but the idea is found in many accounts of the 1990s.[2] A distinction was repeatedly made between the 'organised' welfare capitalism of continental Europe, especially Germany, and the liberal market capitalism of the Anglo-Saxon kind.

Within this debate, Peter A. Hall and David Soskice directly addressed the question of whether the variety of capitalisms could be maintained under conditions of globalisation. Their provisional answer was that it could. Such optimism has since largely disappeared in the North. To give just one example: Wolfgang Streeck was one of the protagonists in the debate about sustainable alternatives to capitalism as well as a champion of 'the German model', characterised by strong and intelligent trade unions, an economy successful on the world market and a political landscape in which social democracy, though not always in government, remained influential and in which neoliberalism was marginal. But now Streeck develops a perspective on capitalism which remains conceptually open but in which, empirically, he only recognises the forward march of neo-liberalism with its individualistic-instrumental emphasis on profit and greed, and in which other social bonds, institutional forms and normative orientations have disappeared and are unlikely to return – just as Marx and Engels had it in *The Communist Manifesto* of 1848.[3]

What is significant for present purposes is that Streeck's analysis is accompanied by observations about the weakening of democracy as a consequence of the transformation of capitalism. The connection is made in two steps: the capitalism of the postwar period, called 'democratic capitalism',[4] was nationally organised, with elected national governments taking responsibility for Keynes-inspired economic steering; it was, thus, compatible with democratic expectations. The democratic idea of the sovereignty of the people identified the sovereign with the nation; this nation in turn was thought of as a community of responsibility, in which organised solidarity was an obligation.[5] However, globalisation and neoliberalism released the capitalist economy from the fetters of the nation-state, which meant, in a first step, that governments could no longer meet expectations of economic regulation and welfare-state redistribution. In Europe, the transfer of competences from elected national governments to central banks and other regulatory agencies such as those of the European Union is an institutional expression of this farewell to democratic steering. In a second step, precisely because of this, citizens turn away from democracy: elections change nothing, therefore participation is pointless. Falling turnouts or an increase in votes for protest parties with weak programmes are expressions of this 'disenchantment with politics' or 'citizen disaffection'.[6] Some analyses assume a fundamental transformation of politics, in which the democratic element has disappeared and been replaced by co-operation between oligarchic-technocratic elites.[7]

The transformation of nationally embedded, regulated Keynesian capitalism, based on industry and on standardisation and homogenisation in both production and consumption, into global neoliberal capitalism, in which services, in particular financial services, creativity and flexibility gain in importance, is accompanied by a political transformation, in the course of which a competitive-party democracy, with a measure of fit between the will of the electorate and national government policy, gives way to a technocratic politics in which political programmes are diluted and in which voters are asked merely to approve measures to which there is no alternative. That at least is the impression given by current academic and political commentary – and it is hard to deny that European political and economic reality corresponds closely to such an image.

For this interpretation, the link between economic and political developments is conceptually necessary because otherwise one would have to ask why, under democratic conditions, there was not a more effective opposition to neoliberal capitalism. The concept of 'democratic capitalism' suggests in the first place that democracy and capitalism are compatible. But the notion of a 'crisis of democratic capitalism' suggests that this compatibility has many preconditions, and cannot be maintained in the long term. It is assumed, quite reasonably, that the latest transformations of capitalism bring with them a transformation of democracy. But here the economic transformation appears as the plain triumph of the ever more effective logic of capital, and the political transformation as nothing other than the weakening or even rejection of democracy.

This account raises more questions than it answers. It is shortsighted in two respects, temporal and spatial. It is historically limited in that it ignores or forgets the origins of the dual transformation. To be sure, there is in Europe a crisis of democratic capitalism, but this is also a democratic crisis of capitalism. That is, the shift from Keynesian to neoliberal capitalism cannot be explained by the inherent logic of capital; it has to be placed in the context of the political and social demands on the reproduction of capital.[8] Secondly, the account neglects the fact that the prescribed exit from the crisis has not only spatial consequences – so-called globalisation – but also global presuppositions. In other words, neither was social-democratic Keynesianism an endogenous achievement of North-Western Europe, nor can its crisis be understood without referring to worldwide political and economic change. The regional limitation of this account will become especially clear if one can show that the relationship between democracy and capitalism is fundamentally different in other parts of the world. In what follows, an attempt will be made to correct the temporal and spatial short-sightedness of such analysis of capitalism. New questions will then be raised about the challenges facing current democracy and capitalism.

The democratic crisis of European capitalism: a historical perspective

Current analysis concentrates on the decline of democratic capitalism, but does not ask how capitalism became democratic and what democratic embedding means for the reproduction of capital. Yet in many European societies capitalism developed before the introduction of universal suffrage – taking this as a formal criterion for the existence of democracy. Such democracy had been on the political

agenda at the end of the eighteenth century as much as free trade
and the abolition of serfdom and slavery were, which made possible
the expansion of wage labour (they were co-original, as Habermas
would say). But in many countries it was introduced only after the
First World War. On closer inspection one can see that European
elites were discussing the introduction of democracy around 1800,
but that they consciously rejected it.[9] So how does one explain the
breakthrough to an egalitarian-democratic idea in the European
societies of the early twentieth century?

Capitalism is an economic form with two characteristics that are
important for answering this question. Firstly, it is based on the
idea – which we have called elsewhere the economic problematic
of modernity[10] – that material human needs are best satisfied indirectly, mediated through the interests of producers of commodi-
ties on a market.[11] Secondly, in capitalism there is a distinction
between a group of economic subjects who decide over production,
and another who are subject to the decisions of the first – for brev-
ity's sake we will adopt established terminology and call them the
dominant and dominated classes. For two main reasons this makes
probable a discrepancy between economic potential and actual need
satisfaction: exploitation in the sense of an appropriation of the
products of labour by those who make production decisions; crises
of market self-regulation, which lead to less being produced than is
possible, or to the destruction of products that remain unsold. The
awareness of such a discrepancy leads then to critique.[12] Whatever
its content, critique will be likely to include the demand that all who
are affected by this state of affairs should be involved in measures to
improve it. When stubborn social problems appear under conditions
in which people are excluded from government, egalitarian-inclusive
self-determination – democracy – is prima facie a convincing means
of tackling the problem in an appropriate way. Such reasoning obviously needs to be made more historically nuanced, but in general
terms it allows us to understand the democratic tendencies at work
in a capitalist economy.

Nevertheless, the foregoing account only explains the demand
for democracy of the dominated class. It does not explain why the
dominant class should accede to it. To a certain extent the force of
argument may be adduced – under conditions of modernity there is
a need for justification[13] – but this alone is insufficient. Other conditions must be in place; we can conceptualise this in ways that are
compatible with the idea of a 'logic of capital'. In historical terms,
the dominant class has been tied to the dominated class in two ways:
firstly, industrial production requires a great number of workers who
under conditions of wage labour must be willing to work, albeit F. W.

Taylor tended to separate motivation from results and Max Weber claimed that modern capitalism was no longer dependent on such motivation. Strikes were historically as effective as they were because withdrawal of labour struck at the heart of capitalism. Secondly, the consumer capitalism that emerged in the twentieth century required workers who purchased the products of their own labour, and this in turn demanded both corresponding purchasing power and the will to acquire the goods produced. Fordism combined mass production with increased wages in order for these conditions to be met.

Because of this dependence on workers, the dominant class could not resist the demand for democracy in the long run. Its introduction enhanced the legitimacy of capitalism and at the same time ameliorated the problems of profitability associated with the prior regime of accumulation.[14] However, Fordism brought with it new problems, which were often associated with democracy: voting rights for workers would lead to policies that went far beyond what was functionally desirable. After the First World War there was a fear of a socialist or communist revolution, and in general the concern was widespread that the granting of social rights might bring about a major socio-political transformation. At the beginning of the twentieth century the idea of democracy was closely associated with a high level of political mobilisation, and with social demands which derived from class struggle and which were opposed to the interests of capital. The move away from supposedly immature democracy and into authoritarian or totalitarian regimes during the 1930s was, among other things, a first attempt by the elites to solve this problem.

After the Second World War democratic political forms were re-established in different ways, a process that can be understood in the light of the experiences with class struggle and civil war. The West German case is exemplary: political organisations with extreme programmes were banned, and the interaction between parties and interest groups was organised in such a way as to avoid the dominance of particular interests and to foster the search for consensus. Democratic theory adapted itself to the new reality: the egalitarian form of democracy was for the first time in history the starting point for all thinking; at the same time, the problem of the limitation of political passions was central.[15] Direct citizen participation outside elections was undesirable, and it was expected that conflict resolution through representative organisations would have a filter effect, so that only reasonable points of view could influence decision-making.[16] This model proved effective until the late 1960s, when it appeared to have reached its limits.

The decade from the late 1970s until the late 1980s was marked by a series of events that at first sight appear unconnected but which led to an unforeseen great transformation in so-called 'modern societies'. We will name a few of them here and add some more in the next section. Significant for changes in the relationship between democracy and capitalism in European societies were: the student revolt of 1968 and the return, in 1968 and 1969, of spontaneous labour protest that was not directed by trade unions; the first post-war recession in the early 1970s, which affected almost all societies, called into question Keynesian demand management, and led to the 'fiscal crisis of the welfare state'[17] that cast doubt on the sustainability of redistribution through taxation; and finally the electoral victories of Margaret Thatcher and Ronald Reagan in Britain and the USA, through which monetarism and supply-side economics became government policy and trade unions were seen as opponents of governments.

This sequence of events can be presented as follows: the demands of workers and students express a crisis which can no longer be solved through the co-ordinated action of trade unions, employers and the state. Because the crisis persists and is even deepened by counter-measures such as wage increases, which fuel inflation, radical solutions such as monetarism gain increasing acceptance, until they become a central plank of government policy. The protests that stand at the beginning of this sequence of events can be described partly as democratic pressure on the profitability of enterprises,[18] and partly as an expression of discontent with alienating living and working conditions. But at the end there is neither the socialism that was hoped for or feared in 1919, nor the destruction of democracy of the 1930s, but the transformation of both capitalism and democracy.

In the first half of the 1970s the crisis was perceived as such by elites and critical thinkers alike. A report of the trilateral commission referred to a 'crisis of democracy', while Jürgen Habermas spoke of a legitimation crisis.[19] But this crisis was not dealt with in the way that was anticipated. The processes that are often summed up as economic globalisation – namely, according to circumstance, neoliberalism, deregulation, structural adjustment or shock therapy – mean that capitalism is freed from its embeddedness in national institutions and thereby from the grip of democratically raised demands. That far, the analysis by Wolfgang Streeck and other critics of today's capitalism in Europe appears correct, and their distance towards the varieties of capitalism thesis is understandable in so far as, for instance, European banks have opened themselves to the global financial market and major European firms have relocated their production – though not their R and D – or adapted themselves to global conditions of production.

My disagreement with these critics lies less in the analysis of

European outcomes than in the account of the causes. The presentation so far should have made clear that the recent transformation of capitalism cannot be attributed, at least not exclusively, to capitalism's internal dynamics. Neither the classical Marxist account of the limitless pursuit of profit, to which Streeck surprisingly appeals, nor regulation theory's more historically nuanced account of changes in regimes of accumulation, enable us to grasp the latest changes in capitalist practice. In order to understand both the temporality and the form of that change, the dynamics of democracy needs to be considered as well. The effective exercise of democratic rights had threatened the profitability of European capitalism and provoked transformative responses by the elites.

The longer-term historical perspective is important, beyond the time-span of the recent politico-economic transformation. In contrast to the interwar years, in which democracy still had few passionate advocates, there has been a widespread consensus about the desirability of democratic political forms since the Second World War and particularly since the 1980s. For this reason the democratically provoked crisis of profitability in Europe – in contrast to Latin America, for instance – did not lead to the cancellation of democracy, as it did in the 1930s. Since this exit option was not open, the flight from democracy's grip, its hollowing out rather than its destruction, provided an alternative for the elites.

Democracy and capitalism: a global perspective

Flight from the grip of democracy presupposes that there is another place – another spatial constellation – from which capitalist enterprise can be carried out more profitably. Let us add to our list of events during the 1960s and 1970s: at the beginning of the 1970s the postwar monetary system, with the US dollar as its leading currency, collapsed; the so-called oil crises of 1972–3 and 1979 shifted the terms of trade for a central raw material to the disadvantage of the industrial countries; US industry was unprepared when Japanese businesses became globally competitive, and other East Asian countries followed suit. From this point onwards, one began to speak of a 'new international division of labour',[20] in which societies for which the adjective 'industrial' made less and less sense no longer had a monopoly on industrial production, as 'newly industrialising' or 'threshold' countries came to the fore, countries that were at a competitive advantage over the old industrial countries, notably due to lower wages and, often enough, to the absence of democracy.

Why is it worth rehearsing these well-known facts? The point is not only to show that the current discussion about the omnipresence of Chinese industrial products on the world market, or about emerging economies or BRICS (Brazil, Russia, India, China, South Africa) has had a thirty-year long preamble. They suggest that the events of the 1980s do not signal the beginning of globalisation but presuppose an already-existing global political-economic constellation.[21] Neoliberalism and deregulation did not create globalisation; rather, these policies exploited a situation of globalised production, responding to problematic democratic pressures by circumventing them.

During the 1980s the full significance of the new global situation was not yet appreciated in Europe: it was assumed that only the less desirable forms of production – with poor working conditions and high environmental impact – would leave Europe, where high levels of qualification would continue maintaining competitiveness and living standards.[22] In stark contrast to the current situation, relocation of production and migration of labour were seen quite positively, enhancing the comparative advantage of the organised variety of capitalism. It should be added that this strategy presupposed that national capacity for action would be maintained, and that even under the new conditions the sedimentation of European/Western domination, which had gone on for a century and a half, would continue to generate a significant difference in the quality of life and work.

Today it is clear that this line of thought rested on false assumptions, and not only economic ones. For these expectations to be met, all or most of the participants would have had to commit themselves to the project, without considering the exit option.[23] But just this did not happen: deregulation opened up the possibility of exit, and gradually – in continental Europe rather slowly – banks and productive enterprises made use of it. We could say that the bourgeois class bade farewell to the project of societal development.[24] Marx, of course, had never assumed that they would participate in it. In *The Communist Manifesto* he and Engels attributed to them the destruction of everything national. But in fact, the economic development of Europe was carried out by a combination of state and economic elites, joined by the trade unions in the 1920s.[25] Since the 1980s and 1990s, European economic elites have abandoned this project.

But the hollowing-out of nationally constituted democracy in Europe stands in contrast to developments in other countries. Post-soviet elites in Russia appear to pursue booty capitalism using national resources under political conditions in which opposition is barely able to express itself. In China the persisting elites pursue an economic development project in which, on the one hand, they themselves acquire unprecedented personal wealth and, on the other hand, national resources are used for wealth creation at large, albeit with enormous damage in the form of exploitation of workers and nature. These are variants of capitalism that the debates of the 1990s took no account of. Moreover, the three remaining BRICS societies – Brazil, India and South Africa – are capitalist societies as well as high-intensity democracies, and so especially instructive for the following discussion. Because my knowledge of India is insufficient, I will limit my observations to Brazil and South Africa.

Democracy and capitalism in Brazil and South Africa

Neither of these societies has been democratic for long. In the twentieth century Brazil experienced the oligarchic Vargas regime (1930–45) and, following a rather short interim, a military dictatorship. One can only speak of a stable parliamentary democracy since 1985, reinforced by the constitution of 1988. South Africa was founded as a state in 1910, since when its population has been segregated according to skin colour and through massive restrictions on political participation of the non-white inhabitants, formalised and reinforced to the point of exclusion through the apartheid regime after 1948. Since 1996, however, the Republic of South Africa has had an egalitarian democratic constitution.

Both societies have undergone an industrial-capitalist development marked by comparable special circumstances. Until the 1920s the Brazilian economy was dominated by large-scale agriculture, maintained originally by slavery. In order to achieve national industrialisation the Brazilian government embarked on a long-term policy of import substitution, made possible by customs barriers. South Africa underwent early industrialisation through gold and diamond finds in the late nineteenth century. The more widespread industrialisation that this stimulated assumed a nationally distinctive character, inspired by developments in other commonwealth countries – in particular Australia – and strengthened in the era of economic sanctions against the apartheid regime.[26] At the end of the twentieth century, in both countries openings to the world market were undertaken in parallel with the advent of neoliberalism. In the last decade both have achieved rapid economic development, which made possible their membership of the BRICS group.

Thus, today, both societies are as democratic and capitalist as European societies. But both their contemporary democracy and contemporary capitalism differ markedly from those of a European stamp, and thereby raise new questions about the relationship between democracy and capitalism. I will have to be content here with a schematic analysis, whose main aim is to raise just these questions.

In contrast to Europe, Brazil and South Africa have witnessed a strengthening rather than a weakening of democracy during the last two decades. Some might want to call the introduction of egalitarian-inclusive democracy and of universal civil and political rights in the constitutions of 1988 and 1996, already mentioned, a 'catching-up' revolution (paraphrasing Jürgen Habermas) with little conceptual or historical significance. However, a closer look suggests that this is not so. Both countries have been governed now for some time by political majorities oriented towards societal transformation. In South Africa, the African National Congress, the most important organisation of the national liberation movement, has governed the country in alliance with the trade unions and the communist party since 1994, with near-two-thirds majorities. In Brazil, candidates of the Workers' Party (PT) have won presidential elections four times in a row. Since 2002, the federal government is formed by the PT in alliance with other parties.

In both cases the government coalitions are a product of the resistance to repressive regimes – the apartheid regime in South Africa and the military dictatorship in Brazil. Members of today's governments have experience of armed resistance, arrest, imprisonment and torture: the South African president Jacob Zuma was a member of the liberation army of the ANC, spent ten years in prison on Robben Island with Nelson Mandela, and was then in exile until the ANC was legalised; the Brazilian president Dilma Rousseff was active in a small revolutionary guerrilla group and was tortured in prison. The resistance, at times violent, was connected in both countries with the mobilisation of broad sections of the population for democratic and social demands, in conjunction with the trade union movement and parties such as the South African Communist Party and the Brazilian Workers' Party. Many members of Brazilian governments over the past decade come from protest movements and movements for participatory democracy which began in the Porto Alegre Social Forum and then achieved worldwide attention.

Despite increasing critique and opposition, the government alliances in both societies continue enjoying considerable support, as the 2014 election victories of Dilma Roussef and Jacob Zuma show. In contrast to Europe, where governments are frequently voted out of office because they not only take no measures against worsening standards of living but often bring them about by budget cuts and tax increases, the PT as well as the ANC can still rely on – though diminishing – electoral majorities. It should be emphasised that party competition and media freedom prevail in both countries, and that the political opposition can count on considerable sections of the economic elite and of the media. Electoral success, therefore, is not attributable to 'incomplete' democracy, as the 'North' is often inclined to assume about the 'South'. Governments are dependent on the votes of a majority of the electorate, are aware of this dependence, and have taken protests seriously enough to gain elections.[27]

However, these governments, which are not only democratically legitimated but arose out of democratic and social movements – and here is the second objection to the generalisation of observations about Europe – leave the capitalist structure of the national economy intact and encourage an opening to the world market. They are therefore sometimes described by leftist critics as 'neoliberal'. In Latin America this is an accusation often levelled with the supposedly more radical governments in Venezuela, Bolivia and (sometimes) Argentina in mind.[28] In South Africa it was directed in particular at the economic policy known as 'Growth, Employment and Redistribution' (GEAR), introduced by Thabo Mbeki, Zuma's predecessor. But it is often unclear what the term 'neoliberal' is meant to mean. It is evident that the PT and ANC governments try to avoid policies that threaten their credibility in the context of a capitalist world economy.[29] To the extent that this world economy operates under neoliberal conditions, such national policies are doubtless compatible with the neoliberalism of the external economy. At the same time, both governments are pursuing a – at least until very recently – relatively successful growth policy led by a democratically legitimated interventionist state that is committed to pursue its objectives without jeopardising its relationship to the world market.

A core component of both government programmes is an expansionist social policy, guaranteeing to the lower income strata benefit payments to a hitherto unprecedented degree. In Brazil the *Bolsa Familia* programme provides poor families with continuous cash payments on condition that they send their children to school and attend to their family's health. Begun under the PT President Lula, it now reaches thirteen million children. In tandem with this the minimum wage has been raised, and economic growth itself has created more and better jobs. As a result of these developments an internal economic demand has emerged in Brazil, which makes the country – which predominantly exports primary sector goods – less dependent on fluctuations in the world economy, as shown by developments since 2008. Similar processes, though on a lesser scale, can be observed in South Africa. The index of social inequality has hardly altered, attributable to the fact that the social and political improvement in the living conditions of the poor population has been statistically effaced by the growing wealth of a small stratum, including now parts of the black population. But fourteen million South Africans now receive social grants, alleviating poverty. In both countries the social structure has changed enormously during the period in which these governments have been in office. There are now middle strata whose living conditions have improved markedly. In Brazil this is discussed under the heading of 'the new middle class', in South Africa under that of 'the black middle class'.[30]

Brazil and South Africa in comparison with 'the North'

Here there is no place for a more detailed account than this short and schematic overview; such an account would have to address criticisms that have been directed at government policies, and not least the question of these policies' long term sustainability.[31] Instead, in an equally short and schematic final section, we will compare these Southern experiences with those of the European welfare states, and then draw some general conclusions about the relationship between democracy and capitalism. The main theme of these reflections will be the mixture of scepticism and reserve with which the Northern analysis of capitalism approaches the South: are these currently successful societies merely catching up with something that began in Europe much earlier, and so destined to run up against the same limits? Or are there reasons to assume that Brazil and South Africa are asking political and economic questions – and finding answers – that are new, and thereby of both analytical and practical interest to the North?[32] I will restrict myself to five remarks.

Firstly, the European welfare state is no model for the link between capitalism, democracy and solidarity.[33] The post-fascist reorganisation of society was based on concertation at the expense of participation, according to a model that had already been developed in the Netherlands in the first half of the twentieth century.[34] The promise of social security was made on condition that high levels of participation were renounced; in the 1970s this was known as the union of 'welfare state and mass loyalty'.[35] During this period these societies did not develop a political culture in which it was understood how to devise common political and economic goals under restricted circumstances. The current crisis makes this clear. In Brazil and South Africa, by contrast, social solidarity programmes, modest though they are, are driven by a democratic movement. Social transformation is the result of a democratic transformation whose radicality is often underestimated. In South Africa for the last twenty years the government has been shaped by a majority population that was hitherto completely excluded from 'conventional' political participation. In Brazil, political discourse has until very recently – until the demonstrations of June 2013 – been dominated in quasi-hegemonic fashion by what was a radical leftist grouping founded only thirty years ago, which had its first successes in connection with social movements and local participative democracy. True, electoral stability in both countries has also been the result of an 'exchange' of votes for social policies. But the strong democratic impulse which characterises today's politics distinguishes both countries from Europe.

The strength of this impulse, secondly, can be gathered from the fact that it has started to turn against the government alliance. The ascent of PT and ANC to government had raised very high expectation of radical and rapid social transformation. In South Africa there is a rather widespread sense that these expectations have been disappointed. In Brazil, in turn, some of the recent protest urges to go further, whereas other parts rather call for a change of direction, towards moderation. In both cases, clearly, long years in office have led to an exhaustion of political energy and to widespread criticism and protest. But the fact that government practices are challenged in election campaigns, in the media and in the streets gives testimony to a continuity of high-intensity democracy rather than of a crisis of democracies still in search of consolidation.

But what, thirdly, about the limits of transformative politics in these societies? For Brazil it needs to be kept in mind that the PT, now accused of corruption, adapted to common political practices because it never had a majority in parliament and needed to keep political allies on board. In South Africa the ANC 'inherited' a state apparatus that dealt rather efficiently with the needs of a minority but was ill-suited for equal treatment of the whole population. The amount of politico-administrative transformation that is needed is often underestimated in the critique – also the scholarly critique – of government performance. Nevertheless there are good reasons to assume that the transformation strategy on which the PT- and ANC-led governments embarked has reached its limits. A main component of this strategy has been the satisfaction of the demands voiced by their core electorates, whether material or institutional. Given the historical legacy of oppression and injustice, such strategy is highly justified and should not be denounced as mere interest politics. But in the pursuit of this strategy, the alliances renounced both a broader transformation of the state apparatus and a public debate about the kind of society one wants to live in, beyond general statements that suffer from lack of concreteness. Stating this, though, one has to bear in mind two further features of the situation.

Fourthly, namely, unlike in Europe in the postwar period, there is no economic and social model that can be simply applied in a technocratic way. European societies, inspired by Keynesianism, rested upon a full-employment economy, with one full-time salary enough to sustain a family, and a level of redistribution that financed social security, education and health. Such a productivist conception of economic and social policy cannot be applied to Brazil and South Africa. In South Africa the official rate of unemployment is 24 per cent. In Brazil the rate has fallen from 10 per cent a dozen of years ago to 6 per cent today, and thus is lower than in many European countries. But in both cases the figure for those who are actively seeking formal waged work hides the far greater number of those who do not participate in the formal labour market. For this reason too, poverty reduction is at the top of the social policy agenda, along with the question of the long-term link between democracy, economy and solidarity. For European societies, in which this once stable link is at breaking point, the 'Southern' discussion should be a matter of great interest.

Fifthly, Brazilian and South African politics face challenges that European elites in the postwar decades did not recognise or did not want to recognise, but which, given the prominence of democracy in both societies, are unavoidably high on the political agenda. I just want to mention three core issues: firstly, today's Brazil and South Africa emerged against a background of oppressive regimes. For this reason, the repression and injustice of the past and the resulting – and justified – political expectations and demands of the present are a key component of current societal self-understanding. In Europe, in contrast, the dominant view is that the past – centrally Nazi totalitarianism and war – has successfully been settled through the creation of liberal-democratic polities allied with one another. Some current debates in Europe, though, show that this is an erroneous assumption, for instance in the emerging North–South cleavage. Secondly, it may appear as if concern for ecological sustainability first arose in the North and was successfully dealt with in environmental policies. It seems more appropriate, however, to consider the North as having exported environmental problems to the South through relocation of industries and intensification of resource extraction, while at the same time placing the burden of future policy change on the South as well. This can be seen in the debate about climate change as well as in the responsibility placed on Brazil and South Africa for protecting the Amazon rain forest and the rhinoceros, respectively, for the sake of all humankind. Thirdly, Brazil and South Africa do not only live with high social inequality that is a long-lasting legacy of European settlement; they also live with cultural plurality in ways that are still unimaginable for many Europeans, in whose self-understanding the democratic nation-state has cultural-linguistic homogeneity as a core presupposition.

On the current tension between democracy and capitalism

The preceding discussion is in many ways too brief and lacking in nuance, but it does allow us to assert that the claim that today's global capitalism is disembedded from its social and political anchorages, and in particular that national democracy is being undermined, is a provincial one. It applies to parts of Europe, but it is not a description of general tendencies in the relation between democracy and capitalism. In today's world there is, as there always was, a tension between capitalism and democracy, but in order to understand that tension today we must see the dismantling of democracy in some parts of the world in connection with the efforts made in building it in others. Here I must restrict myself to some concluding remarks in the form of theses, less for reasons of space than because they point towards a research programme that yet remains to be carried out.

1. The tension between democratic form and capitalist dynamics is well known. One of the more convincing accounts of it is Hannah Arendt's observations about the nation-state and imperialism in *Origins of Totalitarianism*.[36] That is a tension, however, that may or may not explode, rather than the history of a dominant logic, that of capital, with merely local countertendencies.

2. The European experience has shown that democratic action can change capitalism. But the power of democracy can in one socio-historical context lead to the embedding of capitalism within a nation-and-welfare-state, but in another lead to its disembedding and to the dismantling of the welfare state. Thus careful contextual investigation is required, and the remarks above were intended as a contribution to it. The social sciences have often assumed that Europe can supply generally applicable concepts and models.[37] Today one cannot escape the insight that European developments occurred in circumstances that were highly specific and that will never be repeated.

3. To a considerable degree, the temporary success of the European connection between democracy and capitalism after the Second World War was based on European (Western) global dominance.[38] The newness of the current situation may consist not least in the fact that the era of such dominance is over. The regression of European democracy is attributable to changed global circumstances. The oil price rises of the 1970s could be addressed through inflation, which

immediately lowered the real cost of this raw material. Today, if time can no longer be bought, to use Wolfgang Streeck's phrase, it is because others in this world are claiming equality of rights and of power in this time, in the present. In Europe there is still a limited awareness of global change, in particular the positive changes that I have sketched in the cases of Brazil and South Africa. A leap of the European imagination will be required for a renewed and improved understanding of the place of European societies in the world.

4. It is highly probable that the current global restructuring is to the disadvantage of Europe; it marks the end of a two-centuries-long dominance, albeit that in the first only the European elites profited from it while the majority of the population did so only after the Second World War. This does not mean that one has to accept greater social inequality and less democracy in Europe as an unavoidable part of global transformations. But one cannot hope that the mechanism for connecting economic strategies with democratic demands will once more be found by virtue of a privileged position vis-à-vis the rest of the world. In contrast, not to accept increasing inequality and a democratic deficit may be made easier by the observation that inequality is being reduced and democracy strengthened in other regions of the world, often under the most difficult circumstances. It is still an article of faith in Europe that the combination of a liberal-democratic nation and welfare state and a market economy is the solution to all socio-political problems. Solutions to new challenges are then sought only in incremental changes. The Brazilian and South African debates make it clear that more radical reorientations must be, but also can be, found. Brazil and South Africa are not so much competitors in a world-capitalist race that Europe is finding more and more difficult, as pioneers in the search for sustainable social and democratic solutions. To be successful, these new orientations must embrace an understanding of democratic politics that aims not at maximising the satisfaction of one's own interest in a perceived zero-sum game but – another Arendtian idea – at the definition of the kind of world in which one wants to live. This question is posed constantly in South Africa, since it is by no means obvious that former oppressors and oppressed wish to or can live together well and in peace. It is a question that would need to be posed globally as well.

Notes

1. An earlier version of this chapter, written within the research project *Trajectories of Modernity – comparing non-European and European*

Varieties (TRAMOD), funded by European Research Council Advanced Grant no. 249438, was published (in German) in the journal *Westend: Neue Zeitschrift für Sozialforschung*. I would like to thank the TRAMOD research group and the participants in the TRAMOD conference 'Economic Modernity in the 21st Century' (Barcelona, 3–5 October 2012); in a seminar at the Institute for Social Research, Frankfurt (January 2014); and in the Canandian Institute for Advanced Research's 'Successful Societies' conference (London, January 2015), as well as in particular Sidonia Blättler, Mauricio Domingues, Sonia Fleury and Aurea Mota for suggestions and critical comments.

2. Peter A. Hall and David Soskice (eds), *Varieties of Capitalism* (Oxford: Oxford University Press, 2000); Michel Albert, *Capitalisme contre capitalisme* (Paris: Seuil, 1998); Colin Crouch and Wolfgang Streeck (eds), *Political Economy of Modern Capitalism: Mapping Convergence and Diversity* (London: Sage, 1997); later: Bruno Amable, *Les cinq capitalismes: Diversité des systèmes économiques et sociaux dans la mondialisation* (Paris: Seuil, 2005). A comprehensive social analysis with similar motivations operates with the concept of 'alternative modernities'; see among others Dilip Parameshwar Gaonkar (ed.), *Alternative Modernities* (Durham, NC: Duke University Press, 2001).

3. Wolfgang Streeck, 'Taking Capitalism Seriously: Towards an Institutional Approach to Contemporary Political Economy', *Socio-economic Review*, 9 (2011): 137–67; Wolfgang Streeck, 'How to Study Contemporary Capitalism?', *Archives européennes de sociologie*, 53 (2012): 1–28; Wolfgang Streeck, *Gekaufte Zeit: Die vertagte Krise des demokratischen Kapitalismus (Adorno-Vorlesungen 2012)* (Frankfurt am Main: Suhrkamp, 2013).

4. Wolfgang Streeck, 'The Crises of Democratic Capitalism', *New Left Review*, 71 (September–October 2011): 5–29.

5. Nathalie Karagiannis (ed.), *European Solidarity* (Liverpool: Liverpool University Press, 2007); Peter Wagner and Bénédicte Zimmermann, 'Nation – Die Konstitution einer Politischen Ordnung als Verantwortungsgemeinschaft', in Stephan Lessenich (ed.), *Wohlfahrtsstaatliche Grundbegriffe* (Frankfurt and New York: Campus, 2003), pp. 243–66.

6. Claus Offe, 'Political Disaffection as an Outcome of Institutional Practices? Some Post-Tocquevillean Speculations', in André Brodocz, Marcus Llanque and Gary S. Schaal (eds), *Bedrohungen der Demokratie* (Wiesbaden: Verlag für Sozialwissenschaften, 2009), pp. 42–60; see also Peter Wagner, *A Sociology of Modernity: Liberty and Discipline* (London: Routledge, 1994).

7. Colin Crouch, *Post-democracy* (Cambridge: Polity, 2004); Cornelius Castoriadis, 'Fait et à faire', in Castoriadis, *Fait et à faire: Les carrefours du labyrinthe*, V (Paris: Seuil, 1997), p. 64. Wolfgang Streeck and Armin Schaefer (eds), *Politics in an Age of Austerity* (Cambridge: Polity, 2013), develop this perspective further. It is worth noting that at the end of the 1990s these developments were often justified and seen positively

as a new understanding of democracy; for instance, by Giandomenico Majone in *Regulating Europe* (London: Routledge, 1996) and Fritz Scharpf in *Governing in Europe: Effective and Democratic?* (Oxford: Oxford University Press, 1999).

8. For a related approach, see Peter A. Hall, 'The Political Origins of Our Economic Discontents', in M. Kahler and D. Lake (eds), *Politics in the New Hard Times* (Ithaca, NY: Cornell University Press, 2013), pp. 129–49.

9. Peter Wagner, 'Transformations of Democracy', in Johann Arnason, Kurt Raaflaub and Peter Wagner (eds), *The Greek Polis and the Invention of Democracy* (Oxford: Blackwell, 2013); see now Bo Stråth, *Three Utopias of Peace and the Search for a European Political Economy* (London: Bloomsbury, 2015).

10. Peter Wagner, *Modernity as Experience and Interpretation: A New Sociology of Modernity* (Cambridge: Polity, 2008).

11. Albert Hirschman, *The Passions and the Interests* (Princeton, NJ: Princeton University Press, 1977).

12. Wagner, *Sociology of Modernity*; Luc Boltanski and Eve Chiapello, *Le nouvel esprit du capitalisme* (Paris: Gallimard, 1999).

13. Wagner, *Modernity as Experience*, chs 12, 13; Peter Wagner, *Modernity: Understanding the Present* (Cambridge: Polity, 2012), ch. 7.

14. Michel Aglietta, *A Theory of Capitalist Regulation: The US Experience* [1976] (London: New Left Books, 1979).

15. Gabriel A. Almond and Sidney Verba, *The Civic Culture: Political Attitudes and Democracy in Five Nations* (Princeton, NJ: Princeton University Press, 1963).

16. Leonardo Avritzer, 'Modes of Democratic Deliberation', in Boaventura de Sousa Santos (ed.), *Democratizing Democracy* (London: Verso, 2007), pp. 377–404.

17. James O'Connor, *The Fiscal Crisis of the State* (New York: St Martin's Press, 1973); OECD, *The Welfare State in Crisis* (Paris: OECD, 1981).

18. Andrew Glyn and Bob Sutcliffe, *British Capitalism, Workers and the Profit Squeeze* (Harmondsworth: Penguin, 1972).

19. Michel Crozier, Samuel Huntington, and Joji Watanuki, *The Crisis of Democracy: Report on the Governability of Democracies to the Trilateral Commission* (New York: New York University Press, 1975); Jürgen Habermas, *Legitimationsprobleme im Spätkapitalismus* (Frankfurt: Suhrkamp, 1973).

20. Folker Froebel, Jürgen Heinrichs and Otto Kreye, *Die neue internationale Arbeitsteilung* (Reinbek: Rowohlt, 1979).

21. Quite apart from the fact, increasingly recognised, that globalisation was set in motion with the Atlantic opening of Europe from the late fifteenth century. From this moment on, a new awareness of the earth and its limits emerged, and with it the possibility of taking possession of it; see, from different angles, Carl Schmitt, *Der Nomos der Erde* [1950] (Berlin: Duncker & Humblot, 1997); Enrique Dussel, *Política de la liberaciòn* (Madrid: Trotta, 2007); and now Peter Wagner

(ed.), *African, American and European Trajectories of Modernity: Past Oppression, Future Justice? Annual of European and Global Studies vol. 2* (Edinburgh: Edinburgh University Press, 2015).

22. Volker Hauff and Fritz Scharpf, *Modernisierung der Volkswirtschaft* (Frankfurt: EVA, 1975); Michael J. Piore and Charles F. Sabel, *The Second Industrial Divide* (New York: Basic Books, 1984).

23. Albert Hirschman, *Exit, Voice, and Loyalty* (Cambridge, MA: Harvard University Press, 1970).

24. Depending on circumstances, the exit option is not only available to the business elites. In other societies workers use it: like the flexibilisation of capital, labour migration can jeopardise a society's ability to create a stable political and economic order. The countries of the South (and today, once again, of Southern Europe) have been far more affected by this, while in the North this question is hardly posed any more.

25. Karl Polanyi, *The Great Transformation* [1944] (Frankfurt: Suhrkamp, 1973).

26. Jeremy Seekings, 'The Making of a High-Wage Economy in South Africa: Market Regulation in a Colonial and Post-Colonial Society', *European Journal of Social Theory*, vol. 19, no. 2 (2016), forthcoming special issue on 'Modernity and Capitalism', edited by David Casassas and Peter Wagner.

27. On the intensity of democracy in Brazil see Avritzer, 'Modes of Democratic Deliberation'; James Holston, *Insurgent Citizenship: Disjunctions of Democracy and Modernity in Brazil* (Princeton, NJ: Princeton University Press, 2008); José Mauricio Domingues, 'Democratic Theory and Democratisation in Contemporary Brazil and Beyond', *Thesis Eleven*, 2013.

28. Their inclusion in the discussion would strengthen our argument about the impact of democracy. For a comparative and critical discussion of social policy in Latin America see Rubén Lo Vuolo, 'The Limits of Autonomy in Latin American Social Policies: Promoting Human Capital or Social Control?', *European Journal of Social Theory*, vol. 19, no. 2 (2016), forthcoming special issue on 'Modernity and capitalism', edited by David Casassas and Peter Wagner.

29. Sonia Fleury, 'Las reformas pendientes: desafíos para la gobernabilidad en Brasil', *Revista CIDOB d'afers internacionals*, no. 97–8 (April 2012): 33–54; Leda Maria Paulani, 'Modernity and Capitalist Progress: the Case of Brazil', *European Journal of Social Theory*, vol. 19, no. 2 (2016), forthcoming special issue on 'Modernity and Capitalism', edited by David Casassas and Peter Wagner.

30. Sonia Fleury, '¿Qué protección social para cuál democracia? Dilemas de la inclusión social en América Latina', *Medicina Social*, vol. 5 (March 2010), no. 1; Ivor Chipkin, in this volume; Jeremy Seekings and Nicoli Nattrass, *Class, Race and Inequality in South Africa* (Durban: University of KwaZulu-Natal Press, 2006).

31. A more detailed account and discussion of transformation-oriented politics in Brazil, South Africa and Europe is in preparation – Jacob

Dlamini, Aurea Mota and Peter Wagner, *Possible Futures: Trajectories of Modernity in Brazil, South Africa and Europe.* The observations in this section are partly drawn from this work.

32. On the idea of 'successful' societies, which in post-Parsonian critical sociology has received too little attention, see Peter A. Hall and Michèle Lamont (eds), *Successful Societies: How Institutions and Culture Affect Health* (Cambridge: Cambridge University Press, 2009).

33. As Claus Offe – 'Demokratie und Wohlfahrtsstaat: Eine europäische Regierungsform unter dem Stress der europäischen Integration', in Wolfgang Streeck (ed.), *Internationale Wirtschaft, nationale Demokratie* (Frankfurt: Campus, 1998), pp. 99–136 – still maintained.

34. Arend Lijphart, *The Politics of Accommodation* (Berkeley: University of California Press, 1975).

35. Wolfdieter Narr and Claus Offe (eds), *Wohlfahrtsstaat und Massenloyalität* (Cologne: Kiepenheuer und Witsch, 1975).

36. Hannah Arendt, *The Origins of Totalitarianism* (Chicago: Harcourt, Brace, Jovanovich, 1951).

37. Jean Comaroff and John L. Comaroff, *Theory from the South* (Boulder, CO: Paradigm, 2012).

38. See Sandra Halperin, *War and Social Change: The Great Transformation Revisited* (Cambridge: Cambridge University Press, 2004), pp. 272–9. In previous work I myself have emphasised the intra-European aspects; see Wagner, *Sociology of Modernity.* While they cannot be denied, today a shift of perspective is long overdue.

10 From Realism to Activism: A Critique of Resignation in Political Theory

Lea Ypi

This chapter presents a critique of realism in political theory.[1] It focuses on two issues central to the realist agenda: the problem of politics as characterised by radical disagreement and the role of motives in conceptualising political action. It introduces an activist approach to political theory which is close to political moralists' concern for justice while also acknowledging the force of some realist critiques. On this approach, norms of justice develop in response to the concerns and commitments of real-life political agents, but also appeal to historically developed moral criteria in critically assessing different practices of political contestation. They are thus sensitive to the circumstances of politics and able to motivate political agents, but also help us avoid the politics of resignation to which some strands of realism seem to give rise.

The 'realism' controversy in political theory

Philosophers, a famous slogan reads, have only interpreted the world in various ways; the point is now to change it. One way to understand the realism controversy in political theory is as a dispute about the meaning and plausibility of this slogan. On one side of the dispute stand those, call them political moralists, who read the argument in a disjunctive form, and then proceed to deny its validity.[2] Political change and moral argument, they contend, are not a matter of either-or: they appear closely intertwined with each other. The choice is never between either interpreting the world or changing it, but rather trying to change it in a way that reflects the most appropriate (collective) interpretation of fundamental moral norms. On the other side of the dispute stand those, call them political realists, who read the second part of the statement as taking priority over the first. Political action and change, they claim, belong to a sphere that is irreducible to the demands of morality and the particular interpretations that follow from it.[3] The domain of the political, so their argument goes, is characterised by profound disagreement and radical conflict amongst a plurality of perspectives. Endorsing moral criteria (however we arrive at them) to orient the reform of political institutions would at best be inconclusive, at worst dangerous.

Political moralists are often accused of understanding political theory as a kind of applied ethics. Their approach, although distinctive in its orientation towards justice rather than the good moral life, is sufficiently informed by moral principles to believe in the possibility of reforming institutions compatibly with some collectively agreed moral principles (either minimal procedural principles or more substantive ones). For their realist critics, to act politically places constraints that no philosophical examination of the dilemmas of moral agents can fully capture. Whatever its merits, justice is *not* the first virtue of political institutions. On the contrary, if we really are interested in the conditions of political action, realists emphasise, we need to draw attention to the exercise of power by those who seek to achieve political aims. That in turn raises questions concerning the basis on which power can be exercised in order to legitimately constrain those who are affected by it.[4] And although justice and morality will have a role to play in articulating the basis for the legitimate use of political power, these are by no means the only criteria influencing political decision-making and the theoretical reflection that accompanies it.[5]

It is easy to see what realists are doing when they warn us that acting politically is different from offering an interpretation of the political world, especially when that interpretation centres on identifying a set of moral values as the Archimedean point on the basis of which political action unfolds. But it is difficult to see what they positively stand for. One thing is to say that in seeking to legitimise the use of power, other considerations (apart from, say, the justice of a system of rules) must be taken into account. Another thing is to say *what* these considerations are. With regard to the former, the critique appears trivial: no political moralist denies that a number of different values inform our attempts to understand political change or that what we call 'the political' is a very complex domain, the analysis of which does not neatly overlap with whatever account of it emerges as a result of abstract moral analysis.[6] With regard to the latter, the issue appears more complex. A realist might resist the call to come up with a more positive set of criteria for how we should understand political action and change, insisting that the point of the critique is precisely to avoid committing to a list of positive values.

If they were to develop their own criteria for interpreting the basis on which power is exercised, realists would be committing the same mistake they ascribe to their adversaries: reifying the political process by imposing on it constraints that are not themselves drawn from political life. But this response sounds implausible. No realist says (or would want to say) that whatever emerges from the sphere of political confrontation is *ipso facto* plausible because it has emerged from that process, or that there is no way in which normative criteria are invoked to adjudicate between different attempts to justify the use of power. So perhaps the critique is more limited: in selecting standards for evaluating political action, political moralists implausibly focus on *distinctively moral* criteria at the expense of *distinctively political* ones. Thus they fundamentally misunderstand the nature of the 'politics first' slogan. In order to examine whether that critique of political moralism has force, we need to consider what the suggested criteria are.

In this chapter I will focus on two ideas that are often invoked to identify the distinguishing line between the conception of the political that political moralists implicitly endorse and an analysis of political action that is more attuned to realist concerns. Although the literature on realism has only recently begun to offer more systematic analysis of these concepts, they appear with sufficient regularity in a number of diverse texts to warrant an attempt to scrutinise them as part of a coherent body of thought. These are, firstly, the issue of radical disagreement and, secondly, the role of motives (other than moral motives) in the analysis of political change. In the following pages I will try to assess the realist critique of political moralism with regard to these two points and outline an alternative (activist) conception of the political that develops in tune with a realist analysis of existing instances of political agency. Although ultimately siding with political moralists on the nature and purpose of political life, this alternative conception is sufficiently attentive to these dimensions of realist critique of political moralism to act as a basis for productive exchange. Or so I hope to show.[7]

Political conflict and the real nature of politics

The first dimension along which to express the disagreement between political moralists and their realist critics concerns the very nature of the domain of the political. On both accounts, politics is marked by sharp conflict concerning both the ends of public life and the means through which such ends ought to be pursued. Political moralists attempt to channel such disagreement by identifying decision procedures able to generate reasonable consent around the fundamentals of social and political institutions. Their realist critics insist that such procedures either undermine the extent to which political agents disagree even on such procedural fundamentals (the unavoidability of conflict thesis) or threaten to depoliticise areas of public life by removing particularly agreed upon principles from the legitimate sphere of contestation (the primacy of politics thesis).

These realist critiques of political moralism are very important, but both of them are also significantly underdeveloped. Consider the unavoidability of conflict thesis. We can interpret the thesis as attempting to capture some descriptive features of society; the fact, for example, that different people hold different values, that these values are plural and often incompatible, and that it is an illusion to think that they will ever generate any kind of agreement, including on minimal norms likely to be endorsed by everyone. Although a political moralist might at first be inclined to dismiss this objection as merely empirical, it is in fact far from that. Realist critiques of political moralism do not limit themselves to pointing out empirical obstacles on the way to realising particular norms (and if they were doing just that, the insights generated by realist critiques would be no different from those generated by straightforwardly empirical disciplines such as sociology, anthropology or political science).[8] What realist critiques urge us to do is reflect on the ways in which such empirical observations might be incorporated in a theory that addresses basic facts of political life (i.e. the issue of legitimate exercise of the coercive use of power) by appealing to norms internal, rather than external, to politics itself. Let us examine in more detail what that might mean.

If we take seriously the unavoidability of conflict thesis, we will come up with two different interpretations of legitimacy demands compatible with norms internal to it.[9] One interpretation leads to the idea that since politics is by its nature inherently coercive and ill-suited to promote a variety of ends, we should seek to contain its reach by theorising alternative associations (economic, cultural, religious) where individuals can pursue their interests and act together in a more spontaneous form.[10] Thus, if we limit our ambitions to the attempt to secure order rather than guarantee justice, we will contain the potential for abusing power in seeking to realise the latter. But the problem with this view is that it conflates the statement that politics is essentially coercive with another one, which appears more controversial – namely, that *only* politics is essentially coercive. Although it is plausible to say that any exercise of political power, however noble its inspiration, is likely to result in a few elites imposing their own standards of legitimacy on the rest of the civic body, it is naïve to suppose that only political elites are vulnerable to a similar critique. If disagreement among individuals exists and is unavoidable, it will shape any association in which they take part. If rules are needed to contain such disagreement, the question of who makes such rules and in what name will apply to all circumstances characterised by division of labour, structures of co-ordination, and collective decision-making. Thus, not just political institutions but also families, the market, religious organisations (to mention but the most relevant examples) will entail some degree of coercion in order to flourish. It is contrary to the spirit of realism to assume that they will spontaneously guarantee the pursuit of agents' ends free from any degree of unilateral interference. Even more importantly, if disagreement pervades all areas of human interaction, the distinctiveness of *the political* as that realm in which collective decisions must be made on the face of such disagreements seems difficult to capture.

The second alternative way of incorporating the unavoidability of conflict in a realistic agenda leads to its positive endorsement in an 'agonistic' account of public life.[11] Here the alternative to political moralism is to celebrate rather than suppress disagreement, maintaining awareness that only in the creative engagement with different forms of political expression is genuine emancipation ever possible. If politics is by its nature paradoxical, then the reassurance that political moralists offer in trying to shape institutions that respond to moral concerns is a false one. As agonistic theorists emphasise, no legal and political arrangement, not even one that is 'relatively enabling and empowering' can ignore the fact that every politics 'has its remainders, that resistances are engendered by every settlement'.[12] It is on behalf of these resistances that the perpetual nature of conflict is celebrated rather than suppressed.

It is at this point that the unavoidability of conflict thesis joins the primacy of politics thesis. Agonistic realism shares with alternative realist accounts the general critique of political moralism: attention to existing historical experiences of political discontent and challenge to the constituted order, scepticism towards universal moral values underpinning political life, and sensitivity to the dynamic of power and exclusion present in all political contexts, even those of a benign sort.[13] But agonistic realism also differs from these accounts in its commitment to the essentially contested character of 'reality' itself, a move considered essential to preserve the spirit of activism necessary to nurture ongoing political contestation. As some of its most prominent advocates put it, 'diminishing coercion on behalf of a more just, inclusive, consensual practice is, it seems to us, clearly desirable, but a politics oriented to replacing coercion with consent leaves those who seek justice and equality ill-prepared for (some of) the battles ahead'.[14]

But let us pause at this point to raise some questions. How exactly do we better prepare those who seek justice and equality for the battles ahead? How should we understand those battles? Where do they come from? Who is involved in them? Who should be prepared? Are justice and equality important to their pursuits? Why, if at all? Who or what stands on their way? What is the reason? At this point, realism, including realism of an agonistic kind, becomes a vague project. Repeating the slogan of the essential contestation of everything, 'even the "real" itself',[15] does little to answer these questions. On the contrary, asking us to cast doubt on reality and implying that we ought to be suspicious of all consolidated facts, all real manifestations of existing political struggles, all determinate content, risks turning political life into 'the night in which all cows are black', to use Hegel's expression.[16] If we are seriously concerned with exclusion and oppression in the public sphere and with how fit marginalised subjects are to face the challenges of their political future, we need to provide more than a theoretical celebration of what they already know all too well: the daily struggle to assert themselves as equally worthy of dignity and respect. What we need instead is an analysis of both the epistemic and practical resources necessary to articulate what they are fighting for, in whose name, against whom and in what form. It may well be that no such package of resources can be elaborated outside these sites of contestation, abstracting from concrete understandings of the circumstances of conflict and from a rooted interpretation of its causes and potentials for remedy. And it may well be that no answer is definitive or sits comfortably with alternative interpretations and discourses. But to dismiss moral attempts to articulate such sources of grievance, to understand the agents involved, to interpret and assess competing critiques for fear that any such commitment to a particular body of thought will serve only to reify some social arrangement at the expense of all others, is itself a reification of scepticism and discontent as the most appropriate form of political engagement. A similar attitude replaces the political moralists' faith on appropriate evaluative standards with a vision that begins by celebrating disagreement but leads to a politics of resignation. After all, what is the point of contestation if those who contest power can never be sure that they are justified in doing so?[17]

This leads me to a final point on incorporating disagreement in political theory: the need to reconcile the primacy of politics thesis with an activist ethics. It is plausible to agree with agonistic realists that in trying to construct our future with others, we would 'do well to look to the events of history and to the essentially contested realities of our own time, in order to inaugurate or maintain futures worth having'.[18] But conflict in modern societies takes many forms, and involves a myriad of different agents. Consider the examples that occupy the headlines of newspapers: the conflict between governments and rating agencies, the conflict between employers and employees, the conflict between secularists and believers, the conflict between foreign residents and anti-immigrant groups, the conflict between national separatists and central organisations. Are agents embedded in these conflicts all the same? Are their reasons equally valid? Do all perspectives bear the same weight? Do all instances of contestation contribute to inaugurate a 'future worth having'? If so, how? And if not, why not?

Of course, agonistic realism cannot be expected to answer all these questions at once. But if it is to avoid the politics of resignation, and really inaugurate 'futures worth having', the relevance of the question concerning how exactly political conflict can give rise to emancipatory exchanges in the public sphere cannot be overstated. If the answer to the problem of the political can only be given by appealing to categories inherent to the political itself, we need an account of how intelligible and plausible principles of political change can flow from within instances of political contestation. To insist on this point is not to undermine that such principles ought, in any case, to remain open-ended and welcoming of future expressions of political contestation. But it would be ill-advised to renounce even the aspiration to elaborate visions of politics able to capture the sources of political dissatisfaction and to provide agents engaged in politics with justified principles on the basis of which to seek political transformation.

All this leaves us with the question of how we might approach the question of disagreement and conflict in a way that turns it into an emancipatory source for political theorists keen to avoid both the abstraction of political moralism and the resignation of political realism. Elsewhere I have discussed the relevance of contestation by defending the need for an activist approach which is sensitive both to practices of contestation and to the nature of claims advanced through them. On this approach, political theory develops principles of justice from its engagement with the concerns and commitments expressed through social and political movements challenging existing power structures.[19] Theories of the political are informed by observation of real-life instances of political contestation and normative analyses emerge in relation to them. They help scrutinise and assess the processes and agents involved in such struggles and contribute to a distinctively political form of engagement. Here, different interpretations of the function and purpose of political institutions enable agents involved in practices of contestation to appeal to them in articulating their grievances and putting forward visions of alternative political orders. In the next section, I shall consider some key features of political theory in an activist mode, examine in what way it contributes to answer the realist critique and clarify how it helps address the second challenge political realists typically address to political moralists: the motivational question.

Political motives and activist political theory

One additional dimension in which realism is thought to have an advantage over its political moralist competitors is its apparent sensitivity to motives that are distinctively characteristic of political action and often necessary to its success. If political theorists are to take politics seriously, realists argue, they should also pay close attention to the fact that moral principles often fail to guide political action in any direct way. One needs to pay attention both to potential instances of ideological distortion and to the way in which the normative principles require a kind of motivational endorsement for which rational persuasion alone may be insufficient. On the one hand, this means that principles for political reform ought to be accessible to politically situated agents and that they should appeal not only to their reasons but also their feelings, emotions and partial interests.[20] On the other hand, realists are careful to caution us about the potential for regress as well as progress in seeking to transform existing political institutions compatibly with certain moral ideals. Failing to take seriously the non-moral dimension of politics, so the argument goes, undermines the fact that moralistic political projects are at best incapable of motivating people to take such projects seriously, and at worst dangerous in either ideologically distorting political goals or prioritising the pursuit of justice at the expense of equally important political values such as legitimacy and stability.[21]

Adopting an activist approach to political theory illustrates that this contrast might be misleading. There is no reason to assume that taking the 'circumstances of politics'[22] seriously comes at the expense of demanding political visions oriented to justice but served by more realistic (embedded) interpretations of political conflict. The pursuit of political change in the name of justice need not be divorced from motivational considerations and from attention to the ideological factors that might distort political discourse. A normative project can be motivationally sustainable if agents embedded in relevant social struggles find the institutional and social conditions governing their lives sufficiently unacceptable to initiate political change in a required direction. And yet that direction ought also to be acceptable by some relevant normative standard. But it is hard to see just what the relevant realist standard is. It is here that the question of how theory relates to political contestation becomes particularly pressing, and where the realist answer seems insufficient.

An adequate account of the criteria for reflecting on the relation between political activism and political theory must be able to tackle the problem of motivational sustainability raised by political realists, but also allow us to introduce a more nuanced understanding of political conflict and its contribution to political change. The development of political theories should be sensitive to social and political struggles rooted in the political demand for justice. It should engage with the concerns and commitments that these movements express. The best way to reflect on this process is to conceive of developments in political theory as closely connected to social and political changes. Such changes reflect processes of moral and political learning whereby certain collective commitments and the principles associated to them are constantly re-assessed in in the course of particular historical (social and political) developments. In the course of such developments, existing interpretations of how political institutions ought to respond to the claims of political agents are challenged, and the engagement with such responses forces us to reflect on the plausibility of available principles on the basis of which we seek to orient our public life.

To illustrate this claim we might use as an example the debate on the normative relevance of the state, and the issue of whether principles of egalitarian justice have value outside state boundaries.[23] On some normative accounts, we should think of these principles as closely connected to practices of co-operation and coercion that only obtain with the boundaries of the state, and that only apply amongst fellow citizens. On other accounts, labelled as 'cosmopolitan', we should expand the reach of global principles to demand the reform of global institutions compatible with egalitarian principles of justice.[24] To some extent, both cosmopolitan theorists and their critics fall prey to the critique of political moralism outlined in the previous pages. Both these families of theories seek to provide normative guidance on an external, moralistic standpoint from which to assess existing political institutions. They emphasise, in the case of cosmopolitanism, the moral relations that obtain amongst all human beings and, in the case of its critics, the value of the principles of co-operation or the negative impact of coercive institutions on the autonomy of citizens subjected to them. From the realist point of view, although cosmopolitan critics seem to capture better their understanding of the nature of political institutions (i.e. their essentially coercive nature), in both cases theorists understand their normative projects to provide criteria that neglect the real (often unavoidable) obstacles that stand in the way of connecting their theories with the concerns of real political action. For political realists, then, the whole debate between cosmopolitans and their critics might be seen to operate at the level of the most adequate moral criteria that allow us to reflect on relations between political agents (be they states or individuals) in a globalised world, thus neglecting the prior question of whether these concerns make sense to such agents, in what way they can help to mobilise them and how, if at all, the normative projects developed connect to their concerns and commitments.

Although I believe political moralists have internal resources to resist the realist critique mounted at this level, relatively little has been done up to this point to explain what these resources are. If we take an activist approach to political theory, we could address the realist challenge by providing an account of the ways in which political theorists can direct their enquiry to try and connect their theories to the concerns of agents whose concerns and commitments are not addressed by the political institutions that are supposed to be responsive to them. For in the latter case, political theory takes its cues exactly from such concerns and commitments and from the claims and practices of contestation that are developed as a result of them.

Consider, for one example, the role played by recent global social movements that seek to expand the unit of analysis from a traditional concern with the state and the provision of goods to its citizens to a more expansive account of claims and obligations across borders. Recent research in political science and political sociology has documented the emergence of new networks of transnational protest (for example, the World Social Forum or Occupy movements) emphasising the negative impact of neoliberal globalisation processes on the lives of millions of citizens affected by such processes, and criticising existing institutions for failing to cope with their demands. These protests have revealed the need for a more global approach to political theory, an approach able to scrutinise the causes of such perverse effects, question the effectiveness of theories focused merely on the distribution of benefits within state boundaries, and propose new normative principles and theories able to capture the concerns and commitments of these alternative agents.

A more detailed account of how different theories of global justice fare with regard to these forms of political agency would be out of place in these pages.[25] But the activist approach to political theory that I have outlined in this section allows us to provide a specific response to the question of motivational sustainability that political realists typically raise. In the case of global theories of justice, for example, rather than seeing such theories of justice as emerging in a purely speculative realm, it is important to analyse them as developed in response to instances of political action, attentive to the conflicts which agents experience and supporting such agents with the conceptual tools necessary to better articulate their views. Normative proposals are therefore a constitutive part of the activity of engaging with existing social and political movements and paying attention both to the specific justification of their projects, and to the interests, passions and emotions of actors whose motivation to participate in the public sphere may not be reducible to rational argumentation.

This sensitivity to the psychological basis for certain kinds of political actions allows it to also grasp the potential for making normative projects developed in connection to such activities motivationally sustainable. For in this case, normative theories develop where there is already public demand for a particular kind of change, and serve to better articulate the rationale for that change and the principles according to which change must be sought. Yet they do so in the awareness that politics is, and remains, an essentially contested enterprise. Therefore, although change at one particular point in time might be demanded to improve the status quo with regard to a specific dimension (e.g. needed reforms to recalibrate the role of the state, and to expand the reach of particular principles of social justice), these principles will remain valid only for so long as the political institutions they will help create by and large respond to the expectations of political agents mobilising to support them. Once new developments in the political sphere bring about new agents demanding political change, the cycle begins again and new principles are sought.

In explaining more specifically how we should approach from a methodological perspective this process of both learning from existing political movements and intervening actively to give them a more coherent direction, we can distinguish three stages, which I have called diagnostic, innovative and heuristic. In the first one, political theorists observe dynamics of political antagonism with a view to understanding the attitudes they reveal, the agents involved in them, the kind of dissatisfaction with political institutions they express and the rational or psychological basis that supports the public voicing of particular concerns. Political theory here performs a diagnostic task because it joins other social sciences in observing empirical reality, seeking to understand the reasons for action of different political agents involved in particular dynamics of political conflict.

In a second stage, political theory (again aided by other social sciences) reflects on the causes of these conflicts and examines whether the existing social ethos, the principles that are generally recognised as valid in the public sphere and available theories of social and political justice can help these political agents identify visions of the public good that reflect their commitments and provide remedies for their concerns. If existing interpretations of the function and purpose of political institutions seem to capture their concerns and commitments, they are preserved and simply modified from within. If they fail, the need for conceptual innovation paves the way to a new stage, in which it is the articulation of new families of theories (or, we might also call them, new normative paradigms) that is at stake.

Therefore, in this second stage, political theory performs an innovating role. That is to say, the kind of empirical and conceptual analysis developed in the first stage lays the foundation for a renewed account of the function of social and political institutions, which adds new content to existing families of theories and in some way supersedes them by providing more adequate principled foundation for the claims of relevant political agents. By relevant political agents, I mean those agents whose claims on political institutions are plausible and acceptable from the point of view of the public standards of justice endorsed up to that point. To give a more concrete example: although, for example, both populist xenophobic movements and alter-globalisation movements active in many Western democracies will seek to challenge existing political institutions and the normative principles underpinning them, the former reject both what is acceptable and what is problematic of the liberal status quo. The latter, on the contrary, seek to expand ideals of equal treatment and reciprocity that obtain within the boundaries of the state, and therefore add new demands for change to existing normative theories.

This is, then, also what distinguishes activist political theory from the agonistic accounts examined in the previous section. Rather than celebrating all kinds of political conflict as important for theory's purposes, we scrutinise political agency with an eye to the kind of collective moral learning processes that we have endorsed up to that point. Politics is, on this account, neither circular nor paradoxical, it is dialectical. The new forms of agency that emerge from the critique of previous ones retain the benefits of the claims of their predecessors that have met demands of public justification, but improve on their shortcomings. This, of course, is not to deny that there is a grey area that often makes it difficult to distinguish clearly between political practices that promote or hinder a particular moral learning process. In those cases, the use of theory to make more situated judgements can only give us negative criteria, telling us simply which agents in politics clearly fall short of qualifying as supporting such collective learning processes and are unable to provide the political resources necessary to articulate future plausible normative theories – consider again the case of racist or xenophobic movements and their frightening resemblance to fascist protests in the early part of the twentieth century. In the more ambiguous cases, on the other hand, the decision on what kinds of concerns and commitments are most critical for the process of normative innovation should be left to processes of democratic decision-making that are also able to capture the concerns of vulnerable minorities.

Finally, a theory or family of theories that can contribute to shifting the boundaries of existing normative interpretations of the function and purpose of existing political institutions in a way that captures the claims of emerging political subjects should also contain heuristic potential. That is to say, the new theory should be able to contribute to existing bodies of thought by adding new questions about the principles and shape of future political institutions. If, for example, an egalitarian interpretation of global political practices is shown to be able to capture better the concerns and commitments of new political subjects, that theory will be more successful in the future if it can also anticipate some questions that the previous institutional setup ignored. Examples of these questions in the global justice debate are the normative and political significance of human rights, the legitimacy of humanitarian intervention, the accommodation of cultural minorities and so on. None of these questions could have been raised by theories focused exclusively on the institutions of the nation-state as the once-plausible answer to the question of social, cultural and economic modernisation that provoked the decline of previous political configurations.[26]

These criteria are of course open to further revision and subject to different interpretations. But they give us some building blocks for thinking of how political theorists should engage with transformations in the political world, what attitude they should take to existing political movements and how they should integrate their activity in theories that are sensitive to dynamics of political conflict but preserve some critical purchase in their work. Once we think of the process of political theorising as developing in conjunction with larger social processes, the risk of developing theories that are irrelevant, unable to motivate existing political agents or vulnerable to ideological distortion is consequently minimised.

Conclusion

In this chapter I have examined a prominent critique to most mainstream approaches to contemporary political theory: the realist critique. Normative political theory, realists maintain, tends to overly moralise discussions on the nature and principles necessary to guide the conduct of existing political institutions. Political moralists produce criteria that ignore the essence of political exchange (conflict and disagreement) and the complex motivations of agents involved in political contestation. Although I believe that the realist charge is in principle answerable, many political moralists have either dismissed the questions or failed to provide a persuasive response. Having assessed the strengths and weaknesses of the realist critique, I have tried to outline where an activist approach to political theory could intervene to fill the gaps. By reflecting on the criteria for how political theorists can engage with existing processes of political contestation, activist political theory seeks to draw a balance between sensitivity to real-world movements conducive to sound normative criteria and sufficient critical distance conducive to a more plausible basis on which to articulate their claims. A similar approach, I hope, sacrifices neither the stringency of normative principles nor their motivational sustainability. Of course, my suggestions and the concrete examples I have used to support my case are by no means immune to critique. The more methodological argument I have tried to present here does not depend on finding uncontroversial examples, which are intended more as illustration rather than carrying the burden of proof. Still, one can only hope that the thoughts articulated here provide a sufficient basis for further thinking about political contestation as neither uncritically celebrated nor unduly ignored, but rather reflectively mediated by normative critique. For it is only then that we will be able to avoid the politics of resignation to which some strands of realism come dangerously close.

Notes

1. I am grateful to Eva Erman, Rainer Forst and Ed Hall for comments on an earlier version of this chapter.
2. The term 'political moralists' comes from Bernard Williams, who criticises authors in the so-called high-liberal tradition (e.g. Rawls) for their exclusive reliance on moral norms in articulating constraints applying to the political sphere; see Bernard Williams, *In the Beginning Was the Deed: Realism and Moralism in Political Argument* (Princeton, NJ: Princeton University Press, 2008). See also Raymond Geuss, *Philosophy and Real Politics* (Princeton, NJ: Princeton University Press, 2008). The label is sufficiently general to capture a variety of other authors (from G. A. Cohen to Jürgen Habermas to Ronald Dworkin, to mention but the most influential ones) who

share the view that moral and political theorising are closely inter-twined, despite their disagreements on how exactly to construct that relation.

3. For excellent discussions and reviews of the recent literature on political realism and the many authors associated to it, see William A. Galston, 'Realism in Political Theory', *European Journal of Political Theory*, 9/4 (October 1, 2010): 385–411; Marc Stears, 'Liberalism and the Politics of Compulsion', *British Journal of Political Science*, 37/03 (2007): 533–53; Enzo Rossi and Matt Sleat, 'Realism in Normative Political Theory', *Philosophy Compass*, 9/10 (2014): 689–701.

4. This is what Bernard Williams calls the 'basic legitimation demand', the idea that 'those who claim political authority over a group must have something to say about the basis of that authority, and about the question of why the authority is being used to constrain in some ways and not others'. Moreover, he continues, 'there is a sense in which they must have something to say to each person whom they constrain. If not, there will be people whom they are treating merely as enemies in the midst of their citizens', p. 135.

5. For more emphasis on the role of legitimacy and the importance of focusing on values other than justice see, in addition to Bernard Williams's classic contribution, Geuss, *Philosophy and Real Politics*; Glen Newey, *After Politics: The Rejection of Politics in Contemporary Liberal Philosophy* (Basingstoke: Palgrave, 2001) and Matt Sleat, *Liberal Realism: A Realist Theory of Liberal Politics* (Manchester: Manchester University Press, 2013).

6. Indeed, here the positions of political moralists and realists seem to overlap; see for example Eva Erman and Niklas Möller, 'Political Legitimacy in the Real Normative World: The Priority of Morality and the Autonomy of the Political', *British Journal of Political Science*, 45/1 (2015): 215–33, and Mark Philp, 'Realism without Illusions', *Political Theory*, 40/5 (2012): 629–49.

7. For more detailed analysis of the concept of avant-garde political agency and the kind of political theory that places it at its centre, see Lea Ypi, *Global Justice and Avant-Garde Political Agency* (Oxford: Oxford University Press, 2012).

8. See Stears, 'Liberalism and the Politics of Compulsion', and Matt Sleat, 'Liberal Realism: A Liberal Response to the Realist Critique', *The Review of Politics*, 73/03 (2011): 469–96.

9. See for discussions Stears, 'Liberalism and the Politics of Compulsion' and Galston, 'Realism in Political Theory'.

10. See the discussion in Stears, 'Liberalism and the Politics of Compulsion', at p. 548. See also the defences of what we might call *modus vivendi* liberalism in e.g. John Gray in *Two Faces of Liberalism* (New York: New Press, 2000) or Chandran Kukathas in *The Liberal Archipelago* (Oxford: Oxford University Press, 2003).

11. See for two prominent examples Chantal Mouffe, *On the Political (Thinking in Action)* (London: Routledge, 2005) and Bonnie Honig,

Political Theory and the Displacement of Politics (Ithaca, NY: Cornell University Press, 1993).

12. Honig, *Political Theory and the Displacement of Politics*, p. 3.
13. For an excellent summary of this position see Bonnie Honig and Marc Stears, 'The New Realism: From Modus Vivendi to Justice', in Jonathan Floyd and Marc Stears (eds), *Political Philosophy Versus History?: Contextualism and Real Politics in Contemporary Political Thought* (Cambridge: Cambridge University Press, 2011), pp. 177–205.
14. Ibid., pp. 204–5.
15. Ibid., p. 205.
16. See Georg Wilhelm Friedrich Hegel in Yirmiyahu Yovel (ed.), *Hegel's Preface to the Phenomenology of Spirit* (Princeton, NJ: Princeton University Press, 2005), p. 94.
17. For a critique of realism that emphasises a similar concern with the justificatory narratives central to these practices of contestation see also Rainer Forst, *Justification and Critique* (Cambridge: Polity, 2014), esp. pp. 1–15.
18. Honig and Stears, 'The New Realism: From Modus Vivendi to Justice', p. 205.
19. Ibid.
20. Galston, 'Realism in Political Theory', and Mark Philp, 'What Is to Be Done? Political Theory and Political Realism', *European Journal of Political Theory*, 9/4 (1 October 2010): 466–84.
21. There may be a partial overlap here between the realist critique and what is often called non-ideal theory; for a discussion of the relation between the two, see Matt Sleat, 'Realism, Liberalism and Non-Ideal Theory, or Are there Two Ways to do Realistic Political Theory?', *Political Studies* (forthcoming).
22. The expression comes from Jeremy Waldron, *Law and Disagreement* (Oxford: Clarendon, 1999), p. 102ff.
23. I have discussed this example at much greater length in Ypi, *Global Justice and Avant-Garde Political Agency*.
24. See for the most recent contributions to this literature, Gillian Brock (ed.), *Cosmopolitanism: For and Against* (Oxford: Oxford University Press, 2013).
25. But see for a detailed analysis Ypi, *Global Justice and Avant-Garde Political Agency*.
26. See for further discussion of this point Jürgen Habermas, *The Inclusion of the Other: Studies in Political Theory* (Cambridge, MA: MIT Press, 1998), esp. pp. 105–14.

11 The World as We Find It: A Suggestion for a Democratic Theory for Our Times

Tracy B. Strong

Wo aber Gefahr ist, wächst
Das Rettende auch.

Hölderlin

We are concerned with the prospects for democracy under the conditions of modernity: two words that need not so much definition as exploration.

When in 1950 Hannah Arendt visited Martin Heidegger for the first time after the Second World War, they went for long walks and she sought to engage him in conversation as to how one was to think of the events that had transpired since their last encounter in 1934. Her early book *The Origins of Totalitarianism* and the later *The Human Condition* were her most extended attempts to come to grips with this new world (although one should mention *Eichmann in Jerusalem* here as well).

This is our problem also – at least one of our problems – if democracy is the activity of a people coming together to deal with what they have in common; that is my first attempt at an exploration. I take it that any theory of democracy must determine an appropriate democratic response to the particular set of problems that confront a given people (or peoples) at a particular time. These problems vary importantly, and what one thinks are the predominant problems of the time may be different from what they in fact are. Identification of the nature of particular problems is thus the first and most important step. As an example: if one understands the problem connected to the practice of segregation in the USA in the first two-thirds of the past century as a problem of civil rights, one will tend to think the appropriate response to be the achievement of voting rights. Such, I might note, was the conclusion of Robert Dahl in his 1956 *A Preface to Democratic Theory*. If one understands segregation as a problem of ressentiment, the achievement of one's identity by the negation of another's, a democratic response requires something additional.

I cannot here given more than an indication of what I think the most important problems that shape this world are. Partly out of lack of adequate knowledge of some of the parts of the world that are of concern to this volume, but more significantly out of the conviction that different peoples have different problems, I am going to restrict myself to the Anglo-American-European West in the twentieth century. I do think, however, that the issues I raise here are relevant to the rest of the world – how could they not be, given the model of the Russian and Chinese revolutions, the erosion of colonialism, the eruption of nationalist revolutions, the predominance of bureaucratic forms of administration (where relations are between roles and not persons, as Weber said), the plundering of the earth as a standing-reserve, the growing inequalities both inside and between nations: the list goes on.

So what is the starting point? The past century saw a new form of warfare, involving not just a few nations but much of the globe; not just armies but entire populations, both actively and passively. A conservative estimate gives 155,000,000 deaths in the wars of the twentieth century, 43,000,000 deaths in genocides, 87,000,000 deaths from famine. And we are not counting those maimed in body and in spirit. What used to be thought of as 'nature' is increasingly treated as a supply dump from which humans may extract what they want. Derrida calls attention to 'the macroscopic fact [that] never before in absolute figures have so many men, women and children been subjugated, starved or exterminated on the earth'.[1] Nietzsche foresaw a period of *Geisterkriege* – wars 'the like of which had never been seen'. These were wars, one might say, for the *logos*: not for how to divide up what there was, but to determine what was to be divided. The question arises of whether we are capable of making sense of these developments.[2] Such wars are, as Raymond Aron wrote, *total* – they are about everything and involve everyone.[3] You may say that the period of *world* wars is behind us, but even more parochial wars tend to be total – about everything and everyone.

My sense is that the standard canon of Western political thought is not capable, or is only partially capable, of coming to grips with these developments. *To what texts might we turn?* This is the central question of a democratic theory for our times. I have recently finished a book that looks at seven thinkers (eight with the opening chapter on Kant) who all tried to think through the questions of the twentieth century 'without a banister'.[4] The phrase is originally Nietzsche's in *Thus Spoke Zarathustra* and elsewhere, and was taken over by

Arendt to designate a time when humans could – and were obliged to – think without the support of anything external to thought, to think on the basis of only that which humans are capable of, and of capacities that are only human. None of those considered in my book – Nietzsche, Weber, Freud, Lenin, Schmitt, Heidegger and Arendt – are liberals; only Arendt has at best half a claim to being some kind of democrat. Yet it is in their thought that I hope to have found resources adequate to a democratic understanding of our times. Tellingly, each of them thinks that two conceptual matrices get in the way of an adequate consideration of the present political and spiritual condition of the West. These are morality and Christianity. I am thus proposing that we try to develop an understanding of democracy that does not rest on moral considerations, but is not composed simply of a set of agreed-upon procedures either. My attempt here is to think about democracy without relying on moral judgements or more-or-less disguised Christian orientations.

Consider this citation from Max Weber:

> [I]t is immeasurably moving when a mature (*reif*) man – whether old or young in years – who truly feels this responsibility for consequences and acts with a whole soul in terms of the ethic of responsibility, arrives at some point where he says; 'I can do no other; here I stand.' This is something truly impressive (*ergreift*). For this situation truly must be possible at some point for each of us who is not inwardly dead. Insofar as the ethics of disposition and the ethics of responsibility are not absolute contraries, but complements, which only in combination constitute a genuine person (*echten* Menschen), one who can have the 'calling for politics.'[5]

Actions taken by such a person have the quality, Weber tells us, of providing the terms by which they are to be judged. Only those who are 'inwardly dead' will not respond to such presence. Such actions, however, are not subsumable under the standard understandings of morality – they create their own rules. More importantly, it is from the acts of those who bring them into existence that the terms by which they are to be understood (which does not mean necessarily accepted) come into being. Thus the Declaration of Independence brought into being something that had no existence before – *novus ordo saeclorum*, it will be called;[6] likewise, the declaration by the Third Estate in Paris on 20 June 1789 that it *was* the National Assembly brought into being something that had no existence. It is for this reason that Schmitt says that the Sovereign in cases of exception acts from 'nothing' and brings about a new order. [7]

The passage in Weber is further noteworthy in that it comes precisely at the moment that Weber considers the justification for the acts of a person who truly has politics as a vocation. It is an act that brings a world into existence; it succeeds in that those who are not 'spiritually dead' are moved by it, presumably to act differently than they had been. This existential Lutheran justification is explicitly not utilitarian; it clearly makes no reference to natural law, nor to the public good, nor to individual glory, nor to historical destiny, nor to God's plan, nor to the necessities of the universe. It rests on nothing but itself. No banister. Most centrally, it makes no appeal to a moral justification for policies.

The question of the place of morality

What is this distress with morality? Nietzsche holds that one can find oneself 'beyond good and evil'; neither Weber's leader nor Freud's hero who dreams without distortion have much to do with morality. The case is even clearer for Lenin (for all of his naïve claim that *after* the revolution basic moral principles, 'known for centuries', would re-emerge) and Carl Schmitt. Most of those who have sought to find an ethics or morality in Heidegger have grasped at straws or transformed him into a version of Levinas.[8] Even Arendt passes morality and the 'rights of man' by with hardly a wave of the hand.[9]

Why this refusal? It comes from the fact that in confronting the particular realities of the world in which they live – or which, in Nietzsche's case, they anticipated – there was a sense that the competence of morality to judge human affairs was not so much wrong as limited. The famous example from Sartre's 'Existentialism is a Humanism' (the young man who has to choose between staying with his infirm mother and joining the resistance against the Nazis) is intended to show that one might find oneself under two incompatible demands, both with a moral claim, without there being an overarching system of reasons that permits choice between them.[10] Choice will have to be made – but on what basis is not and cannot be clear, for there is no basis from which to make it.

What, however, are the consequences of this for our understanding of morality? Many of those who think about the relation of morality to human life assume that unless the validity of morality is independent of time, place and person, it cannot be a truly moral doctrine. This is held to be the case of moral doctrines in both the Kantian and post-Kantian forms, as well as in the various forms of utilitarianism. There are two aspects to a response to this position. The first is that various moral demands can at a given time make contradictory and incompatible claims upon us and hence that the application of a moral system cannot, in such circumstances, provide a directive as to what one should do. As such, the position is one that Bernard Williams explored at length. In *Ethics and the Limits of Philosophy* Williams argued that any moral system that held as basic tenets firstly that moral obligations could not conflict with each other (if properly understood), and secondly that in the end moral considerations carried an obligation that trumped all others, was necessarily false to our experience and to our intelligence. Indeed, at times, the justification of a choice will come only in how it turns out. Williams wrote: 'The only thing that will justify his choice will be success itself.'[11] Thus morality – *as a final system* – must be refused.

The second aspect follows, I think from the first and relates also to our experience. The fact that there are circumstances in our lives for which moral doctrine does not provide the (or an only) answer does not either mean that morality can *ad libitum* be rejected whole cloth, nor that it must fatalistically devolve into relativism. As Stanley Cavell has written:

> Morality must leave itself open to repudiation. It provides one possibility of settling conflict, a way of encompassing conflict which allows continuance of personal relationship against the hard and apparently inevitable fact of misunderstanding [. . .] Other ways of settling or encompassing conflict are provided by political, religion, love and forgiveness, rebellion, and withdrawal. Morality is a valuable way because the others are often so inaccessible or brutal; but it is not everything.[12]

The underlying premise here is that to the degree that moral principles are not derived from this world but from something beyond it (whether this be a Platonic or theological realm), the events of the twentieth century have made the belief in or the acceptance of such principles impossible for any person who faces the world as it has shown itself. The First World War had a devastating effect on the confidence that reason might solve human affairs. Arendt quotes Winston Churchill writing in the thirties: 'Scarcely anything, material or established, which I was brought up to believe was permanent and vital, has lasted. Everything I was sure, or was taught to be sure, was impossible, has happened.'[13]

Here is what Arendt says about morality:

> Even though we have lost yardsticks by which to measure, and rules under which to subsume the particular, a being whose essence is a beginning may have enough of origin within himself to understand without preconceived categories and to judge without the set of customary rules which is morality.[14]

If our 'essence is a beginning' – that is, if or when our being brings something new (an 'origin') into the world – then the 'preconceived' and the 'customary' will be inadequate to understand what has come to be. In such a circumstance, it can also be the case that we might encounter 'a position whose excellence we cannot deny, taken by persons we are not willing or able to dismiss, but which, *morally*, would have to be called wrong.'[15] Such a position, one might say, would be 'beyond good and evil'.

Some of the problems associated with this position can be seen in attitudes towards the various cultural revolutions that shook the world during the late 1960s. All my thinkers think that there is something *radically* wrong with contemporary Western civilisation and that if change is possible and is to occur, it will have to be radical change. Secondly, and more problematically, these thoughts can give rise to a deep suspicion of morality as a justification for *any* political action. This is not the old suspicion that morality might be a kind of personal judgement, an understanding that persists in the thought of philosophers like A. J. Ayer and Charles Stevenson.[16] It was rather that the categories of 'good and evil' seemed to be available to almost anyone. Thus a particular kind of moral relativism developed in the wake of the Second World War. The energy and apparent clarity of purpose that the Nazis brought to the justification of their enterprise called any singular grounding of the moral enterprise as a way of organising human affairs into radical doubt. The question 'what if the Nazis had won?' inescapably seemed to suggest that moral categories were relative to success and success relative to power. If that was so, the only answer was power – and power, it was thought, was not a moral category. As Stanley Cavell has written: 'Someday, if there is a someday, we will have to learn that evil thinks of itself as good, that it could not have made such progress in the world unless people planned and performed it in all conscience.'[17] The problem with the moral point of view after the death of God is that one retains the ability to think of what one does as good, and avoid seeing what one is *in fact* doing.[18]

The problem, it is important to note, does not lie so much with the crimes that the Nazis committed, horrible as those were. What is of greater importance is a general collapse of the possibility of transcendental moral standards. Arendt writes that the crimes of the Nazis pose no 'moral problems'. What, however, *does* pose a problem – and it is the problem of our age – is this:

> Morality collapsed into a mere set of mores – manners, customs, conventions to be changed at will – not with criminals, but with ordinary people, who, as long as moral standards were socially accepted, never dreamt of doubting what they had been taught to believe in.[19]

The problem is not so much Hitler as it is *us*. It is simply the case, she continues, that 'no one in his right mind can any longer claim that moral conduct is a matter of course'.[20]

Finally, the possibility of human extinction – that we can destroy all life on the planet – means that there can be no other terms to understand human life than those that it makes available to itself. This is what the death of God was to come to mean – that now humans will 'play dice with gods at gods' table, for the earth is a temple for the gods'.[21] Arendt's reminder and urging to love this earth, and her distress about the fantasies she saw in the public reactions to the launching of Sputnik, reflect the same thought.[22]

I will return to this below, but that which had been difficult and rare for Nietzsche, Weber, Freud and the others suddenly and facilely became the property of everyone who might think to claim it. And illegitimately so: as Cavell quickly goes on to say about the moral understanding: 'Not just anybody, in *any* way, can repudiate it.'[23] The question then becomes who, in what way, and when, *can* repudiate it. The answer I will come to suggest below is that these criteria are met in the realm that we call the political. There is another question.

The fate of Christianity

Marx proclaimed the 'criticism of religion to be the premise of all higher criticism'.[24] He meant that if left without critique, religion made impossible an understanding of the human. Religion did so because it posed an impossible requirement for true knowledge of an other: such knowledge was to be like the knowledge of God. And because knowledge of God was not possible, so also was knowledge of other human beings.

As noted, I am approaching these questions through texts that notoriously not only have little to do with Christianity, but reject it. Consider this passage in Weber:

> For weakness it is to be unable to look the fate of the age full in the face. The destiny of our culture, however, is that we shall once again become more clearly conscious of this situation after a millennium in which our allegedly or supposedly exclusive reliance on the glorious pathos of the Christian ethic had blinded us.[25]

How has the 'Christian ethic [. . .] blinded us'? At the very end of *On the Genealogy of Morals*, Nietzsche writes that humans would 'rather will the void than be void of will' – '*lieber* [. . .] *das* Nichts *wollen als* nicht *wollen*'. He means that even after the death of God, the structure of willing characteristic of the Socratico-Christian West will persist. That structure consists in the pursuit of something (truth, a banister) that is destined to fail, precisely because it is pursued. Yet one never gives up trying. The genius of Christianity was to have established that it was possible to attain truth, but in heaven. Nihilism consists in attempting to do something that cannot be done.[26] Cavell: 'The reason consequences furiously hunt us down is not merely that we are half blind, and unfortunate, but that we go on doing the thing that produced these consequences in the first place.'[27]

Contrast the Christian approach to a more ancient one. The Greeks retained a sense of human frailty in that human action was measured against the eternality of the natural world. Several points emerge from this consideration.

1. First is that the nature of contemporary human action is to initiate world processes, the consequences of which cannot be determined;

2. Second, the modern attitude towards such processes is to seek to render the world of human affairs stable at the expense of the natural world – a reversal of what Arendt takes to have been characteristic of the Greeks;[28]

3. Thirdly, the pursuit of the desire to make the world knowable – the aim of modern science – has paradoxically introduced human unpredictability into the natural world. Unleashed with this are sets of occurrences about which humans can make no human action. Events occur for which there can be neither forgiveness nor punishment. (One has only to think of the actual and coming ecological crises). Arendt: 'It is therefore quite significant, a structural element in the realm of human affairs, that men are unable to punish what has turned out to be unforgivable.' In *The Human Condition*, she refers this to Kant's understanding of 'radical evil' – and her experience with Eichmann will lead her to modify this to the idea of the 'banality of evil'. But, importantly, such events 'transcend the realm of human affairs and the potentialities of human power, both of which they radically destroy wherever they make their appearance. Indeed [. . .] the deed itself dispossesses us of all power.'[29]

If matters look bleak, it is because they are. In her 1967 Introduction to a re-issuing of Karl Jaspers's 1931 *Man in the Modern Age* Arendt writes: 'Jasper's forebodings of an imminent catastrophe [. . .] were denounced by respectable critics. It is of course the case that many of his predictions were vindicated.'[30] In her Introduction to Jaspers's 1960 *The Future of Germany* she warns again against the transformation of the political system into a 'dictatorship of the politicians', a warning that does not seem completely improbable.[31]

What might be a vision of politics that engages this? A speculation

It is also the case that being without a banister opens up possibilities. As Arendt remarks in the beginning of *The Life of the Mind*:

> [The] possible advantage of our situation following the demise of meta-physics and philosophy would be twofold. It would permit us to look on the past with new eyes, unburdened and unguided by any traditions, and thus to dispose of a tremendous wealth of raw experiences without being bound by any prescriptions as to how to deal with these treasures. '*Notre heritage n'est précédé d'aucun testament*' ('*No will and testament gives rise to that which is our legacy*').[32]

She goes on with a warning:

> The advantage would be even greater had it not been accompanied, almost inevitably, by a growing inability to move, on no matter what level, in the realm of the invisible; or, to put it another way, had it not been accompanied by the disrepute into which everything that is not visible, tangible, palpable has fallen, so that we are in danger of losing the past itself together with our traditions.[33]

How so? In the essay *La comparution (The Compearance)*, Jean-Luc Nancy poses a double question: 'how to exclude without fixing (*figurer*)? And how to fix without excluding?'[34] The answer to his question is difficult. I think it would go something like this:[35] any understanding of citizenship – essential for an understanding of democracy – presupposes insiders and outsiders. Let us consider the problem of the outsider – for Nancy here the 'Arab', but for others the 'Turk' or the 'Mexican' or the 'black' or the Moslem or the Sikh (or the 'male' or the 'female' or the 'gay'). I clearly know that the out-sider is in some sense different from me – not to admit this would be to deny the actuality of our presence to each other. (It follows from this, for instance, that 'race' cannot be relegated, as does Rawls, to the private world in the conversation of justice: part of what justice requires is not avoiding that an other is what that other is to me).[36] I think I also have to say, following the analysis in Stanley Cavell's *The Claim of Reason*, that I cannot fall back on the (again Rawlsian) claim that the other and I could or do have common understandings of primary goods. I may claim precisely that we do not, that the other is not (really, fully) human ('I just can't stand their smell [. . .] they are not like us, you know').

When I say something like that about the other, what is it that I am missing about them, or what is it that I want to miss? Take the case of the most clear-cut attempt at denial of that which we have in common with another being that is human. Cavell:

> What [a man who sees certain others as slaves] is missing is not something about slaves exactly and not exactly about human beings. He is missing something about himself, or rather something about his connection with these people, his internal relation with them, so to speak.[37]

Cavell goes on to point out that my actions show that I cannot *mean in fact* that the other is not human, or is less than human.

> When he wants to be served at table by a black hand, he would not be satisfied to be served by a black paw. When he rapes a slave, or takes her as a concubine, he does not feel that he has by that fact itself, embraced sodomy. When he tips a black taxi driver [. . .] it does not occur to him that he might more appropriately have patted the creature fondly on the side of the neck.[38]

No matter what the slave owner, or the Frenchman in Nancy's essay, can claim (and assert that they truly believe), their *actions* show that they hold something quite different. He can allow that the others have qualities (their cuisine or their music, say), but what he cannot allow is for them to see themselves as he sees them. For then, he would see himself as they see him. His power consists in requiring that the others have no existence for him except that which he allows. Montesquieu saw this as the central quality of tyranny in *The Persian Letters*.

So what counts is in fact what *we do*, not what we claim to believe (and do believe). What is missing is the act that is an acknowledgement of the other. It is not simply a matter of knowing (all there might be to know) something about the other, but acknowledgement of the other. Picture: You are late, you know you are late, I know you are late, you know that I know you are late. Knowledge does not suffice: you *have to do something* – in this case say 'I am sorry.' Cavell again:

> [A]cknowledgment goes beyond knowledge not in the order, or as a feat, of cognition, but in the call upon me to express the knowledge at its core, to recognize what I know, to do something in the light of it, apart from which this knowledge remains without expression, hence perhaps without possession [. . .] [A]cknowledgment of the other calls for recognition of the other's *specific* relation to oneself, and that this entails the revelation of oneself as having denied or distorted that relationship.[39]

Acknowledgement is to express that which we are often inclined to suppress, especially that which surpasses the standard conventions of a time, no matter how beneficent these might appear under most circumstances. It is to recognise the place of others in a world that is in common. It is necessarily a revealing (to oneself, to others) of something about oneself. To hear as one's own the voice of the other is to recognise something about one's relation to the other – that there is the relation of being human – and to recognise *one's constant temptation to deny that relation*, that is, to exclude and fix the other *as* other. My existence as human depends on theirs, and this in turn on the acknowledgement that no one's soul or self or body is his or her own. This is what Arendt, following thoughts like these, will call an 'enlarged consciousness' and it is the basis of the political or public realm she evokes.[40] Likewise, Arendt's judgement on Eichmann is that no one could rationally want to share the earth with him. We verge here on territory that is only beginning to be explored. Acknowledgement in the case of the reconstitution of the self along the lines of this journey both introduces contingency in any conception of justice (there may be a first word, but there is never a last) and makes impossible the 'core-periphery' conception of a just political society so dear to the hearts of liberals.

It also introduces a whole new set of questions and problems for a truly democratic theory for our modern, post-modern, Western times. Here it is important to see that that 'being human' is something that is attained, not something that one has as given equipment.[41] As Weber noted, bureaucracies are not relations between human beings but between roles, and having a role is comforting – one knows what to do.

Such recognitions, however, have to take actual place. That is, one cannot acknowledge in any meaningful sense the human race. A consequence (but not a premise) of acknowledgment is that one must consent to live with certain people and not with those with whom one has not consented. Consent here is neither tacit nor explicit: it is what one has done by living in a particular place and time. (I may not think of the government as *my* government, but it remains *our* government.) Here is the difference between the political and what one might broadly call the economic realm. An economic act is one's own, and it is purely one's own. *In politics, however, the consent I have given speaks not only for myself but also speaks for – makes a claim on – others. I speak for – I claim to speak for – the others with whom I associate myself. Likewise they speak for and claim to speak for me.* They do not speak for me in the way that I spoke for my child when she was quite young; rather, they speak – that is they can legitimately claim to speak – what is in my mind; at times, they may even know it better than I do. Thus, as Americans, we acknowledge that the Constitution is the final arbiter of what it means to be an American, even if I may not always know, or agree with you, as to what that means in any particular instance. Likewise I speak for them – that is, when I speak politically I am making a claim which I take to apply to those who find themselves (albeit and especially when unthinkingly) with me. As Ralph Ellison says at the end of *Invisible Man*: 'Who knows but on the lower depths I speak for you?'

My saying 'I am an American' is a claim about myself that is necessarily a claim about any who make that claim, and only about those who make that claim. This is the stuff of the political and it is necessarily democratic. Since nothing guarantees that you will automatically accept or acknowledge my claim, conflict, discussion, argument, struggle, voting and so forth are necessary: this is, as Andreas Kalyvas argues, the stuff of politics.[42] Importantly (as opposed to, say, in arithmetic), I cannot compel you to accept my position: here it is worth reflecting on precisely what happens when one persuades or is persuaded.

But if the political is for these reasons more extensive – that I speak not only for myself but my words must carry the claim to speak for others – *the political is also for that reason perhaps the most fragile of human activities*. It rests on nothing other than acknowledging and being acknowledged. I can speak for myself in other realms, but in politics the judgement of others – and the possibility of being refused – is ever immediately present. Others may want to silence my voice; I may even not note or know that I am silenced – there are so many others speaking. If the political depends on the possibility of acknowledgement of a claim that I make as a claim about us, if my claim falls on deaf ears and fallow ground, then I cannot act politically. Note that I do not mean that others must accept what I say: the political requires only that they acknowledge it as a claim. One of the reasons for the contemporary cynicism about politics in my country is, I suspect, that many simply do not feel that they can be heard.[43]

All this rests on the sense of the importance of the fragility of a life that is human. Indeed if it were not fragile, it would not be human.[44]

The space in which this happens – and from which we are constantly falling out – is the space we have for 2,500 years named the *polis*. Arendt returns explicitly to Kant's *Third Critique* and derives from it an understanding of political thinking as representative in that it involves an 'enlarged mentality'. As Nietzsche wrote: 'One is always wrong: truth begins with two.'[45] A bit later, he will elaborate:

What I am most in need of, for my health and my own recovery – that would be the belief that I was not alone, that I did not see alone – an enchanted suspicion on companionship and similarity of sight and desire, a response in the confidence of friendship, a blindness for two without suspicion and questioning, a delight in foregrounds, in surfaces, in proximity, in neighbours, in all that has colour, skin and appearance.[46]

And requiring that there be two always leaves a question open; for one may withdraw, refuse, turn away, as so many have done.

'A blindness for two.' This calls for acceptance of the risk of contingency in human affairs. And given the demands of fragility – which is why the human and the political are, as Aristotle saw, coterminous – although nothing is more a sign of the weakness of our humanity than to want to give life solidity and permanence. To call for the valorisation of fragility is nothing less than to call for a place for tragedy in human affairs. To want to reject it, is to seek to remove the tragic from human experience. We live in a time when the rage to know (and not just in the social sciences) is pandemic. The effect of this is to attempt to remove all that is unknown from the world, or, as in Carl Schmitt's critique, to relegate that which cannot be known to the individually relative and subjective. What is central here is that we retain the unknown, acknowledge it as unknowable, on the grounds that it is only if there is that which we do not know that there can be hope for human reason.

The question remains: what kind of human being must one be to do this? In his notes, Wittgenstein jotted this down:

> There is no tragedy in this world [the one I am in], and thus there is nothing that is without limits [das *Unendliche*], which in fact is that which gives rise to tragedy [as its result].
>
> It is so to speak as if everything was soluble in the aether of the world; there is nothing hard.
>
> This means that hardness and conflict do not come into a commanding position [*wird nicht zu etwas Herrlichem*], but rather seem a defect.[47]

What does it mean for 'hardness' to come into a 'commanding position'? Likewise Nietzsche, through the mouth of Zarathustra, sets a new commandment to his 'brothers': to 'become hard'.[48] What does he mean? Few passages in Nietzsche have taken more criticism than this one. And his language *is* dangerous. Jonathan Glover, for instance sees this as a 'rejection of unmanly compassion, support[ing] the domination, even the cruel domination of others'.[49] Yet such readings are thin: at the beginning of the section Glover cites, Nietzsche presents an exchange between the diamond and the 'kitchen-coal'. The latter asks the former 'Why so hard? Are we not close relations?' The diamond responds: 'Why so soft? – Are you then not my brother?' Democracy must raise the question of human excellence. There are two ways of seeing excellence in human beings. The first is to claim that some are simply more, better, superior to others. Nietzsche is often read this way. But there is another. Remember that diamond and coal are close relations, even brothers. Diamond's response to coal is not to tell him that he is lesser, but to ask him *why he is not more*. A second way of seeing excellence is to ask why most humans are not more than they are, why they live, as Thoreau remarked, 'lives of quiet desperation'. (It is understandings of this kind that motivated the work of Theodor Adorno, Max Horkheimer and others of the Frankfurt School – a quality, alas, mostly lost in their present-day would-be descendants.).

Why are most (of us) not more? We are, in Nietzsche's/Zarathustra's diamond words, 'weak'. To be weak here means to acquiesce to norms ('tablets') that are consequent to weariness, to submission to the forms of the society that is. As Nietzsche says: 'One span' away from another world, humans would from weariness prefer to 'die of thirst'.[50] Note that he tells us that another world is within our reach, but it is one which we do not reach. Our weariness will not be overcome by gaining more knowledge about the world – indeed, that is simply a continuing expression of weariness. When Cavell speaks of acknowledgement here he does not mean simply that one should add the normative to our knowledge ('do what we ought'). It is rather to respond to something about oneself.[51] This is why the foregrounding of the moral is misguided. And it is precisely this response that requires that one become 'hard'. *The issue that must be faced in modern times is that the words 'good' and 'evil' have become too promiscuous.* When Nietzsche calls to 'break the good and the just'[52] he is reflecting on what one might call the moralisation of morality in the present period. The 'moralisation of morality' means simply that what is *called* 'good' is taken – without immediate dishonesty – to *be* good. Cavell again: 'the moralisation of moral theory has done to moral philosophy and the concept of morality what the events to the modern world have often done to the moral life itself: made it a matter of academic question'.[53] As Arendt wrote:

> We can no longer afford to take that which was good in the past and simply call it our heritage, to discard the bad and think of it as a dead load which by itself time will bury in oblivion. The subterranean stream of Western tradition has finally come to the surface and usurped the dignity of our tradition. This is the reality in which we live. And this is why all efforts to escape from the grimness of the present into nostalgia for a still intact past, or into the anticipated of a still better future, are vain.[54]

To persist in a vain enterprise is mere vanity. We need to tone the 'insane and independent energy of reason'. [55] When morality is moralised, we will and do justify the consequences of reason – a justification that leads increasingly to the destruction of lives and peoples – we have but to look around. Since Machiavelli at least, we have tended to see politics as theatre, played by characters who fill their roles: prince and mass, sovereign and populace, capitalism and proletarians, white and black, leaders and led. And if all we are is characters playing a role – this was Weber's fear for the modern age – then there is nothing to be done about those roles – merely to play them out. Rather we need to start from the conviction that no one actually is, as him or herself, any thing in particular. And precisely from that lack of definition we might start to find ourselves in acknowledgement of an other, of others. That we are no thing – nothing in particular – is the foundation of democracy: this was the promise of the *Internationale* and of Walt Whitman, of Rousseau and Nietzsche. These are our texts.

Notes

1. Jacques Derrida, *Spectres of Marx* (New York: Routledge, 1994), p. 85.
2. Here are some other facts about the present:
   The enormous increase in capital transfers across the entire world; by 1997, on a typical day that world capital markets would move $1.3 trillion at a time when the total yearly value of world exports was $3 trillion. By 2007 daily capital market transfers were 3.2 trillion, which is equivalent to $2.2 billion a minute. Yearly total world exports are now up to 17.09 trillion.
   The rise of regional, and international, policy pursuing bodies: worldwide, there are at least 49,411 registered NGOs with the WANGO, of which, tellingly, the fewest proportionally and almost absolutely are in China.
   The efforts of global corporations and financiers to divorce themselves from state regulations and tax regimes; with a few exceptions, it no longer makes sense to think in terms of national financial markets. They are increasingly being integrated into a single global one, as cross-border holdings of financial assets and cross-border flows of capital grow. Today, for example, foreigners hold 12 per cent of US equities, 25 per cent of US corporate bonds and 44 per cent of Treasury securities, up from 4, 1 and 20 per cent, respectively, in 1975. Cross-border capital flows create stronger links among national markets and clearly show that despite the past decade's financial crises and the backlash against globalisation, the world capital market continues to integrate and evolve.
   The increasing governing of nations on principles of economic

growth; and the rise of businessmen where there once were politicians. As Peter Mandelson, the EU trade commissioner, said recently, 'it's most likely that businessmen and entrepreneurs, rather than diplomats, ministers and special commissioners, will provide for economic and political rapprochement between Russia and the EU'.

3. Raymond Aron, *The Century of Total War* (New York: Praeger, 1981).

4. Tracy B. Strong, *Politics without Vision: Thinking without a Banister in the Twentieth Century* (Chicago: University of Chicago Press, 2012). Some material in this chapter is adapted from my book.

5. Max Weber, 'Politik als Beruf' ('Politics as a Vocation'), in Weber, *Gesammelte Politische Schriften* (Tübingen: Mohr, 1965); Max Weber, *The Vocation Lectures*, eds David Owen and Tracy Strong (Cambridge: Hackett, 1997), p. 92.

6. Thus Arendt entitles Chapter Five of *On Revolution* (Viking: New York, 1963) 'Novus Ordo Saeclorum' – the motto of the United States and derived from a passage in Virgil.

7. See Joseph Lima and Tracy B. Strong, 'Telling the Dancer from the Dance: On the Relevance of the Ordinary for Political Theory', in Andrew Norri (ed.), *Stanley Cavell and the Claim of Community* (Redwood City, CA: Stanford University Press, 1999).

8. See e.g. Donovan Miyasaki, 'A Ground for Ethics in Heidegger's Being and Time', *Journal of the British Society for Phenomenology*, 38, no. 3 (2007): 261–79; Michael Lewis, *Heidegger and the Place of Ethics* (London: Continuum, 2005); Joanna Hodge, *Heidegger and Ethics* (London: Routledge, 1995); and see the discussion by Herman Philipse, 'Heidegger and Ethics', *Inquiry*, 42 (1999): 439–74.

9. See the extended discussion in my *Politics without Vision*, Chapters 2 through 9.

10. This is a consequence of Bernard Williams's argument against the existence of 'external reasons': 'Internal and External Reasons', *Moral Luck* (Cambridge: Cambridge University Press, 1981), pp. 101–13. The implication is that there may be beings for whom (in some areas 'we' would normally think moral) moral reasons are not relevant.

11. Bernard Williams, *Moral Luck*, p. 18.

12. Stanley Cavell, *The Claim of Reason* (Oxford: Clarendon, 1979), p. 269. See the account in Richard T. Eldridge, 'Stanley Cavell and Ethics', in Eldridge, *Stanley Cavell* (Cambridge: Cambridge University Press, 2003), pp. 21–45. On the question of why relativism is not a consequence of Nietzsche's, see Babette Babich, *Nietzsche's Philosophy of Science* (Albany, NY: State University of New York Press, 1994), pp. 51–6.

13. Cited in Hannah Arendt, 'Some Questions of Moral Philosophy', *Responsibility and Judgment*, p. 30. Jonathan Glover, *Humanity: A Moral History of the Twentieth Century* (New Haven, CT: Yale University Press, 2007), ch. 1 and p. 408ff., refers to a 'fading of the moral law' (although his heartfelt and often moving book is designed to put it back in focus: 'The best hope of this is to work with the grain

of human nature, making use of the resources of moral identity and the human responses.') One can only wonder about the saliency of these 'resources' and whether the 'grain of human nature' exists and is straight (p. 409). Kant warned us about this.

14. Hannah Arendt, 'Understanding and Politics', in Hannah Arendt, *Essays in Understanding* (New York: Schocken, 1994), p. 321.
15. Cavell, *The Claim of Reason*, pp. 268–9.
16. Charles Stevenson, *Ethics and Language* [1944] (New Haven, CT: Yale University Press, 1965). See though Colin Wilks, *Emotion, Truth and Meaning: In Defense of Ayer and Stevenson* (Berlin: Springer Verlag, 2002).
17. Stanley Cavell, *Must We Mean What We Say?* (New York: Scribners, 1970), p. 136.
18. One has only to look at the 'bringing of democracy' to Iraq. Hence Arendt will speak of the fragility of facts in her 'Truth and Politics' in Hannah Arendt, *Between Past and Future* (New York: Viking Press, 1961).
19. Arendt, 'Some Questions of Moral Philosophy', p. 54.
20. Ibid., p. 61.
21. Friedrich Nietzsche, *Thus Spoke Zarathustra*, 'Seven Seals', 3, in Giorgio Colli and Mazzino Montinari (eds), *Werke: Kritische Gesamtausgabe* (Berlin/New York: de Gruyter, 1966), VI.3: 296.
22. It is for this reason that she opens *The Human Condition* with a discussion of Sputnik. See Hannah Arendt, *The Human Condition* (Chicago: University of Chicago Press, 1958).
23. Cavell, *The Claim of Reason*, p. 269.
24. Karl Marx, 'Preface to a Contribution to the Critique of Hegel's Philosophy of Right'.
25. Weber, 'Politik als Beruf'.
26. I cannot resist noting that Groucho Marx was admitting to a form of nihilism when he said, 'I don't want to belong to any club that will accept me as a member.'
27. Cavell, 'The Avoidance of Love', in *Must We Mean What We Say?*, p. 309. This understanding of nihilism was present in my doctoral thesis (1968), and later my first book (1975). As Cavell says: 'Nietzsche was not crazy when he blamed morality for the worst evils, though he may have become too crazy about the idea.' That said, Cavell also has a complex respect for Christianity. See Espen Dahl, 'On Acknowledgment and Cavell's Unacknowledged Theological Voice', *The Heythroth Journal*, 51, no. 6 (2010): 931–45.
28. Compare Max Weber, 'Wissenschaft als Beruf', in Weber, *Wissenschaftslehre* (Tübingen: Mohr, 1966), p. 604; Max Weber, *Vocation Lectures*, p. 23: 'Now the gods have been deprived of the magical and mythical but inwardly true qualities that gave them such vivid immediacy.'
29. Arendt, *The Human Condition*, p. 241. Importantly, this development is related by Nietzsche to the death of the political. In 1871, with his

attention still turning around the problematic of *The Birth of Tragedy* and the problem of political identity, he writes: 'From what does the art of the state disappear? From science. And this from what? A turning away from wisdom, a lack of artistry.' Nietzsche, *Werke: Kritische Gesamtausgabe*, III.3: 156.

30. Babette Babich, 'Jaspers, Heidegger, and Arendt: On Politics, Science and Communication', *Existenz* 4, no. 1 (Spring 2009).

31. Hannah Arendt, 'Foreword', in Karl Jaspers, *The Future of Germany* (Chicago: University of Chicago Press, 1967).

32. The citation is from René Char and was one of Arendt's favourites; she uses it in at least four places, including as the epigraph to Chapter Six of *On Revolution*.

33. Hannah Arendt, *The Life of the Mind* (New York: Harvest Books, 1978), p. 12.

34. Jean-Luc Nancy, 'La comparution – The Compearance', *Political Theory* (April 1996): 393.

35. I am importantly indebted here to Cavell, *The Claim of Reason*, as well as to email exchanges with Utz Lars McKnight (University of Alabama) and Linda Zerilli (University of Chicago).

36. See here Utz Lars McKnight, *Race and Political Liberalism* (Lund: University of Lund, 1996), ch. 1.

37. Cavell, *The Claim of Reason*, p. 377. Here it is worth noting that the Nazis kept careful records of those incarcerated in the camps.

38. Ibid.

39. Ibid., p. 428 (my emphasis). The question of acknowledgement has been best explored in recent political theory in Patchen Markell, *Bound by Recognition* (Princeton, NJ: Princeton University Press, 2003).

40. See Charles Louis de Secondat Montesquieu, *The Persian Letters*, trans. C. J. Betts (London: Penguin Books, 1973). Indeed, this may be what Montesquieu was trying to capture in his telling of the undoing of the Troglodyte community. Letter 11 of *The Persian Letters* concludes with the words of a doctor from a neighbouring country who had been wronged by the Troglodytes: '"Away with you!" he said, "for you are unjust. In your souls is a poison deadlier than that for which you want a cure. You do not deserve to have a place on earth, because you have no humanity, and the rules of equity are unknown to you."'

41. For Rousseau, for instance, kings, slaves, gentlemen, bourgeois and so forth are explicitly not human.

42. It is this recognition that is at the basis of the attraction of some on the Left to Carl Schmitt. See, e.g., Chantal Mouffe, 'Carl Schmitt and the Paradox of Liberal Democracy', in David Dyzenhaus (ed.), *Law as Politics: Carl Schmitt's critique of liberalism* (Durham, NC: Duke University Press, 1998), pp. 159–78.

43. A 2007 Rasmussen survey found that 16 per cent believe that government reflects the will of the people; 11 per cent say that Congress is doing a good or excellent job. At December 2010 the rate lowers to 9 per cent. See http://www.rasmussenreports.com/content/pdf/1066 (last

accessed 29 June 2015). When the President can proclaim, 'I am the decider', it is no wonder that Carl Schmitt's decisionist model enjoys analytical popularity.

44. My sentence calls to mind Martha Nussbaum's *The Fragility of Goodness* [1986] (Cambridge: Cambridge University Press, 2001), a book I greatly admire. My difference with her is that she relates the question of fragility to ethics or morality; I relate it to the political.

45. Nietzsche, *The Gay Science*, 26, in Colli and Montinari, *Werke: Kritische Gesamtausgabe*, V.2: 195. Cf. Ecclesiastes, 4:9.

46. Nietzsche, *Human, All Too Human*, in Colli and Montinari, *Werke: Kritische Gesamtausgabe*, IV.2: 7.

47. Ludwig Wittgenstein, *Culture and Value*, eds Georg Henrik von Wright, Heikki Nyman and Alois Pichler (London: InteLex, 1998), p. 12. Translation extensively modified.

48. Friedrich Nietzsche, *Thus Spoke Zarathustra* – On Old and New Tablets, in Colli and Montinari, *Werke: Kritische Gesamtausgabe*, VI.1: 264; see also *Dawn of Day*, 541; *Beyond Good and Evil*, 62; *Gay Science*, 28.

49. Glover, *Humanity*, p. 16.

50. Nietzsche, *Thus Spoke Zarathustra*, in Colli and Montinari, *Werke: Kritische* Gesamtausgabe, VI.2: 256.

51. See the excellent discussion in Markell, *Bound by Recognition*, pp. 34–5.

52. Nietzsche, *Thus Spoke Zarathustra*, in Colli and Montinari, *Werke: Kritische* Gesamtausgabe, VI.2: 263.

53. Cavell, *The Claim of Reason*, pp. 269–70. See my discussion in 'Nihilism and Political Theory', in John S. Nelson (ed.), *What Should Political Theory Be Now?* (Albany, NY: State University of New York Press, 1983), pp. 243–63.

54. Hannah Arendt, *The Origins of Totalitarianism* [1951] (New York and London: Harvest Books, 1978), p. 381.

55. Stanley Cavell, *The World Viewed* [1971] (Cambridge, MA: Harvard University Press, 1979), p. 92.

12 Epilogue: Democracy as Capacity for Self-Transformation

Gerard Rosich and Peter Wagner

Democracy is the hegemonic political form today, and at the same time it is often diagnosed as being in profound trouble, even as having reached the end of its possibilities. To arrive at a more adequate understanding of the current state of democracy, in the light of the observations and reflections of the preceding chapters, we proceed in three steps. First, we briefly portray the three dominant views of democracy as underestimating historicity in favour of conceptuality. Secondly, as an alternative, we try to identify the key tensions with the concept of democracy that are actualised in different ways under changing historical conditions. On this basis, finally, we outline the main reasons for the current trouble with democracy.

Three views of current democracy

According to the affirmative narrative, democracy is in its best state ever. After a long history of breakthroughs and setbacks, the democratic imaginary has finally imposed itself all over the world. A wide range of democratic institutions exists with considerable popular support, or at least consent, and there is no other political form that competes against it. At this moment, some contemporary thinkers and politicians do not hesitate to close the historical gap between reality and ideality, which had allowed for unlimited political progress to happen: nowadays reality and ideality are finally matching. Therefore, any critique of the existing democracies is only possible from an instrumental or technical perspective, not from a normative one – from a reformist, not from a radical one, to use Luc Boltanski's distinction.[1] From this moment on, we only have to manage and administer efficiently the democratic institutions in order to keep together the form and content of democracy. The temporal gap between the idea of democracy and its actuality is closed; to criticise democracy would be tantamount to a rejection of democracy *per se*. Accordingly, the troubles that democracy faces are external and not generated by its own dynamics. They are associated with the other or the outside: religious fundamentalism, power relations, cultural difference and so on. Democracy itself is a stable political accomplishment.

In contrast, the existing critical narrative corresponds roughly to the inverted view. In short, it assumes that what is commonly understood as democracy is only a technique of government which conceals that the real constitution of political power is in fact non-democratic: reality and ideality are always in conflict. The critical task is to unveil in any allegedly democratic institution its anti-democratic element due to the imbalance of power relations or violence, be it symbolic or material. Only in exceptional moments, normally revolutions, does democracy become real. Contemporary theories on biopolitics or governmentality are forms of this narrative. A wide variety of answers is given to the question about what it is that is concealed: class struggle, gender domination, racial supremacy, bare life, national domination, etc. If the affirmative narrative reifies democracy and is unable to accommodate change or crisis, the critical narrative is in its optimistic version idealistic and messianic, and in its pessimistic version dystopian and apocalyptic. It understands stability as the sedimentation of power relations that hampers any democratic aspiration.

These two narratives have co-existed for a long time. More recently, a new proposal to escape from the irreconcilable opposition between them has been to state that democracy is a conundrum in itself. In this view, democracy's essence is paradoxical or aporetic; its institutionalisation is phenomenologically unfeasible or would turn out to be self-destructive. In the former case, an assumed property of democracy entails its contrary – for instance, the democratic self blurs the difference between the self and the other. In the latter case, an essential property negates or abolishes another essential property – for instance, the principle of freedom and the principle of equality are not reconcilable and therefore the enforcement of a real democratic polity is not possible by virtue of its own presuppositions. There is a third variation of this theme, which suggests that democracy includes the possibility of its self-cancellation because it does not impose any limits, in accordance with its premises, on any form of democratic agency. Nathalie Karagiannis's contribution to this volume provides a critique of this perspective, showing that the alleged paradoxical nature of democracy only emerges when we consider self-cancellation itself as a democratic action.

Though all of these narratives offer insights for the analysis of specific historical constellations of democracy, they are not plausible as the *general* theory of democracy as which they are often proposed. The affirmative narrative helps to analyse democratic institutions when they have been in place and are stable for a long time: so-called consolidated democracies. When used as a theory of democracy, however, they tend to mistake a *finite* and *temporary* state of stability for a situation of *absolute completeness* of democracy, under which all the possibilities of the democratic imaginary are subsumed – and those that are not are considered as anti-democratic. The critical narrative offers a plausible hypothesis for situations where the democratic institutions once enacted by the demos have become self-sustaining, with the forms of domination they contain, and the active participation of the demos is no longer necessary for their reproduction. Lastly, the paradoxical narrative is suitable for those moments in which the demos is, in the words of Cornelius Castoriadis, at the same time and place, the instituting and the instituted, i.e. revolutionary or foundational situations, or inversely, for moments, as Nathalie Karagiannis points out regarding the state of exception and totalitarianism, in which a democratic regime ends by a political decision. Other allegedly paradoxical features of democracy only appear by the effect of assuming *possible* contents of a democratic regime as *necessary*. Both the meaning and the outcome of democracy are defined in such an axiomatic manner that their interplay can only be paradoxical.

This short summary – to some extent a caricature – of the current assessments of the state of democracy serves us here to illustrate that which we did not want to do in this book. When one starts from the assumption that human beings are the instituting actors of any political formation, it becomes immediately clear that the key problem of these approaches is that they do not engage with the actual experiences of democracy, with the contexts in which people live and elaborate their political self-understandings and interpretations. Concepts are created, used and received by human beings to guide their actions and constitute a common space of interpretation. Against the background of novel and unprecedented experiences, new practices emerge and others disappear and with them new concepts are created or change their meaning in order to produce a new common space of interpretation. Political concepts do not refer to any external reality that exists independently of the presence of human beings. They are tools of self-institution that transform or create the reality to which they refer, and since plurality is the condition of human beings on earth, there is no a priori consensus about their meaning. Democracy is one of these concepts, and its peculiarity is that it neither provides an unambiguous meaning nor supports a single institutional setting. It is the explicit recognition of the collective capacity of a self-instituting polity. Thus, it is no surprise that its meaning is contested from the very beginning, from the moment it implies the interaction of the human beings that constitute a collectivity. This is one of the reasons why it is often accompanied by an adjective that qualifies it: liberal, representative, parliamentary, organic, direct, etc. At the same time, knowing that under democracy the political reality is self-instituted by a plurality of actors and is the result of collective action, strife over its change or conservation is a normal consequence, which opens the space for critique and progress. Thus, rather than inviting for conceptual stabilisation, democracy implies the capacity of a society for self-transformation.

Tensions within the concept of democracy

Democracy, as we understand it here, is the collective capacity of being autonomous, of giving oneself one's own laws. As such, it is not automatically associated with any particular institutional form, be it the constitutional state or the parliamentary system; nor with any historical formation, i.e. modern times against ancient, archaic or medieval times; nor with any anthropology of the human being or ethnology of peoples. It is a particular way, an ethos, of dealing both with the plurality of human beings and with the need of creating rules for life in common and stabilising them. Desirable as it is to speak in comparative terms of the presence or absence of a democratic regime, and to record the varieties of its eventual formation and analyse its meaning and inner workings, this should not be done by conceptual presupposition based on one particular experience, the one of 'modern' democracy in recent Europe and North America. Rather, it is necessary to explore a wide range of historical sources in order to capture the variety of institutions in which expressions of this political imaginary of democracy are present.[2]

Historically speaking, many of the troubles with analysing democracy arise because democracy is equated with the institutional order that recently emerged in 'the West'.[3] Conceptually speaking, in turn, troubles arise when the capacity of acting autonomously is disconnected from instituting an order. According to a time-honoured intellectual tradition, these two phenomena imply different logics, each with their own dynamics. Though there can be an order without being democratic, however, it is difficult to imagine a democracy without creating order. Autonomy, to give oneself one's own laws, already contains the need of having an order and institutions, namely to establish the law that henceforth is to guide one's own actions, or in other words, to control the outcome of one's own actions. In the same move, a tension is created: once there is a law to be followed, there is a limit to autonomy. Emphasising this tension may lead to the erroneous view that to have an order is in principle anti-democratic or that it is ontogenetically prior to the exercise of collective autonomy. The tension increases as times elapses and the self that gives the law is no longer exactly the same as the one that obeys the law. A democratic order will always need to remain aware of its capacity for self-transformation so as to avoid domination, a situation in which the self that obeys the law has not created it.

That is why the concern for stability – present in all three narratives, even though as something unattainable in the third one – can itself create trouble for democracy, namely when its purpose and effect is to limit this capacity for self-transformation. In the affirmative view, lack of stability causes deep troubles: fiscal crisis, political violence, populism and even regress of democracy, to just mention current crisis topics. In turn, not being able to entrench the capacity for self-transformation in a democratic order means to legitimise the critiques of democracy, claiming that contemporary democracy conceals domination. The insistence on stability becomes then an unambiguous support for the maintenance of the status quo by those who benefit from it. Sometimes it is even an argument used against transformative democratic action that would create a new order as a consequence of the *instability* of the existing one. Andreas Kalyvas's contribution to this volume is a critique of the still-dominant intellectual tradition that has understood the democratic imaginary as a particular justificatory repertoire based on popular sovereignty which is conceptualised so as to legitimise state power. In his words, 'the question of democracy does not pertain solely to *where* sovereignty lies and *who* possesses it but mainly to *what* sovereignty is and *how* it is manifested and enacted'. In contrast, when the capacity for self-transformation is asserted, this ability helps to overcome moments of critical instability on the one hand, and on the other hand it is also a means to overcome domination that is crystallised in the contingent institutional order.

Thus, it is not instability that spells trouble for democracy, but the lack of capacity for self-transformation, in particular in situations in which transformations may be needed for democracy to prevail or to move closer to fulfilling the normative promises of the democratic political imaginary. In other words, the main problem for understanding the prospects for democracy today is to identify that which in the current socio-political situation requires self-transformation but may exceed the existing capacity for self-transformation. In what follows we will make a brief attempt into this direction. Because we are referring to events in the present, it is very difficult to avoid the distorting effect of being an actor and an observer at the same time. The analysis can either be influenced by manufactured public opinion or biased by one's own normative commitments. In turn, historical comparisons can be fruitful in order to assess which are recurring troubles with democracy and which are the dilemmas which democracy can neither escape from nor ignore. However, any particular chosen comparison might induce the error of seeing the present as determined by the past. Thus, we will first embark on a brief conceptual reflection which is sensitive to historical experiences without being determined by them. Subsequently, we will address the present without, hopefully, being captured by it.

Democracy is the political form that is based on the commitment to autonomy, to give oneself one's own law and to follow those self-given laws. First of all, therefore, democracy requires a 'self'. This self is by definition a collectivity, the membership of which needs to be defined. And this collectivity needs to be capable of action, which leads to further requirements: it needs to be sufficiently separate from its 'outside', other collectivities; it needs to be capable of collective decision-making; and it needs to be capable of implementing its decisions.

In theory (as discussed in Chapter 1), the sovereign democratic nation-state is the political form that fulfills all these criteria. The democratic self is the people. Its boundaries towards the outside are defined through the concept of 'nation', binding members of one nation to each other and excluding members of other nations. Internally, the rights-holding individual is the unit citizen, and the aggregate preferences of these citizens constitute the collective will. This will is implemented by the sovereign state. The state defines and protects the external boundaries by means of tariffs, passports, the military and other devices. Internally, it implements the collective will by means of law-making in parliament, law-enforcing through the police and the judiciary, and law-application through a neutral bureaucracy.

One can see the sovereign democratic nation-state as the arrangement that translates the democratic political imaginary, which forcefully arose in the late eighteenth century, into an institutional form. One may even suggest that the idea of building such nation-states guided much political action from then on until the present. However, it would be untrue to say that the sovereign democratic nation-state has been the dominant political form at any time before the end of the Second World War. This discrepancy between the political imaginary and existing institutions was often dealt with by evolutionary assumptions using organicist metaphors. In those terms, the seeds of democracy were sown with the US Declaration of Independence and the French Revolution, but they needed a long time to grow and blossom, and their fruit has emerged in many parts of the world only recently. Such a view harmonises a much more conflict-ridden political history, and it makes underlying tensions in the democratic commitment disappear.

We can sketch a different history, using the terms introduced above. True, the past two centuries have seen powerful state apparatuses emerge, which were effectively capable of governing populations and controlling boundaries. But hardly any of them, before the 1950s, came close to that proximity between those who govern and those who are governed, between making law and obeying the self-made law, that is the key requirement of democracy. Rather, in contrast, those 'modern' states operated on the basis of a double exclusion, the one or the other being dominant depending on circumstances of time and space: internally, these states excluded major parts of the population on their territory from political rights, either entirely (such as women, native populations or slaves) or by restrictions related to property and taxation. Externally, many of these states were either empires dominating populations outside their core territory or, vice versa, political entities dominated by imperial powers, thus not sovereign at all. A fact neglected by much of political theory is that the most cited examples for the road to modern democracy have been explicit empires, such as Great Britain and France, or operated in a quasi-imperial way through territorial expansion and subjugation of native populations and slaves, such as the USA. In turn, in situations in which inclusive-egalitarian, non-imperial democracy was tried out, such as in Weimar Germany or republican Spain, it soon proved untenable.[4]

We want to suggest that these are not small stains on an almost impeccable history of advancing democracy, but that the core tensions within democracy can thus be recognised: it is extremely difficult to create and sustain a political constellation in which everyone affected by a law or policy has a say in making it and in which the law or policy is actually implemented for all those, but only for those, involved in making it. A polity with limited, partial participation rights has no evolutionary tendency to become more inclusive and egalitarian. Rather, it has the opposite tendency of aiming to improve the situation of those who participate in decision-making by dominating others, either within the same polity or members of other polities.

Seen in this way, the tension between the democratic imaginary and institutional practices is not historical and contingent, it is systematic. And the post-Second World War democratic nation-state, which was inclusive-egalitarian and ever less explicitly imperial, only appeared to stabilise – or, as political scientists like to say, consolidate – democracy. The general 'crisis of democracy' was announced as early as the mid-1970s, and it has never been resolved since. Rather, the current trouble with democracy is the one in which the inherent tensions in the democratic commitment become most clearly visible, because neither internal nor external domination is any longer possible – or at the very least, no longer justifiable.

The current trouble with democracy

Tracy Strong, in his contribution, evokes a series of current challenges that a (still absent) democratic theory for the present would need to address, and he underlines the limits of classical Western theories of democracy in facing these challenges. After reading his contribution, one could be inclined to think that the challenges are of such a nature and, at the same time, the collapse of the political realm in our time is so deep that democracy is no longer a political option. In the face of this situation, Lea Ypi suggests that an activist approach to political theory, with no need to assume a strong and all-embracing notion of the self, together with a 'vanguardist' understanding of the normative role of the state as the agent of feasible progress in the global sphere, can occupy the space that the demos has left empty. The radical insight into the current challenges and the search for new forms of agency, necessary as they are, should not lead to abandoning the commitment to collective autonomy, but should stimulate reflections about the particular intensity that the general tensions in democracy acquire today. In the light of the preceding reflections, the current trouble with democracy results from: firstly, the end of imperialism and the growing global interdependence; secondly, the need for recognition and the weakening of the self; and thirdly, the need for new institutions and the inability to create and stabilise them.

1. As we argued above, imperial domination has been a way of addressing domestic democratic pressures. From the age of the discoveries until the end of the Cold War, however, empires have also been the target of resistance, and thus provided the impetus for the democratic aspirations of the subordinated peoples. Furthermore, one of the consequences of empire-building has been the creation of wide and varied networks interconnecting polities and creating relations of domination based on enforced dependence. What today is called globalisation has one of its sources in past empires. The

creation of the United Nations after the Second World War, the decolonisation of the 1960s and 1970s and the end of the Soviet 'empire' have altered the political picture. The polities that were either enforcing or suffering dependence are now, in general, both politically independent entities. But the relation of imperial dependence had created social, economic and political bonds that do not disappear with formal political independence. The end of the age of empire thus generated a situation of global interdependence between formally independent polities. Thus, a historical moment has been reached in which collective decisions are taken within (mostly) democratic states, but many of the issues that the 'people' in a state want to determine are of a global nature. There is little left that the 'people' can decide or determine.[5] Therefore, collective autonomy is no longer possible in the full sense of the term. Gerard Rosich addresses this situation when he criticises the idea that individual autonomy and cosmopolitanism can be the solution to this lack of collective autonomy, and Manuel Garretón shows how the endeavor for instituting 'Latin America' as a political actor gains contemporary significance and momentum as a response to past dependence, either colonial or neoliberal, and as a political strategy to face an anti-democratic globalising dynamics.

2. As Geneviève Fraisse has outlined, the democratic self has been constituted by a series of formal exclusions, mainly gender and racial exclusion, though as Carlos Forment reminds us, workers have also been in various moments excluded from the collective self. The nation as container of collective autonomy had clear and strict boundaries regarding who was a member of the nation and who had political rights. The history of nation-states is a history of exclusion and of struggle for recognition as full members.[6] As a result of these struggles, full inclusion of all members of a collectivity has now been achieved in many polities. However, the struggles for recognition have produced two effects: first, struggles have been led based on a discourse of rights and thus have achieved recognition as individual rights-holder, not as a specific collectivity; and as a consequence, second, they have weakened strong and substantive notions of the self, which are now seen as exclusionary. Thus, the liberal-constitutional state, which considers the individual human being as the only existing political entity, seems to be reinforced by virtue of its capacity to accommodate these struggles. Ivor Chipkin and Carlos Forment analyse in their contributions current struggles for recognition based on claims to rights in liberal-constitutional states. They show how notions of collective selves can be effective in struggle: over security in the first case, and over work in the second. As these notions are weak and temporary, however, at least

compared with earlier notions of class, they seem unable to sustain a link to democracy in general. Ultimately, the lasting effect is often that only individual autonomy is taken into consideration, evacuating the question of historical injustice and its present significance. Additionally, the current degree of interconnectedness, as explained above, has created new associative bonds that are different from the national ones, without being able, at least until now, to create new political, collective selves. Summing up our first two observations, there is little to determine and there are weak selves, something which in combination makes the exercise of collective autonomy highly precarious.

3. If we believe dominant discourses on democracy, we seem nevertheless to be living in strong and viable democratic polities. But, clearly, no new democratic political institutions have yet been created that are capable of facing the transformations outlined above. To the contrary, rather, the understanding of democratic institutions has changed from a communicative or conflictive perspective to a procedural one, because existing democracies cannot handle the challenges in substance and their remaining legitimacy resides in observance of procedure. As a consequence, disaffection of citizens with existing democracy has widely been noted. This disconnection between the people and the institutions has created a new vicious circle. The institutions have substituted the government *by* the people with government *for* the people, using technocratic forms of decision-making and assuming that expertise is a primary qualification for governing. However, this creates a crisis of legitimacy because the technocratic governments tend not to provide what they promised, and subsequently are not confirmed in elections. For the same reasons that there is inability of the 'people' to exercise collective autonomy, there is also inability of the governments to implement decisions: they do not have enough power for decisive action in either the domestic or the international sphere. And it is at these moments that it is clear to both the governing and the governed that there is a democratic insufficiency which is difficult to overcome. While the governed blame the governing for not heeding legitimate demands, the governing blame the governed for irresponsible behaviour, in particular extremism and populism.

The political troubles that this democratic gap creates have not been addressed by a new understanding of democracy, but by creating institutions that are not democratic and are beyond people's effective control, with the justification that they would engage in an efficient way with current problems: new kinds of supra-polity global institutions, from Non-Governmental Organisations like Amnesty International to international economic institutions such as the

International Monetary Fund or the World Bank or judiciary ones such as the International Criminal Court; from global state associations like the United Nations to regional ones like the European Union, BRICS or G20, etc. However, these institutions are neither democratic in form nor have as their main goal to address the troubles with democracy in contemporary times. Their main concern is merely the stabilisation of the dynamics launched by what they call globalisation. Such stabilisation may at some moments be necessary, and it may also be achieved by those means. But the commitment to democracy has been eradicated from the agenda. Implicitly, the idea is very present that important policy objectives can only be achieved at the price of abandoning the democratic imaginary because our current conditions allow us no longer to realise it. The new and widespread normative political discourses praising human rights and a post-sovereign world order provide a smokescreen for the current trouble with democracy, because it is highly doubtful whether they are of a democratic nature. These new paradigmatic norms are justified through transcendental moral standards which in turn cannot be the outcome of collective autonomy, since autonomy is a capacity that has no groundings outside itself and where every decision can be contested; or, as Tracy Strong points out, democracy has 'no banister'.

The persistence of democracy

Despite this troubled picture, there are signs that the democratic imaginary is alive and is the main driving force in some struggles. On the one hand, the inability of governing elites to address the most pressing issues of our time provokes protest movements. They focus on different issues according to local circumstances – in Latin America, South Africa, India, Europe. But they have in common the claim that elite governance is the problem and democratic participation (at least part of) the solution, not the other way around.[7] On the other hand, there are contexts in which collective autonomy has been successful in recent times in transforming the societal self-understanding and in achieving considerable institutional stability as well. As Peter Wagner shows in his contribution, Brazil and South Africa, despite ongoing disputes and struggles, are significant examples for contemporary democratic experiences.

True, it is difficult to yet assess the lasting global relevance of these events, to recognise whether they can be considered 'avant-garde' actions, in Lea Ypi's sense, or 'exemplary' actions, in Alessandro Ferrara's sense,[8] leading towards a constructive self-transformation of democracy. Brazil and South Africa could stand as examples for strong social movements bringing about democracy, or the transformation of a very limited democracy. Certainly, under current conditions it is difficult to sustain such democratic experiences based in individual states if they cannot be well embedded in the global sphere. The problem is that the global sphere is marked by anti-democratic trends and its impact might be too strong for any single democratic collectivity.

One strategy to counterbalance the impact of these trends could be, as Manuel Garretón has tried to show for Latin America in his contribution, to promote regional integration. But such integration would need to be oriented at radically new democratic standards, as it to some extent is in Latin America, and would need to let some 'regional self' emerge that defines the democratic collectivity in new terms. Otherwise, regional integration at such is not necessarily an answer. European integration has often been hailed as an example for democratic reconstitution under current conditions. But the experiences with the recent crisis within the European Union are sobering. Technocratic government is at the centre of crisis resolution, and its implementation shows the re-emergence of subterranean historical imperial tendencies,[9] with the difference that now there is no 'outside' to be conquered and imperial domination develops internally. The current Greek situation within the EU is telling: democratic self-determination in a small and dependent polity is obstructed by the political elites in the dominant states of the Union, legitimating themselves through technocratic expertise. New political movements in Europe are successful in disintegrating and discapacitating the existing states, but in contrast to Brazil and South Africa they have not (yet) been able to bring about a democratic self-transformation.

These brief examples, all of them with still open long-term outcomes, offer at least two insights. First: the democratic imaginary is alive. In situations of oppression or crisis, it is forcefully actualised by social movements that call for democracy, freedom, justice and solidarity. Second: under current conditions of global interdependence the lasting success of such movements requires more than the winning of 'local' power in existing states. The perspective needs to be a broadening of the democratic impetus by creating federations of movements and institutions that are able to sustain the democratic experiences and, at the same time, address the challenges of the present. This requires a self-transformation of current democratic forms – a transformation that may spell trouble for those only interested in stability, but current stability is neither very democratic nor susceptible to generate answers to the challenges ahead.

Notes

1. Luc Boltanski, *De la critique* (Paris: Gallimard, 2009).
2. Marcel Detienne, *Les Grecs et nous* (Paris: Perrin, 2009).
3. As argued earlier: Peter Wagner, *Modernity as Experience and Interpretation* (Cambridge: Polity, 2008), part II.
4. The major exceptions to this alternative view of the history of democracy are the Scandinavian countries during the twentieth century. In turn, radical confirmation of this view is provided by South Africa up to 1990, in which democracy stabilised when it was practised as domination by a minority over a majority.
5. Current processes aspiring towards independent state formation seem to suggest, though, that this little is still of enough importance and relevance in local contexts.
6. Nation-states have also been the outcome of struggles for national emancipation from imperial or colonial domination. However, they had to set clear boundaries and define nationality. This created a great problem in contexts where the boundaries of these former colonies were decided by the interests of the empires. For instance, decolonisation in Africa took place against the background of the partition of Africa between European empires in the Berlin conference in 1885, and the creation of new nation-states in Europe out of the collapse of the Ottoman and Austro-Hungarian empires against the background of the Paris conference in 1919.
7. For recent analyses, see Breno Bingel and Mauricio Domingues (eds), *Global Modernity and Social Contestation* (London: Sage, 2015).
8. Alessandro Ferrara, *The Force of the Example* (New York: Columbia University Press, 2008).
9. Gerard Rosich, 'La independència i/de la Unió Europea', in *Revista Mirmanda*, 2015.

Index